RUSSIAN RESEARCH CENTER STUDIES 16

Soviet Taxation

The Fiscal and Monetary Problems of a Planned Economy

Soviet Taxation

THE FISCAL AND MONETARY PROBLEMS OF A PLANNED ECONOMY

FRANKLYN D. HOLZMAN

Harvard University Press · Cambridge · 1962

Second Printing

Distributed in Great Britain by
Oxford University Press
London

The Russian Research Center of Harvard University is supported by grants from the Carnegie Corporation, the Ford Foundation, and the Rockefeller Foundation. The Center carries out interdisciplinary study of Russian institutions and behavior and related subjects.

This volume was prepared under a grant from the Carnegie Corporation of New York. That Corporation is not, however, the author, owner, publisher, or proprietor of this publication and is not to be understood as approving by virtue of its grant any of the statements made or views expressed.

Library of Congress Catalog Card Number 55-5061
Printed in the United States of America

To

MATHILDA

PREFACE

This study was prepared during the tenure of a fellowship at the Russian Research Center, Harvard University. I am very grateful for the financial assistance of that organization, without which the work would not have been possible. I am also indebted to Clyde Kluckhohn and Helen Parsons, Director and Administrative Assistant of the Center, for the warm cooperation and generous assistance which left me free of all responsibilities other than my research.

My work naturally owes much to the men under whom I studied economics, first at the University of North Carolina and then at Harvard University. I feel a particular intellectual debt to Edward M. Bernstein of the International Monetary Fund, whose courses at the University of North Carolina first stimulated my interest in economics.

For help in the actual writing of this book, I am most deeply indebted to three persons. Alexander Gerschenkron originally suggested and supervised the entire study, which began as a doctoral dissertation, "Taxation in the Soviet Union" (unpublished, Harvard University, 1951); he has read several drafts of the manuscript, and contributed many valuable suggestions throughout. My wife, Mathilda, also read the manuscript more than once, and discussed with me many of the problems which arose in the course of formulating and writing down my ideas. Nancy Nimitz edited my final draft of the manuscript. In her efforts to improve the readability of the book, she spent considerably more time on the manuscript than any other reader. Her contribution was by no means confined to suggestions of style, however; she checked my reasoning page by page and made innumerable substantive suggestions. Although I originally was perturbed by the delay in publication which editing entailed, I now feel that it was well worth waiting for.

My daily contact at the Russian Research Center with Gregory

Grossman and Raymond P. Powell was invaluable. Both discussed various parts of the manuscript and generously shared with me their materials. I am particularly indebted to Professor Grossman for help in formulating Chapter X, although he made helpful suggestions concerning other chapters as well, and to Professor Powell for valuable criticisms of my first two chapters. Others who were of help in improving the content of the book are: Joseph Berliner, James Coogan, James Duesenberry, Alexander Erlich, Donald Hodgman, Alex Inkeles, Naum Jasny, Robert Lampman, Wassily Leontief, Demitri Shimkin, Robert Solow, and Warren Wilhelm. Special mention is reserved for Dan Throop Smith, who read the entire dissertation and offered many useful suggestions. Technical assistance was provided at the Russian Research Center by Elizabeth Fainsod, who expedited my work in many ways; Boris Syssoeff, who gave bibliographical assistance; Ada Dziewanowska, Rose DiBenedetto, and Margaret Dalton, who patiently and carefully typed successive versions of the manuscript; Robert Campbell, who checked footnotes; and Nick DeWitt, who drew the original from which Chart 1 is taken. I am also indebted to Isabella Stevenson Diamond, head of the United States Treasury Department library, for generously lending me materials.

Grateful acknowledgment is made to the *Journal of Political Economy* for permission to reprint parts of my article "Commodity and Income Taxation in the Soviet Union," which appeared in October 1950 (University of Chicago Press; copyright 1953 by the University of Chicago); to the *American Economic Review* for permission to reprint from "The Burden of Soviet Taxation," which appeared in September 1953; and to the *National Tax Journal* for permission to reprint from "The Soviet Budget, 1928–1952" which appeared in September 1953. Raymond P. Powell and James F. Coogan generously granted permission to quote from their doctoral dissertations, and Peter Wiles to cite from his then unpublished essay "Retail Trade, Retail Prices and Real Wages in the U.S.S.R."

Because of the time lag between the completion of this manuscript and its publication, events of the past year or two may not be adequately recorded here. The book includes, I believe, all relevant material available in this country by August 1952, when the penultimate version of the manuscript was completed. In September 1952 I left the Russian Research Center at Harvard and since then have not had the opportunity to read systematically current Soviet materials. Nevertheless, an attempt was made to append to various parts of the manuscript summaries of the major events of 1953.

FRANKLYN D. HOLZMAN

University of Washington
Seattle, Washington
February 22, 1954

CONTENTS

LIST OF TABLES

FOREWORD

Professor Holzman's study is a valuable addition to the still small but rapidly growing number of scholarly, Western writings on the Soviet economy. In broad outline, Soviet Russia's system of taxation is fairly familiar, but this is the first really thorough and systematic survey of the subject. The different kinds of taxes, including among others the notorious turnover tax, the income tax, and the various agricultural taxes, are here all described in careful detail. While attention is focused on the present-day levies, their antecedents are traced from the Soviet beginnings. Annual data on the different sorts of taxes are assembled for the entire period of the five-year plans.

While Professor Holzman has rendered an important service in collecting and presenting in convenient form a great amount of information, his study is far from being just a factual reference work. In a field where all too often facts are compiled for facts' sake, his approach is refreshingly analytic. The ultimate concern is to explore a number of basic issues, and the facts are discussed with this aim in mind.

On one of these issues, the burden of Soviet taxation, Professor Holzman breaks distinctly new ground. This first attempt to compile systematic measures of this category is made with a due regard to the novel pitfalls posed by the special nature of the ruble price system, particularly the absence of any clear-cut economic boundary between indirect taxes, profits and charges for the factors of production and between direct taxes and the now largely compulsory government-bond subscriptions. For this reason and because of the deficiencies in Soviet statistics, the calculation must be somewhat arbitrary and inexact. But granting the inevitable limitations, it certainly is very illuminating to know that the Soviet government directly or indirectly taxed away from two-fifths to over half of the average household's money income in the late thirties; that the government's exactions reached about 55 to 65 per cent in 1948; and that while they declined thereafter they were still around the prewar level in 1953. The alternative figures obtained for any one year refer to alternative definitions of the tax burden, which Professor Holzman wisely decided to consider. The larger figure for 1948, for example, involves the additional supposition that taxes include the retained profits of Soviet enterprise, social-security collections, and bond deductions.

In order to calculate the tax burden, Professor Holzman had to compile his own series of statistics on household money incomes. Regrettably, except for one year, he was not able to take into account the income-in-kind of farm households, which is still a significant item in Soviet agriculture. But his measures stand nevertheless as a further, striking commentary on the costs to the Russian people of the Soviet industrialization drive.

Limitations in the statistical data preclude a definite determination of the distribution of the tax burden by income classes. As Professor Holzman explains, such a distribution in any case cannot be easy to interpret. While the ultimate concern is with the "equity" of the tax system, it is necessary to bear in mind not only the lack of any clear-cut delimitation of the tax burden but also the fact that the government in any case controls the distribution of income directly according to principles which are not yet entirely clear. The very tentative inquiry that is attempted nevertheless will be of interest for the critical methodology, for the fresh information assembled, and for the novel, though altogether provisional, conclusion that taken together Soviet taxes probably are more or less proportional to income. Considering budgetary expenditures as well as taxes, the net effect might tend to be mildly equalitarian. Under the five-year plans, the government has relied for its revenue primarily on indirect taxes, especially the turnover tax. This sales tax must be a source of embarrassment to Soviet economists, but, contrary to a common supposition, the turnover tax (while certainly harsh in the case of bread) may not have been markedly regressive generally, at least in recent years. For the most part other taxes tend to be either proportional or somewhat progressive. It is to be hoped that Professor Holzman will continue his inquiries on this interesting question, and so provide a firmer basis for appraising it.

The magnitude and distribution of the Soviet tax burden have an interest of their own, but they are considered here also as part of a larger inquiry. In a planned economy of the centralized Soviet type, taxes necessarily lose a good deal of the importance they have in a market economy as an independent factor affecting economic decisions. But clearly they still must have a role. What is the nature of this role? How sensible are the Soviet taxes from the standpoint of economic efficiency? In general, taking into account all aspects, what is the rationale of the Soviet tax system? The questions are intricate, but happily Professor Holzman does not shrink from grappling with them, and his careful and thoughtful efforts to deal with these aspects add at once a further dimension to his study, and one moreover which as much as anything else distinguishes it from most previous accounts of Soviet finance. As a result, this volume must be accorded a place among the very few serious inquiries to date on the large theme of the working principles of Soviet economic planning.

This pioneer work necessarily is often tentative and exploratory, but Professor Holzman faces difficulties squarely and confides in the reader regarding limitations. For specialists, the value of this study will be much enhanced as a result of the careful documentation throughout. I am sure the more general reader will find in these pages further perspective on some of the momentous topics of the day.

Abram Bergson

SOVIET TAXATION

INTRODUCTION

Any nation which attempts to devote a large share of its resources to purposes other than current consumption by the population faces difficult financial problems. The lower the absolute level of total output, and the larger the share of output diverted from current consumption, the more difficult of solution these problems become. This is true of backward areas attempting to industrialize more rapidly than the natural propensities of their citizens permit, and of nations fully mobilized for war or semimobilized for cold war. The Soviet Union has experienced each of these conditions: it was converted from a relatively backward agricultural nation to a leading industrial nation in the space of a generation; it was mobilized for total war from 1941 to 1945; it is presently semimobilized for cold war and for further forced industrialization. This book is a study of the financial problems of the Soviet Union over the periods of industrialization and war, with particular emphasis on the tax system.

Soviet taxation is a neglected field of study. Three books on Soviet finance were published in the mid-thirties, but these dealt with taxation only peripherally; [1] no comprehensive work on the subject by a Western economist has yet appeared. The aim of this book is to present such a comprehensive picture of the Soviet tax system, its relationships to the rest of the financial system and to the problems of the Soviet economy as a whole.

The subject is complex and permits of no simple treatment. Taxes relate to the Soviet economic system in many different ways: through problems of resource allocation, incentives to work, distribution of income, and price administration in a planned economy. Presentation is further complicated by the necessity of treating the subject both historically and theoretically. In addition, statistical analysis is needed not only to provide a foundation for the historical and theoretical sections, but also to answer questions of a purely empirical nature. Finally, the fact that so little has been written about the Soviet economy, especially from the monetary point of view, makes it necessary to carry the research into related fields. Thus in Chapter 2, for example, where the fiscal problems of combating inflation are discussed, it was not possible to refer to other writers on the causes and nature of the Soviet inflation; nor was it possible, in estimating the "burden" of Soviet taxation in Chapter 10, to rely on others for estimates of personal income; in these instances and many others, laborious digressions had to be undertaken.

The book is divided into four parts, with considerable overlapping between the parts. In Part I an attempt is made to work out the theoretical considerations necessary for an understanding of the functions and structure of the Soviet tax system. The approach is from the general to the particular: the first two chapters deal with the relationships between taxes (taken as a unit) and other economic tools at the government's disposal in dealing with basic fiscal problems; the third with the Soviet choice among different forms of taxation; the fourth with the most important form of taxation in the Soviet Union, the indirect or commodity taxes. Only a schematic representation of Soviet taxes is presented in this part of the book, and no more information about the economy is provided than is absolutely necessary to the discussion.

Part II is essentially historical and descriptive: taxes are described in detail, and changes in each of the major taxes are traced throughout the Soviet period. An understanding of many of these changes is facilitated by the discussion in Part I, particularly Chapters 3 and 4. Data relevant to this section were so plentiful that it threatened to outgrow all the other parts combined; considerations of proportion and space dictated the use only of the more important materials, and for general Soviet economic background the reader must be referred to other books on the Soviet economy.

The two chapters in Part III are devoted to statistical analysis. Broad trends in Soviet finance are traced through the planning period (i.e., since 1928) and explained in the light of theory developed in Part I; and the "burden" or average rate of taxation is computed in terms of definitions established in Part I.

Part IV is reserved for a critical evaluation of Soviet tax policy. Information from the previous three parts is collated and reëxamined in terms of generally accepted criteria such as containment of inflation, equity, the preservation of incentives, efficient allocation of resources, and effectiveness in implementing political objectives. This, then, is the broad framework of the book; a more detailed summary of the problems studied and results arrived at follows.

The first chapter of Part I, "Taxation and Direct Economic Controls," is concerned with the significance of taxes in the Soviet context. Those unfamiliar with the economy may be misled by the emphasis commonly placed on "planning" and "controls" into thinking that money and money taxation are not important. While it is true that the Soviets rely more heavily on direct economic controls than any other nation in the world today, and while direct economic controls, where they are used, do substitute for money and the market mechanism, it is not true that money and the market mechanism have been wholly supplanted. The structure of the Soviet economy is examined with the purpose of discovering the areas in which the market mechanism functions and the areas in which direct economic controls supersede the market. As a result of this investigation, it is deduced that the principal function of Soviet taxes is the prevention of inflation in the market for consumers' goods. We also deduce that taxes are not essential to the maintenance of a high rate of investment, since this allocation of resources is accomplished primarily by the use of direct economic controls. In this respect the Soviet pattern differs only in degree from that which characterized the American economy during World War II.

The prevention of inflation has always been the primary explicit financial objective of the Soviets. In their first three five-year plans, they planned for a steadily declining price level in the consumers'-goods markets, a stable or declining price level in the market for producers' goods, and only a mildly rising wage level. The reasons for their failure to avoid inflation in the prewar period are considered in Chapter 2. From 1928 to 1940 prices of consumers' goods increased more than tenfold, and prices of producers' goods and raw materials about threefold. Repressed inflation in the market for consumers' goods rose to a peak for the prewar period in 1932, when food prices in the free market were roughly 15 times state ration prices. By raising the prices of rationed goods and increasing the quantity supplied, repressed inflation was all but eliminated by 1937–38, only to reappear in 1939 and 1940 as the war clouds gathered. The average annual wage rate increased from about 700 rubles in 1928 to over 4000 rubles in 1940; no comparable increase in productivity has been claimed even by the Soviets. In every year of this period the actual wage rate turned out to be higher than the planned rate, in some years by as much as 15 to 20 per cent; on the other hand, actual increases in productivity typically fell below the planned increases.

The interaction between inflation in the factor markets and inflation in the consumers'-goods markets is also analyzed in Chapter 2. In most capitalist countries the interaction is reciprocal; high prices of consumers' goods induce workers to press for higher wages; higher wages, in turn, induce higher prices by increasing both costs and effective demand. However, this is not quite so true of the Soviet Union. Here higher wages do induce higher prices, but because workers are not organized and can exert little pressure on the wage level, rising prices alone are not sufficient to explain the rapid rise in the Soviet wage level in the prewar period. The basic cause of wage inflation, as we shall demonstrate, must be found elsewhere. The significance of this analysis for Soviet fiscal policy is that an anti-inflationary program which attempts only to keep supply and demand in the final output markets in equilibrium cannot succeed. Second, because wages do *not* follow prices, the Soviets are free to rely on price-increasing commodity taxes without fear of inducing a spiral inflation.

Wage inflation, though not the only factor in the picture, was certainly the focal point of Soviet inflation. Increases in wages, unaccompanied by compensating increases in productivity, pushed up the prices of both producers' and consumers' goods by increasing money costs of production. In the case of consumers' goods, causation operated through demand as well as supply: household incomes rose much faster than consumers'-goods output. Finally, unpredicted increases in wage rates created an extra problem above and beyond that of closing the very large *planned* inflationary gap. To the extent that the household sector earned more income than the fiscal authorities had anticipated, with no compensating increases in output, tax revenues tended to fall short of the amounts needed to prevent the development of repressed inflation in the consumers'-goods markets. Because of the central importance of wage inflation among Soviet financial problems, we consider in some detail how and why wages are "bid up" in defiance of plan, and the measures taken by the Soviets to stop wage inflation.

Taxation, it should be noted, is not the only financial tool of the Soviet planners; there are also bank credit, profits of state enterprises, the amortization fund, sales of government bonds, and so forth. Discussion of the interrelationships among these instruments of Soviet financial policy is undertaken as a prerequisite to a better understanding of the role of fiscal policy in the over-all Soviet financial plan. The fiscal problems created by the inflationary Soviet monetary policy are discussed at length.

This completes our discussion of the relations of the tax system as a whole to the economic system; attention is turned next (Chapter 3) to the Soviet choice among different forms of taxes. The outstanding feature of the Soviet tax structure is the heavy reliance placed on indirect or commodity taxes. Those familiar with Marxist literature in public finance may find this difficult to understand, in view of the vehemence with which indirect taxes were attacked by these writers. The basic argument — an argument of considerable merit — was that sales and excise taxes were inequitable (or regressive), falling most heavily on the poor and on the members of the working classes. Why, in spite of their ideological bias, have the Soviets relied so heavily on indirect taxes and so little on direct taxes? Why, with such large indirect taxes, are direct taxes levied as well? Why tax at all in an authoritarian society — why not just reduce wages? Why is taxation in kind rather than money taxation used to extract "forced savings" from the agricultural sector of the economy? These questions are discussed in Chapter 3. The answers take us further afield: taxes must be considered in relation to a large number of problems, including maintenance of a rational system for pricing the factors of production, conservation of the effectiveness of differential wages in allocating labor, market administration, the costs of tax collection, and problems of controlling the agricultural sector of the economy.

In Chapter 4, attention is turned to the Soviet system of indirect or commodity taxation. Our first task is to define what we mean by a commodity tax under Soviet institutional arrangements. Should the retained profits of state enterprises be regarded as taxes? Can we assume that the incidence of the Soviet sales tax is entirely on the household? Is the tax on profits of state enterprise a direct tax or an indirect tax? Further problems are created by the fact that economic categories which are considered factor costs of production in the West (e.g., interest as the cost of or return to capital, rent, returns for exceptional entrepreneurial ability) are not explicitly taken into account by the Soviets. To the extent that cost of production is thereby understated, should it not be argued that the Soviet commodity tax is overstated? Is it possible to measure the degree to which the Soviet commodity tax implicitly includes these neglected costs of production? Our second task is to rationalize the use, by the Soviets, of both a sales and a profits tax. Why not just levy one of these taxes? We discover that the use of the two forms of commodity tax confers substantial administrative advantages. The need for two taxes instead of one is also related to the problems of maintaining managerial incentives and of insuring the right product-mix in the case of enterprises producing more than one commodity.

The history of Soviet taxation falls into two distinct periods, separated by the Tax Reform of September 1930. (From about 1918 to 1921, the Soviet economy was essentially a barter economy; money taxation all but disappeared.) In Chapter 5, we survey the tax system which existed from 1921 to 1930, and show why the transition from the quasi-planned economy of the twenties to the fully planned economy of the thirties necessitated reforms. In Chapters 6, 7, and 8, the development of commodity taxation, taxation in kind, and all other taxes (i.e., income taxes, sales of government bonds, taxes on the income of collective farms and coöperatives, and others), respectively, is traced. The nonspecialist may wish to skip lightly over these four chapters.

The last section of Chapter 6 may prove to be of special interest, however. An attempt is made to assess the claim of the majority of Western economists, a claim, incidentally, denied by Soviet economists, that the structure of indirect tax rates is regressive. Substantial statistical and methodological problems had to be confronted and the results must be considered quite tentative. To some, the most interesting part of this section may be the attempt to break down into component parts the turnover tax on bread, which returns more revenue to the budget than the tax on any other commodity. The tax on bread (and on most other food products) cannot be considered a tax falling entirely on the Soviet consumer of bread; it reflects also the tax in kind negatively expressed in the very low price paid by the state for grain to the collective farms and farmers. How much of the tax on bread is paid by the consumers of bread, and how much by the producers of grain (in the form of the below-cost price for grain)? The answer to this question is important for assessing the equity of the turnover tax viewed as a sales tax on the consumer, and for determining the relative incidence of Soviet taxes on the urban and rural populations, respectively. For the year 1940 we find that the turnover tax on bread was 86 per cent of price, and that the part paid by the consumer amounted to from 68 to 80 per cent of price, still a very substantial tax. A very tentative estimate for 1953 indicates, however, that the total turnover tax on bread had fallen to between 60 and 72 per cent, and the share paid by the consumer had declined to within the broad range of 40 to 65 per cent. Other considerations must be taken into account, however, in computing the tax in kind on the agricultural producers and this is done in Chapter 7. The tax in kind on grains is estimated there to have been between 5 and 15 per cent in 1937, a good crop year, but to have roughly doubled by 1939. These figures are surprisingly low and must be regarded with considerable caution.

The general reader may also find interesting the discussion in Chapter 8 of sales of government bonds to the population. In this section reasons are adduced for classifying as taxes rather than as voluntary purchases in the Western sense sales of bonds by the Soviet government. Among other things, we find that considerable social pressure is brought to bear upon the population to subscribe from two to four weeks' wages a year and that these amounts are deducted from workers' wages every month just like direct taxes; most bonds are not redeemable until their full term has expired; a series of conversions (1930, 1936, 1938), and the 1947 currency reform have together resulted in extended maturities, reduced interest rates, and a reduction by two-thirds, in 1947, of the value of all outstanding obligations; finally, rampant inflation (until 1948) has steadily reduced the "real" value of these highly illiquid assets.

Only two chapters are included in Part III, primarily because a good deal of the statistical material proved to be inseparable from the analyses in earlier chapters. Almost complete series of budgetary receipts for the past 25 years are presented in Chapter 9. Trends in total receipts and in the relative amounts of different taxes are analyzed. War and postwar fiscal and monetary policies are discussed and some important questions are considered. Why did the Soviets not rely more on taxation and less on credit creation to finance the war? For what reasons did the Currency Reform of December 1947 take the particular form it did? What was the approximate amount of currency in circulation just before the Reform? With regard to the amount of currency in circulation at the time of the Reform, most Western estimates have been in the neighborhood of 400 billion rubles. This is much too high. My own estimate is of the order of 100 billion rubles. This finding has important implications for estimating the amount of resources devoted by the Soviets to the war effort and for evaluating the efficacy of Soviet fiscal policy during the war years.

Are the Soviet people heavily taxed? Has their "tax burden" increased or decreased over the past 25 years? Do Soviet citizens pay higher taxes than citizens of the United States? These are the principal questions to which answers are provided in Chapter 10. Because the concept "tax burden" is not unique, several different estimates are presented. Whichever the series selected, the level of taxes is discovered to be extraordinarily high. The "tax burden" increased steadily and rapidly from 1926 to 1936, roughly doubling over the 10-year period; in 1936, the household paid back to the state in the form of taxes 60 per cent of its total money income. The "burden" declined during the relatively good years, 1937 and 1938, but increased again in 1939 and 1940 as the Soviets mobilized for war. In 1948 the "burden" is estimated to have been almost 69 per cent. The substantial concessions to the consumers embodied in the price cuts from 1949 to 1953 are reflected in the drop to 57 per cent again by the latter year. Many difficulties, both methodological and statistical, were encountered in making these estimates; these are discussed only briefly in the text but in great detail in an appendix.

The evaluation of Soviet taxation in Part IV is an extension of the analysis in Part I. The analytical material was thus divided because Part I is essential to an understanding of Parts II and III, while the factual material provided in Parts II and III is essential to the analysis of Part IV. The Soviet tax system is evaluated in terms of generally accepted criteria: preservation of incentives, equity, allocation of resources, containment of inflation. Soviet fiscal authorities, like those of all other nations, are faced with the basic problem of choosing between methods of taxation which are equitable and those which tend to preserve work incentives. In practice, it is usually not possible to satisfy both these criteria simultaneously: taxes which best preserve incentives are usually inequitable; equitable taxes rate very poorly from the point of view of preserving incentives. Soviet choice between taxes is all the more critical because of the very high level of taxation which is imposed.

How have the Soviets resolved this dilemma? To what extent do the Soviets rely on economic incentives? What is the impact of the tax system on incentives? Is it meaningful to talk about the equity of the Soviet tax system per se when the state has substantial powers to determine not only taxes but also virtually all factor and final output prices and, in addition, can substantially redistribute income by budgetary expenditures on health, education, transfers, and subsidies? What standards of equity should we have in mind in examining the Soviet tax system? In connection with allocation of resources, considerable attention is devoted to examining the possible effects of the Soviet subsidy program, subsidies being viewed here as negative taxes. The assumption is made that relative prices do play a role in Soviet production and investment decisions. Finally, the apparent absence of inflation since the Currency Reform of 1947 is discussed and the reasons are examined. Has Soviet fiscal policy been changed? Or have physical and financial controls reached a higher level of stringency? The analysis presented favors the latter explanation. To evaluate the Soviet fiscal system, answers to these and other questions must be provided.

It was my original intention to make a study of the whole Soviet budget, dealing not only with receipts but with budgetary expenditures as well. It soon became apparent, however, that budgetary expenditures could be treated in only the most superficial manner in a book written from the public-finance standpoint, because of the general lack in economics of an adequate theory of public expenditures. In any case, in dealing with the Soviet economy, budgetary expenditures are probably more appropriately treated as part of a larger study of investment decisions, because of the overwhelming importance of the state in economic activity (some investment is financed by the state through other channels than the budget). For purposes of this book, then, the procedure was to take the amount of expenditures as given, and to examine the problems involved in financing it. Though investment is a major item, other important expenditure categories are financed by the budget: welfare expenditures, defense, administration, transfer payments, and so forth. In discussing relations between taxes and the development of the economy, we cannot therefore accurately speak of the rate of investment, since the taxes serve to finance other activities as well; instead we shall speak of the rate of government expenditures or, more typically, of the rate of "nonconsumption" expenditures of the state. "Nonconsumption" is defined in Chapter 2 to include "all activities from which the household sector of the economy receives money income (including transfer payments) but which do not result in the output of goods or services for which the household can spend its income."

As we have noted, the most important Soviet taxes are indirect taxes which are collected through state enterprises. In Western nations the incidence of taxes levied on enterprises falls in part on the enterprises themselves and in part on the consumers. To the extent that such taxes are shifted forward into higher prices, they are, in effect, paid by consumers (i.e., the real income of the consumers is reduced); to the extent that they are shifted backward and reduce profits, they are paid by the enterprises. (For simplicity, secondary effects of taxation on employment, sales, and so forth are ignored.) Private enterprise, with very minor exceptions, no longer exists in the Soviet Union. Therefore taxes collected from Soviet enterprises are borne completely by the consumer (taxed commodities sold for final use by one enterprise to another or to a government organization constitute a minor exception), and the focus of our study of Soviet taxation is accordingly the household.

From the point of view of Soviet enterprise, the price-increasing taxes may be regarded simply as monetary transfers from one government account to another, like transfers between the United States Post Office Department and the budget. This is recognized by the Soviets, and explains why the transfer of enterprise profits to the budget is not dignified as a "profits tax"; it is labeled simply "deductions from profits." This should not be taken to imply that the deduction from profits and other monetary transfers from state enterprises to the budget serve no important functions, for they do. Soviet enterprises are set up to operate on an independent financial basis and with financial incentives. As we shall see, the accumulation of funds in enterprise accounts due to their role as instruments of tax collection, or for any other reason, tends to reduce the efficiency with which such enterprises are operated and can lead to inflation in the factor markets.

It should be pointed out that throughout the book taxation, except where otherwise noted, refers to the sum of taxes levied by the whole hierarchy of Soviet political subdivisions, namely, the union, republican, and local governments. In the Soviet Union, the subordinate political units have little or no autonomy in the sphere of taxation; the consolidated state budget is the significant economic magnitude and object of policy decision, and very little importance attaches to the distribution of the total tax burden among the constituent budgets. This is not true of the United States, where the federal, state, and local governments do make autonomous decisions regarding tax matters.

A word about sources: the historical and statistical materials presented are based almost entirely on Soviet sources. The first difficulty posed by the statistical data stems from the radical and frequent changes in Soviet economic structure, institutions, and financial policies over the past thirty years. This creates serious problems of comparability of data over time. In many instances, Soviet economists have revised figures for earlier years to make them more comparable with current figures; more often than not, these revised figures have appeared without identification. It is this failure of Soviet economists to annotate their data sufficiently that often leads to "unexplainable" discrepancies between figures which purport to describe the same economic magnitude.

A second major difficulty was lack of data for the war and postwar periods. The alternative of estimating missing magnitudes was preferred to the omission of a large part of the statistical analysis for the period since 1940. All sources and methods of computation have been described in detail and included in appendices.

In view of the suspicion with which many persons view Soviet statistics, we should comment on the possibility that some of the data used in this study have been deliberately falsified. The grounds for suspicion are well known: the usual amount of secrecy which has surrounded Soviet economic information, particularly in recent years; the ambiguity observed in Soviet data; and most important, the fact that the Soviet government uses economic statistics liberally for propaganda purposes, and has shown itself not unwilling to present or omit data with the deliberate intent to mislead.[2] The question of falsification has been argued at length in Western literature on the Soviet economy, and the commonly accepted conclusion is that Soviet statistics are not generally falsified in the sense of being freely invented. For a persuasive statement of this position, the reader is referred to Professor Bergson's recently published book on Soviet national income.[3] Professor Bergson stresses, however, that even if Soviet statistics are not falsified outright, they must be handled with great caution. All figures must be checked and rechecked; the footnotes in fine print must be read carefully; methods of collecting and combining raw data must be studied; and the data must be tested for internal consistency. Wherever possible, these precautions were taken in the course of writing this book.

PART I: THEORY

Chapter 1

TAXATION AND DIRECT ECONOMIC CONTROLS

Taxation is as prominent a feature in Soviet economic life as it is under capitalism. In fact, because of the commanding role of the state in economic affairs, the average rate of taxation in the USSR is perhaps the highest in the world today. The functions commonly performed by taxes are modified in the USSR, however, by extensive use of direct controls over resources and prices. We shall therefore begin by considering briefly the role of money, hence money taxation, in the functioning of the Soviet economy.

THE PROBLEM

Inability of the free-market mechanism to meet the needs of sovereign governments, particularly in times of national emergency, has led many Western nations in recent years to adopt direct physical controls over economic resources.[1] Such controls ordinarily supersede money and the market mechanism as the allocator of scarce resources. For example, it would be impossible to explain in terms of federal fiscal and monetary powers the fact that almost all the steel and aluminum produced in the United States during World War II went into defense industry, the sole customer of which was the government. The explanation is that manufacturers of these products were constrained to give priority to government orders.

What we have said of the recent United States experience applies with even more force to the situation of the Soviet Union. Given Soviet conditions in the late 1920's, when the decision to industrialize was made, it was inevitable that considerable reliance should be placed upon direct physical controls. Not only did Soviet plans envisage the diversion of an almost unprecedently large share of national output away from the household: this diversion had also to be accomplished under conditions of such extreme national poverty that strong household-sector resistance was certain to be encountered.

Furthermore, the Soviets were not impelled by ideological considerations to reverence the market mechanism as they have felt impelled to respect other fetishes — for instance, the labor theory of value as an instrument of economic analysis. If anything, the reverse was true.[2]

Does the extensive use of direct physical controls by the Soviets mean that monetary phenomena, including those associated with taxation, can be disregarded? It does not, because physical controls, though used to a greater degree in the Soviet Union than elsewhere, are still not all-pervasive. The free market continues to function in some sectors of the Soviet economy. As long as it survives, or as long as the physical allocation system contains loopholes which cannot easily be plugged, financial planning remains important, and has a *real* impact both on the size and composition of the national output and on the division of that output between the household and the government.

In the next section we shall review briefly the main outlines of the Soviet economy, with the purpose of delineating the areas in which the market mechanism and direct physical controls, respectively, are primarily responsible for the direction and extent of economic activity.

AREAS OF DIRECT CONTROL AND FREE MARKET IN THE USSR

The Soviet economy is a money economy. With the exception of peasant labor, paid partly in kind, all factors of production as well as finished commodities are valued in monetary terms by the state, and every material transaction has a monetary counterpart. Budget expenditures are matched by receipts; interorganizational transactions are financed by transfers in the State Bank from the account of the buyer to the account of the seller; wages are paid in currency; consumer purchases are made with currency.

The economy consists of the following important sectors:

(1) Households viewed both as suppliers of labor and as consumers.

(2) Enterprises owned by the state but operating on a relatively independent financial basis. This category includes those enterprises in industry, distribution, transportation, and other branches of the economy which keep their own accounts and finance most of their operating expenses and part of their investment requirements from

their own earnings. However, the budget has typically supplied them with the bulk of the funds designed to meet their investment requirements, as well as large subsidies to cover operating costs in the industries where state policy has been to keep prices below cost. The surplus funds of enterprises which earn profits in excess of their planned needs are transferred to the budget.

(3) The state apparatus, defined here to include all organizations and activities completely dependent on budget finance, such as ordinary administration, defense, social and cultural organizations and institutions, and the machine tractor stations (MTS).

(4) Collective farms and other so-called coöperative organizations.

Allocation of the components of production among producing firms and government organizations is to a large extent planned in advance; in the case of the more important materials, distribution may even be accomplished directly. Referring to the most critical materials, the so-called "funded" commodities, Professor Bienstock says:

> "Funded" commodities may not be disposed of by agencies producing them . . . they are distributed to the users . . . by direct order of the Economsoviet, in quantities and purposes fixed in advance by the Plan. This group of commodities includes the most important producers' goods, about 300 items in all, including raw materials, fuel, machines and other equipment, motor vehicles, etc. To make the best possible use of the generally limited supply of such essential goods, the government undertakes their distribution to individual users for specified purposes.[3]

This quotation refers to the prewar period. By 1950, according to a Soviet economist, the number of "funded" commodities had grown to include more than 1500 items.[4]

Next in importance are the so-called "quota" commodities. Quoting Bienstock again:

> A "quota commodity" is supplied by the People's Commissariat of the producing industry to any individual user, provided the aggregate quota allotted to the user's industry or region in the procurement plan is not exhausted. Purposes are not specified in advance. Commodities in this group, while also scarce, are less urgently essential than the "funded" ones to plants or ultimate consumers. They include, for example, timber, glass for chemistry equipment, electric fans and irons, petroleum, matches, etc.[5]

The allocation of the remaining resources is completely decentralized, i.e., they may be bought freely whenever available. In actual practice this sharp trichotomy among commodities does not exist. On the one hand, distribution of commodities which may be purchased "freely" is not utterly decentralized; the planned allocation of funded and quota commodities to some extent predetermines the uses to which decentralized materials can be put, because of factor complementarity in production. On the other hand, Soviet economic literature clearly indicates that direct controls over both funded and quota commodities are frequently evaded.

A substantial degree of planning in the allocation of labor, enforced by various forms of compulsion, has characterized the Soviet economy only since the late 1930's. Before 1938 the labor market was relatively free; in fact, there was a very high degree of labor turnover in industry.[6] Measures introduced since this date have reduced the mobility of labor: workers are prohibited from leaving their jobs without the permission of their plant managers; the government is empowered to transfer skilled workers anywhere in the country without regard for the workers' wishes; boys of 14–17 years of age may be drafted for training in certain trades and compelled to work at assigned jobs for a specified number of years, and so forth. Although these measures may have been conceived originally as temporary expedients to meet the threat of war, and later the actual war situation, most of them have never been rescinded.[7]

In spite of the apparent severity of these controls, there remains a considerable area in which the labor supply is not controlled and in which, if compulsion is resorted to, it is not effective. This is evidenced by the high rate of voluntary labor turnover, and by the differential wages and other inducements used to attract labor from one area or industry to another even in the postwar period.[8]

The collective farms (*kolkhozy*) belong in the controlled sector in two respects: (1) a large part of their output is centrally planned and sold under compulsion to state organizations at very low fixed prices, and (2) the amount of nonagricultural raw materials and producers' goods available to them depends on the plan for the distribution of industrial output. To the extent that they contribute goods to the free collective farm markets, they constitute part of the uncontrolled area of the economy. These collective farm markets are markets in which the peasants and the collective farms sell (or barter) their surplus foodstuffs, usually to the urban population. Prices in these markets are set freely by supply and demand.

The consumers' coöperatives are the next largest class of so-called coöperatives in size. They serve primarily as an instrument of distribution, however, and therefore do not affect the basic variables in this analysis. The producers' coöperatives do not account for a significant percentage of total output and need not be considered here.

By controlling the relative amounts of equipment and labor which may be employed in different industries and in various sectors of the economy as a whole, the planners determine, within fairly narrow limits, the relative shares of total national output destined for consumption and for nonconsumption purposes. This allocation is a significant one embodying one of the fundamental policy decisions in the economic plan, namely, the decision as to the rate of investment.

The direct controls which more or less predetermine the consumption-investment ratio are fortified by broad monetary controls. State organizations and industrial enterprises are required to keep all their funds, with the exception of small cash working balances, in the form of bank deposits. Although the total amount which may be drawn down by an enterprise or organization is limited only by the size of its deposits, the amounts which may be spent for specific purposes — wages, other ordinary operating expenditures, and capital investment — are, in theory, delimited by the quarterly or yearly plans of the enterprise. (Actually an enterprise which economized on labor would probably be allowed to spend its extra funds for raw materials or equipment if these were available. The reverse is not true, however; economies in the use of raw materials or equipment should not, in theory, increase the cash available to an enterprise for expenditures in wages.)

The Soviets prefer the market mechanism to rationing for the distribution of consumers' goods. Rationing was indeed employed from about 1928 to 1935 and again during and immediately after World War II, but only because of the inability of Soviet fiscal machinery to cope successfully with repressed inflation in these periods. Since the Currency Reform of December 1947, consumers' goods have again been distributed primarily by the market. At present the consumer is free to choose among the goods offered for sale by the state at planned prices, and the distribution of these goods among consumers is related to the size-distribution of consumers' money incomes.

THE ROLE OF TAXATION

Having identified the functioning elements of the Soviet economy, we are now in a position to evaluate the role of taxes. Direct controls, as we have seen, are an important determinant of economic activity in the enterprise sector, particularly in the allocation of scarce equipment and raw materials. By means of these controls the planners can determine within fairly narrow limits the relative shares of national output destined for household consumption and for government purposes. In other words, achievement of a desired rate of non-consumption expenditures, measured in "real" terms, is primarily dependent *not* upon the ability of the Soviets to raise the appropriate amount of funds either by taxation or credit creation, but upon their ability to allocate directly the means of production.

Consumers'-goods markets. Nevertheless, taxes are essential to the smooth functioning of the Soviet economy. If the state decided not to levy taxes, but simply to print money or commandeer resources, serious inflation in the markets for consumers' goods would immediately result. Since prices, with the exception of those in the collective farm markets, are administered, inflation would at first be repressed, but its effects would be none the less harmful. Repressed inflation in the market for consumers' goods tends, first of all, to reduce the household incentive to work. This takes the forms of withdrawal of some workers from the labor force, especially among marginal groups such as the elderly, or wives with children; reduced effort on the job; excessive absenteeism, lateness, and so forth. The net result of these phenomena is reduction of the national output. Direct controls over labor, including the well-known severe penalties for absenteeism and lateness, reduce somewhat the scope of the problem. Nevertheless, Soviet economists have noted that the elimination of wartime repressed inflation by the Currency Reform in December 1947 was followed by a rapid increase in the number of persons seeking jobs.[9]

Secondly, the distributional inequities which accompany repressed inflation usually make it necessary to ration consumers' goods. As we have noted, rationing has twice been used by the Soviets. In both cases they did their best to restore the free market as rapidly as possible. Rationing is costly to administer, and requires resources which could otherwise be used to satisfy the direct needs of the household or the state. Furthermore, rationing is much less efficient than the free market as a method of distribution; its use tends to reduce the amount of satisfaction derived by the household from a given bill of goods. (I am abstracting from the possibility that rationing may make for more equitable distribution of goods and for this reason increase consumers' welfare.) If, therefore, repressed inflation and the rationing it would necessitate were permitted to become permanent conditions of the Soviet economy, the state could hardly avoid one of two disagreeable alternatives: reduction in the rate of nonconsumption expenditures, or reduction of consumer welfare below the feasible minimum.

Repressed inflation in the consumers'-goods markets involves still further strains on the economy. The desire of individuals to make use of involuntary currency holdings constitutes a chronic threat to the allocation of resources between consumption and nonconsumption uses desired by the state. Perhaps the most likely leakage is through the collective farm market system, where prices set freely by supply and demand sensitively reflect repressed inflation in the state sector of the economy. The greater the differential between state prices and collective farm market prices, the greater would be the incentive of the peasant and of the collective farm to devise some subterfuge for defecting on obligatory deliveries to the state in order to sell greater amounts to consumers on the collective farm market. High *kolkhoz* market prices might also lure peasants out of collective farms into independent farming, and one might expect some workers in state factories to quit their jobs to become self-employed, either producing consumers' goods for the free market or engaging in illegal speculative activity.

Raw-Material and Equipment Markets. Inflation in the enterprise sector of the economy has also contributed to Soviet economic difficulties; this was especially true of the prewar period. Inflation in the raw-materials and equipment markets has always been repressed, because prices of these commodities are very rigidly controlled.[10] To the extent that physical rationing of essential resources is successful, the deleterious effects of such inflation are of course mitigated. But to the extent that commodities can be purchased freely, or controls on directly distributed items circumvented, the logic of the "plan" may be destroyed; shortages develop here and surpluses there. This has in fact been a fairly common occurrence. Soviet economic literature gives many examples of commodity hoarding by industrial enterprises; in the conservative phraseology of one Soviet economist, enterprises will refrain from using surplus funds to buy supplies only when they are already "clearly and significantly oversatiated." [11] Still another undesirable effect of repressed inflation may be distinguished. The existence of widespread shortages combined with price controls means that not all enterprises can find industrial commodities to buy with their surplus funds. When funds accumulate which cannot be spent, plant managers lose some of their incentive to operate their plants efficiently and to show bookkeeping profits.[12] Thus, regardless of whether surplus funds are used for inventory hoarding or just lie idle, serving to lessen managerial incentives, the result is reduction of the national output.

Labor Market. The Soviets were conspicuously unsuccessful in preventing open inflation in the labor market in the thirties and during the war. Like all other factors of production, industrial labor was continually in short supply; unlike the price of other factors of production, the price of labor (i.e., the wage rate) was not effectively controlled. Bank supervision of enterprise expenditures for labor was hardly effective in the prewar period, nor was there much direct allocation of labor. As a result, managers used excess funds to compete for workers, driving up wage rates rapidly and continuously. As will be demonstrated statistically in Chapter 2 (Table 3), wage rates increased more than fivefold from 1928 to 1940, and in every year of this period for which data are available the actual wage level exceeded the projected level.

Soviet wage inflation had an impact on real national output through at least three channels. First, the unplanned increase in the average wage rate was one of the principal factors responsible for the development of repressed inflation in the Soviet consumers'-goods markets. This effect was accentuated by the fact that projected increases in productivity were typically underfulfilled (see Chapter 2, especially Table 5). Accordingly, part of the loss to national output immediately caused by repressed inflation in this market is ultimately due to wage inflation.

Second, the tremendous turnover of the industrial labor force, which exceeded 100 per cent annually over a good part of the prewar period (Chapter 2, Table 2), may be attributed primarily to the ability of managers of enterprises to bid workers away from each other by offering higher wages. The effect on output of such a huge labor turnover is not difficult to imagine, and was in fact discussed with considerable alarm by Soviet economists and administrators at the time.

Finally, wage inflation together with the failure of productivity to increase on schedule upset Soviet plans for stabilizing the price level of raw materials and producers' goods, and caused an expansion of the subsidy program far beyond original intentions. The cost-price system as an accurate indicator of scarcity relationships between components of production was thoroughly disrupted in the process. (The relation between wage inflation, subsidies, and allocation of resources is discussed in Chapter 11, and the reader is referred to that chapter for an expanded statement of the problem.) We are not sure how much Soviet planners rely on relative prices and relative money costs of production in making decisions about the direction and methods of production, but it is hard to believe they can entirely avoid being influenced by these factors. To the extent that they are influenced by a distorted cost-price system, misallocation of resources results, and the level of national output must fall short of the level which might otherwise be achieved. It is safe to say that if the price system were *not* used because of distortions introduced by subsidies or for other reasons, the level of output would certainly suffer. It is difficult to conceive of a reasonably efficient solution of Soviet allocation and production problems without the use of a pricing mechanism.

To summarize: it is clear that direct controls are heavily relied upon by the Soviets to divert an extraordinarily large portion of the national output into investment. Nevertheless, in most markets a substantial degree of freedom still exists; money, prices, and incentives, rather than physical controls, are the prime movers. Because of the very high level of government expenditures maintained, taxes are essential to the efficient operation of these markets.

Chapter 2

TAXATION, INFLATION, AND THE FINANCIAL PLAN

THE FINANCIAL PLAN

The success of Soviet tax policy cannot be judged by inspecting the budget accounts alone. Inflation developed in the prewar period despite the fact that budgetary surpluses were recorded almost every year; this was possible because the budget is but one of several elements in the Soviet financial system, each of which has its place in the inflation picture. We shall preface our inquiry into the problem of inflation with a description of these other elements of the financial plan.

In addition to the budget accounts, the important elements are (*a*) on the receipts side: retained profits of enterprises and depreciation reserves; (*b*) on the expenditure side: investment financed by retained profits and depreciation reserves, and short-term loans by the State Bank (*Gosbank*). Receipts and expenditures are not necessarily equal; currency in circulation serves as the balancing item. For purposes of illustration, a rough approximation of Soviet financial accounts for 1936, a year for which most of the data are available, is presented in Table 1.

All items in Table 1 are reflected in one form or another in the accounts of the State Bank; the funds which it does not collect or disburse directly (as the agent of the budget) are handled by banks which keep their balances with the State Bank. Funds which the Bank does not disburse directly include those for budget-financed capital investment and that part of depreciation reserves which is used for replacing old or constructing new equipment; these funds are transferred to the so-called long-term investment banks for final disbursement. The investment banks also handle the retained profits of enterprises. It should be noted that investment banks are not credit-

TABLE 1 Soviet National Financial Accounts, 1936 (estimate; billions of rubles)

Receipts		Expenditures	
Budget receipts (including bonds)	94.4	Budget expenditures	92.5
Retained profits		Investment and other expenditures financed outside budget	
State enterprises	8.9		
Collective farms	1.5[a]	From retained profits	
Others	?	State enterprises	8.9[c]
Depreciation reserves	4.9[b]		
		Others	2.6[d]
		Depreciation	?
		Short-term credit (State Bank)	8.1
		Long-term loans to collective farms and farmers	1.5[e]
	109.7		113.6
Currency issue	1.6	Currency withdrawal	0
Discrepancy	2.3		
Total	113.6	Total	113.6

For sources and references, see Appendix.

creating organizations: this function is reserved exclusively to the State Bank.

An excess of budget receipts over budget expenditures can be used by the State Bank to offset its short-term credit operations or to retire currency from circulation. On the other hand, if expenditures are larger than receipts, or if the net increase in short-term credit operations of the State Bank exceeds the surplus of receipts over expenditures, new currency enters circulation. This relationship is not upset by changes in voluntary savings by the population (other than increases in hoards), since savings are deposited in banks which in turn invest most of their funds in government securities; funds from all purchases of government securities are included in budget receipts. However, an increase in cash hoarded by the population does upset the relationship, since it means that part of the income created by the state through its expenditures is not respent to increase either budget receipts (via sales and profits taxes) or the retained profits of enterprises. A desire on the part of the population to hold more money therefore increases the increment to cash in circulation resulting from a given amount of new short-term loans.

The short-term credit operations of the State Bank determine the issue of new currency not only in the accounting sense indicated above, but also in a more substantive sense. In the early 1930's, when the basis of the present Soviet credit system was established, the State Bank was made the *only* source of currency issue in the USSR. At that time the Bank was given the authority to extend short-term credit to finance (1) goods in transit, (2) seasonal production processes and expenses, (3) "other temporary needs connected with the production and turnover of goods." [1] In 1933, the Bank was assigned a further function, (4) the task of financing a large percentage of the permanent working capital needs of trade organizations.[2] Since 1939, credit has also been extended by the State Bank (5) to finance a part of the permanent working capital of heavy industry; and after 1943 the Bank (6) advanced large credits to enterprises in the liberated areas for reconstruction, especially for the purpose of rebuilding their working capital.[3] With the exception of the period from 1941 to 1943 — years of great internal disruption, when the budget ran deficits which were met by currency issue — credit created to finance the above-noted operations has been the sole source of new currency in circulation. Increases in currency in circulation occur whenever net receipts from other financial operations, primarily the surplus of budget receipts over budget expenditures, are not large enough to offset the new quantity of short-term loans.

It is important to understand why an increase in short-term credit outstanding which exceeds the surplus from other financial operations is almost certain to involve an increase in the circulation of cash currency. There is a fairly rigid dichotomy in the Soviet Union between transactions in which the household is a participant (i.e., transactions between households, or between state enterprise and the household) and those entirely outside the household sector (between enterprises and organizations). The former are conducted almost entirely in cash money; the latter, with minor exceptions, are handled by means of clearing operations of deposit money in the State Bank.[4] Workers use cash to purchase goods and services from the state or from each other; they may also hoard cash. Enterprises use cash only to pay wages; purchases of raw materials and equipment from other enterprises are paid for by a credit to the account of the buyer and a debit to the account of the seller in the State Bank. Every extension of short-term credit by the State Bank is resolved eventually into increased payments for either the labor or the nonlabor components of production. An increase in credit which is not eventually spent on wages simply involves an equal increase in bookkeeping payments to the state. But any credit increase which is used to finance wage payments must be converted to cash; part of this cash may not return to the state.

For example, if an additional 2 billion rubles of short-term credit had been extended to state enterprises in 1936 (Table 1), and these funds in their peregrinations around the economy were never used to finance wage payments, it can be shown that they would finally result in 2 billion rubles of additional budgetary receipts or enterprise profits; the financial balance would not be upset and cash currency in circulation (the balancing item) would not increase. If, on the other hand, the 2 billion rubles were paid entirely to workers, it might conceivably result in a 2-billion-ruble additional increase in cash in circulation: this would follow if the population hoarded the whole increase in income instead of spending part of it on goods and services. In reality, the increase in cash circulation would be much smaller, since part of the new income would undoubtedly be used to purchase consumers' goods from the state, thus increasing either budget receipts (via the sales and profits taxes) or the profits of state enterprises. Budget receipts from the income tax would also tend to increase slightly. We see from this example that increases in cash in circulation can come only from increases in short-term credit which are eventually spent on wages.[5] It is also clear that the increase in cash held by the population is never as great as the increment to wages.

The state is of course concerned with the increase in bank-deposit money which results from an extension of short-term credit, as well as with increases in cash in circulation. Both forms of currency constitute claims for goods and services, albeit not for the same goods and services. Some of the difficulties created by the existence of more currency claims (either bank deposit or cash) than there are goods and services to be bought at given prices in consumers' goods and factor markets were indicated in the previous chapter, and need not be repeated here.

If more new short-term loans are extended than is consistent with financial stability, the nature and direction of inflation depends largely on the kinds of economic controls which are employed. One of the most important of these controls is State Bank supervision over expenditures by enterprises, to be discussed in greater detail below. Funds which accumulate to the accounts of enterprises either from operating receipts or from short-term credit are not segregated automatically into cash and noncash components; [6] the segregation is determined by enterprise production and financial plans. The Bank's responsibility is to insure that the amount of currency converted to cash in order to pay wages does not exceed the amount called for by plan. Even if the volume of short-term loans were not so large as to upset financial stability in the aggregate, misallocation of funds by the State Bank between cash and noncash currency could cause inflation in one sector and deflation in the other.

In the prewar period there undoubtedly were inflationary pressures in both sets of markets. Those in the labor market were expressed openly, since the price as well as the allocation of labor were poorly controlled; inflation in the market for raw materials and equipment was repressed, since prices were rigidly controlled and allocation of many commodities was accomplished physically. In all probability, the rigidity of price and allocation controls over raw materials and equipment caused the conversion into cash for wages of a larger percentage of enterprise deposits than would otherwise have been the case.[7]

Inflation in the factor market leads, of course, to inflation in the markets for final output.[8] Most important, wage inflation increases the effective demand for consumers' goods without an automatic, commensurate increase in the quantity or price of goods supplied; repressed inflation accordingly develops in the consumers'-goods market unless taxes are increased. Taxes may be increased for another reason as well: increased wage rates raise the cost per unit of commodities purchased by the state, i.e., the cost index of a unit of budget expenditures, including subsidies, rises.[9] This makes it necessary for the state to increase taxes if it is to achieve its previous level of "real" expenditures. If there were open inflation in the nonlabor-factor markets, a similar rise in the cost index of budget expenditures would ensue. However, as we have pointed out, inflation in this market has been effectively repressed.

Since there was inflation in Soviet factor markets, at least until 1948, it is quite obvious that the Soviets financed too large a part of total state activity by short-term credit, and too small a part by taxation. If the Soviets had financed their entire expansion by taxation, it is unlikely that inflation could have resulted. No increase in currency would have occurred, and it seems highly improbable that the velocity of circulation could have increased sufficiently to have supported even the expansion of economic activity which actually took place, let alone inflation. So austere a policy, however, would in all probability have stifled economic activity. Some increment to both deposit currency and cash currency was undoubtedly warranted in the prewar period as it is at present, because of the rapidity of Soviet economic expansion.

The relation between taxes and short-term loans best calculated to produce financial stability in certain simple economic models is a function of many variables, as Professor D. H. Robertson has demonstrated; estimating the relationship is no simple matter.[10] Moreover, it is beyond the scope of this book to discuss Soviet bank policy in detail.[11] Therefore we content ourselves here with inferring from the actual course of events that the combination of banking policy and fiscal policy, at least until 1948, was on the whole inflationary, although this was not equally true for each individual year, as we shall see later. We then assume, for purposes of analysis, that bank policy was the sole offender, and proceed to examine the problems which confronted the tax authorities. Although this assumption is perhaps extreme, there is some evidence to support it.

First, as Professor R. P. Powell has indicated, Soviet banking theory is not very sophisticated. In general the Soviets hold to what Robertson calls the "principle of productive credit" [12] (more commonly referred to as the "real bills" or "commercial loan" credit policy; this doctrine asserts, in brief, that from the standpoint of monetary stability the right amount of credit will be created if commercial banks restrict their loans to those borrowing for short-term bona fide commercial purposes). Powell concludes that for this reason Soviet financial plans may well have been inherently inflationary.[13]

Second, even if the *plans* were not inflationary, there is some evidence that the short-term credit program, in its execution, may have been largely responsible for the development of inflation. In the prewar years for which data are available, actual extension of short-term credit quite consistently exceeded plan.[14] Budget receipts, on the other hand, were larger than plan from 1929–30 to 1936; from 1937 to 1940 budget receipts were below plan, but less so than budget expenditures, i.e., budget surpluses were larger than planned. Budget surpluses were underfulfilled only in the years 1931 and 1932. This creates the presumption that banking rather than budget operations were primarily responsible for the development of Soviet inflation, if it is meaningful to assign responsibility to any one factor alone.

METHOD OF ANALYSIS

For purposes of analysis, inflationary pressures will be subdivided into two categories: those which have and those which have not been correctly anticipated by the tax authorities. Anticipated inflationary pressures are defined as those which can be offset by the planned tax program. Successful prediction of the inflationary gap requires good projections of the values of the many economic variables which affect the gap: short-term bank credit, velocity of currency circulation, wage rates, employment, productivity, output of consumers' goods, rate of investment, and so forth. In the prewar period the Soviets were conspicuously unsuccessful in anticipating changes in some of these variables, particularly wage rates, and this led to the generation of *unanticipated* inflationary pressures. The distinction between these two categories of inflationary pressures is empirical, and exists only as long as the Soviets are unable to predict all pressures or prevent their occurrence.

There is some overlapping in the foregoing list of variables. Excess bank credit and increases in the velocity of currency in circulation are largely reflected in higher wage rates and increased employment. We will not be concerned with bank credit or velocity as such in the discussion which follows. The authorities seeking hints for tax policy would find it extremely difficult to translate changes in these variables into operationally significant units, particularly since their conception of the relation between bank lending and financial stability is faulty, as we have indicated. Rather, the tax authorities are guided by such things as changes in household income and demand for consumers' goods. For their purpose, changes in wage rates and in employment, the size of queues outside the state stores, and prices in collective farm markets are all much more pertinent than changes in bank credit and currency velocity.

Our classification of inflationary pressures is not unlike classifications used by Western writers in recent years to characterize inflationary processes in capitalist countries. A. G. Hart, for example, distinguishes between demand-pull and cost-push inflation; [15] R. Turvey and H. Brems, and also Bent Hansen, distinguish between inflation in the factor markets and inflation in the market for final output.[16] Wage inflation, the major unanticipated factor in Soviet inflation, corresponds primarily to inflation in the factor market, or to cost-push inflation. Our anticipated inflationary pressures are similar to demand-pull inflation and inflation in the market for final output. The classifications do not exactly match, as we shall see, because wage inflation affects final demand as well as cost. Nevertheless, the similarity between these other classifications and the one used here may facilitate understanding of the analysis which follows.

ANTICIPATED INFLATIONARY PRESSURES

The budget occupies a more prominent position in the economy of the Soviet Union than is the case in most Western nations. For example, it has been estimated that in 1937 Soviet budgetary receipts were 36 per cent of gross national product, in comparison with 17 per cent for the United States in the same year.[17] This relatively greater magnitude is due primarily to the very high level of ***planned nonconsumption*** expenditures incorporated in the budget each year. Nonconsumption is defined here to include all activities from which the household sector of the economy receives money income (including transfer payments) but which do not result in the output of goods or services for which the household can spend its income. The more important nonconsumption categories financed by taxation are: investment in fixed and working capital; expenditures on defense; expenditures on administration, and on the so-called social and cultural categories such as education, health services, social security, and so forth.

It is estimated that since the inception of the industrialization drive in 1928, net investment, the first nonconsumption category, has constituted between 20 and 30 per cent of national income.[18] This is probably the highest rate of investment sustained over an extended period of time by any nation. Part of this investment has been financed by enterprises from their retained profits, part has taken the form of budget expenditure. The method of financing chosen does not, of course, affect the impact on the consumer, which is determined solely by the *level* of investment — its share in gross national product. The burden on the consumer will remain unchanged, but the budget will be larger, if the state prefers to subsidize investment or operating expenditures in some industries instead of pricing their output sufficiently above cost to enable them to finance themselves. This has in fact been the Soviet policy: mark-ups over cost have been high in the consumers'-goods industries and low in the producers'-goods industries; profits have then been redistributed through the budget.[19]

The second nonconsumption category, defense, was not very significant in net national output before 1936,[20] but loomed large in the years just preceding World War II, overshadowed all other budget expenditures during the war, and in the postwar period continues to absorb a substantial portion of the national output and of total budget expenditures. As for the final item — government expenditures on education, health, and the other social and cultural services — this understandably occupies a more prominent position in the economy than is the case in Western countries, since in the Soviet Union the state has taken over many of the social functions which are discharged by the private sector in capitalist nations.

The sum of all these expenditures creates a tremendous inflationary potential in the form of large amounts of excess purchasing power in the hands of the household; this must be offset somewhere in the economy if monetary stability is to be achieved. Voluntary savings cannot be expected to close much of the gap; as in other countries where standards of living are low, the rate of personal voluntary savings in the Soviet Union is very low.[21] Nor could inflationary pressures be eased by external borrowing, since the Soviet Union was not able (at least until World War II) to obtain substantial net physical or financial aid from foreign countries. Therefore taxation remains the primary instrument for achieving monetary stability. Conversely, the major tax problem is the absorption of the enormous excess purchasing power created by the state-planned nonconsumption expenditures.

In the past 15 years the state has never failed to take away more than half of consumers' money incomes in the form of money taxes.[22] The great magnitude of the excess purchasing power, as well as the fact that the tax system is part of a planning apparatus, limit the types of tax which are effective.[23] Despite these considerations, the tax problem would be relatively straightforward if the plan were rigidly adhered to in all respects.[24] Under these ideal circumstances, the required tax could be estimated as follows: Planned taxes on the consumer *equal* planned consumer income *minus* planned cost of consumers'-goods output to be offered for sale *minus* personal voluntary savings *minus* retained profits of enterprises which produce consumers' goods. Since the plan is not strictly adhered to, this formula does not provide fiscal stability. It could, however, be modified to recognize the probability of various unplanned movements in output and wages; we shall discuss these modifications later in this chapter.

UNANTICIPATED INFLATIONARY PRESSURES

The picture we have presented so far of inflationary pressures in the Soviet Union is essentially static, since it takes into consideration only the excess demand generated by the initial gap between voluntary savings and nonconsumption expenditures. But highly inflationary situations are characterized by changes in economic variables leading to secondary reactions throughout the economy. Unless these changes are prevented by the use of controls, they destroy the effectiveness of the tax formula set forth above for maintaining monetary stability.

The Soviet inflationary potential can be traced to two conditions, other than the high rate of nonconsumption, which have consistently characterized the Soviet economy: (1) planning for a very high degree of utilization of the components of production;[25] (2) easy availability of funds for use by enterprises and organizations. Soviet planning for full utilization of resources has the effect of creating a very strong real (as opposed to monetary) demand for labor, equipment, and raw materials. It also renders the supply of these factors relatively inelastic, at least in the short run. Given these real demand and supply conditions, earnest competition for the components of production in the factor markets is inevitable. The easy availability of funds to enterprises and organizations translates real demand into effective demand, and makes an inflationary process in the factor markets possible.

Both direct and monetary controls have been used by the Soviets in their efforts to prevent the development and to offset the effects of inflation in the factor markets. As was noted in Chapter 1, these controls include direct allocation of important materials and equipment, allocation of certain classes of labor, almost universal price control, and State Bank control over expenditures by enterprises and organizations.

The fact that prices of the nonlabor factors of production have risen relatively little over the past 25 years does not mean that the controls were successful. The practice of directly allocating important raw materials and equipment undoubtedly contributed something to price stability, and strict enforcement of price controls contributed even more. But the decisive factor was the profligate use of subsidies.[26] These were required to offset the effects of wage inflation on the costs of producers' goods and raw materials.[27]

Until the late 1930's the state attempted little direct allocation of labor, and imposed few restrictions on the flow of labor from one enterprise to another. For obvious reasons it is much more difficult to allocate men than materials and equipment; accordingly, the Soviets preferred to accomplish the distribution of labor through market forces. But the market was extremely turbulent. Managers competed very actively for workers, and workers, aware of their strong bargaining position, moved from job to job seeking higher wages. The extreme fluidity of the labor market is clearly reflected in the official labor turnover figures for large scale industry, which are presented in Table 2.

TABLE 2 Inflow and Outflow of Workers in Large-Scale Industry (percentage of total number of workers)

	1928	1929	1930	1931	1932	1933	1934	1935
Inflow	100.8	122.4	176.4	151.2	127.1	124.9	100.5	91.6
Outflow	92.4	115.2	152.4	136.8	135.3	122.4	96.7	86.1

For source, see Appendix.

In the absence of extensive direct allocation of labor, wage inflation must be prevented by controls over the price of labor and over the sums of money which enterprises may expend on this factor.

As we shall see, neither of these controls operated at all effectively before 1939.

Evasion of Wage Controls. Let us first consider wage controls. The plan for an enterprise usually specifies the categories of jobs to be filled, the rate at which each category is to be paid, and the total amount of cash which may be spent on wages, i.e., the authorized wage fund or payroll. If the plans are enforced, how do wage rates become inflated?

Managers of Soviet plants have resorted and still resort to all sorts of devices for paying higher than planned wage rates in competing for workers. They are substantially aided in their efforts by the complexity of the Soviet wage-payment system. Unauthorized upgrading, for example, can be accomplished easily and with little chance of detection because of the large number of piece-rate schedules which are used, and because many of these schedules are progressive. It has been reported that some factories use hundreds of different rates at one time; there were, for example, up to 700 rate schedules in effect in the factories of the railroad transport system in 1937.[28] It is not only difficult to apply correctly so complex a system; it is almost impossible, and very costly, to audit it properly.

As part of the incentive program, elaborate systems of bonus payments to workers have been established to reward good productivity and output performances. It has been reported that many plants have as many as 75 bonus systems in operation simultaneously.[29] Again, complexity lends itself to misuse. There are numerous reports of instances where funds reserved for bonus payments have been used to pay higher wages unaccompanied by either output or productivity increases.[30]

Several writers claim that enterprises pad payroll plans in order to have extra cash available for competing on the labor market.[31] Other enterprises gain access to uncommitted cash funds by reducing, below plan, the number of workers paid from their authorized wage fund. This is done by contracting with another enterprise or organization to take over part of the planned task, usually a job requiring a large labor input, or else by hiring outside workers to come in and do the job, listing the cost of their services under some miscellaneous classification such as "other monetary expenditures" instead of under wages. Although the funds which are freed by this second method are used to pay higher wages or to hire additional workers, this is not reflected as excess wage payments, even though the outside workers usually cost the enterprise more than their own workers would have.[32]

A fertile field for evading wage-fund limitations was opened up when cash available to enterprises for paying wages was tied to gross output performance; this was the rule from 1933 to 1935, and has been the rule since 1939. It has led to manipulation of gross output figures in various ways. Some enterprises have falsified gross output by including in it canceled orders and waste (*brak*).[33] Workers are not supposed to receive remuneration for *brak* attributable to negligence, but apparently the regulation is not strictly observed.[34] The relation of the wage fund to gross output is particularly easy to manipulate where an enterprise produces more than one commodity (in Soviet terminology, an assortment); enterprises which find themselves short of cash can try to produce that combination of commodities which requires the least expenditure on wages per unit of gross output, even when this deviates from the combination called for by plan. A similar manipulation of the planned assortment, induced by the Soviet practice (abandoned in 1949) of measuring gross output in 1926–27 prices, was to concentrate on the production of that commodity which yielded the largest gross output, valued at the preindustrialization prices, per unit of input (including labor) measured in current prices.[35] Manipulation of assortment to minimize wage-fund requirements or to maximize gross output obviously produces the largest variations in cash requirements and availabilities when it is attempted on an interenterprise scale by a higher administrative body (e.g., the trust, central administration, or ministry).[36]

There is a further source of extra funds arising from the tie between the authorized wage fund and gross output. Although gross output is related quite directly to the efforts of labor actively engaged on the production line, it depends only indirectly upon the efforts of overhead personnel — bookkeepers, statisticians, administrators, etc. — the need for which may remain constant over a wide range of output. Yet the wages and salaries of many of these persons are included in the regular wage fund of the enterprise. If the plan of gross output is exceeded, that part of the authorized increase to the wage fund which need not be spent on more office workers can be used to bid up wages.[37]

The foregoing examples are sufficient to indicate the ingenuity with which Soviet managers and accountants have evaded wage controls. Many other subterfuges could be cited, but this is hardly necessary. Some legal loopholes which facilitate wage inflation will be described in the following section on State Bank control over wage expenditures.

A continuous upward wage movement is supported by the tendency for the current year's *de facto* inflated wage level to gain legal status in the succeeding year. In submitting plans for the following year, directors of enterprises naturally submit wage plans which will enable them to procure the labor they need, i.e., wage plans based on *going* or *inflated* wage rates rather than on previously planned rates. Because of the resistance of workers to a reduction in money wages, higher planning units are not likely to reject these wage plans and call for lower estimates. The process is repeated each year, and the wage level consequently tends to move steadily upward.

State Bank Control over Wage Expenditures. Attempts to check wage inflation by preventing illegal practices of the sort described above have been going on for the past twenty years. It was natural for the State Bank to be drawn into the campaign because of its central position in the economy with respect to cash currency: enterprises and organizations are supposed to receive all their cash for wage payments from the Bank, and to deposit there all cash receipts from sales to the population. The Bank's powers until 1939 were too limited to have a noticeable effect on wage inflation; the legislation of 1939, which is still in force, suffers from serious defects but represents a considerable improvement over previous decrees.

From 1931 until February 1933 the Bank had virtually no authority. It was obligated to honor all requests by enterprises for cash even when such requests were for wage payments in excess of plan. Each enterprise or organization was required to submit to the Bank a certificate (*spravka*) regarding its planned wage expenditures. The Bank's duty was confined to checking cash disbursements of enterprises against planned wage payments and informing the Commissariat of Labor or the Workers' and Peasants' Inspection (*RKI*) of overexpenditures. Any disciplinary action had to be taken by these organizations.[38]

The authority of the Bank was increased in 1933. Enterprises were obligated to submit to the Bank so-called "standard certificates" (*standartnye spravki*) indicating the amount of their authorized wage expenditures. The Bank was obligated to honor *all* requests for cash not exceeding the absolute amount of the authorized wage expenditures, as well as requests for additional funds from enterprises which were overfulfilling their production programs. Presumably the Bank was *not* to permit expenditures for wages to increase at a faster rate than output, once the basic authorized wage fund had been exhausted. It is not clear just how firm a stand the Bank was able to take in the face of insistent demands by enterprises for cash.[39]

Apparently control by the Bank in this period was not successful, for in 1935 most of the responsibility for overexpenditures was shifted to the enterprise and to its superior administrative organizations. Enterprises were required to submit an accounting report to the Bank showing their actual wage expenditures for the preceding period and the Bank was obligated to disburse the required amount of cash. The Bank's only control functions appear to have been to check the correctness of enterprise estimates of their own wage requirements, and to make sure that enterprises did not spend on other things funds reserved for wages. Accordingly, while this decree was in force, the Bank disbursed cash to enterprises without regard to the amount of the authorized wage fund or execution of output plans.[40]

In 1938, a new experiment in Bank control was initiated. A group of 210 enterprises which had persistently overexpended their wage funds were required to submit to the Bank not only the accounting reports previously required, but statements of authorized wage expenditures and percentage fulfillment of output plans. Armed with this information, the Bank was supposed to tie cash disbursements to fulfillment of production plans in a manner to be described below. The experiment was declared a success,[41] and on August 15, 1939 the new controls were applied to all *industrial* enterprises. They were applied, with modifications, to various other classes of enterprises and organizations at about the same time.[42] The main provisions of the 1939 decree, which differs only in details from later decrees, may be summarized as follows:[43]

1. Basically, wage-fund expenditures are tied to fulfillment of the plan of gross output. Overexpenditures for wages are allowed if the output plan is overfulfilled (and by the same percentage); similarly

underfulfillment of the output plan involves a proportional reduction in the allowable expenditures for wages. Exceptions are noted below.

2. The Bank must automatically provide funds for a relative overexpenditure (i.e., relative to output fulfillment) of up to 10 per cent in the first month, and only in the first month, in which such an overexpenditure occurs. This is called a primary overexpenditure. The enterprise is supposed to take immediately corrective measures designed to prevent recurrence of overexpenditures.

3. The Bank is not authorized to disburse funds to an enterprise which repeatedly overspends its wage allotment unless the enterprise secures permission from its central administration or trust.[44] In the latter case, the additional funds are to be taken from the total wage fund of the central administration or trust, that is, they are to be redistributed from the wage funds of sister enterprises.

4. Overexpenditures in any month amounting to more than 10 per cent, whether primary or repeated, require permission of the ministry, and the funds must be redistributed from the wage fund of other enterprises in the ministry.

This decree, though superior to previous decrees, has two major weaknesses. First, according to the 1939 decree, the Bank is permitted to make a primary overpayment of the wage fund of 10 per cent. "Primary overpayment" has been interpreted to mean overpayment in any month which follows a month in which the enterprise has kept within the authorized wage fund.[45] This liberal interpretation, which one writer implies is contrary to the intent of the decree,[46] in effect allows 10 per cent overspending of the wage fund every other month. The second weakness, quantitatively more important, lies in the provisions allowing overexpenditures in successive months, or in excess of 10 per cent, if permission is obtained from one of the higher administrative organizations.[47] Soviet writers claim that permission is usually granted mechanically without investigation into the merits of each case.[48] Since it is usually to the interest of the higher organization to support member enterprises in their requests for extra funds, the system of control is inherently weak.

Some flexibility with respect to wages and other cost items must be maintained to compensate for the errors and oversights which are inevitable in large-scale planning, and also to meet unforeseen developments.[49] This no doubt explains the loopholes left in provisions (3) and (4). The Soviets have not yet solved the difficult problem of creating the necessary degree of flexibility without having enterprises and higher organizations take advantage of the situation.

In spite of the weaknesses of the 1939 decree, a substantial reduction in overexpenditures was reported almost immediately. Overexpenditures of more than 25,000 enterprises are reported to have declined from 8.7 per cent in September 1939 to 5.8 per cent in October and November and 5.5 per cent in December.[50] According to N. Zabozlaev, overexpenditures decreased every year in the period 1939 to 1945 except for 1942; in 1945, overexpenditures of industrial enterprises, expressed as a percentage of the authorized wage fund, were "1½ times lower" than in 1939.[51]

It is not clear that Bank control over wage expenditures is primarily responsible for the reduction in the rate of wage inflation. The controls over labor mobility, which were introduced just before and during the war and are generally still in effect, certainly play an important role in restricting managerial competition for labor. Although the wage overexpenditure problem has been reduced, it has not been eliminated. At the time of writing (1952), Soviet economic literature is still devoting considerable space to attacking most of the malpractices described above and to suggesting ways of reducing still further overexpenditures of the wage fund.

Wage Inflation: Planned and Unplanned. Having examined the reasons for Soviet inability to curb wage inflation, let us look at the available time series relating to wages. From 1928 to 1940, the average annual wage increased almost sixfold and the annual payroll about fifteenfold. The figures are presented in Tables 3 and 4. Part of the phenomenal increase in the average wage is undoubtedly a consequence of the Soviet policy of using wage differentials to allocate labor. Wage differentials set by the state were supposed to attract both new labor and workers engaged in old industries and jobs into industries where expansion was rapid, or where productivity was higher. It is much simpler for political reasons to adjust wages upward than downward. In the Second Five Year Plan, for example, wage increases were *planned* for workers in *every* branch of the national economy; these increases ranged from about 13 per cent for trade to 31 per cent for water transport and 50 per cent for wage earners in agriculture; in no branch of the economy was a reduction in wage rates planned.[52]

TABLE 3 Average Annual Wage Rate, Planned and Realized, 1928–1942

Year	Wage rate (rubles)		Increase (per cent)		
	Planned	Realized	Planned [a]	Unplanned [b]	Total [c]
1928	690 [d]	703		2	
1929		800			14
1930		936 (879 [e])			17
1931	941	1127	7.1 [e]	20 [f]	20
1932		1427			27
1932	(994) [g]				
1933	1523	1566	6.7	3	10
1934	1625	1858	3.8	14	19
1935	2031	2269	9.3	12	22
1936	2465	2856	8.6	16	26
1937	2978	3038	4.3	2	6
1937	(1755) [g]				
1938		3467			14
1939		[3867] [h]			[11] [h]
1940		4069			[5] [h]
1942	(4100) [g]				

For sources, see Appendix.

[a] Planned increase is increase from the realized wage of one year to the planned wage for the subsequent year.

[b] Unplanned increase is increase of realized over planned wages for the same year.

[c] Total increase is the increase from the realized figure of one year to the realized figure for the subsequent year.

[d] This figure is for the year ending October 1, 1928.

[e] The planned wage rate for 1931 is coupled (in the source) with a realized figure for 1930 which differs from other realized figures in our series. Nevertheless, in obtaining a figure for the planned increase in the average wage rate, it is more meaningful to use the figures which have been coupled together, and this has been done.

[f] The unplanned increase may be too high because of the discrepancy mentioned in footnote e. That is to say, 941 rubles may be a somewhat low wage rate because it is based on a preliminary realized wage for 1930 which is too low. Hence the increase from 941 to 1127 may be high.

[g] These are the figures contained in each five-year plan for the last year of the plan period.

[h] Average wage was unavailable for 1939. Interpolation was used to obtain the figure entered. The basis for the interpolation was the total wage bill figures for 1938–1940 presented in Table 4.

A comparison of planned and actual wage rates for each year indicates, however, that much of the increase cannot be attributed to deliberate design on the part of the planners. Actual wage rates exceded planned rates by 12 to 16 per cent in four of the six years for which both figures are available.[53] Comparison of plan and ful-

TABLE 4 Annual Wage Bill (Payroll), Planned and Realized, 1928–1942

Year	Wage bill (billion rubles)		Increase (per cent)		
	Planned	Realized	Planned[a]	Unplanned[b]	Total[c]
1928		8.2			
1929		9.7			18
1930		13.6 (12.5)[d]			40
1931	15.3	21.4	22[d]	40[e]	57
1932	26.8	32.7	25	22	53
1932	(15.7)[f]				
1933		35.0			7
1934	38.1	44.0	9	15	26
1935	49.8	56.2	13	13	28
1936	63.4	71.6	13	13	27
1937	78.3	82.2	9	5	15
1937	(50.7)[f]				
1938	93.6	96.4	14	3	17
1939		116.5			21
1940	129.3	123.7	11	−4	6
1942	(133.2)[f]				

For sources, see Appendix.

[a] Planned increase is increase from the realized wage of one year to the planned wage for the subsequent year.

[b] Unplanned increase is increase of realized over planned wages for the same year.

[c] Total increase is the increase from the realized figure of one year to the realized figure for the subsequent year.

[d] The planned wage rate for 1931 is coupled (in the source) with a realized figure for 1930 which differs from other realized figures in our series. Nevertheless, in obtaining a figure for the planned increase in the average wage rate, it is more meaningful to use the figures which have been coupled together, and this has been done.

[e] The unplanned increase may be too high because of the discrepancy mentioned in footnote d. That is to say, 941 rubles may be a somewhat low wage rate because it is based on a preliminary realized wage for 1930 which is too low. Hence the increase from 941 to 1127 may be high.

[f] These are the figures contained in each Five-Year Plan for the last year of the plan period.

fillment figures for the Five Year Plans reveals much more dramatically the inability of the planners to contain wages. A 44 per cent increase in the average wage rate was anticipated in the First Five Year Plan period; the actual increase was 121 per cent. A 25 per cent increase was scheduled for the second Plan period; the actual increase was 113 per cent. From 1937 to 1942, the average annual wage was to rise by 53 per cent; this increase was virtually achieved by 1940.[54] The deviation of actual wage rates and total payroll from plan is much more significant for this analysis than the absolute increases in these figures. Planned or anticipated wage increases are presumably taken into account in financial planning. Unanticipated increases cannot, by definition, be planned for.

A rough idea of the impact of unplanned wage increases on the consumers'-goods market can be gained by examining the situation in a specific year. The average annual wage rate in 1931 was 1,127 rubles, or almost 20 per cent above the planned rate of 941 rubles. This resulted in an increase in unanticipated income to wage earners of roughly 3.5 billion rubles. Actually, overpayment of the wage fund was 6 billion rubles, but 2.5 billion can be attributed to greater than planned employment in the socialized sector of the economy. To the extent that this increase in unplanned employment was in industries producing for government use, the inflationary impact on the consumers'-goods market was, of course, greater than 3.5 billion rubles; the inflationary impact is also increased to the extent that the higher level of employment in the socialized sector represents a decrease in employment in agriculture or private enterprise. For reasons to be discussed in the next section, only a fraction of this excess is absorbed automatically by taxes. Since total consumer money income in 1931 was about 30 billion rubles (see Chapter 10), of which 21.4 billion constituted the wage bill, effective demand of the population increased, as a gross approximation, by about 10 per cent of total money income and 15 per cent of the income of the non-agricultural population.

Unplanned wage increases have an impact through costs as well as demand. Since profits are a residual (see Chapter 4), they tend to be squeezed between rising costs and fixed prices. As a result, either investment financed from retained profits of enterprises or the deductions from profits, or both, must be reduced. Enterprises which are operating at a planned loss, i.e., enterprises subsidized by the budget, suffer additional losses. This necessitates an increase in subsidies. From the budgetary point of view, both of these factors operate to reduce the budget surplus, the first by reducing receipts and the second by increasing expenditures. In addition, all budgetary expenditures allocated to pay current wages must be increased. If the state is to maintain the real level of budgetary expenditures planned, an increase in budgetary receipts is called for. This will be recognized as the counterpart of the increase in budgetary receipts required to restore monetary equilibrium in the consumers'-goods market.

Other Deviations from Plan. Inflationary pressures not anticipated by the planners are also generated by underfulfillment of the plans for increasing productivity and consumers'-goods output, and by overfulfillment of the plan of nonconsumption output. These deviations are mentioned because they have not been uncommon in Soviet experience, but it should be clear that planning failures in these areas are not dynamic in the same sense that errors in wage planning are. Wage inflation has its roots in the motivations of managers and workers in a labor-short, overliquid economy. Under these conditions the strong upward pressure of wages remains a constant threat to financial stability. Failures of productivity and production, on the other hand, are the result of negative rather than positive forces: inability of labor to master new techniques, shortages of important materials, bad weather conditions leading to a poor crop, and so forth.

Soviet expectations of increases in productivity have often been too optimistic. For example, in every year of the Second Five Year Plan the anticipated reduction in costs of production in industry was underfulfilled; this is true even after adjustments are made for increases in the prices of the inputs. The data are presented in Table 5. With respect to production, Soviet practice seems to have

TABLE 5 Planned and Realized Cost (*sebestoimost'*) Reductions in Soviet Industry, 1933–1937 (per cent)

	1933	1934	1935	1936	1937
Planned reduction in costs	−1.5	−4.7	−6.7	−7.4	−8.2
Actual reduction in costs (deflated for increases in prices of inputs)	+0.5	−3.7	−4.1	−4.0	−0.1

For source, see **Appendix**.

been to sacrifice output of consumption goods wherever this was necessary to secure fulfillment of the investment plan. Some relevant data for five-year plan periods are presented in Table 6. It should be borne in mind that unless output of consumers' goods falls behind within the period of an *annual* plan, the financial plans are not upset.

TABLE 6 Targets and Fulfillment of Industrial Consumers' Goods (percentage increase)

	First Plan Period 1927–28 to 1932–33		Second Plan Period 1932–1937		Third Plan Period* 1937–1940	
	Target	Fulfillment (1932)	Target	Fulfillment	Target	Fulfillment
Cotton goods	69	−2	87	27	21	17
Woolen goods	180	−6	142	15	34	14
Shoes	142	37	120	100	29	25
Paper and cardboard	171	55	119	62	40	−2
Matches	122	2	114	29	47	38
Soap	176	64	180	39	44	31

For source, see Appendix.

* "Fulfillment for the Third Plan Period is that in 1937–1940. Half of the goals were used in computing the schedule percentage increases during those 3 years" (Jasny, *The Soviet Economy*, p. 20).

It is not difficult to understand why these productivity and output failures disrupt the financial plan and add to inflation. The tax plans anticipate certain rates of increase in productivity and production. If the anticipated increase in productivity does not take place, and if wages are not reduced accordingly, there will be an excess of money in the hands of the consumers relative to the value of consumers' goods to be purchased at given prices. The only instance in which failure to achieve productivity goals does *not* result in excess purchasing power is if productivity increases according to plan in the consumers'-goods industries but not in the producers'-goods industries.

Underfulfillment of the production plan for consumers' goods means fewer goods available for sale to consumers; consumers' incomes, however, usually remain undiminished. Moreover, because the Soviets obtain the bulk of their budget receipts from sales taxes on consumers' goods, the inflationary effect of an underfulfillment of consumers' goods production is multiplied. Again, any *overfulfillment* of planned output of nonconsumption goods which is not attributable to increased productivity involves an increase in consumers' incomes unaccompanied by an increase in supplies of consumers' goods.[55] Each of these occurrences generate some repressed inflation, unless taxes are adjusted upward.

Overfulfillment of the productivity plans has, of course, the opposite effect, i.e., it tends to reduce inflationary pressures. But this has been the less frequent occurrence.

TAXATION PROBLEMS AND POLICIES

For purposes of analysis, inflationary pressures were subdivided into two empirical categories: anticipated and unanticipated. These categories were shown to be similar to Hart's cost-push and demand-pull, and Turvey-Brems' inflation in the factor and final-output markets. For convenience, these alternative designations will be used in the following discussion wherever they convey accurately the meaning intended.

It is most important to recognize that although the two types of inflation, for which we have several sets of names, can be kept in separate analytical boxes, they interact in the real world. The most direct interaction is from excess demand in the factor market to excess demand in the market for final output. Applied to the Soviet economy this simply means that a rising wage level (relative to productivity) increases the demand for consumers' goods relative to the supply at given prices. In a capitalist economy, supply and demand tend to inflate apace as the upward pressure of rising wages on costs induces frequent retail price revisions. Also, the returns to nonwage factors of production are likely to be bid up in a capitalist economy and to have an impact on the market for final output. As we have seen, this does not happen in the USSR, because prices of the nonwage factors are successfully controlled.

Interaction from the final-output market, especially the consumers'-goods market, to the factor market is very important in capitalist countries, but of little significance in the Soviet Union. In Western nations, particularly those with strong labor movements, wages tend to follow final-output prices. In periods of rising prices, workers and unions can be expected to exert all their efforts to keep wages rising commensurately. In some industries, and in some countries, wages are actually tied to a cost-of-living index, and are adjusted regularly to changes in the index. In the USSR, though wages have tended to rise concurrently with retail prices, it is doubtful that the movement in wages can in any sense be considered functionally related to the price rise. Soviet workers belong to unions, but wage determination is not a function of Soviet trade unions; workers have no means of arguing as a bloc for a wage increase, regardless of how rapidly retail prices rise. The key to Soviet wage inflation lies not in rising retail prices, but in the scarcity of Soviet workers relative to demand. And the real stimulus to wage inflation comes from the demand side, in the competition of Soviet managers for industrial labor — a competition in which labor serves as a not unwilling accomplice.

The direction of interaction of inflationary pressures is very significant for Soviet tax policy. Most obvious, perhaps, is the fact that the Soviets can rely almost solely on indirect, price-increasing taxes without fear of wage-price spiral repercussions. If wage inflation were related functionally to changes in consumers'-goods prices, the Soviets might consider it expedient to collect a larger percentage of budget receipts by income taxation, rather than relying primarily on commodity taxation, as now.

A more important, though less obvious, implication is that the absorption of excess demand in the consumers'-goods market will not prevent inflation in the factor markets; however, prevention of excess demand in the factor markets *will* reduce excess demand in the consumers'-goods markets by eliminating unanticipated wage increases. This means that the state cannot prevent wage inflation by taxing the consumer, but can reduce the impact of wage inflation on the consumers'-goods markets by preventing managers from bidding up wages. The question to be asked here is: can managers be prevented from bidding up wages by taxation, or must other devices such as monetary or physical controls be used? The answer to this question depends on the stage, temporally speaking, at which the additional taxes are levied.

Taxation to Prevent Inflation. It was tentatively suggested earlier in this chapter that in the prewar period the Soviets financed too little of their economic expansion by taxation and too much by State Bank credit; otherwise the period could hardly have been so highly inflationary. In theory, inflation could have been avoided if the Soviets had planned for (and properly executed) the financing of a larger part of the working-capital requirements of Soviet enterprises by taxation and retained profits, and less by short-term credit creation. This does not have to be proved; it follows from the logic of a simplified model of economic systems with which we are familiar.[56] Theoretically, if taxes are levied sufficiently early to eliminate the need for Bank credit, excess funds which may be used to bid up wages are never made available to managers of enterprises, and inflation is avoided.

Let us suppose, however, that the Soviets plan for (and execute) much more Bank credit and much fewer taxes than is consistent with stable finance. Can taxes be used to absorb the excess deposits of enterprises *before* these deposits are actually converted to cash and used to bid up wages? If this were attempted, it would have to be accomplished by the present Soviet profits tax or some similar type of tax. The reader is referred to Chapter 4, where the cost-tax-price structure of a typical Soviet enterprise is outlined in detail and discussed. The profits tax is seen to be a residual deduction into the state budget after an enterprise's receipts have been used to finance the following outlays: operating costs of production, investment from retained profits, the turnover tax, and the deductions into the Director's Fund. If either operating costs or the costs of investment from retained profits are greater than the plan calls for, because the average wage has been bid up above plan, prices cannot be adjusted upward to compensate; therefore some other outlay or outlays must be reduced. The turnover tax, typically estimated either as a percentage of price or as so many rubles per unit of output, remains unaffected by changes in cost. The deduction into the Director's Fund which is a positive function of profits is very moderate for firms which underfulfill their profits plan, and can be ignored here. This leaves the profits tax as the only item which may be reduced to compensate for above-plan costs. If the profits tax were *not* a residual but a fixed percentage of price or an absolute amount per unit of output sold — in other words, if it were as invariant to changes in cost as the turnover tax is now — it would be impossible for managers to bid up wages above plan. In fact, no deviation of any sort from the financial plan of the enterprise would be possible, since no degree of freedom would remain in the cost-tax-price structure.

It is doubtful that planning, even under the best circumstances, could ever attain sufficient precision to eliminate the need for slack — in this case, the residual item in the cost-price structure. Moreover, Soviet planning is still fairly crude, as is quite obvious both from the economic literature and from comparison of Soviet plans and their execution.[57] Therefore it would not appear feasible for the Soviets to enforce a profits tax which was not a true residual.[58]

Compromise solutions are possible, of course. The state might collect the profits tax as a fixed amount, but immediately subsidize those enterprises which had spent too much on wages. There is some evidence that this is the procedure actually followed with some enterprises. The method would have the advantage of alerting the authorities to each overfulfillment of expenditures for wages as well as to underfulfillment of productivity plans. It is quite possible, however, that the subsidies would be handed out mechanically, very much as wage expenditures are supervised at present, and that reduction of enterprise deposit accounts by collection of the profits tax as *planned* would have little actual effect on managerial behavior. There is also the possibility that if the rules of the game were obeyed (i.e., if managers kept expenditures within the limits of the plans and subsidies were handed out only in merited cases), the necessary flexibility required to compensate for the errors in, and crudity of, planning would be lost, bottlenecks would develop, and real output would suffer.

The tentative conclusion is that the profits tax must continue to be a residual, and therefore cannot be an effective instrument of fiscal policy. Once the financial plan is drawn up in such a way as to be basically inflationary, taxation, *unaided*, cannot alter execution of the plan to prevent the development of inflation.

The foregoing discussion should not be taken to mean that wage inflation cannot be resisted, given a basically inflationary financial plan. Bank controls over expenditures on wages, described earlier, represent an explicit attempt to prevent wages from being bid up, and may be accurately described as an instrument for repressing inflation. Direct controls which reduce the mobility of labor also tend to repress inflation in the labor market. These seem to be the measures upon which the Soviets must depend to prevent wage inflation in the absence of a major revision in banking policy. If managers are prevented by physical controls and Bank controls from bidding up wages, then the profits tax, even though a residual, may serve to absorb excess deposits into the budget. In this way, and only in this way, is it possible to convert an *ex ante* inflationary financial plan into an *ex post* stable financial balance sheet.

Before turning to the next section, we should like to raise the question of whether the Soviets, given the nature of their economic system and goals, are really free to finance a decidedly larger proportion of their nonconsumption expenditures by taxes rather than by credit. It is commonly asserted of capitalist countries that economic development proceeds most rapidly and efficiently in a mildly inflationary climate. This is true for two reasons: profits expectations are maintained at a high level, thereby helping to prevent drops in the level of private investment; a little excess liquidity in the economy also helps "grease the wheels of trade" without serious side effects. In the Soviet Union inflation is of course not needed to maintain the rate of investment, since this is determined quite independently of expectations of money profits. It is, however, just as important in the USSR as it is in free-enterprise economies to keep the wheels of trade well greased. As we have indicated, Soviet planning, both physical and financial, is very imperfect. The consequences of errors in planning are seriously magnified because the Soviets plan for such full utilization of physical resources and at the some time allow a large degree of decentralized decision making. If each enterprise had at its disposal only *just* enough funds to carry out planned tasks — if there were no recourse to subsidies or to credit, and no allowance were made for failure of productivity to increase as planned, or for waste — then the number of bottlenecks and economic breakdowns which would ensue would be very large indeed.

Suppose, for example, an enterprise is not allocated sufficient fuel to carry out its production plan. If its funds were sufficient to purchase only the quantity of inputs *planned*, it would have no way of acquiring more fuel and production would come to a halt. If, on the other hand, funds are available via subsidy, loan, or residual profits, then the enterprise might be able to get additional fuel and prevent a production breakdown. If the deficit item falls in the "quota" or "decentralized" classifications (see Chapter 1), and the commodity is available, procurement can be accomplished by legal means through ordinary market processes. If the item is "funded" and presumably unobtainable through legal channels without an allocation order, then procurement may have to be extralegal. In the latter case, bribery, persuasion, collusion among officials, doctoring of books, and many other practices may have to be resorted to.[59] Whether the transaction is legal or illegal, however, it is facilitated by the availability of extra funds. The same type of activity could be accomplished by barter, but it would necessarily be on a much more limited scale.

Some financial slack, then, contributes to the smooth functioning of the system; individual production units with access to financial resources can compensate for errors in planning, and for unforeseen developments. On the other hand, financial slack is frequently used for purposes for which it is not intended, e.g. to bid up wage rates, and to hoard scarce materials. It is conceivable that improper use of financial resources by enterprises may create even more problems than the legitimate use of financial reserves serves to eliminate. For while bottlenecks attributable to errors in planning *can* be corrected as soon as they become manifest, there is no obvious way to cope with the invisible bottlenecks created by enterprises which hoard for future use materials which are needed in the present by other enterprises. (To some extent, the seriousness of hoarding and the initial misallocation of resources which results is mitigated by the large amount of illegal trading between enterprises.[60])

The truth of this last speculation cannot, of course, be verified. Accordingly, there is no conclusive answer to the question we raised earlier: whether it is actually feasible for the Soviets to reduce substantially the proportion of the working-capital needs of enterprises which are financed by credit. One conclusion is clear, however. As long as the Soviets plan for overfull employment of their resources, there is no distribution of financial resources which will prevent bottlenecks — visible or invisible — from developing.

Our demonstration that the profits tax cannot serve as an effective fiscal instrument is, in reality, a special case of the more general problem just described. There is a basic inconsistency in Soviet policy. On the one hand their financial objectives have always been non-inflationary; their plans have consistently called for stable or falling prices for everything except labor. On the other hand, their physical planning has been both crude and too ambitious (in terms of availabilities) to permit the use of a deflationary financial policy. The Soviets put their faith in the "principle of productive credit," expecting Bank policies based on this principle to bring them financial stability. They did not realize that the productive-credit principle was not inconsistent with inflation; they also did not realize that considerable slack was necessary for economic planning, as they practiced it. If the principle of productive credit had not already existed and had not inadvertently provided them with financial slack, no doubt the Soviets would have had to invent it.

Taxation to Offset Inflation. Until 1948, the Soviets were unable to *prevent* wage inflation. Therefore they were constantly confronted with problems of tax policy relating to the effects of upward wage pressures and what we have called unanticipated inflationary pressures. There were several alternative courses of action open to the tax authorities.

First, they might have attempted to construct their tax system with built-in flexibility against deviations from plan of the types mentioned above. An examination of the actual structure of the tax system, with its extensive commodity taxation of consumers' goods, inconsequential commodity taxation of producers' goods, and very moderate personal-income taxation, would lead one to conclude that this has not been done. Wage inflation is offset most effectively by income taxation. If the Soviets relied exclusively on income taxation, the effect of unplanned wage increases might be reduced automatically by as much as one-half. The present moderate schedule of income-tax rates could conceivably absorb 5 to 10 per cent of the increased wages, but not more. Obviously, commodity taxation has no automatically compensating features with respect to wage inflation. Furthermore, the high rate of commodity taxation on consumers' goods aggravates the inflationary impact of a decline in the output of consumers' goods, since it also involves a substantial automatic decline in commodity-tax receipts; the low rate of commodity tax on producers' goods (and on a large proportion of government services) fails to provide an automatic increase in commodity-tax receipts to compensate for increase in output of nonconsumption goods and services.

There is one other automatic device which the tax authorities might use to offset wage inflation. A substantial part of the household income which in periods of repressed inflation cannot be spent in state or coöperative stores flows into the free collective farm markets. Prices in these markets accordingly rise relative to prices in the state and coöperative stores, and the higher prices may call forth additional supplies. In 1937, a year of very little, if any, repressed inflation, prices in the collective farm markets were at roughly the same level as state prices. On the other hand, during the war, when repressed inflation was at a peak, free market prices were at least 10 times the state prices.[61] If the state placed a heavy tax on purchases or sales in the free market, or on incomes earned there, a substantial degree of flexibility would be built into the Soviet tax system. The authorities have not availed themselves of this device, however; no important taxes are levied on the collective farm markets. The explanation may lie in the administrative difficulties entailed in collecting such taxes.

Second, the Soviets might confine their tax policy to offsetting only the anticipated inflationary pressures, leaving the marginal year-to-year unplanned pressures to accumulate and be eliminated eventually by currency reform. This was essentially the policy adopted in the war period, although the repressed inflation which developed then may have been due not only to unanticipated pressures, but also to the unprecedentedly large anticipated inflationary gap. Repressed inflation was finally wiped out by the currency reform of December 14, 1947, which is discussed in later chapters. It is doubtful that a fiscal policy of this sort would be adopted in an otherwise fully planned economy in any but an emergency situation of the magnitude of World War II.

Third, the tax authorities might try to anticipate "unanticipated" increments to consumer income. The Soviets lived with wage inflation for many years. It is not unreasonable to expect that after the first few years they would recognize the existence and fiscal impact of unplanned wage increases, and would plan high enough levels of taxation to absorb an "estimated unplanned increment" to consumer income as this increment develops. In this case the tax formula would be: planned taxes on consumer *equal* planned consumer income in current period *plus* expectation of unplanned consumer income in current period, *minus* planned cost of consumers' goods output (to which could be added the loss of tax receipts due to expected underfulfillment of consumers' goods output) *minus* planned retained profits of enterprises which produce consumers' goods *minus* personal voluntary savings. Evidence concerning possible use of this policy is discussed below.

Fourth, the tax authorities might content themselves with mopping up the "unanticipated" increment to purchasing power in the period *after* it has been generated. This would have one advantage over the previous method, in that the increment could be estimated more accurately and the required levels of taxation calculated more precisely. It would have the disadvantage of permitting a degree of repressed inflation to exist all the time, i.e., it would permit the current period's contribution to repressed inflation until its elimination in the succeeding period.[62] The tax formula in this case would be: Planned taxes on the consumer *equal* planned consumer income in current period *plus* actual unanticipated increment to consumer income in previous period *minus* planned cost of consumers'-goods output *minus* planned retained profits of enterprises producing consumers' goods *minus* personal voluntary savings.

Taxation and Inflation in the Prewar Period. There is little written material which discusses Soviet tax policy in terms of the last two alternatives. But statistical series which have been collected[63] are rather suggestive; they are presented in Tables 7 to 10, and the reader is also referred to the series on wages (Tables 3 and 4) presented earlier. On the whole these data indicate application by the tax authorities of the fourth alternative. There is some evidence for believing that application of the third was also attempted, though not too successfully.

The series show, first of all, that the course of Soviet inflation was not smooth, but was marked by periods of more or less rapid expansion. The time sequence will be apparent as we proceed. The initial

TABLE 7 Receipts from Turnover Tax and Special Markups, Planned and Realized, 1931–1941 (billions of rubles)

Year	Planned	Realized	Deviation from plan (per cent)
1931	9.393	10.601	+13
1932	15.126	17.140	+13
	0.985[a]	1.761[a]	+79
1933	21.796	23.000	+6
	1.700[a]	3.200[a]	+88
1934	29.228	29.254	0
	6.300[a]	8.361[a]	+33
1935	52.023	51.900	0
1936	62.690	65.900	+5
1937	76.8	75.9	−1
1938	83.3	80.4	−2
1939	92.4	96.9	+5
1940	108.3	105.9	−3
1941	124.5	93.2	−25

For source, see Appendix.

[a] Figures so denoted are special markups from sales in commercial stores. For 1935 and 1936 the turnover tax figures are inclusive of special markups. The funds from special markups are usually entitled "commodity fund" in statistical collections.

TABLE 8 Currency in Circulation and Short-Term Loans Outstanding of the State Bank, January 1, 1929–1941 (billions of rubles)

Year	Currency in circulation	Income-velocity of currency in circulation	Short-term loans	Govern-ment securities	Total loans and securities	Increase over preceding year (per cent): Currency	Increase over preceding year (per cent): Total short-term loans
1929	2.10	9.2					
1930	2.86	7.9	4.4		4.4	+36	
1931	4.36		6.7		6.7	+52	+52
1932	5.67	9.9	10.5	4.1	14.6	+30	+118
1933	8.41	8.1	10.5	6.0	16.5	+48	+13
1934	6.86	12.5	14.2	6.0	20.2	−18	+22
1935	7.73	13.9	17.2	6.1	23.2	+13	+15
1936	9.71	13.8	26.7	6.1	32.8	+26	+41
1937	11.26	13.8	34.8	6.1	40.9	+16	+25
1938			40.7	6.1	46.8		+14
1939			44.9	6.1	51.0		+9
1940	16[a]	14.8	47.9	6.1	54.0		+6
1941	16[a]		55.0	6.1	61.1	0	+13

For sources, see Appendix.
[a] Estimated.

expansion covered the period of the First Five Year Plan, and reached a peak in 1932. In this period, currency in circulation increased between 30 and 48 per cent annually. The annual increase in the average wage rose from 14 per cent in 1929 to 27 per cent in 1932; the annual increase in the wage bill mounted from 18 per cent in 1929 to 53 per cent in 1932. Retail trade turnover, which rose by 26 per cent in 1929, increased 47 per cent in 1932; the increase in short-term credit reached a peak of 118 per cent in 1931; and budget expenditures showed large and steady gains. This is indeed the picture of an inflationary movement gaining momentum.

Unsuccessful attempts were made to stem the inflationary tide. Realized budget revenues were 7, 12, 9, and 13 per cent above planned revenues for the years 1928–29, 1929–30, 1931, and 1932 respectively; since these increases were implemented primarily by larger than planned receipts from the turnover tax and the special markups, it is quite clear that as inflation developed the Soviets raised prices in (and perhaps diverted additional supplies of consumers' goods to) the regular state ration stores and particularly the commercial stores. This can be recognized as an application of the fourth alternative — the mopping up of excess demand after it has manifested itself on the market. It is also quite clear that this policy was not successful, for, although budget receipts did increase by very large amounts, budget expenditures in 1931 and 1932 increased by even larger amounts, so that actual budget surpluses in these years were smaller than had originally been planned. The most dramatic evidence of failure is the spread which developed between government prices and collective farm market prices; prices of foods sold in government stores in 1932 are estimated to have been roughly double the prices which prevailed in 1928; [64] collective farm market prices, however, are reported to have reached a *peak* in 1932 from which they subsequently declined; [65] and one writer claims that the prices of some foods were as much as 15 times the ration prices in the cooperative stores in 1932.[66] This indicates an extraordinary degree of repressed inflation in the consumers'-goods markets.

The year 1933 was relatively very deflationary.[67] Currency in circulation actually declined by 18 per cent, in contrast to the very large increases experienced in the years immediately preceding. Other magnitudes increased but at very much reduced rates. The percentage increases between 1932 and 1933 declined as follows: average wage, from 27 to 10 per cent; wage bill, from 53 to 7 per cent; retail trade turnover, from 47 to 23 per cent; budget expenditures, from 33 to 16 per cent. The unanticipated increase in the average wage rate was only 3 per cent in 1933. A partial explanation of this sudden retardation of inflation is found in the budget figures; actual budget receipts were 15 per cent higher than planned receipts, resulting in a budget surplus of 4.5 billion rubles rather than the 1.8 billion rubles which had been planned. The *unplanned* increment to the budget surplus amounted to almost one-third of total currency in circulation in 1933; the budget surplus, as a percentage of total budget receipts, was by far larger than that of any other year in the prewar period. Receipts from the turnover tax were again overfulfilled, though by a small amount; receipts from the special markup, however, were 88 per cent above plan, indicating the importance of sales in the commercial stores for offsetting (perhaps releasing is the better word) repressed inflation. The measure of Soviet success in eliminating repressed inflation is indicated by the fact that prices in the collective farm markets declined by from 30 to 50 per cent in 1933.[68] Repressed inflation still prevailed, however, and collective farm market prices were to fall for several more years before they reached the same level as state prices.

The size of the budget surplus, together with the decline in collective farm prices, suggests that 1933 was a year in which the fourth alternative was applied on a sufficiently large scale to compensate, at least in part, for previous failures. Application of this policy may also explain in part the relatively small increase in average wages and insignificant overfulfillment of the average wage plan from 1932 to 1933. In addition, the initiation of Bank control over wage expenditures in that year probably acted, at least temporarily, as a restraining hand on managers of enterprises in their competition for labor.

A second inflationary surge began in 1934 and continued through 1936. This was primarily a cost inflation; the excess demand currently generated by wage increases, and so forth, was apparently mopped up fairly readily. There were substantial increases in wage rates and the wage bill, and in budget expenditures, though the rates of increase were somewhat less than those experienced during the First Five Year Plan period. The increase in costs due to wage inflation finally led in 1936 to an upward revision in the prices of industrial raw materials and equipment ranging from 50 to 300 per cent.[69] This was the first significant revision of these prices in a decade. Subsidies, which had enabled the Soviets to keep prices steady in the face of rapidly rising costs, were presumably eliminated at this time. More will be said about this later.[70]

In the consumers'-goods markets, repressed inflation was gradually "worked off," as is indicated by the rapid increase in the income-velocity of circulation of currency in these years (Table 8). Collective farm market prices fell constantly in this period and are reported to have reached, by December 1936, a level of about one-third of the March 1932 level.[71] This was accomplished mainly by raising the prices of (taxes on) commodities sold by the state; this left less cash in the hands of households for purchases on collective farm markets. The prices of commodities sold in the commercial stores remained considerably above ration prices, but showed a decline in 1933 and 1934.[72] The increase in receipts from the turnover tax and special markups was due to a relative shift in the volume of sales from state stores to the commercial stores,[73] and to some rise in the price of rationed supplies. These trends showed up in the budget not simply as surpluses each year, but surpluses which were very substantially overfulfilled. Furthermore, overfulfillment was not due to a reduction of expenditures, for these were also overfulfilled, but to a very large overfulfillment of receipts.

It is interesting to note that about this time (1935–36), the commodity tax ceased to contribute significantly to the rising retail price level, i.e., to the price level of consumers' goods sold in state stores. Until 1935 the Soviet *rate* of nonconsumption expenditures was increasing steadily; [74] the increase was especially marked in the years of the First Five Year Plan. This resulted in a continually increasing percentage element of tax in price. Since 1935–36, the percentage of tax in price has not increased significantly, and at times has even declined; therefore the rising level of retail prices since 1936 is primarily a result of the cost inflation. Even in the period before 1936, the cost inflation was quantitatively more important for the rising price level than the increase in the rate of commodity taxation.[75]

The second trough is encountered in 1937, the year which is generally considered the most stable in the prewar period. Cost inflation slowed up as it had in 1933. Prices on the collective farm markets declined still further,[76] and are reported to have been roughly in line with state retail prices, an indication that repressed inflation may have been nearly, if not completely, eliminated. No doubt the excellent crop in 1937 was a stabilizing factor. The year 1938 is again regarded as fairly stable, though, as Tables 3, 4, and 7 to 10 indicate, the wage bill, the average wage rate, and the budgeted magnitudes were increasing at much greater rates than in 1937; some repressed inflation was perhaps being generated.

Repressed inflation was clearly being generated by 1939, for it is reported that collective farm market prices for selected food products were 78 per cent higher than state retail prices on January 1, 1940. It is very difficult to understand from the budget data just what happened in these years. Not only were substantial surpluses returned ever year, but realized surpluses were much larger than planned. Unlike the situation in previous years, however, the surpluses were not a result of overfulfilling budget receipts by larger percentages than budget expenditures; rather, both receipts and expenditures were underfulfilled, receipts by the smaller percentage. Minister of Finance A. Zverev mentions only the underfulfillment of

TABLE 9 Total Budgetary Revenues, Expenditures, and Surpluses (Planned and Realized) 1928–29–1941 (billion rubles)

	Receipts			Expenditures				Surplus	
Year	Planned	Realized	Deviation from plan (per cent)	Planned	Realized	Deviation from plan (per cent)	Increase in realized (per cent)	Planned	Realized
1928/29	7.73	8.3	+7	7.68	8.1	+5		0.05	0.2
1929/30	11.6	13.0	+12	11.6	12.3	+6	52	.0	0.7
1931	21.8	23.8	+9	20.3	23.1	+14	88	1.5	0.7
1932	27.5	31.0	+13	27.0	30.7	+14	33	0.5	0.3
1933	35.00	40.2	+15	33.2	35.7	+8	16	1.8	4.5
1934	48.9	53.7	+10	47.3	50.7	+7	42	1.6	3.0
1935	65.9	67.4	+2	65.4	66.4	+2	31	0.5	1.0
1936	78.7	83.8	+6	78.7	81.8	+4	23	.0	2.0
1937	98.1	96.6	−2	97.1	93.9	−3	15	1.0	2.7
1938	132.6	127.5	−4	131.1	124.0	−5	32	1.5	3.5
1939	156.1	156.0	−0	155.4	153.3	−1	24	0.7	2.7
1940	184.0	180.2	−2	179.9	174.4	−3	14	4.1	5.8
1941	216.8	177.0	−18	210.5	191.4	−9	17[a]	6.3	−14.4

For sources, see Appendix.

[a] The figure is the per cent increase in *planned* budget expenditures for this year, which was preferred because of the effect of the outbreak of war on realized expenditures.

receipts in his budget messages, attributing it in both 1937 and 1938 to failure of some commissariats to produce as much output as planned, failure to lower costs according to plan, and poor administration by the financial authorities.[77] Underfulfillment of planned output could only explain the reduction in receipts if it was entirely in output of consumers' goods; otherwise it would explain the reduction in expenditures. Failure to reduce costs according to plan would tend to increase expenditures in the case of commodities purchased by the state, and would also tend to reduce receipts by squeezing profits. These explanations, it must be admitted, are not entirely satisfactory.

The year 1940 differs from its predecessors in several respects. Wage inflation was of less significance than in any previous year. The average wage increased by 5 per cent and the wage bill by 6 per cent; the realized wage bill was actually 4 per cent *less* than planned. The increase in budget expenditures was the smallest of the decade. The budget surplus was larger than had been planned

TABLE 10 Retail Trade, Planned and Realized, 1928–1941 (billion rubles)[a]

Year	Planned	Realized	Increase in realized (per cent)	Deviation of realized from planned (per cent)
1928		12.0		
1929		15.1	26	
1930		18.9	25	
1931		27.5	46	
1932	35.0	40.4	47	+15
1933	49.0	49.8	23	+2
1934	60.0	61.8	24	+3
1935	80.0	81.7	32	+2
1936	100.0	106.8	31	+7
1937	131.0	125.9	18	−4
1938	140.5	140.0	11	0
1939		163.4	17	
1940	189.0	175.1	7	−7
1941	197.0			

For sources, see Appendix.
[a] The data given here are for state and coöperative trade, including restaurants, etc., but excluding collective farm market sales.

because, as in the immediately preceding years, receipts were underfulfilled by a lesser amount than expenditures. The realized budget surplus was very large, and is perhaps responsible for the fact that cash currency in circulation actually *declined*. Despite this apparent abundance of disinflationary indicators, 1940 is usually considered a very inflationary year. As we have seen, inflation was not wage-induced; the new Bank controls over wage expenditures, together with direct controls over labor mobility, seem to have reduced wage inflation to a manageable size. But inflation may have resulted from a decline in the supply of consumers' goods, probably as a consequence of accelerated war preparation. Consumers' goods are reported to have been in very short supply in 1940.[78] Also, as was mentioned above, 1940 inherited some repressed inflation from 1939, and perhaps from 1938 as well. A serious attempt was made to release this repressed inflation in 1940; there were three substantial tax increases (on January 24, July 15, and October 22) which raised the price of bread by 18 per cent, of beef by 50 per cent, of butter and sugar by 33 per cent, of potatoes by 80 per cent, and of shoes and textiles by 100 per cent.[79] We have no data on the course of collective farm market prices over 1940 and therefore cannot say whether the authorities actually succeeded in reducing the extent of repressed inflation. It is noteworthy that the budget surplus planned for 1941 was larger, absolutely, than that for any previous year. Before concluding the discussion of the year 1940, it should be noted that both in this year and in 1939 prices of industrial goods were again raised in adjustment to the cost (wage) increases which had taken place since 1936.[80]

The data which have been presented are all in support of the fourth alternative policy. Realized budget receipts exceeded planned receipts every year from 1928 to 1936; from 1937 to 1940 receipts were underfulfilled but expenditures were underfulfilled by an even larger amount. In other words, the surplus was larger than planned in the period from 1937 to 1940, as well as in all previous years except 1931 and 1932. In 1931 and 1932 the policy was not applied successfully; excess demand increased faster than it could be mopped up. In 1933, the tide of inflation was stemmed and even turned back. From 1934 through 1937, taxes more than offset new additions to purchasing power, and supplies of consumers' goods apparently increased, with the consequence that repressed inflation was almost completely "worked off" by the latter year. The cycle was renewed in 1939 when substantial repressed inflation was again allowed to develop. The tax authorities took measures to eliminate this in 1940, with what success we do not know. If the planned budget surplus for 1941 is any indicator, that year might well have been very disinflationary had it not been for the outbreak of war.

We noted earlier that the tax authorities may have attempted the third policy alternative: allowing in advance for unplanned wage increases in order to offset them as they develop. The evidence, admittedly inconclusive, is contained in the wage data of Table 3. The Soviets *planned* rather large annual increases in the average wage after 1931; it is hard to believe that such a growth would have been planned if the authorities had been in control of the wage situation. We may infer from the increase originally planned for the Second Five Year Plan — 25 per cent, or less than 5 per cent a year — that a lower rate was preferred; even this rate may be higher than the desired rate, since it conceivably includes a discounting of unplanned wage increases. The rates contemplated in the later annual plans, however, were for the most part higher: 1933, 6.7 per cent; 1934, 3.8 per cent; 1935, 9.3 per cent; 1936, 8.6 per cent; 1937, 4.7 per cent.

Data on the total wage bill are also significant (Table 4). Although unplanned increases exceeded planned increases in 1931 and 1934, the two were almost equal in 1935 and 1936, and the planned exceeded the unplanned from 1937 to 1940 by ever larger amounts. This tempts one to believe that the Soviets tended more and more to include in their planned figure an allowance for unwanted but probable increases in the wage bill. In other words, as the years rolled on the authorities tried to meet wage inflation not only by measures to prevent its occurrence, but by estimating in advance the degree to which it could *not* be prevented. If this policy was in fact applied, it was not very successful; if it had succeeded there would have been no need to resort to the fourth alternative.

The war and postwar periods differ substantially from the period just described. The wartime period was, of course, unique; there were several abrupt deviations from "normal" Soviet fiscal practice. The postwar period, after the Currency Reform of 1947, was a period of deflation, marked by little increase in costs and a declining retail price level. The course of events since 1940, including the Currency Reform of 1947, is described in detail in Chapter 9.

Chapter 3

ALTERNATIVE METHODS OF TAXATION [1]

In the previous two chapters we have considered the character and extent of Soviet inflation and some of the general tax problems which it presents. The purpose of this chapter is to examine the principal alternatives open to the Soviet authorities in solving the inflation problem. Four main alternatives are distingushed: (1) to vary wages and the nonwage costs of production inversely (e.g., to offset an increase in the rate of government expenditures by lowering wages); (2) to levy an income tax or other direct tax on the population; (3) to levy a commodity tax; (4) to levy a tax in kind.

Commodity taxation is defined to include not only the positive taxes actually levied on state enterprises and selling organizations (turnover, payroll, and profit taxes), but also the retained profits or operating losses of these organizations (subsidies, in the latter case, being looked upon as negative taxes). For purposes of this chapter, then, *all deviations* of price from cost are considered a form of commodity tax. Some of the methodological difficulties ensuing from this definition are discussed in Chapter 4.

CONSISTENCY OF THE FACTOR-PRICING SYSTEM AND WAGES POLICY [2]

The first method of approach, namely, to vary wage and nonwage payments inversely, is incompatible with a policy of pricing the components of production to reflect their relative scarcity. It does not matter here whether wages or the prices of nonwage components of production are the object of manipulation. We can readily see that in either case the effect would be (*a*) to change continuously the relation between the price of labor and other components of production as the rate of nonconsumption expenditures changes and (*b*) to upset fortuitously the relative prices of all other commodities, both producers' and consumers' goods, to the extent that the proportion of wage costs to total costs differs from product to product and from industry to industry. Rational economic decisions based on the money costs of the factors of production would accordingly be impossible.

Rational pricing of the factors of production is, however, essential to the economically efficient operation of complicated industrial economies; any other procedure would almost certainly involve a reduction in the final output which can be produced from a given fund of resources. It is therefore clear that the first method cannot be considered a suitable fiscal alternative. The evidence indicates that although the Soviets have varied the prices of nonwage components of production by their program of subsidies to industry (this is discussed in some detail in Chapter 11) they have not used this approach as a method for offsetting inflationary pressures. Instead, relative wages are set to reflect, more or less, differences in productivity, and the inflationary gap is bridged by taxes. Taxes do affect resource allocation, as we shall see later. Yet it is generally true that variations in the rate of nonconsumption expenditures can be offset entirely by changes in income taxation, relative costs of production remaining unchanged. The same holds for the commodity tax if it is levied entirely on consumers' goods, or even when it is levied on raw materials and intermediate products *if* the rates are set to reflect differential rent.

It should be mentioned that varying wages could be considered a plausible alternative to taxation only if the Soviets kept two sets of accounts, one for costs and one for payments to the factors of production. They could then vary the latter without affecting the former, and collect what would be in effect a hidden tax on wages, i.e., a payroll tax. Actually, only one set of accounts is maintained by the Soviets.

THE "MONEY ILLUSION," POLITICAL DISCONTENT, AND ECONOMIC INCENTIVES

The term "money illusion" identifies the opinion generally held among economists that workers are more conscious of the impact on their economic position of changes in wages than of changes in prices.[3] A corollary to the money illusion is the hypothesis that workers are more sensitive to changes in direct taxes than to changes in indirect taxes.

There are several reasons why this should be so. A taxpayer's liability under direct taxation is unambiguous. This is especially true under the pay-as-you-earn system which is common in most countries today: a person's gross income and his income net of tax are reported side by side. Perception of the gross-to-net-income relation is much more difficult where taxes are indirect, particularly if each commodity is taxed at a different rate, as in the Soviet Union.

Furthermore, an indirect tax is not paid all at once in one large sum but in dribs and drabs which depend on the time pattern of taxpayers' expenditures. The amount of tax paid by each person depends also on the types of commodities purchased, since different commodities are subject to different rates of tax. Both the time element and the differential-tax element make it very difficult for the taxpayer to get a clear impression of his tax liability.

A further element of the illusion is that it is possible to hide a commodity tax from the ultimate taxpayer by levying it at an early stage of processing. Even when the tax is levied at the retail level, many consumers, through ignorance, never realize that part of the price they are paying is tax. This naïveté is relatively less important in countries like the United States and Great Britain, where unions as well as independent scholars continually point up the relation between indirect taxes, prices, and real wages. In the Soviet Union, as we shall see, the effect of indirect taxes on real wages is consciously obscured.

To the extent that the individual *is* aware of indirect taxes, he can try to avoid their full impact in either of two ways: he can confine his purchases to those commodities subject to a low rate of tax; or he can choose to save, rather than spend, a larger share of his income. These two consumer options, combined with the vagueness of the level of tax burden on each individual, create an atmosphere in which the average taxpayer undoubtedly takes more kindly to indirect additions to his tax burden than to direct taxes.[4]

We see from the foregoing that the money illusion has both economic and political significance which will hardly be ignored in framing a nation's tax policy. It is axiomatic that no nation likes to burden its population with high taxes. The Soviet Union is no exception to this rule, but its political and economic objectives have left no reasonable alternative to high taxes. Present use of commodity taxation rather than income taxation for meeting the bulk of its revenue needs undoubtedly represents a conscious attempt to use the money illusion to minimize the impact on the population of their tremendous tax burden.

Here a time distinction must be drawn: it is true that the USSR has always relied primarily upon commodity taxation, but for different reasons in different periods. In the early 1920's indirect taxes were used because direct taxes were costly to collect and difficult to administer, and failed to provide a dependable revenue. The advantages of commodity taxation in this regard became less crucial as the USSR developed culturally and economically. As the average rate of taxation increased in the late twenties and early thirties, however, it was the illusion effect of indirect taxes which assumed primary importance.

Soviet economists deliberately fostered the illusion by ceasing to mention that commodity taxes were taxes on the population which reduced the purchasing power of the wage-earner's ruble. Instead they were represented as the device for drawing into the budget "the accumulation (saving) of socialized industry." In 1936, for example, Minister of Finance G. F. Grinko, speaking of the large increase in planned budget revenues, said:

> This increase in the revenues of the state is entirely due to an expansion in the work and an increase in the accumulations of the socialized economy. We are keeping taxation and duties on the population, and also loans, more or less on the same level as last year. This is clearly shown by the following brief comparisons:
>
> a) Assessment on the profits of economic organizations will increase by 63 per cent as compared with 1935.
>
> b) The proceeds from the turnover tax will increase by 20 per cent.
>
> c) The proceeds from loans, taxes, and duties on the population will increase by 3 per cent.[5]

The illusion has been intensified by the Soviet practice of levying the turnover tax on most commodities before they reach the retail network. It would be untrue, however, to say that deception was the first advantage sought by this practice, which seems to have been determined chiefly by administrative considerations.

The Soviet consumer is of course aware of the high prices he pays for most commodities, though he may not know how much tax is included in price or even that he is being taxed. Still, popular discontent with high prices is bound to be weaker and less specifically directed against the government than resentment over high taxes. Even in the Soviet Union not all prices are set by the state (e.g., the free collective farm market exists), but there is no country where the state is not entirely responsible for taxes. The use of the money illusion by the Soviets to cushion the political reaction to its economic policies is submitted as the principal reason for the dominance of the commodity tax and relative neglect of the income tax in the Soviet budget.

Having identified the primary political motive for exploiting the money illusion, we may now explore its relevance to economic motivation. Not only does the money illusion make indirect taxation more palatable; it also accounts for the fact that commodity and income taxes of equal size have different effects on work incentives — a consideration particularly important in a country where almost all income is earned income. Analytically we shall distinguish two areas of impact of taxes on incentives: the effect on differential wages as a factor in choosing between jobs, and the effect on the work-leisure ratio.

The Soviets rely heavily on differential wages as a means of attracting labor to jobs requiring greater skills, and to jobs in expanding industries or in areas where work conditions are undesirable (arctic or desert regions, for example). In a country like the USSR where the face of the economy changes continually, rapid and efficient allocation of labor is of considerable economic importance. The greater the wage differentials appear to the labor force, the more effective the wage policy is likely to be in directing labor into desired channels. Evidence of the significance attributed by the Soviets to income incentives is provided by the pattern of rationing chosen when scarcity has made this imperative, as in the early thirties. In this period, money wage differentials lost their efficacy for allocating labor; differential rationing was employed as a substitute.

The incentive effect of relative wage differentials may also be vitiated by visibly high levels of taxation. The exclusive use of income taxation, for example, would be unsatisfactory under the Soviet pay-as-you-earn system because workers are perhaps as likely to base job decisions on differentials in take-home pay as on gross wage differentials. On the other hand, gross wage differentials retain much of their incentive effect even with very high levels of commodity taxation. This facet of the money illusion is undoubtedly another important reason for Soviet use of commodity taxation.

Taxes also affect the work-leisure ratio, since they are levied on the type of income derived from work rather than on income from leisure. The direction of their influence in this area, however, is not always easy to determine, since taxes on work income produce two opposing effects. The *income effect*, which is related to the average rate of taxation, causes a person to work harder to recover the income taken away by taxes. The *substitution effect*, which is related to the marginal rate of taxation, lessens the incentive to work because the tax reduces the reward for effort (i.e., it reduces the cost of additional leisure).

It is often argued that high taxes (especially progressive taxes) reduce work incentives—that the substitution effect tends to predominate over the income effect. This would indeed be true if the demand for leisure typically increased as income increased, thus reducing the importance of the income effect generated by a high average rate of taxation. But even if this assumption can be granted, the net result of the income and substitution effects is still difficult to predict, especially in the Soviet Union where the lower- as well as the higher-income groups pay a high average rate of tax.

Prediction is difficult because we do not really know how the supply curve of labor is shaped in the Soviet Union. Ordinarily it is assumed that the supply curve of labor is upward sloping except in the case of the very wealthy; this means that persons are willing to work more when they are paid higher wages, and less when the effective rate of wages is reduced by, say, taxation. Backward-rising supply curves other than those of the very wealthy may exist, however; the very poor must work at least as much as is necessary to subsist, and a tax which reduces their earnings has a strong income effect, forcing them to seek additional employment. More generally, a fairly good case can be made for the hypothesis that the supply curve of labor is kinked rather than continuous, because reactions to increases and decreases in wage rates may not be symmetrical in the short run. For example, for classical economic reasons the supply of labor may increase in reaction to an increase in wage rates; this curve is upward sloping. But the curve may also be backward rising: the supply of labor may increase in reaction to a *decline* in wage rates or to the imposition of a new tax because, as Duesenberry and others have emphasized, persons tend to resist a decline in their standard of living, measured in wage goods.[6] We see from these conflicting hypotheses that the effect of taxation on the labor-supply curve is in general ambiguous. With regard to the Soviet Union in particular, we can say only that it does exhibit one condition which favors, though it does not assure, an upward-rising curve. The choice facing a worker is not always between work and leisure, but may be between work as an employee of state or coöperative organizations and self-employment. The possibility of self-employment as well as leisure increases the probability that taxation will reduce the incentive to work for the state. The possibility is of course less real in the case of the Soviet industrial worker, for whom self-employment is not likely to be a very profitable alternative. The private handicraftsman is severely discriminated against by the income tax. Furthermore, self-employed handicraftsmen are allowed to use only the most primitive tools; their productivity is accordingly low. Finally, since most workers cannot grow much of their own food, the turnover tax on food is difficult to evade.

Self-employment is a real alternative in rural areas, however; it has been so profitable that the authorities have been forced to take direct as well as fiscal measures to reduce its scope. These measures include laws specifying the minimum number of labor days a collective farmer must work on the collective farm, and limitations on the size of individually cultivated plots of land. In addition, income earned cultivating one's own plot of land is subject to a direct tax, whereas income earned working for the collective farm is not taxed at all. (Another form of self-employment occasionally reported is illegal commodity speculation. Commodity speculation flourishes under conditions of repressed inflation and it is doubtful that it is very significant in the USSR today.)

Even granted the limited possibility of self-employment, however, the fact remains that the slope of the labor-supply curve in the Soviet Union is not known. It is clear, in theory, that if this curve is positively sloped, the state will tend to prefer indirect taxes in order to reduce the disincentive effects of a lower net wage rate. If the curve is negatively sloped, direct taxes will be preferred, to magnify the incentive effect of wage reductions from taxes. But as long as we cannot claim to know whether work incentives are in fact reduced or increased by changes in the rate of taxation, we cannot legitimately argue that the Soviets prefer commodity taxes because, *inter alia*, they reduce work incentives less.[7]

Failure to resolve the work-leisure problem defined above would seriously impair our analysis if the impulse to work less could be gratified freely in the Soviet Union. Such is hardly the case, however. The possibility of self-employment really exists only for the rural population, as we have seen, and even here it is limited by direct controls. Denied the opportunity to withdraw completely from the labor market, the industrial worker can do little to *reduce* the quantity of work he offers, for absenteeism, the other possibility, is discouraged by severe penalties. On the other hand, his incentive to *increase* the quantity of work offered is sustained by progressive piece rates and premiums calculated to offset the disincentive effect of taxes on overtime work.

Given the small scope for reducing the amount of labor offered, it follows that the Soviets actually do not have to worry too much about the effect of taxes on the amount of work performed. To the extent that incentives to reduce work remain unspent, political and social dissatisfaction undoubtedly accumulate. But taxes cannot significantly affect output in a more immediate sense — by seriously upsetting the work-leisure ratio.

It remains to consider one other distinction between commodity and income taxes, in relation to work incentives, which may have influenced the Soviets to prefer the former. A difference frequently adduced between the two is that commodity taxes are usually regressive and income taxes progressive. Progressive taxes have higher marginal rates than average rates, while regressive taxes have lower marginal than average rates. It can be argued for several reasons that regressive taxes have a less adverse effect on work incentives than progressive taxes. Persons with low incomes have to pay high average rates of tax; the income effect induces them to work hard. Equally, persons with high incomes find that the cost of leisure rises with income, since the marginal rate of tax declines; this maintains intact their incentive to work. Finally, regressive taxes increase the disparities in income determined originally by the relative wage structure, and therefore increase the effect of differential wages in allocating labor. Because regressive taxes have this relatively favorable effect on work incentives, one might expect the Soviets to favor commodity taxation, which is normally regressive.

An attempt is made in Chapter 6 to determine whether the Soviet turnover tax is in fact regressive. The very tentative conclusion reached in that chapter is that the turnover-tax rate structure was either mildly regressive or roughly proportional in the prewar period, and is closer to proportionality at present. It is also tentatively concluded that not one but many considerations go into the determination of the rate structure. On the basis of these conclusions, it seems highly improbable that the turnover-tax rate structure is manipulated with the specific purpose of increasing work incentives. On the other hand, it is not inconceivable that concern with the effect of high marginal rates of taxation on incentives was a factor, though not the most important one, in the Soviet decision to collect only a small part of their revenue requirements by direct taxation.

PLANNER AUTONOMY AND CONSUMER WELFARE

Soviet economists stress the importance of the commodity tax as an instrument of price policy. The real meaning of the statement is revealed by considering the significance of consumer sovereignty in the Soviet Union and the relative impacts on consumer sovereignty of the commodity and income taxes.

Consumer sovereignty may be defined as the power of consumers to determine what is to be produced, hence the power to determine the allocation of resources between different industries. This is usually accomplished through the market mechanism, although other ways in which the consumer could be allowed to exert an influence on patterns of production are conceivable (e.g., consumer polls). In economic theory, a high degree of consumer sovereignty is usually assumed to prevail in a competitive economy, even though sovereignty in most capitalist countries is weakened by many deviations from the competitive norm, such as monopoly, imperfect knowledge, and the influence of advertising.[8] It must also be conceded that the concept of consumer sovereignty is only meaningful in the short run, in connection with commodities which are already in production; the average consumer has no way of expressing demand for commodities not actually on the market, nor of foreseeing the development of new products. Despite these limitations, the concept has a limited validity and is unquestionably useful in understanding the Soviet economy and the Soviet choice between commodity and income taxation.

It should be stressed that the discussion which follows relates entirely to the sphere of consumers' goods, and to the factors of production needed to produce them. Decisions as to the rate of investment and the specific nature of much of the investment are decisions over which the consumer in the Soviet Union has no sovereignty whatsoever.

A distinction must be made between consumer sovereignty and consumer choice. Given a market for consumers' goods, sovereignty implies choice, but choice does not imply sovereignty. Consumer choice means only that the distribution of a group of commodities is accomplished through the market; the quantities offered and the prices set may be determined by the planners independently of any consumer pressure. In a highly planned economy like that of the Soviet Union, there are advantages to adopting, as fully as possible, consumer choice, combined with a minimum of consumer sovereignty. The adoption of consumer choice enables the Soviet authorities to avoid the high cost of direct distribution of consumers' goods by rationing, and tends to maximize consumer satisfaction from a given basket of consumers' goods. Consumer sovereignty, on the other hand, implies an economic power other than the over-all planning board and one not necessarily in agreement with the board. Given a substantial degree of sovereignty over the structure of the consumer bill of goods, it is conceivable that consumers could seriously hamper the autonomy of the planning board. This potential interference increases in importance with the degree of complementarity of productive factors, the size and specificity of capital equipment, and the scarcity of productive factors.

For purposes of illustration, let us assume that the income tax is the only fiscal instrument available to the Soviet planners, and that no form of commodity tax (defined as *any deviation* of price from costs, including profits and losses of state enterprises) can be used. If then the distribution of consumers' goods were accomplished through the market, a reasonable degree of consumer sovereignty would prevail. The planners in this case could produce the bill of goods in accordance with their own preferences, but they would have to place the goods on the market at cost, and would not be able to adjust prices for purposes of equating supply and demand. It does not matter here whether price equals average cost or marginal cost; the significant assumption is that the state cannot alter price to equate supply and demand once a rule of price formation has been established. The price of goods in excess supply cannot be lowered to clear the market, nor can the price of goods in short supply be raised to prevent inequitable distribution or the need for rationing. Most of the burden of adjustment would then have to be borne physically, by shifts in the allocation of the factors of production. If a new allocation were made, the real income of the nation would be reduced by the cost of making the adjustment; if the factors of production were not reallocated, resources would continue to be squandered in making commodities for which demand has declined, and rationing would have to be introduced for equitable distribution of commodities priced too low relative to demand.

The use by the state of nonproportional or discriminatory commodity taxation decreases considerably the extent of consumer sovereignty, since the state can use price adjustments to equate supply and demand without necessarily responding to the price changes by subsequent shifting of resources. An attenuated sovereignty is still retained by the consumer, of course; we can imagine planners offering for sale a bill of goods which would not be purchased entirely at any price, or at prices so low that idle balances would remain in the hands of consumers after the market had been cleared. In other words, consumers might decide not to spend the normal proportion of income in the current period, in anticipation of a more desirable selection of commodities at a later period. In this unlikely event there would indeed be pressure on the planners to alter their pattern of resource allocation, but the example stretches, for economics, the meaning of "sovereignty."

It is clear that the ability to equate supply and demand by price adjustment (i.e., the commodity tax) as well as by adjustments of output allows the planners considerably more freedom from consumer interference than would be possible if the income tax were the sole available fiscal instrument. This is not, of course, to imply that freedom from consumer interference requires a commodity tax of the present size. Price flexibility could be achieved with a much smaller markup over costs than is now the case, and the rest of the nation's revenue needs could be met by income taxation, if policy so dictated.

The problem of consumer sovereignty (as well as of consumer choice) has actually been of less importance in the Soviet Union than in most other countries because of the low standard of living in that country. Priority in the production of consumers' goods must be given to the basic necessities, and these comprise the bulk of the consumers'-goods output.[9] It goes without saying that these are the commodities which stand at the top of the consumers' preference scale. The situation simplifies fiscal and price planning as well as production planning; the state has to do with highly inelastic demand schedules for most of the commodities it supplies to the consumer and from which it collects the preponderance of budget receipts. In 1936, for example, when 62.7 billion rubles of receipts were planned from the turnover tax, 21.2 billion were to come from bread products, 5.9 billion from sugar, and 6 billion from alcohol.[10] Thus the state does not have the difficult problem of estimating the elasticities of demand for a great variety of commodities in order to be sure of "just" clearing the market for each commodity; where demand is inelastic, any of a fairly large range of prices will clear the market without the need to alter supply significantly.[11]

In theory, this inelasticity of demand provides the state with a simple device for making adjustments necessary for fiscal stability. If the economy were suffering from a general condition of overdemand, for example, one solution would be to raise the price of bread sufficiently to mop up the excess purchasing power, and to store the small excess of grain which would result. In practice, the state may be hesitant about using this device for any but minor adjustments, because of the great importance to the population of the commodities involved. When there is substantial inequality in the distribution of income (and this is the case in the Soviet Union as it is in the Western nations), there is an upper limit beyond which the price of a necessity must not be raised. That limit is the price which excludes the lowest income group from the market, thereby forcing it to live at a below-subsistence level. This undoubtedly explains the Soviet recourse to rationing rather than to still higher prices for necessities in the early thirties and during World War II.

In discussing the superiority for planning purposes of discriminatory as compared with proportional commodity taxation, we have abstracted from the important problem of consumer welfare. We must now recognize that the goal of the planning board is not simply to maximize its autonomy from consumer influence in planning, but to choose (or compromise) between this goal and the goal of achieving the highest level of consumer satisfaction consistent with the level of investment and other government expenditures to be undertaken.

The proposition is generally accepted that in an economic system in which resources are already optimally allocated and costing is rational, consumer welfare is reduced less by proportional commodity taxation than by discriminatory commodity taxation.[12] Unlike discriminatory taxation, proportional taxation does not distort the proportionality of price to marginal cost between commodities — a condition for efficient allocation of resources.[13] This is really just another way of stating what has already been said, namely, that a proportional commodity tax allows the consumer more sovereignty over the allocation of resources in production than a discriminatory tax. Consumer sovereignty and consumer welfare are opposite faces of the same coin.

In applying the proportionality criterion to Soviet taxes, allowance must be made for the fact that the consistent or rational factor-pricing condition is violated. In particular, the price before tax of food products sold by the state to the population is substantially less than cost of production. This is a result of the tax in kind levied on agricultural producers (discussed later in this chapter). There are other deviations from consistent costing but these will not be discussed here.[14] Given the inconsistent costing system, the optimum structure of commodity taxation would be one which is proportional between commodities only after discrepancies in costing have been taken into account. In the Soviet case, therefore, *true* proportionality requires the tax on agricultural products to be a greater percentage of retail price than the tax on industrial consumers' goods, since the cost to the state of agricultural commodities is below cost of production to begin with. Similar adjustments must be made for other deviations from consistent factor pricing. In the discussion which follows we will continue to use the term proportional taxation for convenience, but this should be understood to mean proportional taxation after adjustments for inconsistent costing have been made.

In the short run, the state is concerned primarily with minimizing the effect of the consumer on the allocation of resources, because of the high cost of changing the composition of output over short periods of time. Prices (taxes) are altered to equalize demand and supply for specific commodities whenever market equilibrium is upset by short-run shifts in demand patterns. These alterations probably result in a nonproportional tax structure.

In the long run, however, a rational production program for consumers' goods would have to grant more consideration to the desires of consumers. In theory, the state should attempt to expand the production of each commodity to the point at which marginal cost and average revenue are equal.[15] As we have already indicated, the application of this policy leads to the best allocation of resources and tends to maximize consumer welfare. Following this policy, the state would collect a rent (or tax, or profit) wherever average costs are below marginal cost. Given the high level of government expenditures in the Soviet Union, the collection of this rent alone would not yield sufficient revenue for monetary stability; an additional tax would be necessary.

If the goal is to minimize the reduction of consumer welfare, the additional levy could be incorporated in a proportional commodity tax; the result would be that marginal cost and average revenue would bear the same ratio for all enterprises.[16] Alternatively, the tax could be conceived of as an additional cost which would raise the average- and marginal-cost curves of all firms proportionately, production of each commodity being carried to the point at which the new marginal cost is equal to average revenue.[17]

A practical policy fusing the short- and long-run approaches might be to equate supply and demand for each commodity in the very short run by varying the commodity tax, but in the longer run to increase production of those commodities with the highest rates of tax, and reduce production of commodities with the lowest rates.[18] This would tend to equalize the rates of tax on all commodities. Statements by Soviet economists indicate that the planners do attempt to achieve the short-run policy suggested above. The writer has not, however, encountered any evidence that Soviet economists are aware of, or interested in, the principle of carrying production to the point at which marginal cost is proportional to price. Nor do they seem interested in the superiority, from the point of view of consumer welfare, of proportional over discriminatory commodity taxation.

Examination of the actual turnover-tax rate structure sheds little light on Soviet production and price policies. The rates are highly differentiated, giving the superficial impression that the short-run policy of equating supply and demand by price (tax) changes is dominant. There are other reasons, however, for the large disparities between rates on different commodities. Most important, as we have already indicated, is the necessity for a discriminatory tax on food products to offset the fact that the price before tax of these commodities is below cost. Aside from this, it is clearly no simple matter to establish the "proper" prices, or to determine where the need for investment is greatest. Considerable knowledge of supply schedules, demand elasticities, stocks, and other facts and relations, is required. Furthermore, the state undoubtedly sets many prices to conform to moral, health, and other noneconomic policy considerations (see Chapter 6). For example, it might wish to discourage vodka consumption by levying a tax on vodka much higher than the taxes on other commodities; a reverse policy might be followed with respect to children's clothing. Finally, the nonproportional commodity tax may simply reflect differential rent.

DIFFERENTIAL RENT

An implicit assumption of the section on consistent costing was that all commodities which are used in further production must receive a valuation other than the sum of the costs of production wherever this is necessary to take into account scarcity relative to demand, i.e., differential rent. This is hinted at by a Soviet writer:

> The function of rent payments by state and coöperative enterprises is above all to assist the economic organs (especially enterprises in extractive industries) to conserve the natural wealth of the country . . . differential rent . . . enables the best use of the extensive natural resources of the USSR.[19]

If, for example, the costs of extracting a ton of scarce high-grade coal and a ton of lignite were equal, it would be uneconomic to price both items on a straight out-of-pocket cost-of-production basis.

Differential rent can be collected either by payment of rent to the state or by commodity taxation, the results of the two methods being equivalent. The Soviets have apparently preferred the second alternative; explicit rent payments have not amounted to much. According to the Soviet writer quoted above: "To the extent that differential rent does not receive independent expression in all branches of the national economy . . . rent is paid in the form of the turnover tax." [20] Obviously, this function could not be served by an income tax.

To the extent that the commodity tax on producers' goods and raw materials does not accurately reflect scarcity relative to demand, an element of inconsistency is introduced into the factor-pricing system. The seriousness of this inconsistency depends on such considerations as the degree of integration in industry, relative percentages of "arbitrary" markup between firms and products, and so forth. The success of the commodity tax in expressing differential rent is also affected by the Soviet policy of granting subsidies to many industrial enterprises.[21]

Most differential rent in the Soviet Union undoubtedly originates in agriculture. However, neither the collective farms nor the Soviet peasant farmers as individuals pay rent, as such, for their land; although all land has been nationalized, it is parceled out to producers and occupied without explicit charge. It may therefore be inferred that there is a large rent element in the taxes, both in money and in kind, which are levied on agricultural producers. A clue to the extent of differential rent is found in the regional variations in these taxes (see Chapters 7 and 8). The differences presumably take into account differences in fertility, local market prices, mechanization, and other factors which might affect the relative profitability of raising crops and animals in different regions. Although some allowance is made in the tax legislation for such differences within a single region, the allowance appears inadequate to take account of the great variety of conditions which undoubtedly exist. Therefore, unless the state has preëmpted to itself the entire rent element of the agricultural sector, some differential rent also accrues to the holders of the better plots of land within each region.

COSTS OF ADMINISTRATION

The turnover tax, which is by far the most important of the taxes we have chosen to call commodity taxes, was originally conceived as a very simple levy. Only 45 rates of tax, each applying to a separate industry or ministry, were contemplated. Furthermore, the taxes were to be collected not from the small and numerous retailers but from industrial producers, agricultural procurement agencies, and wholesalers, who were relatively large in size and few in number. The system later became more complex both with respect to the number of rates and the number of organizations paying the tax;[22] nevertheless it remains, on the whole, a relatively simple form of tax.

The income tax on workers and salaried employees is also comparatively cheap and simple to administer, because the Soviets use the "pay-as-you-earn" system of collection through place of employment. The number of tax-paying units involved here is clearly much larger than in the case of the turnover tax, since every organization (production, wholesale, retail, social, and cultural) must compute and pay the income tax. In addition, the income of a very large number of persons — most of the population in terms of numbers, though a less important group in terms of the amount of taxes paid — cannot be taxed through an organization but must be taxed individually. Artists, professional people with private practices, petty entrepreneurs and shopkeepers, and the entire agricultural population fall into this category.

Still, since the Soviets are not dependent on income taxation for revenue, administration need not be very costly, even where the tax is paid on an individual basis. If the Soviets did rely heavily on direct taxation, loss of receipts through evasion and incorrect computations would be important; the cost of preventing marginal losses would be high. This consideration would have been particularly relevant in the earlier Soviet period, when illiteracy was common and the rural population was not organized into collectives subject to easy state control.

High marginal costs of taxation are not so serious in the case of the turnover tax, in spite of the more complicated nature of each individual auditing problem, because the number of payers is smaller and accounting procedures are standardized.

FUNCTIONS OF DIRECT TAXATION

We have deduced the main theoretical and practical advantages to Soviet planners in placing primary reliance on commodity taxation, which, since 1930, has provided the bulk of budget revenue. With the exception of the war years, receipts from direct taxes on the population have never provided more than 10 per cent of total tax revenue. Soviet authorities have not abandoned this comparatively unimportant tax entirely, however, because it serves certain minor functions to which commodity taxes could not easily be adapted.

First and foremost, the commodity tax cannot be made sufficiently discriminating to serve as an instrument of Soviet class policy. Income taxes, on the other hand, can easily be made to discriminate against some groups in the population and in favor of others. This use of direct taxation is stressed by Soviet economists, and is clearly evident from the structure of Soviet income-tax rates. Most nations relate income taxes uniquely to the level of personal income. The Soviets, on the other hand, divide taxpayers into groups based on type of occupation or income, and a different rate applies to each group at identical levels of income.

This discriminatory policy was particularly important in the late 1920's and early 1930's, when the state had committed itself to the elimination of the private entrepreneur in the city and of the kulak in the rural areas. In 1934, for example, the city population was divided into the following categories:[23]

(1) Workers and salaried employees; coöperative artisans and domestic workers;

(2) Writers and artists;

(3) Noncoöperative artisans without hired labor; private-practice doctors;

(4) Persons working for themselves (excluding doctors); house-owners; persons receiving income from sale of dairy or garden products;

(5) Noncoöperative artisans or domestic workers with one or two hired employees; owners of certain types of machinery;

(6) Petty business men; artisans and domestic workers with more than two hired employees; persons living on monetary capital; religious workers.

Some sample rates of income tax for these groups in 1934 are given in Table 11.

The discriminatory character of the income tax is obvious from these schedules. One cannot accept completely, however, the Soviet explanation that these differentials are an expression of class policy alone. Class policy undoubtedly accounts for the discriminatory rates paid by the sixth category; this is particularly clear in light of the fact that persons in this category were also subject to an excess-profits tax which increased their income-tax obligation by 50 per cent. But for some other categories, the explanation is not quite this simple.

TABLE 11 Average Income-Tax Rates in 1934 (per cent) [a]

Yearly income (rubles)	Population categories (see text)					
	1	2	3	4	5	6
1,000	0.76	0.90	2.50	3.75	4.00	4.80
5,000	2.79	2.80	9.32	13.98	15.50	19.90
10,000	3.50	8.75	18.36	27.39	30.70	35.85
20,000	3.50	19.98	29.38	44.00	49.40	54.58

For source, see Appendix.

[a] The marginal rates were much higher. For example, the rates for income between 15,000 and 20,000 rubles was: category 1, 3.5 per cent; category 2, 34 per cent; category 3, 44 per cent; category 6, 77 per cent. (*See Sobranie zakonov i rasporiazhenii SSSR* [Collection of laws and decrees of the USSR], 1934, no. 27, art. 211b, pp. 372–373).

For instance, there is no indication that the state wants to discourage private medical practice. Yet doctors with private practices pay a discriminatory tax which seems to reflect the fact that they typically receive much larger incomes from their private practices than from their work for the state. The state exercises no control over the fees charged in private practice. The discriminatory tax on income from private practice would therefore seem to be a device for skimming off into the budget the "rent" element in private fees. This explanation also seems to apply to the taxation of other professional persons with private practices, and to those artists who reap excessive royalties from a "hit" book, play, or musical composition.

Even where the state controls the incomes of highly paid artists, such as leading ballet dancers, the discriminatory tax may be used for the purpose of reducing the rent element in income. Two answers may be submitted to the obvious question why the state does not simply pay such persons less to begin with. For status reasons it may be desirable for leading artists to appear to receive very high basic salaries; alternatively, the state may want to attract persons into the arts by paying high gross salaries. In both instances, the money illusion is exploited and the income tax is used to reduce such salaries to a more reasonable net level.

Turning for a moment to direct taxation of the peasants, we find that the richer peasants or kulaks were treated in a manner similar to the elements in the city. In the late 1920's they were taxed at a higher rate than the poor (*bedniaki*) or average (*seredniaki*) peasants, and in the 1930's at a higher rate than the collective farmers. Futhermore, kulaks were taxed on their actual income, whereas the collective and private farmers paid a tax based on average "norms" of income from each hectare of each crop under cultivation and from each animal owned. The norm basis provided the collective and private farmers with an incentive to work hard, exceed the norms, and thereby achieve a lower effective rate of tax. The kulaks were placed on an actual-income basis to prevent them from adding to their wealth by extracting more than the norm of income from their holdings. The kulaks were also forced to discharge their total tax liability in one payment, while other groups could pay in installments. Today the kulak class has officially been eliminated, but the private farmer still exists and pays a 100 per cent higher rate of tax on income from most sources than the collective farmer does.

Direct taxation of the peasant population reflects, then, the same elements of state policy as the income tax on the urban population. The tax on the kulaks was primarily political in character; it was designed to destroy the kulak as an agricultural producer. The tax on the private farmer is somewhat less oppressive and is perhaps more accurately described as a penalty on those farmers who refuse to join the collective farms. It also may be used to extract the rent element from the incomes of those private farmers who have large surpluses to sell at the high collective farm market prices.

On a strictly economic level, the system of direct taxes is used extensively to adjust various incentives which implement state policy. This is particularly important in the agricultural sector; since it is not state owned, adherence to the over-all plan must be achieved to a great extent by the use of indirect controls. For example, if the plan calls for an increase in the output of one crop at the expense of another, the tax on income from the former may be reduced or eliminated, while the tax on the latter is raised. Because of persistent shortages in the USSR, income from crops which have industrial uses (e.g., cotton, flax, hemp) has often been exempt from taxation, or subject to very low rates; the same has sometimes been the case with income from animal husbandry and beekeeping. A parallel policy is used to encourage settlement of frontier regions, particularly arctic and desert areas: both settlers and enterprises are freed from many types of taxation and are charged specially reduced prices on many commodities imported from the rest of the country.

Under certain circumstances, monetary stability in the Soviet Union might require the use not only of a general commodity tax paid by all households but also of differential taxes on the rural and urban populations. Rural households earn much less money income, aggregate and per capita, than urban households. A commodity tax designed to bring in enough revenue for aggregate stability but undifferentiated between urban and rural households could achieve stability in both urban and rural sectors only if the market for commodities sold and taxed by the state were free and perfect knowledge prevailed. If, however, the urban and rural markets are distinct and the state does not want to, or cannot, distribute the available supply of consumers' goods to the two sectors in proportion to their money incomes, at least one of the two sectors will, in theory, be in monetary disequilibrium unless some other tax is levied. In fact, however, it is doubtful that direct taxation of the urban and rural populations has to date been used deliberately by the Soviets to distribute real income between these sectors in a different ratio from money income earned.

Supplies and incomes of the agricultural and urban sectors may also get out of alignment for fortuitous reasons. In such circumstances, direct taxes could be used to restore equilibrium, although they are not the only method for dealing with this problem. Sales of government bonds, which are a more flexible fiscal instrument than direct taxes, would be even more useful for this purpose. In addition, equilibrium could probably be restored by raising or lowering the turnover tax on food products relative to the tax on industrial consumers' goods, since the former are bought primarily by the urban population.

It was indicated in Chapter 2 that the income tax has more built-in flexibility against wage inflation than the commodity tax. This is, of course, an important advantage of income taxes in general, though of limited significance in a country where they are comparatively little used. The income tax is superior to commodity taxes in another respect which has more relevance to the USSR, however. Commodity taxes are not flexible against declines in the output of consumers' goods. This characteristic was particularly apparent during the war, when the reduction in output of consumers' goods caused receipts from commodity taxation to shrink seriously. Partly for this reason, greater reliance was placed on income taxation and several new direct taxes were introduced. In 1943, direct taxes on income brought in roughly three-tenths as much revenue as the receipts from commodity taxation, in comparison with less than one-tenth in the prewar period. Under similar circumstances, income taxes may again increase in relative importance.

TAXATION IN KIND OF AGRICULTURE

The Soviets are attempting to industrialize at a much faster tempo than would be possible if determination of the rate of investment were left to the time preferences of the population. This policy has resulted in a high rate of forced savings for the economy as a whole. Ordinarily forced savings take a monetary form; they are the result of very high money taxation, or of compelling the population to hold a larger than normal portion of its income in the form of liquid assets, or of price rises which depreciate the value of both income and liquid assets. Each of these processes contributes to forced savings in the Soviet economy in both the industrial and the agricultural sectors. In addition, the agricultural sector is also forced to save by a non-monetary device, taxation in kind.

Taxation in kind takes the form of compulsory deliveries to state and coöperative procurement agencies of a specified part of the outputs of collective farms and individual farmers at very low prices. These prices are a fraction of the retail price at which the state resells the same commodities, and they do not cover the cost of production. The difference between the cost of these commodities to the state (procurement price plus the costs of processing and distribution) and retail price is usually siphoned into the state budget by the turnover tax. That portion of the turnover tax which is collected by virtue of the low procurement price is, in effect, a tax on the agricultural producer rather than on the general consumer, and is the monetary equivalent of the tax in kind. Part of it represents land rent, of course; the remainder represents savings exacted from the rural population over and above savings exacted from the population as a whole through monetary devices.

The industrial sector is almost 100 per cent state owned; all output goes to the state automatically, and the incomes earned in the production process are paid in cash. In the agricultural sector, the only state-owned producers are the *sovkhozy* or state farms, which account for a very small share of total agricultural output. The typical producers are the collective farms and individual farmers, both of which receive a large part of their income in the form of produce. This form of organization of agriculture creates two serious problems for the state. Since the bulk of the turnover tax is collected in the form of markups on agricultural products (food being the principal item of personal consumption in the Soviet Union), the incidence of the turnover tax on the agricultural population considered as consumers is necessarily very slight. Another form of tax on the peasantry must be substituted for the turnover tax if a high rate of saving is to be maintained. Secondly, the state must somehow secure a substantial share of the output of the agricultural sector for urban consumption, industrial use, and export.

The state has several alternatives in solving these problems; it may: (1) compel collective farms and peasants to deliver a specified part of their output either for no remuneration or for a very small one; (2) compel collective farms and peasants to deliver a specified part of their output for a remuneration which at least covers costs of production; (3) do away with collective farms (*kolkhozy*) and replace them by state farms (*sovkhozy*); (4) levy a very high money income tax on peasants and collective farms with the purpose of forcing them to sell a sufficient portion of their output to pay the taxes.

Soviet choice of the first alternative, which is a tax in kind, is not hard to understand in the context of the Soviet type of planned economy. The more precisely the planners can predict the important economic variables (quantities, demand, costs, etc.), the simpler is their task. By abstracting from unpredictables like bad harvests, the tax in kind enables the state to obtain the quantities of commodities it needs at planned costs. Since the state has no legal claim to agricultural output, except through taxation, this method is the only device which insures procurement at planned cost with any degree of certainty under the collective farm system of agriculture. Professor Dobb points out that before taxation in kind was instituted,

> the supply of agricultural produce forthcoming depended in the main on the structure of prices (although it was capable also of being influenced by such things as taxation policy), with the resulting instabilities and incalculable movements, seriously restrictive of economic planning. . . With the campaign for collectivization went a system of "forward contracts" [an early form of the tax in kind] with collective farms (as also with individual peasant economies), in an attempt to secure firm guarantees

of supply upon which the production plans of industry for the coming year could be built.[24]

A crucial feature of the tax in kind, and one which stabilizes agriculture from the state point of view, is that it is based on the number of acres sown or owned rather than on actual output. This system gives the state and those who buy food from the state (primarily the workers) maximum protection from fluctuations in agricultural output. Conversely, it causes the impact of output fluctuations to fall on peasant producers, for they must deliver a fixed amount of produce to the state regardless of the success of the crop.

Under the state-farm system, the peasants would not bear the burden of crop fluctuations. Peasants employed on state farms are paid money wages like factory workers, and depend mainly on state stores to satisfy their food needs. If state farms were substituted for collective farms, the consumer sector as a whole would suffer from the fluctuations in agricultural output, whereas under the present system the worker is protected at the expense of the peasant from fluctuations in food supplies. This may reflect the ideological preference of the Soviets for the working class, or perhaps just recognition of the fact that when there are food shortages the peasant has a better chance than the worker of scrounging enough food to feed his family. Another important consideration militating against wholesale introduction of state farms is the fact that this would seriously complicate price and tax planning in the consumers'-goods markets; the volume of food which could be offered for sale in state and coöperative stores would vary arbitrarily from year to year, depending on crop results. These seem to be the more important reasons for preferring taxation in kind to widespread use of a state-farm system.[25]

An alternative to taxation in kind is compulsory deliveries at a price equal to cost of production. It might be argued that this system has one advantage over taxation in kind, in that agricultural products would be costed in a manner comparable to other economic goods and services. This argument is not very substantial, however; any cost distortion which arises from paying a below-cost procurement price can easily be remedied by adding to procurement price a turnover tax of appropriate size. This is in fact the Soviet practice.

Compulsory deliveries at cost price, while insuring the state a stable quota of agricultural output, would not take care of the problem of taxing the agricultural sector. The money income of both the collective farms and the peasants would be substantially augmented by the additional receipts from compulsory deliveries; this would necessitate a twofold or greater increase in the income tax on the collectives and peasants. It would probably be simple enough to raise the tax rate on the collectives, since the tax is not very large to begin with. But increasing the income-tax schedule for the peasants would be politically undesirable, since it already is much higher than the income tax on the workers.

Finally, high money incomes from the *compulsory deliveries*, together with the high money taxes on agricultural producers which would be required to absorb these incomes, would have the additional disadvantage of discouraging *voluntary sales* of agricultural products on the collective farm markets. It is the high marginal utility of cash to peasants and collective farms which encourages them to forego increased food consumption for money income and the industrial products which the money enables them to buy. The collective farm markets are an important supplementary device, which the state has shown no indication of giving up, for prying agricultural products out of the rural areas. It would be possible, of course, to tax peasant money income from compulsory deliveries at a higher rate than income from sales on the collective farm markets, and thereby preserve the incentive to sell on these markets at the same time that money income from compulsory deliveries is severely reduced by taxation. But this seems to be an unlikely alternative to the present policy of treating money income from compulsory deliveries in a specially favored category.

The fourth alternative is to levy a very high money income tax on peasants and collective farms with the purpose of forcing them to sell enough of their output to pay the taxes. A tax of this sort, to be at all effective, would have to be based on agricultural production rather than on money income itself; a tax on money income would be equivalent to a tax on sales of agricultural output, and this would give the farm population (particularly the individual peasant producers) an incentive to consume more of their output and sell less. Even if the tax were based on production, it would be difficult for the state to predict how much agricultural output would be offered for sale as a consequence of a given rate of income tax. For example, if the state wanted to increase its purchase of agricultural output, increasing money taxes would not necessarily increase agricultural production so long as the agricultural population could pay the tax by cutting down its purchases of industrial consumers' goods or agricultural equipment. Given the chronic shortage of food in the USSR and the typically inelastic demand for food products, this response is a real possibility; it might prove impossible to reduce the food consumption of the peasant farmers to a level consistent with the needs of the nation as a whole for food.

A reduction in the marketable food surplus could also occur if the fourth alternative were employed. This could occasion higher prices, and a spiral inflation might result from a terms-of-trade struggle between the industrial and agricultural sectors. Spiral inflation could of course be avoided by fixing the prices at which agricultural output must be sold, but the problem of procuring an adequate part of total output for the nonagricultural needs would remain unsolved.

In summary, taxation in kind enables the state to impose a high rate of forced saving on the agricultural sector; at the same time it gives the state the direct control over agricultural output necessary for the Soviet brand of planning in a sector of the economy which is not formally state owned.

Chapter 4

THE STRUCTURE OF SOVIET COMMODITY TAXATION

The intent of this chapter is to analyze the structure of commodity taxation in its impact on managerial incentives, plan administration, and other problems relating to the functioning of Soviet enterprise. We shall attempt in particular to explain the complex rationalization by Soviet economists of their commodity tax system. Accordingly, our explanation may do less than justice to Soviet reality. Scattered information from Soviet sources does suggest gaps between theory and practice, and wherever possible these are mentioned.[1]

DEFINITION

The commodity tax is defined here to comprise the total markup over commercial cost, i.e., the total receipts of state enterprises minus their explicit commercial costs. In the case of agricultural commodities, the equivalent of commercial costs will be procurement price plus distribution costs. While this definition is expedient from a statistical point of view, it is conceptually deficient because the tax, as here defined, *implicitly* includes certain elements of cost which are not *explicitly* paid for by the enterprise. The explicit commercial costs of a Soviet enterprise typically include payments for wages, raw materials and intermediate products, depreciation, and short-term interest. They do *not* include returns for exceptional entrepreneurial ability, costs of capital, costs of depletion, and rent — all of which are explicitly cost categories in capitalist enterprises. Furthermore, it is generally pointed out by Western economists that depreciation costs are understated in the Soviet Union, both because the life of fixed assets is usually overestimated and because depreciation charges are calculated in terms of original cost without upward adjustment for the effect of inflation on the cost of replacement.[2]

Returns to entrepreneurial ability are properly not a part of supply price in the Soviet Union, since the state owns industry and any residual returns belong to it already. Therefore, no modification of our definition of commodity tax is required here.

Differences in managerial ability do exist, of course, and are rewarded to some extent through the Director's Fund, which is part of the commodity tax as we have defined it, through output premiums, and through salary differentials. There is no way of knowing whether differential managerial ability is fully recognized by these means, however. To the extent that managers are *not* fully rewarded for exceptional ability, the difference between the real worth of the manager (i.e., his marginal value product) and his actual monetary remuneration accrues to the state through the commodity tax.

Capital formation by state enterprises, which constitutes the bulk of Soviet investment, is financed primarily by interest-free grants from the budget. The cost of capital is therefore not included in the explicit cost-price structure of state enterprises, but is reflected implicitly in the markup over cost. The same is true of depletion cost, and of the depreciation reserve to the extent that it is understated. Differential rent, as the Soviets themselves recognize (see Chapter 3), is expressed through the commodity tax rather than by formal rent payments.

Our definition of commodity tax would be much more satisfactory from a theoretical point of view if it were possible to deduct the above-mentioned charges (except entrepreneurial returns) from the Soviet markup over commercial cost. This would be difficult to do with any degree of authority, since no method has been devised for approximating the value of any of these charges. One writer has assumed that retained profits of enterprises, which are a part of the commodity tax, represent return to capital;[3] another has assumed that the turnover tax is the only commodity tax, and that the rest of the markup represents the above-mentioned costs.[4] These methods are rejected here because the various elements constituting the markup are arbitrary in size and tend to vary in a nonsystematic manner from year to year. Furthermore, there is not much evidence to indicate that they are related to the real economic categories they have been taken to represent.

Our definition of the commodity tax does have the advantage of varying more systematically over time; furthermore, it is operationally fairly satisfactory. The markup over commercial cost has the virtue of being a distinguishable aggregate under Soviet economic accounting practices. The costs of capital, depreciation, depletion, and rent appear to comprise a very small part of the total commodity tax, and the error involved in not deducting them is probably small. As Professor Hodgman says: "Although it is theoretically desirable

Price Structure		*Functional Relations*	
TURNOVER TAX			PERCENTAGE OF PLANNED PRICE
PROFITS	Profits tax	Final residual in most cases	ORIGINAL RESIDUAL
	Director's Fund	1, 2, or 5 per cent of planned profits; 15, 30, or 45 per cent of over-planned profits	
	Retained profits	Function of self-financed investment requirements	
MARK-UP FOR SOCIAL INSURANCE			3.7 TO 10.7 PER CENT OF PAYROLL
COST OF PRODUCTION			WAGES RAW MATERIALS SHORT-TERM INTEREST DEPRECIATION

Chart 1. Simplified model of Soviet wholesale price structure. This model is not drawn to scale, nor could it be in a representative sense since scale differs among products and industries. The turnover tax has tended to be small (prewar) or nonexistent with the exception of oil products (postwar) in the producers'-goods industries and very large, averaging 50 per cent of price, in the consumers'-goods industries. In all industries, profits rarely exceed, say, 20 per cent of cost of production. For details see the text of this chapter and Chapter 6.

to include entrepreneurial-type profits, rent, interest, and the wage elements included in 'other money outlays' in value-added by a given industry, . . . the omission of these . . . elements . . . is judged to have no significant effect . . . since (they) . . . are small relative to salaries and wages and payroll taxes."[5]

DESCRIPTION

The total commodity tax, as we have defined it, is composed of the following elements (see Chart 1):

i. turnover tax;
ii. profits,
  a. retained profits,
  b. deduction into the Director's Fund,
  c. profits tax (or deductions from profits);
iii. social-insurance markup (payroll tax).

The turnover tax is a sales tax levied primarily on consumers' goods. It is not a price-determining factor, however, as is the case with sales taxes in a free-market economy. Instead, the state independently sets the price of each commodity with a view to securing both equilibrium in separate commodity markets and aggregate fiscal stability. The turnover tax is then used to draw into the budget the bulk of the difference between price and cost.

In the prewar period the turnover tax was usually included in either factory price or wholesale price, and was levied as a percentage of one of those prices. For example, if the turnover tax were 50 per cent of the factory price it would constitute a 100 per cent markup over the rest of the elements constituting price. In the case of agricultural produce, turnover tax was sometimes levied as an absolute amount per unit of output, sometimes as a percentage of retail price. In the postwar period, the tax on both agricultural and industrial consumers' goods has more commonly been levied simply as the difference between the wholesale price and the retail price minus trade discount. The tax is levied on all state, coöperative, and other organizations and societies which manufacture and sell commodities. The attempt is made to tax each commodity only once in the production-distribution network. To this end, the practice in the thirties was to have the tax on industrial commodities paid by the factory, and on agricultural commodities by the procurement organization. More recently, the tax on many types of commodities has been paid by large-scale wholesale trading organizations. The tax is paid daily by organizations with large turnover and as infrequently as once a month by smaller organizations. The rates of tax are differentiated by commodity, to some extent by the region where the commodity is sold, in the case of some agricultural commodities by method of procurement, by types of producer (state, coöperative, invalid, etc.), and by use (household or industrial consumption).[6]

The surplus or residual which remains after the enterprise has met all its cost obligations, paid its social-insurance markup, and paid its turnover tax, is designated profits. This surplus usually amounts to from 5 to 15 per cent of commercial cost,[7] and is divided into planned and unplanned profits. Planned profits (or planned losses) can be defined as that part of the surplus which results from operating at the planned level of average cost, selling at the planned price, and producing and selling the precise amount of output planned. Unplanned profits can be defined as additional profits due to operating at lower than planned cost and producing more than planned output.

First lien on profits is held by the Director's Fund, an incentive-oriented arrangement permitting employees of an enterprise to share in the profits. The Fund acquires 1, 2, or 5 per cent of planned profits and 15, 30, or 45 per cent of unplanned profits; in both cases the differentiation is designed to equalize inequlties between industries resulting from factors beyond the control of the enterprise.[8] The funds may be spent by the director of the plant, in consultation with the trade union representatives, with little or no interference from higher authority. It is stipulated by law that not less than 50 per cent of the fund shall be devoted to new housing for employees; the remainder is to be spent on social and cultural projects, bonuses for good management, premiums for workers with outstanding records, and improvements to plant and equipment. The Fund is limited to 5 per cent of the payroll.[9]

A second part of profits remains with the enterprise, or within the chief administration, trust, or combine to which the enterprise belongs; it is used to finance planned investment in plant and equipment or to build up working capital. The distribution of these retained profits among enterprises affiliated with a trust, combine, or chief administration is decided upon by these higher organizations.

Residual profits after deductions have been made for the Director's Fund and for internal investment constitute the profits tax.

This, it should be noted, is a relatively informal procedure compared with that determining the profits tax on private enterprises in most Western nations. The typical Western tax is legally related by a schedule to either the rate of profits on investment or the absolute amount of profits. Soviet enterprises, as we have said, simply hand over to the budget all profits in excess of their planned requirements for investment and payments into the Director's Fund. The upper limit on the rate of deductions into the budget is set only by the payments into the Director's Fund, which are fixed by law as a modest percentage of profits. The lower limit is fixed at 10 per cent of total actual profits. This sum is paid into the budget by every enterprise, even when its internal investment requirements (determined by central planning authorities without specific reference to profits) exceed available retained profits. Enterprises showing losses also pay a minimum tax which is designed to permit financial control by the Ministry of Finance. A simple example will clarify this explanation. Assume planned profits of 10,000 rubles and unplanned profits of 1,000 rubles, making a total profit of 11,000 rubles. Assume deductions into the Director's Fund at 5 per cent of planned profits, or 500 rubles, and 45 per cent of unplanned profits, or 450 rubles, making total deductions of 950 rubles. Then if the investment from retained profits is zero, the surplus available for deductions into the budget is 10,050 rubles; if the investment is 3,000 rubles, the surplus is 7,050 rubles; and if the investment is 10,000 rubles, the surplus is 50 rubles. The actual deductions are 10,050, 7,050, and 1,100 rubles, respectively, since the minimum deduction is 10 per cent of profits. Hence in the last case there is a deficit of 1,050 rubles, which is made up by a subsidy from the budget.

Enterprises not affiliated with a trust or chief administration pay their deductions directly into the budget; enterprises subordinate to higher organizations pay through these higher administrative units. Payments are based on the quarterly profits plan and are made twice a month.[10]

The social-insurance fund, from which old age and sickness insurance payments are made, is financed by a markup over cost which fluctuates from 3.7 to 10.7 per cent of the payroll, depending on the type of work and working conditions characterizing the particular industry.[11]

We shall not be concerned with the social-insurance markup in the following discussion, since it has only fiscal significance, but shall concentrate on explaining the need for the combined use of the turnover and profits taxes. It is frequently asserted that there is no essential difference between the two, because both constitute a markup on cost.[12] From the point of view of the consumer, the taxes indeed serve an identical purpose, and if their only function were the absorption of excess consumer purchasing power, the turnover tax alone would probably suffice. The turnover and profits taxes are related to the economic system in several other ways, however. They differ in fiscal reliability, costs of administration, frequency of computation and collection, effect on incentives, and so forth. In most of these respects the taxes serve somewhat different functions and in some cases their combined use is required for either to function effectively.

As most of the turnover-tax receipts originate in consumers'-goods industries, the discussion which follows centers on these industries.

ADMINISTRATIVE AND FISCAL CONSIDERATIONS

The Soviet state is a huge establishment requiring an enormous and constant flow of revenue to meet its expenditures. The turnover tax is well adapted to this task — better adapted than the profits tax. First and foremost, it is impervious to fluctuations in costs; because it is a sales tax, receipts from it depend exclusively on the rate of tax and the quantity of goods sold. Receipts from the profits tax also depend on the quantity of goods sold, but in addition are a function of cost of production. If production is conducted at higher than planned cost because of wage inflation, inefficiency, or some other reason, receipts from the profits tax decline. But budget expenditures are hardly likely to decrease under the conditions which cause profits to decrease; it is important, therefore, to divorce budget receipts as much as possible from such fluctuations in costs. This is one reason for using the turnover tax rather than the profits tax to collect the bulk of the state revenue. It would also be desirable to divorce budgetary receipts from fluctuations in output and sales, but neither tax has this property. As was explained in Chapter 3, the decline in production and sales of consumers' goods during World War II was the reason for the sharp decline in the importance of commodity taxation in that period.

By its very nature, a profits tax cannot be calculated over short periods of time. The production process is not usually a steady one with an invariant day-to-day relation between cost outlays and sales receipts, and any attempt to calculate profits daily, or even weekly or monthly, would involve enterprises in very irregular shifts from profits one day to losses the next, depending on the flows of costs and sales. Sole reliance on a profits tax would therefore be unsatisfactory either from the budgetary point of view or from the point of view of the individual plant. If the profits tax were paid frequently enough to meet the budgetary requirement for a constant flow of revenue — if it were paid daily or weekly, say, as a percentage of planned quarterly profits — the enterprise would find itself in financial difficulties owing to fluctuations in receipts. On the other hand, monthly or quarterly payments which might suit the enterprise would not provide the state with the steady flow of funds required for its operations. Frequent payments which would not embarrass the individual enterprise might be contrived, but these would require more frequent computation of actual profits, which would be both complicated and costly. Here again the turnover tax has distinct advantages: it is easy and inexpensive to calculate, can be calculated for as short a period as is necessary, and is not likely to be financially embarrassing to enterprises, since it is tied to sales receipts.

What are the advantages of the profits tax, then? Turning from the needs of the budget to those of the enterprise, we see that just as the budget needs a continual flow of funds to meet its huge expenditures, so does each plant require enough funds to cushion it against day-to-day fluctuations in the relation between cost outlays and sales receipts, and against any other unexpected events. Basically this problem is met by endowing each enterprise with adequate working capital and making short-term credit available to enterprises in financial difficulties. Profits also serve this function, however, and are especially important in industries where fluctuations in costs and receipts are large.[13]

From an administrative point of view, the use of two forms of commodity tax is extremely convenient, if not essential, in the consumers'-goods industries. The commodity tax must serve at least three functions in addition to the basic function of providing revenue; it must (1) equilibrate the supply of and demand for different commodities (or groups of similar commodities), (2) allow for differences in average cost among firms producing the same commodity, (3) allow for differences in internal investment requirements of different firms.[14]

Theoretically it would be possible to tailor the turnover tax to fit the needs of each individual plant, thereby solving all of the above problems at one stroke. But this would require a separate tax rate for every plant in the country, and would be a tremendous administrative task. There are other objections. It is doubtful whether, under these conditions, the taxes could be levied with sufficient precision to enable the successful establishment of uniform prices for identical or similar commodities, or (if prices are rigidly fixed) to assure each enterprise the funds necessary to carry out its investment program without suffering losses. Second, the turnover tax is used to collect the largest part of the Soviet budgetary receipts. For this reason, it is important to keep the tax apparatus simple and easy to administer, so as to assure the state of a steady flow of receipts. Third, from the point of view of over-all economic planning, it is useful to relate the cost of a commodity or group of similar commodities to price by a single magnitude which will give a rough indication of the market relation. If individual rates are set for each plant, no such magnitudes emerge as a by-product of the tax process. Special attempts to calculate these market relations would require computations which might prove expensive.

Consideration of these problems prepares us to appreciate the logic of the Soviet solution. The state first establishes the turnover tax for individual commodities or groups of commodities in such a way as to adjust price roughly to correspond to market demand. This is accomplished on a *centralized* basis for the nation as a whole. Then variations between firms in average costs and internal investment requirements are ironed out locally by the trusts or chief administration through the profits tax.

In theory, the turnover tax should be kept fairly stable over time, with adjustments only for relatively long-run shifts in supply or demand schedules, or for important changes in policy regarding self-financed investments by trusts and other organizations. Shorter-run or minor fluctuations in costs, prices, and internal investment should be absorbed by corresponding changes in the profits tax.[15] This policy, if adhered to, would aid in maintaining a simple turnover-tax structure and thereby facilitate planning. The extent to which this policy was not adhered to is discussed in Chapter 6.

THE INDICATOR OF ENTERPRISE PERFORMANCE

Although Soviet industry is owned by the state, enterprises have operated since the early 1920's on a relatively independent financial basis — the so-called *khozraschet* basis. Concerning it Baykov writes: "There is no adequate English equivalent of the Soviet expression *khozraschet*. The notion implies that cost accounting is applied to definite quantitative and qualitative tasks prescribed by the plan as well as to financial results." [16]

One of the most significant results of placing firms on a *khozraschet* basis is that it makes possible the computation of per-unit profits, per-unit costs, and so forth. In the absence of *khozraschet* it would not be possible to test firm performance satisfactorily; incomplete measures such as gross output would have to be relied upon. The most comprehensive test of firm performance — in Russian terms the "indicator" (*pokazatel'*) which provides a weighted index of all other "indicators" — is the deviation of rate of profits earned from rate of profits planned.[17] Under capitalism, because of the existence of the free market, the rate of profits per se serves as a measure of the profitability (over-all performance) of the enterprise. In the Soviet Union, the markup over cost of each commodity is set by the state, and is therefore not an indicator of profitability in any market-determined sense. But the degree of correspondence between the actual rate of profits and the planned rate (based on planned costs and prices) provides the authorities with a fairly comprehensive "indicator" of whether an enterprise's performance is up to expectations. (An important exception to be noted is the case of product-mix, discussed below.) The absolute rate of profit may also be useful in comparing the performance of enterprises producing the same product. It could scarcely be used as a basis for comparing firms producing different commodities, however, because intercommodity differences in profits are determined administratively rather than through the market.

It is important to distinguish between the Soviet rate of profit used to measure enterprise performance and the rate of profit as it is usually conceived in Western economic theory and practice. The Soviet rate of profit is computed from the relation of profits to cost of production; the Western rate of profit usually represents return on investment. This does not detract from the usefulness of the Soviet concept within the Soviet context. It does mean, however, that even if the rate of profit were market-determined, it could not be used as a basis for deciding in which industries investment should be expanded.[18]

The use of the turnover tax, which automatically siphons off into the budget the bulk of taxable surplus, makes the ratio of actual to planned profits a much more sensitive indicator of firm performance than would be the case if the entire gap between costs and price were treated as profits. Without the turnover tax, the level of profits planned for many plants, particularly those producing consumers' goods, would be very high; hence deviations from plan, unless extraordinary, would not be very large in percentage terms. When the turnover tax is used, the level of planned profits is much smaller, and the same deviation from plan constitutes a much larger percentage of the planned-profits figure.

To illustrate this point, let us assume that the plan calls for a firm to produce 1000 units at a cost of 500 rubles per unit to be sold at 1000 rubles per unit, and that the plant is inefficient, each unit actually costing 518 rubles to produce. If there were no turnover tax, actual profits would be 482,000 rubles instead of the 500,000 rubles planned. This would constitute a deviation from plan of 3.6 per cent, or the plan would have been 96.4 per cent fulfilled. But if a turnover tax of 48 per cent were imposed, actual profits would be only 2000 rubles, in comparison with planned profits of 20,000 rubles. Deviation of actual from planned profits would be 90 per cent; plan fulfillment would be only 10 per cent. The difference between these hypothetical fulfillment percentages illustrates the role of the turnover tax in making this important barometer of firm performance more sensitive.

It may be contended that the importance of this point is largely psychological—that it would be possible for the Soviets to instill in their economists and managers as strong a reaction to a 1 per cent deviation from planned profits as is now evoked by a 20 per cent deviation. But since in all other phases of human experience 1 per cent deviations would continue to have very mild connotations, the use of the turnover tax probably constitutes the more satisfactory approach to this problem.

There is an economic as well as a psychological rationalization for this procedure. The bulk of the markup over cost is purely a result of the high planned price set by the state; it is necessitated by the high rate of nonconsumption expenditures, and has little or nothing to do with the efficiency at which a plant operates. The efficiency with which a plant is managed is manifest only in the small marginal variations in markup which are due to over- or under-plan movements in the levels of cost and output. By using the turnover tax to siphon off the larger part of the markup, the rate of profits fulfillment tends to reflect these marginal variations much more sensitively.

It has been pointed out that the percentage of markup over cost differs substantially from commodity to commodity in the Soviet Union. In particular, consumers'-goods industries have large markups and producers'-goods industries relatively low ones. If the turnover tax were not employed to equalize the rate of profits among industries and plants, a given percentage of underfulfillment of the profits plan in a consumers'-goods plant would be of much greater significance than in a producers'-goods plant. Use of the turnover tax to equalize the rate of profits between industries tends to generalize or universalize the significance of the "percentage deviation from plan" as a measure of firm performance. Even with the turnover tax, however, it must be recognized that the rate of profits will differ somewhat from industry to industry, owing to different internal investment requirements and to seasonal fluctuations in demand and cost which make it necessary for some plants to keep large amounts of working capital or profits.

In actual practice, deviation from planned profits is not the only indicator used, nor does it always provide the planners with desired information. Other less general criteria, such as gross output and fulfillment of the wage fund, are also used to check the performance of an enterprise. Most authorities, and in particular those concerned with financial matters — the Ministry of Finance, the State Bank, and the tax authorities — will concentrate their attention on profits. The Ministry of Internal Trade and the chief administration in charge of sales for an industry would tend to be more interested in the gross output of an enterprise; the chief administration, for example, might have contracts for forward deliveries dependent on this output. Other groups in the supervisory network might be interested in still other indicators of performance. The particular indicator of most concern to a plant would probably depend on the relative importance of the different lines of authority descending to the plant.

Gross output seems to be of equal importance to profits as an indicator, if not more widely applied. This is probably a result of the chronic commodity shortage which has plagued the Soviet economy.

Profits can be a spurious indicator of performance. Many cases have been reported of managers increasing profits by allowing the quality of their products to deteriorate. In plants manufacturing more than one product the practice has frequently been to concentrate on the more profitable of the products regardless of the plan. Other managers succeed in increasing profits by selling at higher than plan prices; [19] still others hide over-plan profits by illegally investing in scarce materials which they hoard, or by paying higher than planned wages.

MANAGERIAL INCENTIVES

One of the principal functions of profits as a special decentralized form of socialist accumulation is "to stimulate the struggle for lower costs and wider accumulation by establishing a direct dependence between the results of economic activity and the financial-economic opportunities which large sums of profits bestow upon enterprises through additions to working capital, capital investment, and the Director's Fund." [20] The implication of this statement and similar ones by other Soviet economists is that profits are important for managerial incentives. Many other factors, both economic and noneconomic, affect managerial incentives. Among these the more important are: premiums for fulfilling and overfulfilling the output plan, premiums for lowering costs, benefits from the Director's Fund, and fear of the consequences of underfulfilling profits and of falling into financial difficulties.[21] Just how important profits and the impact of taxes on profits are on incentives of Soviet management, in comparison with these other considerations, the present state of Western knowledge about the Soviet Union does not allow us to say. In this section these other facets of the managerial incentive problem will not be dealt with, since they are outside the scope of the book; the discussion will be confined to presenting and rationalizing the Soviet viewpoint regarding the relation between profits, taxes, and incentives. The partial nature of the presentation should be kept in mind.

Retained profits are invested within the trust, combine, or chief administration in which they occur. Although part of the profits earned by one plant may be redistributed by the trust for investment in some other plant, the presumption is that there is some correlation between plants in which profits are earned and plants in which investment takes place. The incentive element appears to stem from two factors: (*a*) the process of expanding a plant exercises the manager's "workmanship" instinct even though the character of the investment may be to a large extent out of the manager's control, and (*b*) the manager's status and importance are related to the size and growth of his firm.[22]

The turnover tax serves the same role with profits with respect to managerial incentives that it serves with profits considered as an indicator of firm performance. In the illustrative example discussed earlier, let us assume that the state directed the plant to invest 10,000 rubles of its profits in additional equipment. Let us again assume that the plant operated at higher than planned cost. If there were no turnover tax, profits would be 482,000 rubles instead of the 500,000 planned; the plant could still invest in additional equipment out of its profits. If there were a 48 per cent turnover tax, however, the plant's profits would be only 2,000 rubles, and it would not be able to carry out from its own profits the investment planned. The investment might still be undertaken, either through redistribution of funds from another plant in the trust or by means of a state investment subsidy; Soviet literature is not clear on how seriously a firm which is inefficient prejudices its claim to funds for investment. Aside from this, the turnover tax does relate the internal investment of firms more closely to their performance than would otherwise be possible, and presumably tends thereby to increase the incentive of managers to operate their plants efficiently.

The foregoing principle is operative even if the incentive role of internally financed investment is disregarded. If a manager did not expect to benefit from profits in the form of internal investment, he would nevertheless be interested in making a good showing for purposes of advancement or for fear of removal. His showing depends to a considerable degree on how successfully planned profits are achieved. Without the turnover tax there would not be much incentive in the consumers'-goods industries to improve performance, since large changes in efficiency would have only a small effect on the percentage of fulfillment of profits. With the turnover tax absorbing the bulk of the markup over cost, however, a manager must keep his firm operating efficiently or find his profit margin cut by a large percentage which cannot help but reflect unfavorably on his ability.

The way in which the Director's Fund (which is formed out of profits) affects the incentives not only of managers but also of workers is clear from the description of its provisions presented earlier in this chapter. It should be noted that the Director's Fund in the consumers'-goods industries operates on a principle similar to the one we have been discussing. It has been pointed out that because the bulk of the taxable surplus is absorbed by the turnover tax, fulfillment of the profits plan is related much more directly and sensitively to changes in productive efficiency than would be the case if profits constituted the entire markup. The Director's Fund operates analogously: a very small percentage of planned profits is deducted into the Fund since these profits are a function of the high price set by the state and other factors unrelated to plant performance; a much higher percentage of over-plan profits is deducted into the Fund, since these are the extraordinary profits which are related much more directly to managerial and worker ability.

THE PROBLEM OF PRODUCT-MIX (ASSORTMENT)

In the last two sections we have considered the use in Soviet industry of what might be loosely termed the profit motive. Like the private entrepreneur under capitalism, the Soviet manager strives to achieve a satisfactory level of monetary profits. From the point of view of the state, this goal satisfactorily serves its purpose in plants which produce only one commodity (except where profits are increased at the expense of quality), because it leads to cost reduction or an increase in output, or both. Multiple-product plants have a third alternative for increasing profits: they may concentrate on producing the commodity which returns the greatest rate of profits. This may not be too serious a problem in the case of an individual plant, where technical relations between multiple products may more or less dictate the quantitative output relations between the commodities in question. But it can be exploited on a much broader scale by trusts or combines which control a large number of plants producing related products. Like individual plant managers, managers of trusts and other higher organizations are interested in maximizing profits, and in so doing they may seriously alter the proportions in which the different commodities are supposed to be produced. It is clear that a conflict of goals exists: on the one hand, the manager attempts to maximize profits for reasons of self-interest; on the other hand, this tends to upset the relative proportions of output as planned by the state. This conflict presumably could not occur under free market conditions, because the relative rates of profit for different commodities would reflect relative consumers' demand for the commodities. In the Soviet Union, the profit margins on different commodities and for different plants tend to vary for many reasons, and the relative price-cost differentials have little connection with the demand schedules of either Soviet planners or consumers.

The Soviets are aware of the problem which is created by lack of uniformity in the rate of profitability of different commodities, particularly as this affects similar commodities produced by the same plant or group of plants. This problem is mentioned continually in the literature.[23] It should be noted that the incentive to produce the wrong assortment exists not only to maximize profits, but in some instances to minimize wage-fund expenditures. This is accomplished by increasing the output of the commodities that require less labor. The problem was complicated until recently by the fact that expenditure on wages was tied to output valued in 1926–27 prices (see Chapter 2), and the assortment which minimized the use of the wage fund was not likely to maximize gross output valued in 1926–27 prices, hence was not likely to maximize the availability to the enterprise of cash for wages.

The problem is ameliorated somewhat by the combined use of the turnover and profits taxes. The grossest cost-price differentials—those due to differential rent and to the state policy of financing most of its expenditures through large markups on consumers' goods—are eliminated by the turnover tax. In addition, a certain amount of differential turnover taxation within groups of commodities serves to reduce the problem further.[24] Complete solution of this problem by use of the turnover tax (i.e., equalization of the rate of profits for all plants) would necessitate complicating the turnover-tax system, hence the planning and collecting of taxes. This is not feasible as a general method of approach since it is considered important to keep the turnover-tax system as simple and as easy to administer as possible.[25]

The Soviets will be plagued by this and like problems as long as they try to combine the advantages of a system of monetary incentives with a price system which does not accurately reflect economic scarcity. In the absence of a consistent cost-price system, the Soviets will be forced in the direction of more and more complicated controls. A relevant example of this is provided by recent Director's Fund legislation: since the end of the war it has been specified that profits may not be deducted into the Director's Fund unless the actual pattern of output corresponds with the planned product-mix.

PART II: HISTORY

Chapter 5

DEVELOPMENTS LEADING TO THE TAX REFORM OF 1930

The present Soviet tax system, with its distinctive emphasis upon commodity taxation, is essentially the product of the Tax Reform of 1930. The Reform brought about a much needed simplification of the intricate system which had evolved in the twenties. On the eve of the revision, 86 different levies were being collected from the socialized sector and 76 from the private sector of the economy.[1] The old system was further complicated by multiple-stage taxation: that is, commodities were taxed at several stages in the production-trade network. The Reform replaced about 60 of the former levies on industry and trade by two taxes — the turnover tax and the deduction from profits — and attempted to make single-stage taxation universal in the socialized sector of the economy. Large strides in this direction had already been made in the last years of the New Economic Policy (NEP).

In this chapter we shall examine the evolution of the tax system before 1930, the conditions which led to reform, and the principal provisions of the 1930 decree. Considerations of space preclude a detailed discussion of the more general economic background of the Reform, which has been adequately treated elsewhere.[2]

ECONOMIC BASIS OF TAXES IN THE EARLY NEP PERIOD

During the period of War Communism which preceded the NEP, Soviet policy for ideological and other reasons[3] was to eliminate money as a medium of exchange as quickly as possible, and to place the economy on a natural or barter basis. Money taxation of the agricultural population was virtually eliminated in favor of direct requisitioning of commodities. Conventional taxation of industry was made unneccessary by the acts of nationalization, which placed all industry in the state budget on a gross basis. The state simply printed whatever money it needed, and the few money taxes which remained all but lost their significance because of the spiral inflation which gripped the economy in this period.

In 1921 the Soviets abandoned War Communism and launched the NEP, a central objective of which was the restoration of a money economy.[4] By this time the country was suffering from hyperinflation, and financial policy was directed first of all at stabilizing the ruble.[5] As money gradually resumed its function as the medium of exchange, money taxation had to be reinstituted to support the government's activities. Concurrently with the process of stabilizing the ruble, sections of industry were gradually shifted out of the budget to a self-supporting status, with money rather than direct allocation governing the movement of their purchases and sales. Thus a large part of nationalized industry again became subject to conventional money taxation as this was reintroduced. The pattern of taxation which finally emerged in this period can be explained largely by the difficulties encountered by the Soviets in trying to reestablish their tax system after the temporary lapse from a money economy. These difficulties led to reliance on simple indirect taxes for the bulk of the tax revenue, introduction of a large number of taxes, and multiple-stage taxation.

Reliance on Simple Indirect Taxes. Reintroduction of money taxation required reconstituting the whole tax administrative apparatus, which had melted away during War Communism. Tax experts were hard to find; because of the serious shortage of skilled workers, tax specialists who had become unemployed when conventional money taxation declined had been quickly absorbed by other administrative agencies. Special attention was paid to the personnel problem by both the Communist Party and the state, and vigorous attempts were made both to shift former tax experts back into tax work and to train new workers.[6] Nevertheless the tax apparatus remained weak throughout the NEP. This was an important reason for the introduction of simple and easily enforceable taxes.

The weakness of the tax apparatus was aggravated by the lack of so-called "tax discipline" in both the socialized and the private sectors of the economy. In the socialized sector the shift from War Communism to the NEP involved a considerable change in the autonomy of the manager. As enterprises or trusts were placed on an independent financial basis (*khozraschet*) after having been in the budget on a gross basis, management assumed many of the normal entrepreneurial functions denied it during War Communism.[7] At first this abrupt increase in the functions of management led, not unnaturally, to problems in control, and a tendency on the part of managers to abuse their newly granted powers. One aspect of the control problem was the difficulty of enforcing tax payment. The difficulty was aggravated by the fact that managers had just been operating in a period in which money taxation did not exist, and were no longer in the habit of paying taxes as such.[8] The strength of the resistance to paying taxes stemmed partly from the financially unsound position of most state industry in this period (enterprises were not making large profits), and it was fortified by the semantic argument, submitted by many economists as well as managers, that it did not make sense for the state to tax state-owned enterprises.

Although the same rationalizations did not exist in the private sector, "tax discipline" here was even worse. Private traders were subject to discriminatory taxes, and naturally took every advantage of the chaotic economic situation to evade them. The lack of "tax discipline" in both sectors was a second reason for the need to construct simple and easily enforceable taxes.

The third and possibly most important reason for the use of simple taxes was the primitive level of bookkeeping and accounting procedures in Soviet enterprises. This may be attributed partly to the vacation from a money economy which had occurred during War Communism, and also to the fact that at this stage in its development the Soviet Union was backward both economically and culturally. A complicated tax cannot be levied and collected unless the accounting techniques of taxpaying units are sophisticated enough to permit calculating the amount of tax payment.[9] Most Soviet enterprises were not competent to estimate any but the simplest forms of taxes.

For these reasons the Soviets placed primary reliance in this period on levies in the form of license fees and sales or excise taxes, all of which were relatively easy to calculate and collect.[10]

Multiplicity of Taxes. The development of the large number of taxes which existed before the Reform was due to several factors. As was noted earlier, private trade and industry were subject to discriminatory taxation, which they tried in every possible way to evade in order to compete successfully with the state and coöperative sectors. These attempts included devising new forms of business operation, falsifying accounts, continually changing the physical location of the business, and so forth. New tricks to evade existing taxes led to the constant invention of new taxes.[11]

Secondly, as trade and industry developed, the relations of enterprises to the government became more complicated. For example, the government charged fees for inspections of bread products and meats, for analysis of the content of metals, for carrying business disputes to the courts, and so forth. In addition, each enterprise was subject to a large number of other fees and taxes relating to everyday business operations: there were fees for weighing commodities, for shipping freight, for establishing proof or origin of goods, for notarization, to penalize waste in nationalized industries, and so forth.

A third reason for the large number of taxes was that enterprises differed in the degree of sophistication of their bookkeeping and accounting. To a certain extent different types of taxes were applied to firms at different stages of development. This is one reason for the concomitant existence in this period of such major taxes on industry as the license tax, excise tax, craft tax, and income taxes on enterprises.

Multiple-Stage Taxation. The most important Soviet tax, which was levied on all enterprises in the production-distribution network, was the craft tax; as we shall see below, this was essentially a sales tax of a somewhat unusual kind. It is commonplace in most countries to tax the incomes of *all* individuals and the profits of *all* enterprises, since these are taxes which cannot easily be shifted to the consumer and which consequently have little impact on the price structure. It is not so common to tax the *sales* of all enterprises. Where sales taxes and other indirect taxes are employed, they are usually (though not invariably) levied on *final* sales; at this point as much of the tax as market conditions will permit is shifted to the consumer.

Use of a general sales tax was expedient because of the complexity and disorganization of the Soviet production-trade network. Commodities sometimes passed through eight or ten channels before reaching the final consumer. Most of these channels were independent units; this was generally true of the private sector, and was true also of the socialized sector in the early NEP period. It was necessary for the state to tax each enterprise in order to insure that no enterprise—and in particular, no private enterprise—escaped taxation. The result was a pyramiding of taxes and of retail prices as each business unit attempted to shift its share of the tax to the next stage in the network, until the final consumer was reached.[12] The limit to a process of this sort is the swelling of price to such a height that the market cannot be cleared. The various middlemen then have to bear part of the burden of the tax, since the total burden can no longer be shifted to the consumer. This in turn creates an economic incentive to reduce the number of middlemen; it was obvious that if their number in the Soviet trade network could be reduced, the chances of avoiding bearing a part of the tax burden—or alternatively, the chances of earning larger profits—would be greater for those who survived. The possibility that multiple-stage taxation might actually result in the elimination of superfluous middlemen was considered one justification of the system in the early NEP period.[13]

Offhand it would appear more reasonable for the state to have raised the rate of the craft tax and levied it at just one stage in the production-trade network, leaving the forces of competition to distribute the burden among the various middlemen and the consumer. This procedure would have reduced the costs of collection considerably. Some Soviet writers have claimed, however,[14] that lower rates of tax on each enterprise evoked fewer attempts at evasion. This was probably an important consideration in the period under discussion, when weakness of the tax apparatus coincided with a desperate need for tax revenues.

PRINCIPAL CHANGES IN THE ECONOMIC SITUATION DURING NEP

If the chaotic economic conditions described in the previous section had persisted, tax reform would have been impossible, at least in the shape in which it was introduced. Developments occurred, however, which made the Reform a logically necessary step. These developments can be divided roughly into four categories: (1) shrinkage of the private sector; (2) growth and unification of socialized trade and industry; (3) improvement in financial accounting; (4) growth of planning.

Shrinkage of the Private Economy. Throughout the NEP period socialized enterprises received preferential treatment in every sphere of economic activity. The state explicitly discriminated against private capital in its tax and credit policies and in the allocation of scarce materials, and also harassed private business through administrative acts.[15] Consequently, the importance of the socialized sector in trade and industry increased rapidly, while the private sector declined in relative importance; after about 1926 it began to decline in absolute importance as well. For example, in 1922–23 private enterprise handled 75 per cent of total retail-trade turnover; by 1925–26 this fraction had declined to 42 per cent, and by 1930 it was only 6 per cent of the total.[16] The trend in industry was much the same: by 1930 private enterprise accounted for only 5.6 per cent of the gross output of Soviet industry.[17] Since private trade and industry were very small by 1930 and still shrinking rapidly, they were no longer of much concern to the tax authorities. Most of the taxes originally developed to contain private capital were no longer needed or in use. The situation called for elimination of the superfluous taxes.

Growth and Unification of Socialized Trade and Industry. Even more important from the point of view of the Reform was the increasing strength and unification of the socialized sector. Very early in the NEP period trusts were formed to organize the commercial activities of factories producing the same kinds of commodities. The trusts in turn formed syndicates to handle such activities as purchases of raw materials and sales of final output. Organization of the syndicate system was accompanied by centralized financial accounting for the more important branches of state industry.[18] In addition, the so-called *torgi* were created to handle state wholesale trade between the large-scale nationalized industries and the provincial areas. By 1930 these organizations were strong and well organized, and controlled the bulk of industry and trade. This unification automatically tended to reduce the number of stages in the production-trade network in the socialized sector; furthermore, it tended to regularize trade procedures and relations, making it feasible to work out the technical details of a system of universal one-stage taxation in the socialized sector.

Improvement in Financial Accounting. Throughout the NEP period the financial condition of state enterprises improved; at the same time, better methods of bookkeeping and accounting were gradually adopted. These developments paved the way for an extensive reorganization of industry, announced on December 5, 1929. Among other things, the Communist Party stressed the necessity of transferring to *khozraschet* state enterprises not already operating on an independent financial basis. The multiplicity of taxes on each enterprise was clearly an obstacle to this end, since it substantially complicated the financial accounting of enterprises attempting to conduct business on a *khozraschet* basis. The difficulty was recognized in the resolution of December 5, 1929, which said: "Construction of a unified *khozraschet* organization demands decisive simplification of levies on industry." [19] Conversely, the widespread introduction of *khozraschet* simplified the tax problem in the sense that identical taxes, and these more sophisticated than had formerly been feasible, could now be applied to all enterprises in the socialized sector of the economy.

Growth of Planning. Simplification of the tax system was also demanded by the rapid advance of planning in the national economy. As the socialized sector was extended (by 1930 it comprised more than 90 per cent of total trade and industrial activity), the plan became more and more effective in superseding market forces as the means of making economic adjustments. Consequently, more precise planning became imperative. But precision in financial planning was seriously hampered both by the multiplicity of taxes on each enterprise and by taxation of the same commodity at many stages. It was very difficult to plan budget receipts accurately. It was also extremely difficult to plan prices. The latter became a serious consideration by the late twenties, when the planners were leaning more and more heavily on price policy as the instrument for mobilizing and redistributing the financial resources of the nation, as well as for achieving market equilibrium for individual commodities. In the NEP period prices were formed largely in the market, by the forces of supply and demand; taxes were shifted to the consumer to the extent permitted by the market and constituted a price-determining factor in the traditional free-market sense. With the extension of planning to the whole economy, the state set the prices of all commodities: taxes no longer determined prices but were set as a percentage of price, and were used to drain off into the budget part of the difference between price and cost. This change in the nature of taxation was completed by the Tax Reform.

In summary: economic conditions in the last few years of the NEP were significantly different from conditions in the early twenties, when the number of taxes proliferated and multiple-stage taxation of the same commodity was the rule. Some changes in the tax system were made even before the main Reform; these were directed at the elimination of multiple-stage taxation in the socialized sector. This was not completely accomplished, however. Furthermore, little had been done to reduce to a reasonable number the multitude of taxes which were still in use in both the socialized and private sectors of the economy.

Before proceeding to the Reform itself, the principal taxes of the NEP period will be briefly described.

PRINCIPAL TAXES ON INDUSTRY AND TRADE DURING NEP [20]

A general picture of the principal taxes on trade and industry in this period is provided by selected figures presented in Table 12.

TABLE 12 Selected Taxes on Enterprise in the Period Before the 1930 Tax Reform (millions of rubles)

<table>
<tr><th></th><th>1923–24</th><th>1925–26</th><th>1927–28</th><th>1929–30</th></tr>
<tr><td>Excise taxes</td><td>241</td><td>842</td><td>1491</td><td>2643</td></tr>
<tr><td>Craft tax</td><td>113</td><td>229</td><td>373</td><td>1941</td></tr>
<tr><td>Socialized industry</td><td></td><td>135</td><td>288</td><td>1797</td></tr>
<tr><td>Private industry</td><td></td><td>94</td><td>85</td><td>144</td></tr>
<tr><td>Income tax</td><td>65</td><td>151</td><td>231</td><td>615</td></tr>
<tr><td>Socialized economy</td><td>8</td><td>65</td><td>78</td><td>421</td></tr>
<tr><td>Population [a]</td><td>57</td><td>86</td><td>153</td><td>193</td></tr>
<tr><td>Deductions from profits</td><td>49</td><td>172</td><td>382</td><td>1005</td></tr>
<tr><td>Industry</td><td rowspan="2">40</td><td>99</td><td>265</td><td>847</td></tr>
<tr><td>Trade</td><td>22</td><td>27</td><td>37</td></tr>
<tr><td>Credit institutions</td><td>7</td><td>47</td><td>86</td><td>116</td></tr>
<tr><td>Customs and other duties and collections</td><td>135</td><td>308</td><td>489</td><td>445</td></tr>
</table>

For sources, see Appendix.

[a] This category includes taxation of private entrepreneurs.

The Craft Tax. The craft (*promyslovyi*) tax was the first tax introduced under the NEP, in July 1921.[21] At first it applied only to nonnationalized trade and industrial enterprises. It was extended on February 3, 1922 [22] to include all state, municipal, and coöperative organizations and enterprises, as well as small craftsmen employing hired labor. Originally the tax consisted of two parts: a license tax and an equalization tax. Under the first part, each enterprise was required to purchase, six months in advance, a certificate or license to conduct business operations. Collection every six months placed an extra burden on the tax authorities, but under the prevailing unstable conditions many enterprises did not survive much longer than six months, and this term was necessary to insure complete coverage. The cost of licenses was differentiated not by income or profitability of enterprises but by geographical location and by various other criteria external to paying ability, such as the number of employees and the types of commodities handled. The equalization tax was designed to compensate for this grossly inequitable levy, and payment of the license served, in effect, as a deposit in advance toward payment of the equalization tax.[23] The latter was set originally at 3 per cent of turnover for all taxable enterprises, and was vulnerable to the same objection as the license tax; since it was based purely on turnover, it was not necessarily related to profitability, i.e., ability to pay. Consequently, firms which did not succeed in earning profits in excess of their tax obligations were forced to pay their taxes out of working capital. A prominent feature of the craft tax at this time was, of course, that it was levied on *every* enterprise and at *all* stages in the production-trade network.

Many minor changes were made in the craft tax over the next six years: private enterprise was discriminated against and exemptions were extended to state and coöperative enterprises; rates on enterprises producing luxuries were raised;[24] the license fee was eliminated, leaving only the equalization tax;[25] the equalization tax was considerably simplified; and so forth.

In 1929 important steps were taken in the direction of single-stage craft taxation of the public sector. Previously trusts had been taxed on commodities sold to syndicates, and syndicates taxed on goods sold by them. Under the law of September 2, 1929, the syndicates were taxed on total turnover and the trusts were freed from taxation on sales to the syndicate.[26] Furthermore, all intercoöperative trade was freed from the craft tax; only gross receipts from sales outside the coöperatives remained subject to taxation. At the same time, the rates of tax on the private sector were increased by about 50 per cent, and technical simplifications to the systems of rates and methods of collection were introduced.

On September 25, 1929, several survivals of multiple-stage taxation on butter, tobacco, sugar, semifabricated textiles, and manufactures in the socialized sector were finally replaced by single-stage taxation of these commodities.[27] At this point the craft tax reached its final stage of development before the Reform.

Excise Taxes. The excise tax provided the budget with more revenue than any other tax during the NEP period. It was a source of some embarrassment to the Soviets to have to introduce an indirect tax of this scope, since indirect taxes had always been decried in Communist literature as regressive on the working class. The extent of their embarrassment is indicated by the fact that at the Eleventh Communist Party Congress in 1922, the paradoxical position was taken that introduction of indirect taxation was not to lead to a lowering of real wages but was to be accompanied by a corresponding compensation to wage payments.[28] With more sophistication it was emphasized that luxuries would be taxed at higher rates than mass-consumption commodities.

The first excises were introduced in 1921 on wine, tobacco, matches, and a few other products; in 1922 and 1923 coverage was extended to a large number of other consumers' goods.[29] The tax on alcoholic beverages provided more revenue than any other excise; just before the tax reform it accounted for about one-half of the total receipts from the excise tax. The other major excises, from a revenue point of view, were those on sugar, tobacco products, textiles, and petroleum products.

The excise taxes were levied on both socialized and private enterprises, the preponderance of revenue originating in the socialized sector. This was the result of levying excise taxes on producers rather than retailers; as was indicated above, the stronghold of private capital was trade, not production. The tax was levied in terms of quantity rather than value, i.e., in rubles per piece or per pound.

When the excises were first introduced, collection difficulties arising from inadequate accounting systems and poor "tax discipline" were common. The tax authorities attempted to cope with these problems by requiring all taxed enterprises to set up special accounts, submit special reports, and undergo frequent audits. These requirements were costly to enforce, but are reported to have been successful in overcoming many of the deficiencies noted.[30] The organization of trusts and syndicates provided the basis for still further reforms. In 1926 centralized payment of the excise taxes was introduced experimentally in the galoshes industry.[31] When the system proved successful, it was extended to the sugar and oil trusts, and to enterprises producing alcoholic beverages. On October 1, 1928[32] centralized calculation and payment of the excise tax was finally extended to all state enterprises and to part of the coöperative sector. This was a big stride forward in many ways. It lessened the burden on the tax apparatus, which now had fewer units to collect from (although spot checking of individual enterprises continued). It also lightened the work of the banks in connection with the receipt of tax money. Most of the accounts relating to excises were thereafter kept by the trust or syndicate rather than by the individual enterprise, an improvement which reduced the administrative forces engaged in this work by one-half.[33] It should be noted that by this time accounting procedures in many enterprises had become sufficiently developed, and their "tax discipline" sufficiently trustworthy, so that much of the costly supervision and accounting formalities which had accompanied the introduction of the excises had already been dispensed with.[34]

Craft versus Excise Taxation. Before the Tax Reform, Soviet economic literature devoted much space to discussing the type of tax on the socialized sector upon which the state should place primary reliance. The controversy centered on the relative merits of the craft and excise taxes, although some writers also considered the deductions from profits, as well as various combinations of taxes.[35] Three distinctions could be drawn between the excise and craft taxes as these were originally conceived. First, the excise tax was levied in terms of rubles per unit of output (either quantity or weight); the craft tax was stated as a percentage of the value of turnover. Second (and correlative to the first distinction), the excise tax was a tax on specific commodities, whereas the craft tax was levied on the total turnover of an enterprise or combination of enterprises, regardless of the number of commodities produced and sold. Third, the excise tax was always a single-stage tax, the craft tax a multiple-stage tax.[36] By 1929 the differences between the two taxes were no longer so clear-cut. As we have seen, the craft tax in the socialized sector had taken several strides toward becoming a single-stage tax, thereby eliminating its main disadvantage with respect to the excise tax. Excise taxes on several commodities had been restated in terms of price rather than quantity.[37] The difference which remained after these modifications was taxation of total turnover versus taxation of specific commodities. Taxation of total turnover was at first preferred for its greater simplicity.

The first step toward unification of the craft and excise taxes was taken on September 25, 1929, when the excise tax on textiles was revoked and replaced by a craft tax.[38] This was followed a few days later (October 1) by a similar measure applied to alcoholic drinks and tobacco.[39] These laws forecast the course of the Tax Reform.

Other Taxes. The income tax, introduced in 1922,[40] was initially a joint income-property tax, with the property provisions aimed at private capital in the cities. The property tax was levied on housing, equipment, valuable metals, precious stones, etc. The property rates were so low (from 0.33 to 1.5 per cent) that it is difficult to believe that the tax constituted a serious burden. The income tax on private enterprise was introduced in its present form in 1926,[41] at which time tax schedules much higher and more progressive than those of 1922 were established. The final substantial revision of these schedules before the Reform was made in 1928,[42] when small private enterprises with fewer than three hired employees were taxed, for example, 4 per cent on an annual net income of from 1,000 to 1,200 rubles, 36 per cent on 8,000 to 10,000 rubles, and 54 per cent on all income over 24,000 rubles. The rates were slightly higher for enterprises having three or more employees, for persons living on unearned income, and for speculators, and somewhat less for persons working for themselves.

A supplement to this tax — a tax on surplus profits — was introduced in 1926.[43] Its basic aim was to reach the extraordinary speculative profits which had been accruing to private trade and industry owing to commodity shortages.[44] In addition, by discouraging extraordinary profits (which resulted from raising prices above those of state-sold commodities), the tax was intended to keep prices of privately sold commodities down. The tax was levied on that part of profits which exceeded normal income, as defined by the financial authorities in view of earnings in the particular industry and area in previous years, and was not to exceed 50 per cent of the income tax on the same enterprise.

In 1923, an income tax on state and coöperative enterprises was introduced.[45] The tax was proportional, and was established at 8 per cent of net profits (defined as income above the customary costs of operations plus deductions into a welfare fund for workers and certain other expenditures). In its final version before the Reform, the tax took 20 per cent of the net profits of state and coöperative enterprises.[46]

The deductions from profits of socialized enterprises served as a supplement to the income tax. In contrast to the income tax, which was a levy on net profits, these deductions absorbed the residue of profits after all other necessary and authorized deductions and expenditures had been made. The rate of the deductions increased from 15.8 per cent of net profits in 1923–24 to 40.0 per cent in 1927–28.[47] As can be seen in Table 12, the deductions were the third largest payment by trade and industry to the budget. In addition to this residual deduction, there were approximately ten other deductions for specific purposes.[48]

Of the taxes which it remains to mention, the customs duties, stamp tax, and various fees for state services were the most important from a fiscal point of view. Other taxes were small, and since they lacked significance for the future tax system of the Soviet economy they will not be discussed here.

THE TAX REFORM OF 1930

Most Soviet writers discussing the Reform attribute to it both the establishment of single-stage taxation and unification or elimination of the multitude of taxes which had developed in the previous decade. Neither claim is entirely accurate; the first of these reforms had been substantially accomplished in the socialized sector before the new law, and the second was not fully achieved by it (a few superfluous taxes remained). Nevertheless, the decree which set forth the new law [49] may properly be regarded as the principal instrument shaping the present Soviet tax system.

The decree was issued by the Central Executive Committee of the Council of People's Commissars on September 21, 1930. It was prefaced by an explanatory note which correctly set forth the need for the Reform as follows:

> With the growth and increasing strength of the socialized sector of the national economy and the sharp decline of the private sector, with the wider application of planning in national economics as a whole and in its individual enterprises, the present system of taxation no longer corresponds to the conditions and the organization of the national economy. The multiplicity of taxes and levies payable to the Budget, together with

the considerable complexity of their assessment and collection, impedes the regulation of production and exchange and, in particular, hampers price policy. The complex relations of the socialized sector of industry and trade with the Budget hinder the planning of individual branches and of the national economy as a whole. The need radically to alter the fiscal system has become more urgent in connection with the reorganization of State industrial administration and the introduction of the credit reform.[50]

The Reform introduced, for the first time, separate tax systems for the socialized and the private economic sectors of the economy. The most significant changes were made in the socialized sector, in which 61 different taxes and collections [51] were revoked and replaced by a turnover tax and a profits tax on state enterprises, and the turnover tax and an income tax on the coöperatives. The Reform was incomplete in the sense that all fiscally unnecessary taxes were not combined with, or eliminated by, the above-named three taxes. For example, several taxes which had been major sources of income to the local budgets, such as the tax on construction and land rent, were retained intact. Also, certain small fees and collections were retained in circumstances in which they served an important nonfiscal purpose.[52] In general, however, most of the superfluous taxes were eliminated, reducing the burden on both the tax authorities and the administrative apparatus of industry, and simplifying the task of financial planning.

The economic reasons for the use of the turnover and profits taxes, taken individually and jointly, were discussed in the preceding chapter. Developments in commodity taxation after the Reform are discussed in Chapter 6. Here we shall summarize the main technical provisions of the decree of September 1930.

The Socialized Sector. (*a*) The turnover tax was levied on the turnover or gross sales of associations (*ob"edineniia*),[53] enterprises not included in associations, coöperative organizations, and joint-stock companies in which the state owned a controlling share of stock. Turnover was defined as sales of commodities which had either been manufactured or procured (in the case of agricultural products) by the above-mentioned organizations. Furthermore, each commodity was to be taxed no more than once.[54] To ensure these provisions, taxable turnover was defined in considerable detail. The rates of tax were defined as percentages of turnover at the production or procurement level. Only 45 rates were established, each applying to a separate association or ministry. The rate varied from about 3.5 per cent on some producers' goods to 87.2 per cent on liquor and 71.5 per cent on tobacco. The associations were allowed to differentiate the tax rate on their member enterprises, since different types of goods were usually produced within the same association. The taxes were to be paid by the associations, and not by the member enterprises. Theoretically, tax payment was to be made by a transfer of the appropriate sum from the account of the payer to the account of the state budget each time the State Bank received evidence of a sale. However, in an appendix to this section of the Reform it was stated that over the first half-year payment of an amount equal to one-third of the planned turnover of each unit as submitted in its quarterly financial plan was to be made each month; the transfer was to be made automatically from the account of the payer to the account of the state budget. A second appendix presented a list of exemptions from the tax; it included a large number of commodities, consumption of which was being encouraged by the Soviets at the time (e.g., agricultural machinery, books, airplanes), as well as certain types of organizations and types of transactions.

(*b*) The deductions from profits were levied on the profits of all state enterprises operating on an independent financial basis. Most enterprises were subject to a tax of 81 per cent of profits; other rates were: water transport, 30 per cent; the State Bank, 50 per cent; trade enterprises and other banks, 84 per cent. The tax was to be paid from current profits, but was based on the planned profits for the year, with a reconciliation at the end of the year for discrepancies between actual and planned profits. As in the case of the turnover tax, the collections were to be made not by the enterprises directly, but by the associations and trusts to which the enterprises belonged. Deductions from industries of all-union importance were received into the union budget; those from industries of republican and local importance were to go into the republican and local budgets respectively.

(*c*) The income tax on enterprises of the socialized sector was levied on the coöperative organizations and on joint-stock companies in which either the state or coöperative organizations owned at least half of the capital.[55] The tax was levied on the net profits of the organization for the current year, but payments were based on planned profits for the year. Generally speaking, net profits were defined as total income minus production, overhead, and trade expenditures and amortization deductions. The rate of tax was set at 20 per cent of net profit, the same rate which prevailed before the Reform. Because a nationalized enterprise earning less than approximately 5,000 rubles would have had to pay a higher tax than a private enterprise with the same net profit,[56] it was provided that enterprises in the socialized sector could pay at the rate assessed private enterprises if this was lower.

(*d*) A single law regarding state fees was substituted for the large number of small, individual payments which had been in use. This law applied to (1) enterprises and organizations of the socialized sector; (2) workers, peasants, and small craftsmen; (3) persons living on unearned income, and enterprises with more than three hired employees. The only state fee retained for socialized enterprises was a fee connected with legal actions, which varied from 2 to 6 per cent depending on the importance of the action. State fees for categories (2) and (3) were more extensive, and applied to notarization of documents (with many different fees depending on the type of document), legal actions, passports, writing letters to the government or to government officials, complaints with respect to taxes, changing one's name, and so forth. In this case the fees were somewhat higher for the kulaks and persons living on unearned income than for the workers and peasants, but in all cases the fees were quite small. There is no way of determining the percentage reduction which took place in this item. After the Reform, most fees were collected into the local budgets; the available data on local budgets do not contain this category as a separate item. In the all-union budget, however, receipts declined from about 140 million rubles in 1929–30 to slightly more than 1 million rubles in 1931.[57]

Private Sector. (*a*) The craft tax, although revoked in the socialized sector of the economy and replaced by the turnover tax, continued in force in the private sector. As in the case of the turnover tax, the craft tax was made to substitute for many of the smaller taxes and fees which had previously been collected from the private sector.[58] It did not substitute, however, for the income and excess-profits taxes, which continued to be levied in the private sector with few changes. Furthermore, unlike the turnover tax, the craft tax did not become a single-stage tax; enterprises at each stage in the production-trade network were obligated to pay it.[59] The tax was simplified, however, and its rates increased. Four rates were substituted for the previous 16 rates. The rates were 5, 10, 30, and 45 per cent of turnover, production and trade in so-called luxury commodities like tobacco and liquor being taxed at the higher rates, and extraction of fuel, raw materials, and construction materials subject to low rates.[60] The tax was levied in terms of current turnover and was payable monthly. This tax was not significant fiscally, since private industry and trade had been virtually eliminated by October 1930.

(*b*) The income tax on private persons covered citizens and juridical persons in the form of private enterprises. We shall consider only the latter here, and briefly. The tax will be discussed in detail in Chapter 8. It had five progressive schedules of tax rates. The three highest applied to juridical as well as physical persons: to enterprises which consisted of persons working for themselves; to enterprises employing fewer than three persons; and finally, to enterprises employing three or more persons, those dealing in money capital or securities, and those executing services of a religious nature. Taxable income was defined as gross receipts minus business expenses. The rates for these three groups were only a few per cent apart throughout the whole schedule. For a net income of 1,000–1,200 rubles the rates were 5.25, 6.0, and 8.0 per cent respectively; the maximum rates on income over 24,000 rubles annually were 75.81 and 86.5 per cent respectively. In comparison, the highest rate on workers was 37.5 per cent.

Miscellaneous Observations on the Reform. The Reform substantially simplified the Soviet tax system, reducing the costs of administration and facilitating financial planning of the economy. In many respects it brought about too much simplification; as will be indicated in the next chapter, modifications had to be introduced in the years immediately following. Before proceeding to the next chapter, however, two further problems require some comment.

We have emphasized the importance of the Tax Reform for financial planning. It may be asked whether the Reform was also fiscally significant, i.e., was it anticipated that the new forms of taxes would enable the state to extract a higher rate of forced saving from the population than would have been possible under the old tax system. Discussions of the Reform never mentioned this problem, which suggests that the fiscal aspects could not have been very important.

It is impossible to deduce the answer from a comparison of the tax statistics in the pre- and post-Reform years; there is no way of determining what part of a change in the rate of taxation is to be attributed to the change in the tax system and what part to a prior decision on the part of the authorities to raise the rate of taxation regardless of the form in which the taxes were to be collected. As it happens, there was a very large increase in budget receipts from 1929–30 to 1931. However, it was not of a greater order of magnitude than the increase from 1927–28 to 1928–29; furthermore, much of the increase can be attributed to the wage-price inflation which was taking place in those years and to increases in receipts from budget categories which were not affected by the Reform, such as taxation of the agricultural sector and sale of government bonds.[61] The evidence, though sketchy, would seem to support the view that the Tax Reform was not very significant from a fiscal point of view.

The second question to be raised is whether one of the aims of the Reform was to intensify economic pressure on private enterprise. Comparison of the major taxes on private trade and industry before and after the Reform indicates that it was. The craft tax, which varied from about 3 per cent to 28 per cent before the Reform, was increased to 5 to 45 per cent. In addition, private traders suffered from the continuance of multiple-stage taxation in the craft tax. The excess-profits tax remained unchanged. The rates of income tax on private enterprise were raised by about 60 per cent on the average relative to the old rate; the maximum rate on income over 24,000 rubles was increased from 55 per cent to 86.5 per cent. In view of the unimportance of the private sector by 1930, this part of the Reform must be considered of minor significance.

Chapter 6

DEVELOPMENTS IN THE TURNOVER AND PROFITS TAXES AFTER 1930

Only the major developments in turnover and profits taxation are considered in this chapter. It is beyond the scope of this book to discuss the institutional changes in these taxes exhaustively. The complexity of the turnover-tax apparatus is illustrated by the statement of I. Chistov that it was necessary to read 800 regulations of the Commissariat of Finance to understand the operations of the turnover tax in 1941.[1]

CHANGES IN THE TURNOVER-TAX SYSTEM IN 1931-32

Defects in the Original Turnover-Tax System. Very soon after the Tax Reform, it became apparent that the new turnover-tax system was excessively centralized with respect to both assessment and collection. This overcentralization represented, in part, a reaction against the complexity of the pre-Reform commodity-tax system. The Reform had specified that the turnover tax was to be paid primarily by associations (*ob"edineniia*) representing branches of industry, rather than by the many individual enterprises and trusts affiliated with each association. The enterprises and trusts were lax in informing the associations of their activities, and understated their gross sales to avoid having to pay the full amount of the tax. This led to losses and delays in tax payments to the budget. If the associations had been made responsible for checking the accounts of constituent enterprises, tax evasions might have been prevented. Instead, this task was handled by the Commissariat of Finance; administration of tax payments by associations of national importance was handled by the national (all-union) Commissariat of Finance, and taxes paid by less important associations were supervised by financial offices of the republican and local governments.

This allocation of authority placed an impossible burden on the all-union Commissariat of Finance, since enterprises affiliated with all-union associations were commonly located far from Moscow and the few other large cities in which the all-union Commissariat maintained offices equipped to handle the task assigned to them. An effort was made to deal with this weakness by allowing the national financial authorities to delegate their work to local financial offices in cases where enterprises belonging to associations of national importance were located outside of Moscow. The expedient did not work satisfactorily for two reasons. First, the all-union authorities did not take full advantage of their mandate to use local administrative aid. The auditing which they managed to accomplish unaided was restricted primarily to examining the records of the associations. Consequently, since primary documents of constituent enterprises were not checked, mistakes in reporting or deliberate understatements of turnover by these enterprises could not be detected.[2] Second, the use which was made of the local financial authorities was not effective. The local and republican governments received no part of the taxes collected from national associations; they benefited only from turnover taxes they collected from associations of local and republican importance.[3] Lacking a financial interest in collecting taxes from national associations, the local authorities apparently carried out such assignments perfunctorily.

Other difficulties arose because only 45 separate rates of tax were established, each applying to a fairly large branch of the economy (represented, usually, by an association). There was no explicit differentiation for heterogeneity of output, differential cost structures, and other variations among individual enterprises. Each association was supposed to differentiate the tax among the commodities produced by the different plants in its jurisdiction, while maintaining the total tax payment to the state at the planned level.[4] Under this system changes in assortment created problems. Such changes resulted either in a change in the total amount of tax collected (if the differential rates were not changed), or in arbitrary changes in the amount of profit earned by individual enterprises (if the enterprise rates were adjusted to maintain total tax payments at a given level). Arbitrarily adjusting the rates of profits of enterprises had an adverse effect on the incentives of managers to improve operating efficiency, since it tended to divorce the earning of profits from the skill with which a plant was managed. Even though profits were to some extent adjusted, shifts in assortment in 1931 led, according to Soviet economists, to large discrepancies (primarily deficits) between the amount of taxes planned and actual collections.[5]

The use of only 45 rates, one for each association, also caused pricing problems. It was not uncommon for plants in different associations to produce the same commodity. Since each association was subject to a different rate of tax, the same commodity frequently appeared on the market at several different prices in circumstances which called for a single price.[6]

One more shortcoming of the original turnover-tax law is mentioned by Soviet writers. According to the law, the tax was to be paid on the basis of planned turnover (gross sales), with eventual adjustment for actual turnover. It was claimed that the so-called "automatism" thus introduced into enterprise finance weakened *khozraschet.* Where actual turnover lagged behind planned turnover, firms had to pay a larger tax than they could afford, and were temporarily depleted of working capital; where actual turnover was greater than plan, the reverse was true. This was an impediment to the efficient management of enterprise operating on an independent financial basis.

Revisions in the Turnover-Tax Law. The law was revised several times in the years immediately following the Reform to correct its shortcomings. As of January 1, 1932,[7] the system of rates was changed from a single rate for each branch of the economy to an individual rate for each major commodity group. This resulted in an increase in the number of rates from 45 to 143. Instead of a single rate of 32 per cent for the oil association, for example, four rates were established: 53.8 per cent on kerosene, except for tractors; 65.0 per cent on gasoline, except for tractors; 40 per cent on lubricating oil, except for tractors; and 16 per cent on crude oil (*mazut*) and all products for tractors. As we shall see, this was the first step in the direction, explored for the next five years, of establishing too many rates.

As the number of rates increased, the character of the tax changed. In its original form the turnover tax was a gross-sales tax patterned after the craft tax of the late twenties. As the tax became more and more differentiated, specific rates (or more than one rate) were levied on individual commodities. In this form the turnover tax resembled a system of excise taxes. This trend was a reversal of the trend in the twenties.

In response to the trend toward differentiating tax rates, assessment and collection of the turnover tax were decentralized. From 1931 to 1934, the Commissariat of Finance issued decrees shifting the responsibility for tax payment from the association to the enterprise or trust. This was done separately for each branch of the economy. Until 1934 a branch of the economy continued to be taxed on a centralized basis until "decentralized" by specific decree; after 1934, decentralized taxation was the general rule.[8]

In 1932, the law was altered to give the local financial authorities an incentive, lacking in the law of 1930, to collect taxes from all-union enterprises. A new regulation allowed local and republican budgets to keep for their own use part of the turnover-tax receipts collected by local and republican authorities from national enterprises.[9]

The decree of 1930 applied the turnover tax to commodity sales only. Coverage was soon extended to services. Beginning April 15, 1931, a tax of 30 per cent was levied on the gross receipts of movie theaters.[10] The receipts from this tax were kept by the republican budgets. All other services (e.g., repair work, autotransport, photography, haircutting, etc.) were taxed either 5 or 10 per cent beginning July 1, 1931; 10 per cent of the receipts were allocated to the local budgets and 90 per cent to the union budget.[11]

On July 1, 1932, a tax of 1 per cent on gross income from sales was levied on the state farms.[12]

The revenue from taxes on services and on the state farms has always been insignificant. For example, during the period of the Second Five Year Plan it amounted to only about 0.3 per cent of total budget income.

SUPPLEMENTS TO THE TURNOVER TAX

If Soviet price policies had been straightforward, the turnover and profits taxes would probably have been sufficient to handle the commodity-tax requirements of the economy as outlined in Chapter 4. But Soviet economic policies were extremely complex, particularly during the early thirties, and their implementation required a multiple-price system. This led to the development, in the thirties, of three supplements to the turnover tax, namely, the so-called budget markups (*natsenki*), budget differences (*raznitsy*), and special markups (*spetsnatsenki*). Although the distinction between these forms of tax was not always clear, it is generally true that they served different functions and were constructed somewhat differently. Before discussing these taxes, it will be useful to review briefly a simple model of the Soviet distribution system.

There are four basic links in the distribution system for industrial goods: the production unit or factory, the wholesaler, the retailer, and the consumer. The model is slightly modified for agricultural commodities; a state procurement agency replaces the factory, and in some cases a processing unit, such as a bakery, may be added to the network. As a commodity proceeds through the distribution system, its price snowballs; as it leaves each stage, the costs and planned profits of that stage are added to price. In the early and mid-thirties, the turnover tax was usually added to price by the factory or, in the case of agricultural output, by the procurement agency; in some cases, however, it was added by the wholesaler. The cost-price structure had the following form:

Factory price (*otpusknaia tsena*) = costs of production (or procurement price) + profits + turnover tax;

Wholesale price (*optovaia tsena*) = factory price + wholesalers' costs + wholesalers' profits;

Retail price (*rynochnaia tsena*) = wholesale price + retailers' costs + retailers' profits.

For purposes of this discussion, wholesalers' and retailers' costs and profits will be lumped together and designated, as is the Soviet practice, the trade markup. The trade markup is equivalent to our costs of distribution. Accordingly, the cost-price structure can be represented as follows:

Factory price = cost of production + factory profit + turnover tax;

Retail price = factory price + trade markup.

There is a need for supplements to the turnover tax because the last equation does not always balance. Lack of balance is due to changes in retail price unaccompanied by corresponding changes in factory price and turnover tax, and to the existence of more than one retail price. There are two methods of applying the supplements: either as a percentage markup of price, or simply as the arithmetic difference between retail price and the sum of factory price and trade markup. The first method is usually used where the "inequality" in the last equation is sufficiently predictable, stable, and uniform to be bridged accurately by a percentage markup; the second method is used where the situation is less predictable or uniform, so that the state can do no more than siphon off whatever funds remain after all other anticipated expenditures and deductions have been made. This separation of functions between percentage markups and arithmetic differences is not always strictly observed, however. Nor is there always a precise demarcation between the different forms of markups and differences.[13]

In theory, the functions performed by markups and differences could be accomplished by appropriate variations of the turnover-tax rates proper.[14] In practice this has not always been expedient. The turnover tax is the most important source of budget revenue. For this reason, as we pointed out in Chapter 4, Soviet policy is to keep the turnover-tax system as simple as possible. As we shall see, turnover-tax administration became quite complicated during the thirties in spite of the use of supplementary taxes. Without the use of markups and differences, the situation undoubtedly would have been even more complicated.

This is not meant to imply that the existence of markups and differences has always been justified. As is the case with many administrative devices, markups and differences have sometimes been preserved after their period of usefulness has passed, and Soviet financial experts have attempted to secure their elimination.[15] In other instances, they have been eliminated as soon as they were no longer needed.

Special Markups. The special markups were introduced in 1932 to facilitate the coexistence of state stores selling rationed commodities at low prices and the so-called commercial stores, which sold unrationed commodities at higher prices. From 1929 to 1935 the Soviets experienced a serious consumers' goods shortage (relative to effective demand), which necessitated the introduction of rationing. Rationed goods were sold in state stores at retail prices which were equal to factory price (including turnover tax) plus trade markup. In order to siphon off part of the excess purchasing power in the hands of the consumers, and to give them a chance to purchase commodities above their ration, so-called commercial stores were established in which consumers' goods were sold at much higher prices. The difference between ration price and commercial price was deducted into the budget primarily in the form of the special markup. The special markup was calculated as the difference between commercial retail price and the delivery price plus trade markup. It was levied at the factory level along with the turnover tax on those commodities destined for the commercial stores; [16] the same commodities destined for state ration stores paid only a turnover tax. In 1935–36, as the Soviets derationed, the special markups were no longer needed and were discontinued.[17]

Budget Differences. The budget differences were first introduced on a large scale with the end of rationing in July 1936. When rationing was discontinued, the retail prices of many commodities were raised. Procurement prices were not always raised by the same amount,[18] and in some instances were not raised at all.[19] This resulted in a spread between retail and procurement price which exceeded the trade markup; the gap was filled by the budget differences, rather than by adjustment of the turnover tax.[20] As will be shown later, the turnover-tax system was so complicated at this time (1936) that it was to be adjusted to derationing only gradually, with budgetary differences substituting temporarily for changes in turnover-tax rates. However, according to Kutler,[21] the technical difficulties in altering the turnover-tax rate structure were so great that the budgetary difference system was retained beyond the transition period originally contemplated.

Presumably discussing the same set of events, Suchkov [22] states that when consumers'-goods prices were increased, the factory prices of commodities destined for the retail market were also raised; the factory price of the same commodities destined for industrial consumption remained unchanged. To avoid complicating the turnover-tax structure, the suppliers paid the turnover tax on goods shipped for industrial consumption, and paid the turnover tax plus a budgetary difference on commodities destined for the retail market. It is not quite clear whether Suchkov and Kutler are discussing two different sets of events or are placing different interpretations on the same set of events.

The most common and appropriate use of budgetary differences is to facilitate seasonal price changes. Prices of agricultural commodities, in particular, are varied during the year to adjust for short-run changes in supply. Since the changes in price are made relatively frequently, and on a relatively local basis, it is much simpler for the financial authorities to collect the difference between retail price (deducting trade markups) and factory or procurement price than to attempt to establish continually new percentage rates of budgetary markup or of turnover tax.

Budget Markups. Budget markups were first introduced in July 1931 in connection with a large increase in the prices of nonagricultural consumers' goods. Like the budget differences just described, the markups were designed to bridge the gap between the new and old retail prices until new turnover-tax rates could be established.[23] Originally they were applied to 17 groups of commodities. Since the rise in price was different for urban and rural markets, different markups were applied in the two cases. The original intention was to maintain these markups only temporarily, and most of them have been either revoked or combined with the turnover tax. As late as 1947, however, they were still applied to some commodities in 5 out of the original 17 groups.[24]

Budget markups were also used during World War II. On April 11, 1942, a double price system similar to that which accompanied rationing in 1932 was introduced. Again rationed commodities were sold at one price and the same commodities were sold unrationed, in the so-called commercial stores, at much higher prices. On January 1, 1943, markups analogous to the special markups of 1932–35 were introduced to collect the difference between these prices. This time they were not collected as "differences" but were levied as a percentage of factory price, and were designated as budget markups.[25] Presumably most of them were removed in December 1947 with the end of rationing and the reëstablishment of a single price system. They are still levied on oil products, however.[26] The shift from a residual or "difference" method of levy in the rationing of 1932–35 to a percentage levy during World War II may indicate a growing ability on the part of the government to maintain a stable price differential to which percentages could be applied.

The markups are used extensively to allow for the fact that commodities are (1) frequently sold at different prices to city and rural consumers and (2) are sold at higher prices when destined for the consumers'-goods market than when destined for industrial consumption. Such forms of differential pricing appear to be a semipermanent aspect of the Soviet economic system. For these purposes the budget markup appears to be quite satisfactory and will undoubtedly continue to be used.

THE NUMBER OF TURNOVER-TAX RATES [27]

Misapplication of the Turnover Tax. It has been noted that in 1932 the system of levy by the turnover tax was changed from taxation by branch of economy to taxation by groups of commodities. At this time the number of rates was increased from 45 to 143. The number of rates continued to increase through the mid-thirties, and by 1937 there were 1,109 rates abstracting from differentiation of rates by zones, or 2,444 rates including zonal rates. The rates were distributed among sectors of the economy as indicated in Table 13.

TABLE 13 Number of Turnover-Tax Rates per Commissariat, 1937

	Number of rates	
Commissariat	Without zones	Including zones
Heavy industry and machinery	56	56
Forestry	10	10
Light industry	149	149
Food industry	592	1387
Procurement	74	614
Craft coöperatives	228	228
Total	1109	2444

For source, see Appendix.

The number of rates would undoubtedly have been much greater had it not been for the introduction of markups and differences. Some increase in the number of rates was to be expected in this period because of an increase in the variety of goods produced and the tendency toward decentralized administration of industry. However, the main cause, according to Soviet economists, was mechanical application, or misapplication, of the principles of financial policy by the employees of the Commissariat of Finance.[28]

Throughout the thirties there was a conflict between applying the turnover tax properly to fulfill its economic functions (Chapter 4) and using it as an expedient substitute for making other cost-price adjustments. Misapplication of the turnover tax resulted in multiplication of the number of tax rates and in wide disparities between the cost-price relations of enterprises in various industries.

In order for *khozraschet* to be effective, it is necessary that enterprises be rewarded or punished by receiving increases or decreases in profits as operating efficiency fluctuates in the short run. If price and turnover tax are both fixed in the short run, then the rate of profit will vary with changes in efficiency (since profits are usually the residual element in price), thereby creating an incentive for the enterprise to improve its operations. On the other hand, longer-run changes in costs (due not necessarily to changes in efficiency but to changes in the costs of raw materials, wages, external economies, etc.) and in price should be recognized by corresponding changes in the turnover-tax rate. If this is not done, a plant may receive windfall profits and losses due to changes in cost and price beyond its control. This weakens the incentive to efficiency.

In theory, the turnover tax should have been administered in the way we have just described. In practice, there was a tendency to adjust the turnover tax in the short run in order to maintain profits at a desired level for different enterprises and commodities.[29] As cost relations between different plants manufacturing the same commodities and having originally the same rate of turnover tax diverged over time, a different tax rate was applied to each in order to preserve a constant rate of profits. This practice multiplied the number of turnover-tax rates. Differences between rates were often no more than 0.1 per cent; it was claimed that many of the new turnover-tax rates could have been avoided by small changes in rates of profit. The largest increase in the number of rates occurred in 1936–37, after subsidies to industry had been substantially reduced. Before 1936, the subsidies substituted, to a large extent, for the turnover tax as a means of making adjustments in the cost-price structure.

The policy of adjusting tax rates in the short run to maintain profits naturally tended to vitiate the significance of deviations from the planned rate of profits as an indicator of the comparative operating efficiency of enterprise.[30] Since the turnover tax was used to prevent plants from suffering losses, or from earning less profits than usual, lower than planned profits no longer served as a warning signal to the planners that a firm was operating inefficiently. According to Kutler,[31] the Commissariat of Finance was just as reluctant to allow increases in profits as decreases, so that differentiation of the turnover tax often occurred to prevent these also. The existence of such a large number of rates caused considerable confusion in turnover-tax administration. Many plants took advantage of the situation to pay at a lower rate than was appropriate and, in some instances, to evade taxation completely.

Apparently turnover-tax adjustments to long-run changes in costs and prices were equally unsuccessful. Gordin cites many examples to prove that in spite of considerable differentiation of tax rates, uniformity in the cost-price structure over the longer run was still not achieved.[32] By this he did not mean that the tax rates should have been reduced in number to the 143 which existed in 1932, since differentiation was legitimate in many cases. What he did attempt to prove was that during the thirties the longer-run changes in costs, taxes, and prices had not been brought into any systematic relation. At this point (1937) the cost-tax-price system needed a thorough overhauling. For example:[33]

i. In the case of leather shoes, the ratio of cost to price for different styles varied from 65.4 per cent to 103.1 per cent.

ii. In the confectionery industry, the ratio of profits to cost for different types of candy varied as follows: 0.5 per cent, 16.0 per cent, 72.4 per cent, and over 100 per cent. This situation existed despite the use of 8 different rates of tax.

iii. The Rosa Luxemburg factory produced a certain type of caramel (*fruktovoiagodnaia*) at a cost of 4,010 rubles per ton and sold it for 3,950 rubles.

iv. In the cotton industry, the cost-price ratio fluctuated from 30 per cent to 60 per cent between and within different commodity groups, and even more between different enterprises.

Gordin cites other examples as well.

If these examples are representative, Gordin is no doubt correct in contending that costs and prices were generally out of line. Granted this, his next contention is easy to accept; it is that changes in turnover-tax rates were often substituted for changes in prices, or at least had been made without concomitant changes in prices when long-run changes in costs occurred.

There were other reasons for the large number of rates. One of these was the use of token taxes on products of heavy industry for purposes of financial control; a second was the use of zonal prices and rates in the case of food products.

Revisions in the Turnover-Tax System. The first step in revising the turnover-tax system was taken on March 23, 1938,[34] by regulation which decreased considerably the number of rates in the food industry, as is indicated in Table 14. In addition, cost-tax-price relations were revised for some industries, zonal rates were eliminated on butter and margarine, rates expressed in tenths of 1 per cent were eliminated in food, and some small rates of less than 1 per cent were abolished. It was necessary to continue zonal rates in many cases because differences in production costs and prices as well as transport costs were significant; without differential zonal tax rates the flow of supplies to some areas might have been seriously decreased.[35]

TABLE 14 Reduction in Number of Turnover-Tax Rates on Food, 1938

Food	Number of rates: Old	New
Sugar	10	2
Meat	254	58
Tobacco	22	9
Fats and oils	39	15
Cosmetics	20	5
Butter	76	10
Margarine	66	16

For source, see Appendix.

The budgetary-difference approach completely replaced estimating the turnover tax as a percentage of price in the textile and hosiery industries in February 1939.[36] The tax was calculated as the difference between retail price (deducting the trade markup) and wholesale price *without* turnover tax. Apparently the situation in the textile industry was much too complex to be handled effectively by a system of turnover-tax rates or any system based on percentages of cost or price. In 1939, just before the change was effected, there were roughly 4,000 different articles of output in the textile industry; each of these commodities was produced by plants with different unit costs. The commodities were divided into 84 broader categories with a different rate of turnover tax for each. Application of only 84 rates to such a complicated network of commodities and cost structures caused some plants to have large profits and others large losses. Furthermore, where a single plant produced more than one commodity, it often attempted to maximize money profits by producing those articles on which profit was greatest, regardless of the plan of output which had been set by the state.

A change in technique was needed, and the Soviets were faced with the choice of either greatly expanding the number of rates of tax in the textile industry or of substituting budget differences for the turnover tax. As we have seen, an effort was being made at this time to reduce the number of turnover-tax rates; therefore budgetary differences were adopted. Henceforth the tax was equal to the difference between retail price minus the trade markup and factory price minus turnover tax. New factory prices were established which insured that no plant would operate at a loss and that plants would make about the same rate of profit on each article produced. Uniform (*edinye*) systems of retail prices as well as raw-material supply prices were established.

The method of tax payment was also revised. In general the taxes were to be paid not by the factory but by so-called selling bases (*sbytovye bazy*). These were large wholesale depots which handled diverse products of many widely scattered plants. To facilitate payment, an average rate of tax was estimated for each base and paid daily by the base into the budget. Every five days or week a reaccounting took place; the difference between the actual tax liability and the amount paid into the budget was computed, and the account of the selling base appropriately adjusted. According to Suchkov,[37] this procedure resulted in a labor economy at the selling bases of 25 per cent.

In the postwar period the turnover tax as a budget difference has been substituted for the turnover tax as a percentage of price for most industries with highly varied cost structures and wide assortments of commodities.[38] For such industries, the system of budgetary differences is the simpler method of levying the turnover tax. Under the percentage system, tax computation required three schedules: retail prices, wholesale or factory prices, and the turnover-tax rates. In addition, where *supplementary* budgetary differences were used, a fourth schedule was necessary. Under the new method the tax is calculated from the retail and wholesale prices. Changes in either price can be made easily without altering the other, and with no need to recompute the turnover-tax rate; *supplementary* budgetary differences are of course no longer needed where budget differences substitute completely for the turnover tax.

It is the opinion of Soviet economists that the new system of budget differences, properly applied, should prevent plants from experiencing the extreme profits or losses which prevailed, especially in textiles, under the old system. It is a simple process to adjust factory price and recompute the turnover-tax payment on the output of an individual plant which has an exceptionally large profit or loss. Under the old system it was difficult to prevent extremes of profits or losses, because each firm was subject to a rate of tax which applied to many other enterprises. Under these circumstances, as we have seen, adjustments usually meant increasing the number of tax rates. With extreme profits and losses eliminated, managers should have more incentive to produce efficiently — to operate their plants in accordance with *khozraschet* principles. Furthermore, since it is now easier to equalize the profit per unit on all commodities produced by a plant, the new system should reduce the incentive to alter the planned product-mix in order to maximize money profit. Whether this has in fact been true, we do not know.

In some industries such as textiles the selling-base system proves to be a simpler method of turnover-tax payment for still another reason. The products of individual enterprises are frequently shipped to more than one destination. In each case the trade markup is different. Since the enterprise usually does not know the eventual destination of its output, it cannot make the appropriate calculations; the selling base can.[39]

Other less important changes were also instituted.[40] For example, industrial coöperatives, which had been allowed special low rates in the early thirties, were taxed on the same basis as other producers; and the number of token rates on heavy industry was reduced.

Recent Developments. Although some simplification of the turnover-tax system resulted from the above-mentioned changes, many deficiencies remained. The literature of the forties complains persistently about shortcoming of the turnover tax.

Azarkh[41] claims that application of the turnover tax in the form of a residual difference between retail and wholesale prices has a serious disadvantage; it transfers the responsibility for correct tax payment from the government tax inspector to the factory bookkeeper, which does not always serve the best interests of the budget. The amount of tax can no longer be estimated by the tax inspector by simply applying the rate of tax to the price per unit multiplied by the output. The establishment of appropriate factory and wholesale prices requires considerable cost-accounting work and is difficult for a tax inspector to check. These difficulties are multiplied when the tax is collected from the selling bases, because of the huge assortment of goods handled by the bases.

The continued use for financial control purposes of token taxation of the output of heavy industry, even while subsidies were simultaneously being received, has been attacked by many Soviet economists. They point out that financial inspectors have been interested primarily in collecting taxes and only secondarily in using their tax audit work as a means of checking enterprise plan fulfillment. Since the amount of tax paid into the budget by heavy industry has always been small, financial inspectors have spent very little time — perhaps an hour or two a month — checking the tax accounts of the largest enterprises. The existence of the turnover tax on these enterprises, presumably serving only as a means of checking their performance, was considered dangerous because it impeded the introduction of really effective means of control.[42]

In those industries in which the turnover tax was paid by selling bases, financial control could no longer be exerted over production via the turnover tax. Tax collectors at the selling bases could do very little to influence production or shipment of goods by the producers, even if they could determine which producers among the many whose products were represented at the selling bases were not fulfilling their plans.[43] Financial authorities complained that it was much more difficult to plan taxes accurately for selling bases than for individual producing enterprises.[44]

It was suggested that the turnover tax on heavy industry be abolished, and that the profits tax be substituted for it wherever necessary. Apparently this proposal was accepted, because the turnover tax on producers' goods was abolished in 1949 except for the tax on oil and oil products; this was retained to reflect the very large differential rent element in the production of oil.

It was pointed out in Chapter 3 that differential rent on natural resources and producers' goods enters price through the turnover tax. Since Soviet economists recognize the importance of differential rent for their costing system, an attempt will undoubtedly be made to incorporate differential rent into price in some other form. It has frequently been suggested, for instance, that the turnover tax could be simplified if rent payments were made explicitly as an element of cost.[45] Although there is no evidence that this is happening, it is one possibility.

A second possibility is that profits are now used to reflect differential rent. The elimination of turnover taxes from producers' goods was but one facet of a more general overhaul of the price system.[46] which included reducing subsidies, increasing profits, and raising producers'-goods prices. The increase in prices which allowed subsidies to be reduced undoubtedly improved Soviet prices as an indicator of direct costs of production. Whether that part of the price increase which allowed profits to be increased actually does reflect differential rent, however, we do not know.

EVOLUTION OF THE PROFITS TAX

The profits tax was altered substantially in 1931; since then few changes have been made in it, and these have been mainly concerned with the Director's Fund.

The profits tax as defined by the Reform almost immediately proved to be inconsistent, from the point of view of managerial incentives, with the Soviet conception of how enterprises on *khozraschet* were to operate. The tax rates were very high (81 per cent on most enterprises), and were not differentiated according to the varying needs of enterprises; an enterprise which was to undertake large investments from profits paid the same rate of tax as one for which no investment had been planned. For reasons which were discussed in Chapter 4, it is clear that in this situation the incentive of managers to operate efficiently was reduced, thereby lessening the effectiveness of *khozraschet*.[47]

To remedy this situation, the law was revised as follows: (1) enterprises whose planned investment was to exceed profits paid a minimum 10 per cent tax on profits for control purposes; (2) enterprises making no capital expenditures paid a maximum 81 per cent tax on profits; (3) all other enterprises paid a tax of from 10 to 81 per cent of profits depending on planned capital expenditures.[48] Of the remaining 19 per cent (100 − 81), 9 per cent was to be deducted into a fund for workers' welfare, and 10 per cent into a fund for investing in plant and equipment. The rates for banks, trading enterprises, and water transport remained at the levels set by the Reform. To further increase incentives, it was decreed that all enterprises in associations and trusts could retain for their own use 50 per cent of profits earned in excess of plan. These funds were to be used to improve the plant, for the welfare of the employees, for payment of bonuses for extraordinary work, and so forth.[49]

The law remained essentially unchanged until April 19, 1936, at which time the Director's Fund was introduced.[50] Henceforth 4 per cent of planned profits and 50 per cent of unplanned profits were to be deducted into this fund, which replaced the fund for improving workers' welfare. The fund for investing in plant and equipment was discontinued at this time.

On January 7, 1941 a regulation was introduced which exempted local industry from the profits tax in order to encourage the production of consumers' goods made from local raw materials. Seventy-five per cent of planned profits were to be deducted into local and city budgets for increasing output among other enterprises in the same political jurisdiction; the remaining 25 per cent could be used by the local government for welfare purposes. Unplanned profits were entirely at the disposal of the plants which earned them, and were to be distributed as follows: 50 per cent for increasing production, 25 per cent for housing, and 25 per cent for workers' welfare.[51]

The Director's Fund was suspended during World War II. It was reëstablished on July 1, 1946 for state industrial enterprises, and over the next two years was introduced into the state farms, the construction industry, auxiliary enterprises in rural areas, and so forth. In the case of state industry, differential rates were placed in effect with the primary aim of equalizing the deductions for industries with different rates of profit. The Director's Funds of consumers'-goods industries received deductions of 2 per cent on planned profits and 25 per cent on unplanned profits. The corresponding figures for chemicals, aviation, automobiles, etc. were 5 per cent and 50 per cent; for ferrous metallurgy, coal, oil, cement, asbestos, peat, and others, 10 per cent and 75 per cent.[52] A few years later these rates were lowered to 1, 2, and 5 per cent of planned profits and 15, 30, and 45 per cent of unplanned profits.[53] It was stipulated in the 1946 decree that the Director's Fund may not be augmented unless each of the following four conditions is met: (1) fulfillment or overfulfillment of the plan of output; (2) correspondence of actual output with planned product-mix (assortment); (3) fulfillment of the plan of cost reduction; and (4) fulfillment of the plan of profits from sales of output.[54] Failure to meet any of these conditions deprives a firm of the right to deductions into the Director's Fund.[55] Previously, only the last condition had to be fulfilled; the first three were added because many firms were maximizing profits (the fourth condition) by concentrating on one or two of the first three conditions at the expense of the others. For example, profits might be increased by raising output above plan at an inefficient cost level; or by concentrating on the most profitable commodity of the product-mix; or by lowering costs substantially at the expense of output. Proper enforcement of this regulation should aid in the achievement of a better-rounded execution of the plan.[56]

A final provision of the 1946 regulation directed that the Fund must not exceed 5 per cent of an enterprise's total payroll. Before the war, no such limitation appears to have been in force. For the year 1936, a Soviet writer, L. Vilenski, says:

> On the average for the five industrial commissariats the Director's Fund per employee came to 6.3 per cent of the average annual wage. However, for several branches this per cent is considerably higher and attains 21.5 per cent for lumber and woodworking, about 25 per cent for the fur industry and the leather footwear industry, and up to 55 per cent for the liquor, macaroni, and food industries.[57]

A new development which seems to be in the offing is decentralization of profits-tax collection. Several Soviet economists have registered dissatisfaction with the existing system, in which the chief administration (*glavk*) pays the profits tax for its member enterprises. In discharging this function the *glavk* may now collect from these enterprises not merely the sum required to pay the tax but the entire amount of profits; it may also redistribute among its enterprises as it sees fit the surplus remaining after taxes have been paid.[58] The system admittedly minimizes the costs of collection by reducing the number of financial workers needed to administer the tax and by simplifying the planning of tax receipts. On the other hand, the chief administrations have often abused or exceeded their authority; for example, they have reportedly transferred basic working capital from one plant to another, an act expressly prohibited by law.[59]

They have also redistributed profits in such a way as to affect managerial incentives adversely.[60] Finally, the indirect method of collecting the profits tax has often delayed receipt of funds by the budget.

A report which appeared recently in *The New York Times* states that the authority of the chief administrations to redistribute the profits of subordinate enterprises has been substantially limited.[61] The text of the decree is not available to me and I do not know whether or not the method of tax payment has been altered.

TURNOVER-TAX RATES

Formidable obstacles stand in the way of analyzing Soviet turnover-tax rates. The basic difficulty stems from the many changes in the turnover-tax system over the past twenty years; rates are not comparable from one period to the next. Originally there were only 45 rates; then there were 143, and then thousands. Originally they were levied as a percentage of factory or wholesale price; later they were levied extensively as a percentage of retail price, as the residual difference between retail and wholesale price, and as rubles per unit of output. In 1930 supplements to the turnover tax had not yet been introduced; subsequently budget markups, budget differences, and special markups were used in varying degrees at different times. A further complication in the years after 1932–33 is introduced by multiplicity of rates for a single commodity. Clearly, it is no easy matter to appraise rates which are differentiated for, say, 4 or 5 zones and 10 or 12 different grades of quality. The difficulty is enhanced by the fact that the spread between rates on a single commodity may be of the order of ten to one, with no information available on the volume of sales to which each rate applies. Finally, at no period during the existence of the turnover tax have rates on food products been comparable with the rates on industrial consumers' goods; this is because the prices at which state and coöperative organizations procure agricultural commodities from the peasants and collective farms are well below costs of production. Turnover-tax rates based on the low procurement prices overstate the tax on the consumer, since part of the burden is borne by producers. Tax rates on industrial commodities, on the other hand, are based on costs of production; the fact that some industrial costs may also have been understated, because of subsidies, does not alter the fundamental distinction between the two systems of rates.

Average Rate of Turnover Taxation: Trends. The average rate of turnover taxation on all commodities sold within a given period can be estimated very simply from statistics of retail sales and available data on tax receipts. Almost all commodities which are subject to the turnover tax are sold by state or coöperative retail stores, and are included in the figure for the value of retail trade turnover. The average rate of turnover taxation, then, is computed by dividing receipts from the turnover tax by the gross value of retail trade turnover for state and coöperative stores. The estimates are presented in Table 15.

TABLE 15 Average Rate of Turnover Taxation, 1928–29 to 1953 (billions of rubles)

Year	Gross value of retail trade turnover (state and coöperative) (billion rubles) [b] (1)	Turnover-tax receipts (billion rubles) [b] (2)	Average rate of tax (2 ÷ 1) (per cent) (3)	Turnover tax as percentage of value of retail trade *not including* turnover tax [2 ÷ (1 − 2)] (4)
1928–29	14.4	3.1[a]	21.5	27.4
1929–30	17.5	5.4[a]	30.9	44.6
1931	27.5	11.7	42.5	74.1
1932	40.3	19.6	48.6	94.7
1933	49.8	27.0	54.2	118.3
1934	61.8	37.6	60.8	155.1
1935	81.7	52.2	63.9	176.9
1936	106.7	65.8	61.7	160.9
1937	125.9	75.9	60.3	151.8
1938	140.0	80.4	57.4	134.9
1939	163.0	96.9	59.3	145.7
1940	175.1	105.9	60.5	153.0
1947	308.0	239.7	77.8	351.0
1948	332.0	247.3	74.5	292.0
1949	348.0	245.5	70.5	239.5
1950	356.0	236.1	66.3	196.5
1951	385.0	247.8	64.4	180.6
1952	391.0	246.9	63.1	171.3
1953	445.0	243.6	54.7	122.8

For sources, see Appendix.

[a] These figures represent the summation of taxes combined into the turnover tax in 1930.

[b] These figures have not been adjusted as have those in Tables 51 and 52 (see pp. 324–327).

The extraordinary magnitude of the turnover tax rate is immediately apparent from Table 15. From 1933 on, the turnover tax comprised more than half of the gross value at market price of commodities sold by state and coöperative stores. This implies that the rate of tax, expressed according to Western convention as markup over factor cost, has been more than 100 per cent since 1933. A "minimum" estimate for markup over cost is presented in column 4, which gives the ratio of turnover tax to the value of retail trade excluding turnover tax. The figure is a "minimum" for markup over cost because retail trade without turnover tax still includes profits and the social insurance markups in consumers'-goods industries, both of which have been defined as taxes (Chapter 4).

Four trends in the average rate of taxation can be distinguished: a rapid increase from 1928–29 to the prewar peak in 1935; a decline until 1938; increases in 1939 and 1940; and a sharp decline in the postwar period. Since these trends are discussed in considerable detail in Chapters 9 and 10, their significance will be noted only briefly here. The rapid increase to 1935 is due to the continually rising rate of nonconsumption expenditures undertaken by the state in this period. The decline in 1936 is attributable to a shift in the distribution of taxes in favor of the profits tax; the further decline in 1937 and 1938 is due to the increased emphasis on production of consumers' goods in those years, as well as to the exceptional crop in 1937. In 1939 and 1940 increased tax receipts were needed to finance a rising level of military expenditures. The extraordinary decline in the postwar period reflects primarily the shift from a wartime to a peacetime structure of production, and secondarily, a renewed emphasis on profits instead of turnover taxation as a means of finance.

Turnover Tax on Individual Commodities. Turnover-tax rates for selected commodities from 1930 to 1940 are presented in Table 16. In general they seem to follow the trends indicated by the aggregate figures in the preceding table, although deviations may be noted. The tax rates on all commodities increased from 1930–31 to 1932–33. Between 1932–33 and 1935–36 the rates on industrial consumers' goods declined, despite a substantial increase in the average rate of taxation. The few rates we have on food commodities indicate that they increased in this period. Unfortunately the method of computing the tax rate on grains was changed in 1935, making it impossible

TABLE 16 Selected List of Turnover-Tax Rates, 1930–1940 (per cent)

	1930–31	1932–33	1935–36	1937–38	1939–40
Kerosene	32	93	88	—	72
Grain vodka	87[a]	91	—	—	84
Tobacco	72	—	—	40–88	—
Rubber footwear	40	86	33	35	—
Textiles, cotton	37	68	30	65	75
woolen	—	64	—	—	—
Sugar	51	67	84	78	73
Butter	13	26	60	67	—
Salt	15	77	—	83	80
Grains (all)	8	—	—	—	—
Rye	—	55	101[b]	—	75[b]
Wheat	—	55	104[b]	—	88[b]
Flour[c]	8	—	—	—	—
Rye 95%	—	15, 30, 50, 76	86[b]	—	82[b]
Wheat 96%	—	35, 43, 50, 76	101[b]	—	93[b]
Wheat 85%	—	45, 50, 74, 88	182[b]	—	245[b]
Wheat 75%	—	45, 60, 74, 88	241[b]	—	342[b]
	1929–31	**1932–mid 1934**	**2nd half 1934**	**1935**	**October 1935–March 1940**
Bread, rye	8.0	21.3	54.0	87.5	85.9
wheat	68.0	27.4	60.1	87.4	86.8

For sources, see Appendix.

[a] Alcohol.

[b] Rubles per quintal.

[c] In the case of flour, there were rapid changes in rates from 1932 to 1934 and these are all listed. The 1930–31 column contains the earliest rate listed for this period; all other columns contain the latest rate listed for the period represented by the column.

to compare the trend for this most important commodity group over these years. The rate of tax on bread, however, is estimated to have increased sharply. From 1935 to 1940, rates seem to have declined, with the notable exception of cotton textiles.

It should be noted that the average rate of tax can change without the alteration of a single individual rate if a change occurs in the proportions of commodities subject to tax. For example, sale of a relatively larger amount of goods with high tax rates raises the average rate of taxation. For this reason, the taxes on food products, and particularly bread products, are very important in determining the average rate of taxation. Table 17 gives a *rough* indication of the *relative* amounts of tax in the prices of commodities produced by different commissariats. Unfortunately, Suchkov has not provided us with two strictly comparable columns of percentages. The gross output (*valovaia produktsiia*) percentages are probably based on values which have been reduced to a 1926–27 price base (the Soviet convention until 1949), whereas the turnover tax is always in current prices. Nevertheless, rough orders of magnitude may be indicated.

TABLE 17 Gross Output and Turnover Taxes by Commissariat, 1939 (per cent of total)

Commissariat	Gross output	Turnover tax
Oil	3.1	8.0
Meat-milk	4.5	7.3
Food	11.7	29.7
Textiles	10.2	13.0
Light industry	7.9	2.6
Procurement	2.5	34.4
Other: coal, machine-building, chemical, metallurgy, etc.	60.1	5.0
Total	100.0	100.0

For source, see Appendix.

It is obvious from Table 17 that by far the largest turnover-tax rates were paid by the agricultural procurement organizations; the Commissariats of Food, Meat-Milk, and Oil also paid relatively high rates. The tax on oil was high because of a large differential rent element in its price. The tax on textiles appears to have been relatively moderate, and the tax on "other" commissariats whose output consisted almost entirely of producers' goods was relatively insignificant, as might be expected.

The absolute amount of turnover-tax receipts from the sale of different groups of commodities is shown in Table 18. Receipts originating in grain products were much larger than those from any other commodity group. This is explained primarily by the importance of grain products in Soviet diet, and to a lesser extent, by the tax in kind on agricultural producers, which enables the state to procure grains at a very low cost. The next largest contributor was alcohol, which has always been an important source of revenue in

TABLE 18 Revenue from Turnover Tax by Commodity, 1936 (Plan) (billions of rubles)

Total receipts	62.7	
Grain products		21.2
Alcohol		6.0
Vegetable oil		2.7
Sugar		5.9
Meat		3.0
Cotton textiles		4.2
Oil		4.7

For source, see Appendix.

Russia: the state takes advantage of an inelastic demand to charge what the traffic will bear.

It is important to note that three commodity groups—grains, alcohol, and sugar—provided more than half of the state revenue from the turnover tax, and that the seven commodity groups listed provided more than three-fourths of turnover-tax revenue. This is significant because of the simplification of financial planning which is implied. No doubt the planning of turnover-tax receipts from a diverse group like textiles is difficult, but the problem must be relatively simple with homogeneous commodities like sugar and alcohol.

IMPACT OF THE TURNOVER TAX ON THE DISTRIBUTION OF INCOME

The predominance of the turnover tax among Soviet taxes is embarrassing to Soviet economists, since Marxist writers have consistently attacked indirect taxation as socially inequitable.[62] In practice, sales taxes have been notoriously regressive in their impact on income distribution, although in theory it is possible to construct sales taxes with almost any degree of progression or regression desired. Furthermore, this form of tax is associated in Russia with the old regime; the Tsars relied on highly regressive excise taxes for the bulk of their revenue.[63]

In spite of ideological difficulties, the Soviets have preferred to rely on indirect taxation because of its manifest superiority for their purposes (as was demonstrated in Chapter 3). The choice was not made without qualms. In the early Soviet period there were open controversies over the social character of indirect taxes. Some writers admitted that the Soviet excise taxes fell most heavily on the working class, but expressed the belief that they would be abandoned after Soviet finances had been stabilized.[64] Others refused to admit that they constituted a special burden on the workers, and defended their position in various ways: by asserting that the distribution of income had tended to become equalized, so that indirect taxation had no socially inequitable effects;[65] or by arguing that since the working class is the governing class in the Soviet Union, taxes paid by the working class are self-imposed, therefore not burdensome;[66] or by pointing out that, in contradistinction to capitalist countries, expenditures from taxes in the USSR are primarily for productive projects, rather than for suppressing the workers and fomenting imperialist war, and therefore do not constitute a burden.[67] Later, in the early thirties, many writers defended the use of the turnover tax on the grounds that the rates were differentiated in favor of the lower-income groups, i.e., that the tax rate structure was progressive.[68] In the more recent Soviet literature, the impact of the turnover tax on the population is not discussed at all; instead, as we noted in Chapter 3, the tax is described as a device for drawing into the budget the "accumulation of socialized industry."

The only Soviet claim among those mentioned above which merits serious attention is that the turnover-tax rate is progressive. Most Western economists believe the opposite: that the Soviet turnover-tax system is extremely regressive on the poorer classes.[69] An attempt has been made to throw some light on this question, with results which are neither very reliable nor quite unambiguous. The very ambiguity of the results, however, warrants the suspicion that positive assertions about the equity of the tax, based only on superficial examination of the problem, are not justified.

Difficulties encountered in handling turnover-tax data were described earlier, and need not be recapitulated. As for the other factor in the problem — consumption patterns — we have little information on these by income group for the period to be analyzed (around 1936), and are forced to rely primarily on common sense.[70] Fortunately, the Soviet picture is not very complicated with respect to income-group variations. For our supply of turnover-tax rates we rely almost entirely on two Soviet handbooks, one for industrial commodities relating to the years 1936–37,[71] and the other for derationed foodstuffs relating to the year 1935.[72] Both handbooks usually give several rates for each commodity, depending on the zone in which it was produced or sold, whether it was sold by a state or co-operative store, the quality of the commodity, and so forth. Our practice was to concentrate on rates for state stores and on the zones which encompassed the most populated regions. Rates were provided for many more commodities than could be discussed; an attempt was made to select commodities which seemed to be either representative of groups of commodities or important in themselves.

Industrial Consumers' Goods. Selected groups of industrial consumers' goods classified by tax rate are presented in Tables 19 and

TABLE 19 Intracommodity Turnover-Tax Rates on Industrial Consumers' Goods, 1936–37 (per cent)

Mittens		Suitcases	
woolen	53	leather	20
half woolen	45	fibre	12.9
waste wool	38	substitute leather	10
wool and cotton	38		
cotton-knitted	25	Rings	
cotton	1	precious metals and stones	45
Candlesticks		ferrous metals	40
ferrous metals	25	other	20.4
ferrous waste	20	Cigarette holders	
nonferrous metals	22 + 50[a]	silver, precious stones	45 + 50[a]
nonferrous waste	20	ferrous metals	40 + 50[a]
china	8	nonferrous metals	20.4 + 50[a]
glass	2	horns	12.7 + 50[a]
Pocketbooks			
silver	45	Sugar bowls	
other metal	20.4	silver	45
leather	5	china	8
substitute leather	5	glass	2
waste	1	metal	1

For source, see Appendix.
[a] Budget markups.

20. In Table 20 rate differences between commodities, and in Table 19, rate differences for different qualities of the same commodity, may be observed. The story told by the latter is unambiguous: the higher the quality of the commodity, the higher the tax rate. Some exceptions to this rule were noted, but these were not conspicuous. Generally speaking, intracommodity tax rates were progressive.

TABLE 20 Turnover Tax on Selected Industrial Consumers' Goods, 1936–37 (arranged by rate of tax)[a]

0–10 per cent	10–20 per cent	30–40 per cent	60–70 per cent
cheap kitchenpots	stationery	cotton blankets	cotton handkerchiefs
false teeth	paper cups and dishes	alarm clocks	hair cosmetics
cheap leather belts	child's harmonicas	phonographs	tooth paste
children's shoes	clay containers for cooling	tooth powder	cosmetics (lipsticks)
cheap shoes	dominoes	sewing machines	shaving cream
cheap metal containers	toys	camera film	nail polish
peat	whistles	linen cloth	electric appliances (irons, hot plates)[b]
nails and other tools	sickles		cotton bed sheets
wooden washboards	ink	40–50 per cent	rouge
charcoal for samovars	child's bicycles	needles	hair remover
wood for stoves	chess boards	pencils[b]	face soaps
shovels	fiber suitcases	notebooks[b]	expensive perfume
scissors	hunting rifles	calendars[b]	quality woolen cloth
washbasin stands		cheap perfume	
drinking glasses	20–30 per cent	coarse wool cloth	70–80 per cent
tables	cigarette paper	mirrors	tobacco
ladders	matches	woolen blankets	cheap shoe polish[b]
cotton mittens	kerosene-lamp burners	suspenders	cheap forks[b]
cheap sugar bowls	oil cloth	artificial silk cloth	playing cards
toys	ice skates	diamonds	kerosene stoves[b]
couches (used as beds)	pocket knives	precious stones	metal cuff links[b]
baby carriages	good washboards	hair restorer	
furniture	shaving brushes	toilet water	80 per cent or more
salad bowls	oilcloth aprons	cameras[b]	oil for lamps
accordions	cheaper rings	expensive rings	cigarette packs
records	linen handkerchiefs	silver sugar bowls	silver forks[b]
fur coats	better shoes		precious cuff links[b]
good quilts	accordions	50–60 per cent	expensive cigarette holders[b]
pianos	tennis rackets	coffee pot[b]	
typewriters		cheap clocks[b]	
dining room and tea service		berets	
		leather belts[b]	
		woolen mittens	
		metal flashlights	

For source, see Appendix.

[a] Commodities in each tax range are ordered roughly by whether they are bought primarily by low- or high-income groups.

[b] Increased by budget markups.

The intercommodity tax picture is equivocal. A large number of luxury items are included in the lowest rate groups: fur coats, pianos, typewriters, good quilts, and phonograph records. Some items in this same rate group would be bought by low-income families: tools, cheap kitchen utensils, peat, cotton mittens, cheap shoes. Most of the items in the three highest rate groups (above 60 per cent) are in the luxury class and are not likely to be purchased extensively by the lower-income households: cosmetics of all sorts, cotton bed sheets, quality face soap, electrical appliances, etc. Tobacco is a significant exception. No clear pattern emerges from the intermediate classes (10–60 per cent). In the 40 to 50 per cent group, for example, we find diamonds and other precious stones, expensive rings and silver sugar bowls along with needles, pencils, and cheap perfume; in the 20 to 30 per cent groups are found accordions, tennis rackets, and leather suitcases along with indispensables to the poor such as paper for rolling cigarettes, and matches.

Food Products. A sample of the rates for food products is presented in Table 21. It should be borne in mind that they are not directly comparable with the rates on industrial consumers' goods because they are based on the low procurement price paid to the agricultural producer; furthermore, they are not necessarily comparable with each other, since procurement prices of different food products may not be uniformily below cost of production. We shall come back to this problem a little later. The outstanding feature of this table of rates is the very high tax on bread. Bread is truly the staff of life in the Soviet Union, and the largest single item of expenditure of the poorer families.[73] As it stood in 1935, the tax on bread added a highly regressive element to the Soviet commodity-tax structure. Sharing the highest rate group with bread are the better meats, certainly available to relatively few persons during the mid-thirties. As in the case of industrial consumers' goods, the intracommodity schedules are typically progressive: as the meats decline in quality, they fall into lower and lower tax groups; expensive salt is taxed higher than cheap salt; good grades of tea fall in the highest rate group, whereas poor grades are in the lowest; chocolate bars bear a heavy tax and other candies a light tax, and so forth. Fish products and poultry are taxed at much lower rates than meat; possibly this is because the compulsory delivery technique (with low procurement prices) was not employed to procure these commodi-

TABLE 21 Turnover Tax on Selected Food Products, 1935 (arranged by rate of tax)

0–20 per cent	30–40 per cent	60–70 per cent
eggs	geese	bacon
ducks	turkeys	sausage
macaroni	meat subproducts	frankfurters
rabbit	evaporated milk	canned brains
fish products	fish products	canned kidney
cream cheese	canned fruit	animal fats
candy, except chocolate	canned peas and cucumbers	vegetable oils
		Holland cheese
cheap tea	cream	cheddar cheese
fruits, berries	margarine	
nuts	sour milk	70 per cent or more
soft drinks		
	40–50 per cent	bread
	canned meat paste	beef
	cheap salt	mutton
	margarine	pork
		veal
20–30 per cent		goat meat
chickens	50–60 per cent	canned meat
meat subproducts	fresh tongue	vegetable oils
canned pork and beans	liver	Swiss cheese
	canned tongue	American cheese
fish products	evaporated milk and cocoa	sugar
canned tomatoes		chocolate bars
cottage cheese	sour cream	quality tea
cream	animal fats	liquor
candy, except chocolate	vegetable oils	cattle
	beer	expensive salt

For source, see Appendix.

ties. The low rates on eggs and cream and high rates on salt and liquor add an additional regressive element to the tax structure on foods.

Analysis of the Tax on Bread, 1940. As we have indicated, one of the principal stumbling blocks to determining whether the turnover tax is progressive or regressive is the fact that part of the turnover tax on food products is a tax not on the household but on the producer. The high tax on food products and especially on bread is the most important single factor leading Western experts to the conclusion that the turnover-tax structure is regressive; at the same time, the existence of the compulsory delivery system for agricultural products has caused at least one Western economist to contest this point.[74] Information has recently become available which makes it possible to separate, *very roughly*, the tax on the producer from the tax on the consumer of bread. Unfortunately, this is the only food product for which such a computation can be made; fortunately, it is a very important commodity for the problem at hand.

The particular figure we speak of is the cost, planned for the year 1941, of producing one quintal (100 kilograms) of grain on a state farm (*sovkhoz*), namely, 22 rubles 50 kopeks.[75] Although the bulk of the bread sold by the state is made from grain delivered by the collective farms, the cost of production for state farms is a more accurate measure of the cost of production on a collective farm than the costs actually recorded by collective farms. This is because the income earned by collective farmers — in other words, the cost of collective farm labor — is a residual (since the collectives are formally organized as coöperatives) [76] and tends to fluctuate with climatic conditions, market conditions, and so forth. Furthermore, the collective farmers are expected to secure part of their income by selling surplus food from their personal plots of land on the collective farm market. Finally, the collective farms do not have their own machinery but are compelled to use the tractors and combines of the machine tractor stations; the amount of their payment to the MTS may not be in accord with the value to them of MTS services received.[77] The state farms, on the other hand, hire and pay workers (farmers) on the same basis as industrial enterprises, and own and operate their own machinery; their cost structures presumably parallel those in industry. Clearly, the most straightforward method of ascertaining the cost of producing grain in values comparable with nonagricultural costs is to use the estimates for state farms. It may be, of course, that real efficiency in the production of grain differs considerably between state and collective farms. Jasny presents some evidence for believing that costs of production may be higher on collective than on state farms, though this is carefully qualified.[78] We shall assume that the cost of producing grain on the collectives is represented by the cost of production on the state farms *plus or minus one-third*, i.e., that the cost of production is from 15 to 30 rubles per quintal. In the light of available material on the differential efficiency of state and collective farms, this range seems adequate. Even if the range were widened to 10 to 40 rubles, however, the results would not be much affected.

Having settled on a range of production costs for grain, our procedure is to substitute these figures for the actual cost to the state of the obligatory deliveries, and to examine the effect of this substitution on the rate of taxation. The new rate of tax is the tax on bread to the consumer; the difference between the old and the new rates represents the part of the turnover tax paid by the producer. A simple example will make this clear. Assume that a quintal of bread sells for 100 rubles, and that this price is composed of a 10 ruble obligatory delivery price, and a 90 per cent (90 ruble) turnover tax. Assume that the cost of producing the grain is 30 rubles, i.e., that the collective farms receive for their compulsory deliveries only one-third of the cost of production. In this case the tax on the household is not 90 rubles (90 per cent) but 70 rubles (70 per cent), since 20 rubles of the nominal turnover tax represents cost of production.

The actual cost structure of bread and the computations necessary to estimate the total tax and its incidence on producers and consumers respectively are, of course, more complicated (see Table 22, sources and methods).

The results are as follows:

Unadjusted rate of turnover tax (including budget markup)	85.9 per cent
Rate of tax (on consumer) based on 15 ruble cost of production	80.4 per cent
Rate of tax (on consumer) based on 30 ruble cost of production	68.6 per cent

If our assumptions are correct, the rate of tax on rye bread paid by the household is not 85.9 per cent, but somewhere between 68 and 80 per cent, probably closer to the lower figure.[79] The agricultural producer, if our estimates are reasonable, bears from 5 to 17 per cent of the 85.9 per cent rate. This does not mean that the tax on the producer is from 5 to 17 per cent; this tax is computed quite differently, as we shall demonstrate in the next chapter.

The foregoing computations show quite conclusively that although the actual rate of tax on the consumer of bread is below the nominal rate, it is still extremely high — one of the highest rates. No *sub-*

stantial modification of the picture presented earlier of the impact of the turnover tax on income distribution is warranted by the moderate decline in the rate of tax on bread alone. We cannot say what the result might be if we could estimate the actual rate of tax paid by the consumer for other agricultural products, but there is some evidence to indicate that the rate of tax on producers of other agricultural commodities is at least as great as that on the producers of bread, and that the tax on the consumers of those commodities is therefore overstated by as much as is the tax on consumers of bread. It is the opinion of competent Western agricultural economists (Chapter 7) that the collective farms pay, on the average, a fair price for the work performed for them by the machine tractor stations; in other words, that the income in kind (which constitutes almost the entire income) of the MTS, if valued in prices which would cover collective farm production costs, would be just sufficient to cover current operating expenditures of MTS. The income in kind of the MTS is in fact valued at the low compulsory delivery prices. Expressed in these terms they seem to cover only about one-fifth of state expenditures on MTS. In 1938, for example, expenditures on the MTS were 7.5 billion rubles, whereas receipts (valued at procurement prices) were only 1.4 billion rubles; in 1939 the comparable figures were 7.9 and 1.8 billion rubles respectively.[80] The huge operating subsidy to the MTS implied by these figures is reduced by two factors. First, part of the expenditures by the budget on the MTS are not for current operations but for investment in the MTS, i.e., investment subsidies. Budget-financed capital investment in agriculture was planned at 2 billion rubles in 1938 and 1.3 billion rubles in 1939.[81] If all of this investment was in the MTS and not in the state farms, the ratio of operating expenditures to receipts would still be about four to one. A second adjustment must be made, however; the receipts must be revalued upward, since, as we noted above, procurement-price valuation seriously understates their true worth as measured by, say, cost of production. If statements by Western economists to the effect that expenses of the MTS are roughly covered by their incomes are correct, then in agriculture as a whole the cost of production must be roughly four times procurement price. Our assumption regarding the cost of grain suggests that receipts of the MTS were adequate to finance anywhere from 50 to 100 per cent of expenditures. This line of reasoning suggests that the higher estimate for cost of production may be nearer the true cost. It also suggests that the gap between procurement price and cost of production for the nongrain crop must be at least as great as that for grain, if not greater. If the gap between price and cost is, *in fact*, less than one to four, we would be forced to conclude that the Western experts mentioned above are mistaken in their judgment and that the state subsidizes MTS services to the collective farms.

The Tax on Bread, 1949–1953. Recent developments in Soviet costs and prices lead us to believe that although the rate of tax on bread may not have been *significantly* overstated in the prewar period by inclusion of a tax on the producer, the same may not be true in the postwar period. These developments, discussed in other chapters, are: the rapid decline in the price of bread as well as of other consumers' goods (Chapter 9), the rapid increase in wholesale costs and prices (Chapter 9), and constancy of the procurement price for grain (Chapter 7). The decline in the price of bread implies by itself a reduction in the rate of turnover tax on that commodity. Estimates similar to those already made for the prewar period show the following results (see Table 22).

TABLE 22 Rate of Turnover Tax on Consumers of Rye Bread, 1940, 1949, 1953 (per cent)

			1953	
	1940	1949	*A*	*B*
Unadjusted	85.9	79.8	59.5	72.0
Minimum cost of production estimate	80.4	75.8	51.6	64.4
Maximum cost of production estimate	68.6	70.0	40.0	52.8

For sources and method of calculation, see Appendix.

1953 *A*: Assuming that costs of processing and distributing bread are the same as for 1949.

1953 *B*: Assuming that costs of processing and distributing bread were reduced by the wholesale-price reductions of 1950 and 1952.

The unadjusted rate of tax declines from 86 per cent, prewar, to 80 per cent in 1949, and then to 59–72 per cent in 1953. The adjusted rate (i.e., the tax on the consumer of bread) in 1953 lies somewhere between 40 and 65 per cent. This adjustment is significant. A "true" tax on the consumer of bread of, say 40–45 per cent would probably represent elimination of the single most regressive element in the turnover-tax structure.

Equity of Turnover Taxation. So far the data show the following characteristics:

i. Intracommodity rates for both industrial and food products are progressive.

ii. Intercommodity rates for industrial products have no clearly defined pattern except for the groups above 60 per cent. These contain a preponderance of commodities bought by higher-income groups. All other rate groups contain commodities seemingly randomly distributed which would be bought by the low- and high-income families respectively.

iii. The most important food product, bread, added a very regressive element to the tax structure before the war, but has contributed much less to regressiveness in the years since 1950. The high tax on meats is a partially counterbalancing factor. Otherwise no clearly defined trend in food products is discernible.

Food is of course an essential item of expenditure for all consumers; for lower-income groups in particular it is much more important than industrial consumers' goods. It is significant, therefore, that the prices and taxes on food products have been declining much more rapidly than those on industrial consumers' goods. In fact, the price cuts of March 1951 and April 1952 touched only food products; and the previous postwar cuts effected, on the whole, larger reductions in prices of food than of industrial consumers' goods. This development — especially the large reduction in the tax on bread — implies, perhaps, a decrease in the regressiveness of the turnover tax in the postwar period.

To summarize, there appears to be no single trend of progression or regression in the turnover-tax structure *as a whole*. In the prewar period the tax was probably regressive at the lower income levels because of the high tax on bread, roughly proportional over the large range of middle-income groups, and regressive in the case of the high-income groups which purchase fur coats, pianos, typewriters, and other expensive commodities bearing low tax rates. In the post-war period, reduction in the tax on bread may have gone a long way toward eliminating regression from the lower end of the income scale, if the whole spectrum of other rates has not changed too substantially in the meantime. The rate system can be viewed as having three dimensions: intercommodity progression, intercommodity regression, and intracommodity progression; values of these dimensions must be carefully weighted before any truly authoritative conclusion about the equity of the turnover-tax system can emerge. On the whole, the coexistence of numerous progressive and regressive elements makes it rather unlikely that the turnover-tax structure deviates sharply in either direction away from proportionality. More can hardly be said without budget studies of Soviet consumers and prices of the relevant consumers' goods.

Why does the turnover-tax rate structure contain, from an equity standpoint, so many conflicting elements? Is it because the Soviets are not concerned with equity considerations, or because so many factors, other than equity, must be considered in setting rates? The consistent progressivity of intracommodity rates argues against the hypothesis that the Soviets are indifferent to the equity of their taxes; the second explanation is the more reasonable one. Factors besides equity which are important in the setting of tax rates were mentioned in Chapter 3 and earlier in this chapter: differential rent, administrative simplicity, moral considerations, and so forth. For example, the high tax on cosmetics probably reflects official disapproval of the use of cosmetics, rather than an equity attitude on the part of the state. The high tax on liquor is a similar expression of moral disapproval. The high tax on bread is no doubt dictated in part by the administrative convenience of collecting a large part of state revenue from a single commodity without need of large supply adjustments (since the demand for bread is inelastic with respect to price). The low tax on musical instruments may reflect a policy of encouraging the arts. The low tax on pianos and other extremely high-cost items may be required if even the highest-income groups are to afford them. This may also be true of the "showcase" commodities such as automobiles, TV sets, and refrigerators (although we have no information regarding tax rates on these commodities): for propaganda purposes it may be desirable that some private individuals own automobiles; yet if a high turnover tax were placed on such an expensive commodity, perhaps no one would be willing to purchase it. Finally, the turnover tax is used to equalize supply and demand in the market for each specific commodity at different points of time. In theory, this can be accomplished with a very large number of intercommodity tax-rate combinations; in practice, it is usually not easy to manipulate relative tax rates with equity considerations in view — the situation is much too complicated. Supply adjustments are called for, but these usually cannot be effected over the short run.

The statistical data at our disposal have been presented and appraised in this section. The significance of the concept of equity in taxation applied to the Soviet economy is discussed in the concluding chapter of this book.

Chapter 7

TAXATION IN KIND [1]

The reasons for Soviet recourse to taxation in kind were discussed in the last section of Chapter 3. The tax in kind is the most important tax on Soviet agriculture; it is levied on the collective farms (*kolkhozy*), collective farmers (*kolkhozniki*), and independent farmers (*edinolichniki*). Each is obliged to surrender a portion of his crop or other agricultural output to the state at prices which are below the cost of production. State and coöperative organizations resell agricultural commodities at prices considerably higher than these obligatory delivery prices plus costs of processing and distribution. The difference between total cost to the state and retail price is siphoned into the state budget by the turnover tax.

The tax in kind is not included in the budget, as such. It is represented in budget receipts, however, to the extent that the low procurement price increases the gap between cost to the state and retail price to the consumer. It is obvious that the part of the turnover tax which results from below-cost procurement prices is a tax on the agricultural sector of the economy rather than on the economy as a whole. Since the agricultural sector does not make explicit payments for the use of land, part of the tax in kind can be taken to represent land rent. An attempt was made in the previous chapter to separate the tax on the producer of bread from the tax on the consumer.

BRIEF HISTORY BEFORE 1933

In its present form the tax in kind is called an obligatory delivery (*obiazatel'naia postavka*). It was initiated in October 1932 and was quickly extended to the more important crops. Before 1932, at least four separate phases of agricultural procurement can be distinguished.

(i) In the period immediately following the Revolution, there was no taxation of the agricultural sector in the sense of a defined obligation to the state; government agents simply came into the villages and took all agricultural output in excess of a bare subsistence ration left for the peasant households. This form of requisition was called the "food quota" (*prodovol'stvennaia razverstka*).[2] Its effect was to destroy the peasant's incentive to increase his output, since any increment was almost certain to be requisitioned by the state.

(ii) With the introduction of the New Economic Policy in March 1921, the "food quota" was replaced by a produce tax or tax in kind. The first article of the decree establishing the tax read as follows:

> In order to guarantee regular and undisturbed farming on the basis of a freer disposal of produce by the farmer, to strengthen peasant farming and increase its efficiency, and to fix more exactly the obligations of agricultural workers toward the state, the distributive quota [food quota] as a means of accumulating supplies by the state is hereby replaced by a tax in kind.[3]

In contrast to the previous open-end requisitioning, the produce tax stimulated agricultural output by defining the obligation of the peasant, i.e., by placing a limit on the proportion of output which had to be surrendered to the state. It was collected in the form of 18 different products. Collections were costly, reducing the net yield of the tax in some areas by as much as 50 per cent.[4]

In spite of the high costs of collection, the produce tax might have been retained if it had not come into conflict with an important goal of the early NEP period, namely, to place the economy as a whole on a stable monetary basis. During War Communism (1918–1921) and the first years of the NEP, the economy was suffering from hyperinflation; most transactions were conducted on a barter basis, particularly those with the agricultural sector.[5] Many economists believed that the introduction of a money tax on the agricultural sector in place of the produce tax would help to force the peasant out of goods and into money, and that this, combined with other measures, would make it possible to stabilize Soviet currency.

A law of May 10, 1923 instituted partial payment of the agricultural tax in money instead of in kind.[6] A decree of April 30, 1924 completed the shift to money taxation by directing that the tax be calculated in gold rubles and collected entirely in money.

In 1924 the Soviets also undertook a monetary reform which apparently was successful in stabilizing the currency.[7] Most Soviet writers claim that the substitution of a money tax on the agricultural sector for the tax in kind was an important factor in the success of the reform; a few believe that the causation was in the reverse direction, that is, that the success of the reform made it possible to do away with the produce tax.[8]

(iii) With the elimination of the produce tax, the state was in the position of having no legal claim to any part of the output of the agricultural economy; state organizations were forced to go to the market to purchase agricultural output from individual peasants. Procurement on such a piecemeal basis was unsatisfactory. In spite of the fact that the gross harvests of the mid-twenties exceeded the prewar level, the marketed surpluses did not.[9] Measures introduced to increase the marketed surplus and the government's share of this surplus proved unsuccessful.[10]

(iv) In 1927–28, state organizations changed their method of procurement; instead of going to the market and buying from individual peasants or middlemen, the procurement organizations went to the villages and "contracted" directly with both households and village soviets for the delivery of agricultural output. This form of procurement was known as *kontraktatsiia*, and was essentially "a purchase by the government for future delivery of an agricultural product not yet ready for the market." [11] At first, contracts were on a voluntary basis. However, as the Soviets extended the scope of their planning and the need for a stable supply of agricultural commodities became imperative, the contracts acquired a compulsory character. By 1929 the state was specifying the amounts to be delivered, the prices, and even measures to be taken to raise productivity and increase output.[12] The total amount of each commodity to be contracted for was usually specified in the state plan, and sometimes this was distributed among the republics. The distribution of contracts throughout the USSR on a local level is described as follows:

> The government in Moscow decided how much of each crop was to be contracted in the whole country and subdivided this quantity among the individual republics. These subdivided their total quotas among the oblasti which in turn subdivided theirs. So the process continued until each village had its quota and distributed it among the individual peasants or kolkhozy.[13]

There were supposed to be some advantages for the peasants and collective farms in selling goods to the state via kontraktatsiia in spite of the fact that prices were below those prevailing in the free market. State procurement agencies had at their disposal supplies of consumers' and producers' goods needed by farmers; some of these could be purchased only by groups or individuals delivering specified amounts of agricultural produce. The procurement agencies also extended credit to the peasants.[14]

Although kontraktatsiia expanded rapidly, especially after the initiation of the First Five Year Plan, and came to encompass the bulk of peasant output, its administration at the local level proved very unsatisfactory. Local authorities striving to meet high procurement quotas demanded the surrender of an unduly large portion of the total output of collective farms and individual peasants. Furthermore, when yields were unexpectedly high, procurement organizations often unilaterally revised deliveries upward, taking all of the benefits for the state and leaving none to the producers. Deliveries from the more successful farms were commonly revised upward to compensate for failure of the poorer ones to fulfill their contracts.[15] This last practice in particular undermined the incentive of agricultural producers to improve and increase output, and was one reason advanced for the abandonment of kontraktatsiia in favor of obligatory deliveries.[16]

A second reason offered by Soviet economists for abandoning the system was the need created by the development of planning for a more stable and predictable supply of agricultural commodities than kontraktatsiia presumably provided. After all, it was argued, kontraktatsiia is a two-sided agreement, with the state as one party and the collective farms or peasants as the other. The state cannot afford to depend on contracts with the agricultural sector; it must have a definite legal claim on agricultural output. The obligatory delivery, which is nominally as well as in fact a tax in kind, presumably satisfies this requirement.

Of the two arguments presented for the shift to obligatory deliveries, the rehabilitation of incentives appears to be the more substantial. Since contracts had become compulsory, hence subject to planning in advance by the state, it is difficult to see the advantage of obligatory deliveries in this respect.

OBLIGATORY DELIVERIES, 1933–1940

Obligatory deliveries were introduced in 1932–33 for grains, rice, potatoes, meat, milk, wool, and sunflower seeds. Between 1940 and 1942 the system was extended to vegetables, flax, hemp, tobacco, eggs, hay, and other crops.

Some commodities, particularly industrial crops such as cotton and sugar beets, are still procured on a kontraktatsiia basis. Since industrial crops cannot be consumed by the peasants, and since there is no private industry, the state is the only purchaser, and obligatory procurement is unnecessary. Producers of industrial crops must be paid a relatively higher price for their contracted deliveries, however, because, unlike the food-producing peasants, they have no income in kind and no free market in which to sell their surpluses at high prices.[17]

"Norms" of delivery. In the thirties obligatory deliveries were estimated according to so-called "norms," which were stated in the form of quintals (100 kilograms) of output to be delivered to the state per hectare (2.47 acres) of crop planned, liters of milk per cow, and kilograms of meat per head of cattle. The norms were usually differentiated by region and by type of producer. Regional differentiation presumably allowed for differences in fertility of the soil, climatic conditions, distance from the market, and other factors affecting differential rent.[18] Since the region over which a norm applies is quite large, intraregional differences must be substantial; this implies that the less fortunate producers in a given region are forced to deliver an unduly large proportion of their crop to the state.

The obligatory delivery regulations also distinguish between collective farms, collective farmers, and private farmers, with norms increasing in this order. It should be noted that collective farms which do all of their own work pay a higher rate of tax than those served by MTS; this provision was nominally intended to encourage the use of the MTS by the collective farms. A sample of the norms for potatoes in 1933 illustrates the policy of differentiating the rate of tax by region and type of producer (Table 23).

In the case of grain (1933), norms were based on the deliveries from collective farms: the rates for collective farmers, private farmers, and kulaks were respectively 5, 10, and 60 per cent higher than the rates for kolkhozy. It is clear that the system of obligatory de-

TABLE 23 Obligatory Delivery Norms for Potatoes, 1933 (quintals per hectare)

	Collective Farms			
	With MTS	Without MTS	Collective Farmers	Private Farmers
Moscow region	12	16	18	20
Ukraine	6	9	11	12

For source, see Appendix.

liveries provides no exception to the Soviet policy of class discrimination in taxation.

As was indicated in the previous section, one of the principal reasons for introducing obligatory deliveries was to prevent arbitrary requisitioning of agricultural output from producers. Therefore it is not surprising that many of the regulations during the thirties explicitly stated that procurements should under no circumstances exceed the norms of delivery.

Even scrupulous adherence to the norms could not, however, prevent inequities. Obligatory deliveries in this period were nominally a tax on *gross* output, and made no formal allowance for differential costs of production within a region. Local authorities were granted discretion within prescribed limits to adjust intraregional norms for varying conditions but there are many reports to indicate that this was not done. The tax therefore fell very heavily on high-cost producers. Moreover, the heavy burden of the tax was extended even to low-cost producers in bad crop years, since it was in fact a tax on *planned* rather than actual gross output; for example, if the delivery norm for wheat was 5 quintals per hectare and the sown area was 100 hectares, the state collected 500 quintals, regardless of whether the yield per hectare was 20 quintals or 10. These inequities might not have been serious if the tax in kind were not typically a large levy; under the circumstances it seems inevitable that many of the weaker peasants and collective farms were forced to operate at a loss.

There is no ambiguity about the intent of the state to exact the tax even if this results in operating losses to the producers. Obligatory deliveries are legally the *first* lien on current output; they have priority over current and capital expenditures, including seed requirements, feed requirements, insurance funds, and payments to the collective farmers (who are last in the hierarchy).[19]

The original norms of obligatory deliveries were apparently much too high — especially the norms for grain. This is shown by the fact that the government had to provide the collective farms with a large portion of their seed grain in 1933, 1934, and 1936.[20] Substantial reductions in norms were put into effect in the period 1933–1936, as the sampling of rates in Table 24 indicates. The norms of delivery for sunflower seeds also declined from 1933 to 1936 (Table 25). Rates for deliveries of potatoes generally rose for the private farmers from 1933 to 1940, but declined for collective farmers (Table 26).

It should be noted that the ratio of delivery to average yield is quite high for grains, higher for sunflower seeds, and relatively low

TABLE 24 Obligatory Deliveries of Grain by Collective Farms served by MTS (quintals per hectare)

	1933	1934	1935	1936	Average harvest yield, 1928–1930	Average adjusted yield, 1932–1934
Ukraine	3.1	3.1	2.3	2.0	9.0	7.1
Central Black Earth	3.0	2.2	2.1	1.7	8.4	7.6
North Caucasus	2.5	2.5	1.9	1.7	7.0	6.6

For sources, see Appendix.

TABLE 25 Obligatory Deliveries of Sunflower Seeds, 1933–1936 (quintals per hectare)

	1933	1934	1935	1936	Actual yield 1932–1934
Ukraine	3.3	3.0	3.0	2.6	6.1
North Caucasus	3.4	3.2	3.0	2.6	6.0

For sources, see Appendix.

TABLE 26 Obligatory Deliveries of Potatoes, 1933 and 1940 (quintals per hectare)

	Collective Farmers		Private Farmers		Yield for
	1933	1940	1933	1940	1932–1934
White Russia	13	12	15	20	97.4
Kursk region	15	10	16	15	. .
Ukraine	11	8	12	14	. .

For source, see Appendix.

for potatoes. These ratios give a rough idea of the gross tax implied by the norms. A more detailed analysis of the tax involved in obligatory deliveries of grain will be presented below.

It should also be pointed out that individual farmers (both collective and independent farmers), were obliged to deliver meat to the government regardless of whether they possessed livestock or poultry or not. In case of nondelivery, they were forced to pay the free market value of the undelivered meat, and after repeated failure to deliver were subject to indictment under the criminal code.[21]

Procurement Prices. To the extent that producers are paid for obligatory deliveries, the real rate of tax in kind is reduced. It may be stated as a corollary to this that if obligatory delivery prices remain stable when the general price level rises, the real rate of tax increases even though delivery norms remain unchanged. In other words, the variations in the real rate of tax which are required by changes in the savings requirements of the economy can be effected in two ways: by varying the norms, and by varying the relation between procurement prices and the general price level.

One would expect delivery norms to remain relatively stable, varying over the long run with changes in the quantities of food required by the nonagricultural population. These requirements define the minimum share of physical output which the state must procure; the maximum is limited by the consumption requirements of the peasant producers. Theoretically, norms could be manipulated between these two extremes. Practically, an increasing real rate of tax (once the state has met its minimum physical requirements) is less likely to be felt by rural taxpayers if the increase is achieved through price manipulation, particularly when this takes the form of constant or slowly rising procurement prices accompanied by relatively larger increase in the price level for manufactured goods.

Unfortunately, the official regulations concerning obligatory deliveries do not mention the procurement prices paid by the state to the producers. The few available data indicate, however, that procurement prices rose very little in contrast to the rapid increase in the price level of consumers' goods.

The procurement price of wheat remained unchanged from 1928 to 1934 at 7–8 rubles per quintal. In 1935 the procurement price was increased by "10 per cent in connection with the abolition of bread rationing and the enormous increase in retail prices of grain and grain products in regular government and coöperative stores." [22] In 1936, the wheat price was increased by another 1.2 rubles, bringing it to 9–10 rubles per quintal. Apparently the procurement price for wheat is still at about this level.[23]

The procurement price for sunflower seeds was 7.5–8 rubles per quintal in 1928; it was increased to 9 rubles in 1931, to 15 rubles in 1935, and to 20 rubles in 1946.[24]

The trends in the procurement prices of other commodities are probably similar. As was noted earlier, the prices for industrial crops sold on a kontraktatsiia basis were considerably higher, since the producers (1) usually sold their entire crop to the state, not receiving any money income from sales at the high free market prices and (2) often did not grow their own food, and therefore had to have enough money income to purchase food at the high retail prices.

RECENT DEVELOPMENTS IN TAXATION IN KIND

It was pointed out above that kolkhoz obligatory deliveries as originally conceived were taxes on planned gross output, based on the sown area of crops and the size of livestock herds owned. It was also indicated that because this system failed to take adequate account of differential costs and the impact of bad crop years, it was a rather unjust form of taxation; the amount of tax levied was not closely related to "ability to pay." An obvious form of tax evasion under such circumstances was to strive for higher yields per hectare and greater productivity per animal, instead of increasing output through expanding sown area and herds.

With the express aim of preventing this type of evasion, the state introduced in 1940 an even more unjust system of levy. Since that year obligatory deliveries have been made on the following basis: (*a*) grains, potatoes, sunflower seeds, and all other output of field crops (and also eggs) are delivered on the basis of the number of hectares of arable land *in possession* of the collective farms; (*b*) products of animal husbandry are delivered on the basis of the total number of hectares of all land *in possession* of the collective farms which is usable for agriculture; (*c*) hay is delivered on the basis of the amount of arable land and meadows *in possession* of the collective farm.[25]

In this form, the obligatory delivery is essentially a property tax, even further divorced from ability to pay than the previous tax in kind. Its inequities are aggravated by the fact that the tax is payable in specific commodities.

It might be argued that this type of taxation is no more unjust than the property tax levied by local governments in the United States. In principle, this is quite true; the two taxes are essentially the same in form. There are two substantial differences, however. First, the tax in kind is the basic form of direct taxation of Soviet agriculture, and absorbs a substantial part of the output of that sector of the economy. For this reason it is significant that the system of obligatory deliveries is not closely related to ability to pay. In the United States, the basic form of taxation is the income tax, which does conform to the ability-to-pay criterion; the property tax is relatively small, so that the injustices which result from lack of correspondence between extent of property and ability to pay are of second-order importance.

Second, there is a market for property in the United States. A person who cannot pay his property tax can presumably sell part of his property and use the proceeds to meet his obligation to the government. There is no market for land in the Soviet Union; furthermore, even if such a market did exist, taxpayers forced to meet an obligation payable only in grain, potatoes, eggs, meat, etc. would have to accept the loss involved in procuring these items at high retail prices on the free market.

It is clear from the above discussion that by levying the obligatory deliveries in the manner indicated, the state assumed more complete control of collective farm production policy than ever before. Kolkhozy are strongly impelled to cultivate every last hectare of land, and to build up their animal husbandry to the extent required by the tax law. To do otherwise is equivalent to accepting a higher rate of effective taxation than is indicated by the norms. This was, of course, precisely the effect anticipated by the Soviet authorities in introducing the new method of calculating obligatory deliveries.[26]

The Soviet criticism of the old method of computing obligatory deliveries is stated concisely in the text of the 1940 regulation:

> A defect of this system of procurement was that obligatory deliveries of meat, wool, and milk by kolkhozy were based on the number of head of kolkhoz cattle. This led to a situation where kolkhozy which had developed socialized herds of cattle and increased them from year to year had to surrender larger and larger quantities of meat, milk, and wool in

the form of obligatory deliveries to the state, while kolkhozy with undeveloped animal farms surrendered less . . . ; kolkhozy without animal farms and with no inclination to organize them were exempted completely from delivery of animal products to the state.

Transfer to a per hectare calculation of deliveries of meat, wool, and milk not only insures elimination of the deficiencies noted in the system of procurement, but serves as a powerful instrument in the development of socialized animal husbandry.

The existing method of calculating obligatory deliveries to the state of grain, rice, sunflower seeds, and potatoes by kolkhozy suffers from the fundamental deficiency that the amount of deliveries calculated on the basis of the plan of sowing is not a stable basis upon which to calculate obligatory deliveries having the strength of a tax; it leads to a tendency on the part of collective farms to try to reduce the plan of sowing grain, sunflowers, and potatoes, and encourages a reduction in the cultivated area of these crops; it does not stimulate the exploitation of new land through irrigation of deserts, draining bogs, and clearing away brush.[27]

The quoted material correctly points out that the new method of assessing the tax creates an incentive to extend agricultural output. The complaint that the old method discouraged increases in herds and sown area is also true, but disingenuous. Such increases are not ends in themselves but a means to greater output, which can also be achieved through qualitative improvements. The real complaint is that increases in output which were not achieved through enlarging herds and sown area were inaccessible to taxation. The obvious remedy — to base the tax in kind directly upon output instead of some magnitude (like sown area) which correlates with output only imperfectly — was unacceptable, since the state would then have to share with collective farmers the burden of bad crop years.

It might be thought that the "per-hectare" principle provided the final answer to the state's requirements. The tax in kind was not only protected (as far as this is possible) from fluctuations in output due to weather; it was also shielded from the instinct of the producer to conserve effort. The vicissitudes of the tax since 1940 suggest, however, that even this solution is unsatisfactory.

The root of the difficulty is still the difference in costs within a presumably uniform region. Norms high enough to compel reasonable effort from fortunate kolkhozy cannot be met by marginal producers. But total procurement quotas for a region assume that the norms *can* be met by all producers; deficits are therefore inevitable unless some kolkhozy pay more than the norm of tax.

In 1947 the per-hectare principle was modified, or nullified, to permit precisely this. The change was ostensibly a temporary one prompted by the severe shortage of labor in some kolkhozy after the war. Procurement agencies were empowered to adjust delivery norms for individual kolkhozy "in accordance with the degree to which they have succeeded in exploiting the land secured to them" [28] —an ambiguous phrase which, if it means anything, means "in accordance with the amount of surplus." The evils associated with kontraktatsiia duly reappeared, and by 1953 the adverse effect on incentives could no longer be ignored. The decree of September 13, 1953 reaffirmed the old per-hectare principle in all its purity; procurement agencies were enjoined to strict observance of norms in the future.[29]

The dilemma created by the refusal to accept output as the ultimate basis for the tax in kind remains. As long as the state clings to norms of delivery based on the quantity of land utilized by a kolkhoz, it must either establish norms low enough to be met by the large majority, or penalize exceptional producers to compensate for the failure of the poor ones.

THE RATE OF TAXATION IN KIND (GRAIN), 1937–1939

An approximation to the net rate of taxation involved in obligatory deliveries of grain can be obtained from statistics which have been collected from Soviet sources by Dr. Lazar Volin. Dr. Volin presents a percentage distribution of the total collective farm grain crop in the years 1937–1939; [30] in Table 27, adapted from these data, a *first* approximation to the net rate of tax is derived.

The reader will note that the rate of tax has been computed on two different bases. The choice between them depends on whether it is more useful to consider payments to farm labor as a cost (the corporate approach) or as part of the distributed surplus (the coöperative approach).[31] Legally, the collective farms are coöperatives, and the collective farmers are the residual claimants to the collective farm output. It must be borne in mind that although the net rate of tax (coöperative form) is computed as the ratio of obligatory deliveries to the distributed surplus, deliveries are not, in the Soviet intent, a

TABLE 27 Derivation of Rate of Taxation in Kind for Grains: First Approximation (per cent of gross crop)

		1937		1938		1939
1. Gross collective farm crop		100.0		100.0		100.0
2. Deduct nonlabor costs paid in kind						
Payments in kind to MTS	13.9		16.0		19.2	
Return of seed loans	1.5		2.0		4.0	
Collective farm requirements and reserves (seed, feed, etc.)	31.7	47.1	35.0	53.0	35.6	58.8
3. Net collective farm crop, coöperative form		52.9		47.0		41.2
4. Deduct payments to collective farmers		35.9		26.9		22.9
5. Net collective farm crop, corporate form[a]		17.0		20.1		18.3
6. Obligatory deliveries		12.2		15.0		14.3
7. Net rate of tax, first approximation[b]						
coöperative form (6 ÷ 3)		23.1		31.9		34.7
corporate form (6 ÷ 5)		71.7		75.0		74.0

For sources, see Appendix.

[a] This includes obligatory deliveries, sales by the collective farms on the collective farmer market, and the so-called decentralized procurements or voluntary sales by the collective farms to state and cooperative organizations.

[b] The percentage of obligatory deliveries to gross yield can be calculated for 1933 and 1934 by using data in Baykov, p. 203. Baykov gives the percentage share in gross yield of obligatory deliveries plus decentralized purchases; he also provides (p. 243) a distribution of this amount between obligatory deliveries and decentralized purchases. The calculated percentages are: 1933, 21.2; 1934, 16.7. Since cost data are not available for these years, the rate of tax cannot be estimated, but it was undoubtedly higher than the rate in the late thirties. The fact that norms of delivery declined from 1933 to 1937 is partial evidence of this.

tax upon this surplus alone; they are paid before all other claims, including costs of production.

If the collective farm is looked upon as a means of organizing not only agricultural production but also the *collection* of agricultural output by the state (one of the original purposes of collectivization), then there is a good reason to consider the tax on the collective farm as a form of tax on the collective farmers. In this case the coöperative form of the tax is the more significant one, because it reflects the changing fortunes of collective farmers due to variations in yield. The corporate approach, on the other hand, is relatively insensitive in this respect, because both the net crop before payment to collective farmers (coöperative form) and payments to collective farmers tend to vary in the same direction as the size of the crop; in deducting the latter from the former to get net crop (corporate form), the fluctuation tends to be removed.[32] For this reason, the collective farmers will be looked upon as the residual claimant, and the coöperative form of tax will be used.

The rate of tax estimated above was designated a first approximation; at least three adjustments are required before the conceptual requirements of a Soviet type of tax in kind are satisfied.

The rate of tax must first be reduced to take account of the fact that the government does pay collective farms for obligatory deliveries, albeit at a price far below cost. The procedure followed here is to reduce the tax element from gross obligatory deliveries by the ratio of the procurement price to the cost of production of grain. The cost of production of grain on collective farms for the years 1937 to 1939 is derived from the planned cost of production of grain on state farms in 1941. The reasons for using state farm cost figures were presented in Chapter 6.[33] The adjustment backward from 1941 to 1937–39 is assumed to be proportional to the change in the average wage over these years.

In addition to obligatory deliveries, state and coöperative organizations procure additional agricultural commodities from the producers at prices which, though below cost of production, are somewhat higher than the prices paid for compulsory deliveries. These are called decentralized purchases or voluntary procurements. An adjustment must be made to include in our estimate the tax element, if any, in the decentralized purchases.

In considering whether the decentralized deliveries involve taxation, the first question which must be asked is: are these deliveries truly voluntary, or are the collective farms and the peasants compelled to sell another part of their surplus, in addition to the obligatory deliveries, to the state? It has been suggested that these deliveries are compulsory because they are included in the state plan for agriculture each year.[34] This evidence alone is not conclusive, however, since the Soviets include in their plans both activities which are predictable, though not directly controlled, and activities which can be indirectly influenced. One factor making for predictability is that many peasants and collective farms, located in inaccessible areas far from a city, have no alternative market for their surplus output. In this case, the state stands in the position of natural monopsonist. Another factor of importance is that producers who sell on a so-called voluntary basis to the state frequently are given an opportunity to purchase manufactured commodities which otherwise would not be available to them. This is a very important economic consideration in the USSR [35] because of the scarcity of industrial goods.

In neither of these two circumstances can sales to the state be considered *wholly* involuntary: in the latter case the collective farm peasants receive a *quid pro quo* in the form of an opportunity to purchase otherwise unavailable manufactured goods; in the former case the state is a natural monopsonist, a situation which does not unequivocally involve taxation, although it may be to some extent a consequence of longer-run government policy.

Data are not available to determine the amount of the decentralized procurement that is payment for value received and the amount that is tax. For purposes of this section the arbitrary assumption is made that half of the decentralized procurements are compulsory and involve taxation to the extent that the decentralized procurement price does not cover the cost of production; it is assumed that the remaining half are free sales, though at below-cost price, and therefore do not involve taxation.

One more factor remains to be considered: payments in kind by the collective farms to the machine tractor stations. Since 1933 the MTS have been paid by the collective farms almost exclusively in kind.[36] The size of the payments vary with the type of operation performed (e.g., ploughing, threshing, harvesting, etc.), the type of crop cultivated, the geographical zone of operations, and so forth. The question to be answered is whether payments by the collective farms to the MTS are fair prices for services rendered, or whether they contain an element of either subsidy or tax.

It is assumed by many Western observers that the collective farms are compelled to overpay the machine tractor stations, and that payments to the MTS should be looked upon as an adjunct to the tax in kind. Students of Soviet agriculture, however, are of the opinion that the MTS receive remuneration more or less equivalent to the value of services rendered. Hubbard says: "On the whole the charges for the use of the MTS tractors and machinery do not seem exorbitant if the work is properly and punctually done. But this is by no means always the case." [37] Maynard points out that during the NEP private persons charged more than 20 per cent of the crop for hiring out animals and implements to the poorer peasants, whereas the MTS charge less.[38] Jasny very roughly estimates the profits of the MTS for 1938 by valuing all MTS receipts and expenditures in terms of 1926–27 prices; the result is an 11 per cent profit.[39] The above statements seem to indicate that the MTS neither earn a large profit nor suffer a substantial loss. It will be assumed, therefore, that the state operation of the MTS involves neither a tax on nor subsidy to the collective farms.[40] No attempt is made to adjust the rate of tax for MTS operations, since no distribution of MTS receipts and expenditures by commodity is available. If we were justified in assuming that the ratio of MTS expenditures and receipts from grains was equal to the ratio of total operating expenditures (total expenditures minus investments in the fixed capital of MTS) to total receipts, the assumption that the MTS were neutral from a tax standpoint would be roughly supported. In 1938, for example, operating expenditures were 5.5 billion rubles and receipts were 1.4 billion, a ratio of about four to one. The ratio of obligatory delivery price (8 rubles) to cost of production of grain (24 rubles — this is the upper limit which we consider most reasonable) is three to one. Revaluation of MTS receipts on a cost-of-production basis eliminates most of the subsidy from the MTS accounts. It is acknowledged that if our assumption regarding the MTS is not in accord with the facts a substantial error is introduced into the results.

We can now proceed to estimate the tax in kind on grain. The results are summarized in Table 28.

For reasons given in Chapter 6, the assumptions underlying the *B* estimates are considered to represent the actual state of affairs more accurately than the assumptions underlying the *A* estimates. Even assuming the higher production costs, however, the rate of tax in kind for grain turns out to be surprisingly low. The rates are considerably below the average money rates of taxation, as estimated in Chapter 10; in the years 1937, 1938, and 1939 these were 57, 53, and 57 per cent respectively. The comparison is the more striking in

TABLE 28 Rate of Tax in Kind for Grain of Collective Farms, 1937–1939 (per cent of net crop, coöperative form)

	1937		1938		1939	
	A	*B*	*A*	*B*	*A*	*B*
Obligatory deliveries	4.3	13.7	9.1	20.6	12.8	23.5
Decentralized purchases	0	1.6	0.5	2.2	4.0	5.1
Total tax	4.3	15.3	9.6	22.8	16.8	28.6

For sources and methodology, see Appendix.

A: Assuming that cost of production of grain on collective farms is 33⅓ per cent below cost on state farms.

B: Assuming that cost of production of grain on collective farms is 33⅓ per cent above cost on state farms.

view of the generally held opinion that the Soviets favor the urban working class over the peasants *and* that a very large part of the peasants' burden is discharged in kind. There are several possible explanations. First, it may not be feasible to levy too high a tax in kind when the form of the tax is such that ability to pay and tax liability are not closely correlated. Second, it is also possible that we are not justified in implicitly assuming, as we have done, that the grain tax on collective farms is typical of (1) the tax in kind for other crops and (2) the tax in kind on the collective and private farmers; these other rates may be much higher (or lower). Third and most important, it should be noted that the tax in kind is not the only tax paid by agricultural population and collective farms; they are subject to direct money taxes (see Chapter 8), though these were until recently very moderate in amount, and they also pay the very heavy indirect taxes on all commodities purchased from state and coöperative stores. The sum of these taxes and the tax in kind may well raise the peasants' tax burden to that of the urban worker. Finally, it must be remembered that before the war about two-thirds of the Soviet population lived in rural areas. A very substantial part of the net output of the agricultural sector had to remain in the rural areas to feed these persons.

The estimates presented in Table 28 are of interest because grain is such an important crop, and because no other computation of a Soviet tax in kind has apparently been attempted in published Western literature. The table is of very limited validity, however, as an *indicator* of the tax burden imposed on the Soviet agricultural sector.

It should be noted that the rate of tax increases from 1937 to 1939. This is no doubt due to the relative excellence of the 1937 crop, and to the fact that the peasant is always the residual claimant, paying a low rate of tax in good crop years and high rate in poor crop years.

We do not have sufficient information to compute a tax in kind in grain for the postwar period. Since the thirties, however, procurement prices have remained relatively stable whereas costs of production have roughly doubled. From this it may be deduced that the rate of tax in kind in grain has been steadily increasing, unless offset by a decrease in norms of delivery.

Chapter 8

DIRECT TAXATION OF THE POPULATION AND MISCELLANEOUS SOURCES OF BUDGET INCOME

We have now discussed the Soviet taxes which are the principal sources of budget income; these are the turnover and profits taxes on industry and the tax in kind on agriculture. It remains to survey a group of taxes which are of slight fiscal importance, but which may discharge important economic or political functions. Emphasis will be placed on the income and agricultural taxes on the population, sales of government bonds, and the taxes on the income of collective farms and other coöperatives.

DIRECT TAXATION OF THE URBAN POPULATION

Income taxation in the Soviet Union differs from income taxation in the United States in three major respects:

(i) The Soviet income tax is a minor source of budget revenue, typically contributing less than 5 per cent of the total. In the United States, on the other hand, the income tax is the major source of revenue; receipts from the personal income tax in 1948 amounted to one-half of federal budget revenues, and to 37 per cent of the combined revenues of the federal, state, and local budgets.[1] As we have seen, the Soviets have preferred to rely on commodity taxation for the bulk of their revenue, for reasons which were presented in Chapter 3.

(ii) For purposes of direct taxation, the Soviet population is divided into two groups: urban and rural. The urban population is subject to an income tax similar in form to the income taxes of the United States, Great Britain, and other Western nations. It is not feasible to tax the rural population in this fashion, since so much of the peasants' income is in kind. Therefore a special type of tax (called the agricultural tax) is levied on the rural population; it differs from the regular income tax in its methods of assessing personal income and of estimating the amount of tax to be paid. This tax is discussed in the next section.

(iii) The Soviet income tax functions as an instrument of Soviet class policy. As was pointed out in Chapter 3, workers and collective farmers are taxed at preferential rates compared with other groups among the urban and rural populations, respectively. This feature of the income tax was particularly important in the period before 1932, when the groups discriminated against were still numerous. Most Western nations do not have separate schedules of tax rates for different social and economic groups in the population.

In most other respects, as we shall see, Soviet and United States income taxes are similar.

Description of Direct Taxes on the Urban Population. (i) *The present income-tax law.* The income-tax law now in force dates back to an edict (*ukaz*) of the Supreme Soviet of April 30, 1943.[2] All persons who are not primarily engaged in agriculture (and therefore subject to the agricultural tax) are subject to an individual income tax. Taxpayers are divided into the following social and economic groups: (*a*) workers, salaried employees, students, and some others; (*b*) artisans and handicraft workers who are members of a coöperative; (*c*) artists of all kinds; (*d*) professional persons, such as doctors and lawyers, who receive income from private practice; (*e*) artisans and handicraft workers who are not members of coöperatives, and other persons having income not derived from state or coöperative employment. There are four schedules of tax rates, one for each of the above groups with the exception of group (*b*), the coöperative artisans; these pay according to the workers' schedule but at a 10 per cent higher rate. The current rates are presented in Table 29.

This system of rates favors the workers, and to a lesser extent the artists. Since the schedules are progressive, it also favors the poorer against the richer; the progression is very moderate, however, and does not significantly affect the distribution of income. It may be noted in this connection that gross-wage differentials within and between the various groups represented in Table 29 are apparently quite large in the Soviet Union;[3] since the income tax is only mildly progressive, take-home pay also varies over a fairly wide range. For example, a worker with a gross annual income of 1,800 rubles has a take-home pay of 1,800 rubles; this is little in comparison with,

TABLE 29 Personal Income Tax on the Urban Population (per cent of yearly income) [a]

Annual income (rubles)	Workers and salaried employees	Artists and writers	Professionals with income from private practice	Noncoöperative artisans, shop-keepers, ecclesias-tical personnel
Under 1,800	0	1.5	2.0	3.0
1,800– 2,400	5.5	5.5	6.0	8.0
2,400– 3,600	6.0	6.0	8.0	12.0
3,600– 4,800	7.0	7.0	11.0	16.0
4,800– 6,000	8.0	8.0	15.0	20.0
6,000– 8,400	10.0	10.0	19.0	25.0
8,400– 12,000	12.0	12.0	23.0	30.0
12,000– 18,000	13.0	13.0	27.0	35.0
18,000– 24,000	13.0	14.0	32.0	40.0
24,000– 30,000	13.0	15.0	37.0	45.0
30,000– 50,000	13.0	16.0	42.0	50.0
50,000– 70,000	13.0	18.0	47.0	57.0
70,000–100,000	13.0	23.0	55.0	65.0
100,000–150,000	13.0	31.0	55.0	65.0
150,000–200,000	13.0	41.0	55.0	65.0
200,000–300,000	13.0	51.0	55.0	65.0
Over 300,000	13.0	55.0	55.0	65.0

For sources, see Appendix.

[a] It should be noted that these are marginal, not average, rates. For example, an artist who earns 2400 rubles would pay 1.5 per cent on the first 1800 rubles plus 5.5 per cent on the next 600 rubles. Coöperative artisans are taxed according to the same schedule as workers, but at a 10 per cent higher rate.

say, the 34,100 rubles take-home pay of a lawyer who has earned a gross income of 50,000 rubles.

It is significant that the maximum rate on workers and salaried employees is only 13 per cent on all income above 12,000 rubles. Many of the better workers, technicians, plant managers, and government officials probably receive annual salaries considerably above this amount,[4] in consonance with the state's present policy of paying wages which are graded in accordance with differential productivity and effort ("to each according to his labor").

The system of exemptions is also constructed to favor some groups and discriminate against others. For example, workers and students earning wages or receiving stipends of less than 260 rubles a month are exempt from taxation,[5] whereas professionals and noncoöperative handicraft workers have to pay tax on all income above 50 rubles a month (600 rubles a year). Other nontaxable maximum incomes are: invalids, 3,000 rubles a year; Heroes of the Soviet Union, Heroes of Socialist Labor, and holders of other orders, 6,000 rubles; inventors, 10,000 rubles. Among those whose income is completely exempt from taxation are soldiers and officials of the Ministry of the Armed Forces, pensioners, prospectors for gold and other rare metals, winners of Stalin prizes, receivers of income from interest and lottery winnings. Workers are allowed to have small gardens (less than 0.15 hectare) without paying tax and miners are exempt from taxation of income from gardens of any size. Those who raise bees and other specialty products are taxed at a specially low rate. All persons with more than three dependents receive a 30 per cent reduction in tax rate.

In general, the tax is paid at the source as a deduction from wage or salary by the employing organization.

(ii) *The tax on bachelors, single persons, and persons with small families.* This tax was introduced in November 1941, and received its present form on July 8, 1944.[6] Because families with three or more children are exempt from it, it is in effect a supplement to the dependency allowances of income and agricultural taxes.

For purposes of taxation, three groups are distinguished: those subject to the income tax, those subject to the agricultural tax, and those who do not have an independent source of income and are not included in either of the above categories (e.g., students with some earnings from temporary work). The tax rates on these groups are listed in Table 30.

The tax is levied on all males between 20 and 50 years of age and on all females between 20 and 45 years of age. Exemptions are similar to those for the income tax, although fewer in number.

TABLE 30 Rates of Tax on Bachelors, Single Persons, and Persons With Small Families

Number of children	Persons subject to income tax (per cent of income)	Persons subject to agricultural tax (rubles)	Persons with no independent income (rubles)
None	6	150	90
One	1	50	30
Two	0.5	25	15

For source, see Appendix.

(iii) *Subsidies to mothers with three or more children.* The program of subsidies to mothers with three or more children was first introduced in 1936. These subsidies, like the tax on bachelors, etc., serve in effect to strengthen the exemption or dependency provisions of the income-tax law, though there is no legal connection between subsidies and the income taxes.[7] The Soviet income tax constitutes much too small a fraction of total taxes on the population for adequate dependency provisions to be attached to it; hence the need for supplementary devices.

The subsidies are granted as follows: upon the birth of a child, each mother receives a lump-sum payment which varies from 200 rubles for the third child to 2,500 rubles for the eleventh, and a monthly stipend beginning with 40 rubles for the fourth child and extending to 150 rubles for the eleventh. The current schedule has been in effect since 1948 [8] (before 1948, the subsidies were exactly half these amounts).[9] This form of dependency provision is actually much better tailored to the needs of lower-income groups than income-tax exemptions: it is much less regressive. Under most income-tax laws, all persons exempt from paying taxes either because they have too low a basic income or because they have a certain number of dependents are treated alike, regardless of how far below the taxable level their income is or how many dependents they have in excess of the requirement for exemption.

The relative importance of the different Soviet dependency provisions, including subsidies to mothers, is illustrated in Table 31. The 30 per cent reduction from the income tax proper for four or more children is the least important, while for persons with five or more children the subsidies are most important. It is interesting to note that because of the subsidies the low-income household receives relatively greater relief than the average-income household. This is not usually true of income-tax exemptions alone.

The subsidies apply equally to mothers subject to the agricultural and income taxes.

Unwed mothers receive larger stipends than those who are married.

Brief History of Income Taxation. The income tax was introduced in November 1922,[10] as part of a combined income and property tax. When the NEP began in 1921, small enterprises were denationalized and private industry and trade were encouraged. The property

TABLE 31 Soviet Dependency Relief (per cent of income)

Number of dependents[a]	Average-income household, 1950 (annual income 12,000 rubles)[b]: Subsidy to mothers: Lump sum[c]	Subsidy to mothers: Monthly	Tax on bachelors[d]	Income tax[e]	Total	Low-income household (annual income 6000 rubles)
1	0	0	5	0	5	5
2	0	0	5.5	0	5.5	5.5
3	0.2	0	6.0	0	6.2	6.4
4	0.5	4.0	6.0	2.5	13.0	16.6
5	0.7	6.0	6.0	2.5	15.2	21.0
6	0.8	7.0	6.0	2.5	16.3	23.2
7	1.0	10.0	6.0	2.5	19.5	29.6
8	1.0	10.0	6.0	2.5	19.5	29.6
9	1.5	12.5	6.0	2.5	22.5	35.6
10	1.5	12.5	6.0	2.5	22.5	35.6
11	2.1	15.0	6.0	2.5	25.6	41.8

For sources, see Appendix.

[a] Dependent as defined here means each person dependent on the household for support, not including the husband and wife.

[b] Based on an average wage of 8000 rubles, with 1.5 persons per family employed.

[c] For purposes of this table the lump-sum payment is assumed to be paid over a 10-year period in ten equal annual payments.

[d] Cf. Table 30. The figure represents the sum which the head of the family would have to pay if he had no dependent children.

[e] Heads of families with 4 or more children receive a 30 per cent reduction of income tax. As in note d, the figures in this column represent the sum which would be due if there were no dependent children.

tax was designed as a levy on the new class of property-holders (so-called nepmen) which emerged as a result of the denationalization.[11] The taxes on both income and property were mildly progressive, with rates extending from .8 per cent to 15 per cent of taxable income, and from .33 per cent to 1.5 per cent of the value of the property. These rates, particularly the property tax rates, are not high by present-day standards in Western countries.

In 1924 the property tax provisions were eliminated, on the grounds that since denationalization of small enterprises had been completed, this type of tax was no longer needed.[12] The remaining income tax provisions were revised to introduce into Soviet taxation for the first time the principle of class discrimination.[13] Payers of tax on income below a certain level were divided into four categories: employed workers; self-employed persons; those receiving income from enterprises, rent, securities, and other income classified by the Soviets as unearned or nonlabor income; and juridical persons such as joint-stock companies. Each of these four groups was divided into subgroups on the basis of the amount of taxable income and five zonal distinctions; a different rate of tax applied to each subgroup. However, all taxpayers whose annual income was above a given minimum were subject to a single progressive schedule of rates, regardless of the social group to which they belonged.

In 1926 progressive schedules of rates were adopted for each group individually. The schedules were discriminatory, with the workers receiving the most favorable rates and those living on so-called unearned income receiving least favorable treatment. Since this date the formal structure of the income tax has remained essentially unchanged, although rates, social classifications, exemptions, and other details have frequently been revised.

The effect of the discriminatory rate schedules introduced in the 1926 law is evident from the data presented in Table 32. The workers,

TABLE 32 Distribution of Income Tax, 1926–27

	Taxpayers		Taxed income		Taxes paid	
	Number	Per cent of total	Amount (million rubles)	Per cent of total	Amount (million rubles)	Per cent of total
Workers and employees	775,000	49.3	1,200	45.5	13.5	10.0
Self-employed workers	418,000	26.5	500	19.0	18.0	13.2
Unearned income	380,000	24.2	930	35.5	105.0	76.8

For source, see Appendix.

comprising roughly half of the taxpayers and receiving half the taxable income, paid only 10 per cent of the total income tax. Persons with so-called unearned income comprised only 25 per cent of the taxpayers, but they earned 35 per cent of taxable income, and paid three-quarters of the income tax.[11]

Rate revisions made in the late twenties discriminated still more in favor of workers and against other economic and social groups, and also improved the position of the lower-income classes in all social groups. These developments are illustrated in Table 33.

TABLE 33 Tax Payments as Percentage of Income, 1923–1930

Monthly income (rubles)	Workers, coöperative artisans			Noncoöperative artisans, independent income			Entrepreneurs, unearned income		
	1923	1927	1930	1923	1927	1930	1923	1927	1930
200	1.56	1.43	1.44	5.52	7.06	7.06	5.52	13.32	14.1
1000	14.20	11.00	11.07	14.20	24.80	31.60	14.20	57.00	61.2
3000	24.30	27.20	27.20	26.04	41.50	57.30	26.04	94.60[a]	100.0

For source, see Appendix.
[a] Rate of tax on 2500 rubles income.

Only minor changes were made in the income tax during the 1930's. Budget receipts from the tax increased, owing to the continually rising level of wages, but the percentage share of income-tax receipts in total budget receipts remained remarkably constant throughout this period, as is shown by the figures in Table 34.

TABLE 34 Receipts from the Income Tax, 1931–1940

Year	Millions of rubles	Per cent of total budget receipts	Year	Millions of rubles	Per cent of total budget receipts
1931	329	1.3	1936	1,205	1.3
1932	533	1.4	1937	1,496	1.4
1933	631	1.4	1938	1,952	1.5
1934	773	1.3	1939	2,537	1.6
1935	875	1.2	1940	3,677	2.0

For source, see Appendix.

The most important development in direct taxation of the urban population during the thirties was the introduction in 1931 of the so-called *kul'tzhilsbor*, a tax earmarked for cultural and housing expenditures.[15] It closely resembled the income tax in its differential class schedules and exemptions, and claimed almost as much from the average taxpayer. In 1943 the two taxes were sensibly combined to reduce costs of administration.

Soviet entry into World War II enormously increased the state's financial requirements while simultaneously reducing receipts from the major source of budget income, the turnover tax (levied chiefly on consumers' goods). Direct taxation of the population accordingly assumed a new significance. Ten days after the German invasion the rates of the agricultural and income taxes went up by 50 to 100 per cent for most taxpayers. Receipts from the income tax probably rose by at least 50 per cent as a result.[16]

Receipts were further increased by the introduction, in November 1941, of the tax on bachelors, childless couples, and small families already discussed. The receipts from this tax during the war years were as follows: 1941, 123 million rubles; 1942, 1,092 million; 1943, 1,266 million; 1944, 2,231 million; and 1945, 3,373 million.

The most important innovation in direct taxation was the war tax (*voennyi nalog*), which was in effect from January 1, 1942 through 1945. It was levied on all men from 18 to 60, and on all women from 18 to 55 years of age. Military personnel and their families were exempt; civilians eligible for military service were taxed at rates 50 per cent above the nominal rates. With small deviations, the tax was proportional up to an income of 2,000 rubles a month; persons with incomes over this amount paid the flat rate of 225 rubles per month. A regressive feature of the tax was the absence of a nontaxable minimum income; all persons with incomes up to 150 rubles a month paid a 10 ruble tax. With the exception of the first and last income brackets, the tax amounted to roughly 10 per cent of income. Some persons in the lowest income bracket paid the highest rate of tax, while some in the highest bracket paid the lowest rate of tax.

The war tax was second only to the turnover tax as a source of revenue during the war years; it brought in 72.1 billion rubles, or well over half of the receipts from direct taxation of the population from 1942 to 1945.[17]

In the postwar period, the share of all direct taxes in budget income has increased a few percentage points in comparison with the 1930's.[18] Unfortunately, no distribution of this total has been made available since 1945. It is, however, evident that the income tax is taking a larger percentage of most wage earners' incomes than it did in the prewar period. This can be demonstrated by calculating the rate of tax for various levels of wages, using the average wage for each year as a norm (Table 35). From these calculations it appears that the rate of income tax on the average worker has increased steadily and substantially since 1930.

The trend is different, however, for other groups in the population, particularly those in the higher income brackets. Nonworkers

TABLE 35 Income Tax on Monthly Wages and Salaries for Selected Years

	One-half average wage			Average wage			Double average wage		
Year	Amount (rubles)	Tax (rubles)	Rate of tax (per cent)	Amount (rubles)	Tax (rubles)	Rate of tax (per cent)	Amount (rubles)	Tax (rubles)	Rate of tax (per cent)
1930	45	0.34	0.75	90	0.72	0.8	180	2.4	1.3
1934	75	0.60	0.8	150	1.6	1.1	300	6.2	2.1
1940	175	2.25	1.3	350	8.5	2.4	700	24.15	3.5
1947	300	11.00	2.7	600	36.0	6.0	1200	108.0	9.0

For sources, see Appendix.

receiving an income equal to four times the average wage paid at the averages rates indicated in Table 36. From 1930 to 1940 these rates followed the trend in rates on the average worker. Since 1940, however, rates for the higher-income, non-wage-earning elements in the population have declined.

TABLE 36 Estimated Average Rates of Income Tax on Nonworkers with Large Incomes [a] (per cent)

	1930	1940	1947
Artists and writers	2.5	17.2	11.5
Persons with unearned incomes or employing other persons	18.3	50.4	31.3

For sources, see Appendix.
[a] Large income is defined as an income which is four times the average wage.

DIRECT TAXATION OF THE AGRICULTURAL POPULATION

The Agricultural Tax (*sel'skokhoziaistvennyi nalog*) is a money tax paid by individual Soviet peasants.[19] It is the counterpart of the income tax on the urban population; like the income tax, it is not a very important source of budget revenue, the principal levy on the peasant population being the obligatory delivery or tax in kind discussed in the preceding chapter. It has, however, important nonrevenue functions. Because it is a tax on the income which the peasant is presumed to receive from his private plot, it can be utilized as a powerful stimulant or deterrent to production in the private sector.

The agricultural tax resembles the income tax in the way it discriminates among social and economic classes; in the early Soviet period, the poor and middle-income peasants were taxed at lower rates than the richer peasants or kulaks; at present, the collective farmer pays at a lower rate than the private farmer.

The basic unit of taxation under the agricultural tax is the family, rather than the individual as with the income tax. This is explained by differences in conditions of employment between urban and rural areas: in the cities, each working member of a family is hired individually and his work is not necessarily related to that of any other member of his family; in the country, the family, as a unit, operates its own small private farm.

The agricultural tax is levied on all persons who earn their living from agricultural pursuits (including animal husbandry, beekeeping, etc.). These persons are divided into two categories: those who work on collective farms (the collective farmers) and those who spend all of their time cultivating personal plots of land (the private farmers). Each household is taxed on the income from cultivating its personal plot of land and from owning animals. The collective farmers are favored by the tax law in two respects: (1) they do not have to pay a tax on income earned working on the collective farm and (2) the private farmer must pay a 100 per cent higher tax rate than the collective farmer on all income earned.

Exemptions may be divided into two categories: (1) those designed to protect weaker groups in the population and (2) those designed to encourage various economic activities. The first group includes: families with only one working adult per three or more children (these receive a 15 per cent markdown); households which have suffered from a natural disaster such as a tornado, drought, etc.; invalids; wives of military personnel; men over 60 and women over 55 years of age with no family to help support them. The second group includes persons cultivating personal plots who work underground in coal mines, prospect for rare metals, settle in frontier areas or live in border regions of the USSR, are agricultural technicians, etc.

In recent years two quite different methods have been employed to compute tax liability. Under the tax law which was in effect from 1939 to 1952,[20] an unusual method was used to estimate taxable income. Instead of attempting to find out the actual income of the peasants, each of the peasants' income-earning activities (sowing a hectare of wheat, raising a pig, etc.) was valued according to so-called norms of income which had been worked out for different regions. Total income was estimated by adding up the income from the individual activities as valued by the norms. Norms were set by the republic for each crop and each type of animal. The republican authorities were allowed to vary the norms by 30 per cent, up or down, for differences in productivity, prices, etc. between regions (*oblasti*). The regional authorities had the power to vary their norms by another 30 per cent to allow for differences between counties (*raiony*). A sample of norms for the Russian Federated Republic is presented in Table 37. Once taxable income had been estimated by the use of norms, the scale of rates listed in Table 38 was applied

TABLE 37 Norms of Income for the RSFSR, 1952 (rubles)

Income per 0.01 hectare sown or planted		Income per head of livestock	
Grain	45	Cows	2540
Potatoes	64	Sheep and goats	180
Vegetables, etc.	140	Pigs	800
Orchards	160	Horses and mules	2500
Vineyards	180	Oxen	1500
Hay	8		

For source, see Appendix.

TABLE 38 Agricultural Tax Rates, 1952

Estimated annual income (rubles)	Amount of tax
Under 2000	12 per cent
2000–3000	240 rubles + 14 per cent on income over 2000 rubles
3000–4000	380 rubles + 18 per cent on income over 3000 rubles
4000–5000	560 rubles + 26 per cent on income over 4000 rubles
5000–6000	820 rubles + 33 per cent on income over 5000 rubles
6000–7000	1150 rubles + 40 per cent on income over 6000 rubles
Over 8000	1950 rubles + 48 per cent on income over 8000 rubles

For source, see Appendix.

to estimate the tax liability of collective farmers. As mentioned earlier, the schedule of rates applicable to private farmers was (and is) 100 per cent higher. Collective farm households whose able-bodied members do not all work on the collective farms paid the tax on a 50 per cent (75 per cent since 1953) higher income than that computed from the norms.

Under the new law, which has been in effect since July 1, 1953,[21] tax liability is estimated much more simply. Payment is based directly on the amount of cultivable land in use by the farmer regardless of how the land is used or of the extent of livestock holdings. The intermediate step of first computing income is eliminated. Rates are differentiated, however, as with the previous law, by republic and region, for type of crop typical of the region, differential fertility, availability of markets, availability of irrigation, etc. For example, the average rate of taxation for the Russian Federated Republic is 8.5 rubles per hundredth of a hectare, with minimum and maximum rates of 3 and 14 rubles respectively; for Western Ukraine the corresponding rates are 4, 2, and 6 rubles respectively; in Uzbek, those using irrigated land pay 22 rubles while those using non-irrigated land pay 8 rubles.

Formally speaking, the tax in effect from 1939 to 1952 may be classified as a produce tax while the present tax is very much akin to a property tax. (It would be a property tax if liability were based on land owned rather than land in use. The distinction is probably not very important among Soviet peasants, however, since they are known to cultivate their private plots very intensively.) Historically speaking, the property tax was prior to the produce tax and was superseded by it in various European countries in the seventeenth, eighteenth, and nineteenth centuries.[22] The produce tax is more equitable than the property tax: a tax based on the output of property is more closely related to "ability to pay" than a tax based on property held (or in use) without regard to whether the property is capable of being used to produce goods or services with which to pay the tax. The use of a progressive rate schedule with the Soviet produce tax of 1939–1952 and its absence in the present agricultural tax (which taxes on a roughly proportional basis) further widens the gap between the two taxes from an equity standpoint. On the other hand, the produce tax is less equitable than the income tax, since norms of income provide only a rough measure of the actual income of a taxpayer. The extensive power of Soviet local authorities to differentiate the income (1939–1952) and tax norms (1953) undoubtedly prevents some of the inequities which would otherwise result from the use of norms. It seems impossible, however, to avoid over-taxation of some households and undertaxation of others, for, in practice, norms can hardly be differentiated sufficiently to allow for the variability of conditions which is likely to exist in areas as large as Soviet counties.

The use of norms greatly simplifies money taxation of the peasants, and this is the principal reason for their use. Taxation of the peasants is relatively costly to administer even with the use of norms since the taxes must be estimated for and collected from each household on an individual basis. The agricultural tax has too little fiscal significance to warrant the extra cost which would be incurred if the tax were to be based on actual income rather than on norms.

Brief History of Direct Money Taxation of the Agricultural Population. The agricultural taxes of May 10, 1923 and April 30, 1924 were the forerunners of the present agricultural tax as well as of the income tax on the collective farms.[23] These taxes were very significant in their time for two reasons. First, all previous taxes on the agricultural sector had been collected in kind. The law of 1923 instituted partial payment in money; the law of 1924 completed the changeover to money taxation. Second, these taxes replaced a large number of smaller individual levies on the agricultural sector, thereby considerably simplifying agricultural taxation.

Although resembling the agricultural tax in effect from 1939 to 1952 in many respects, the taxes of 1923 and 1924 were constructed much more crudely. For example, only three income categories were used for the purpose of applying the progressive-rate principle; the income norms were based on ownership of arable land rather than on the amount of land to be cultivated, the former being much simpler to administer; all calculations were made in terms of one *desiatina* (2.7 acres) of arable land rather than in terms of money. The tax underwent substantial structural changes during the late 1920's, as tax administration improved,[24] and by 1928 very closely resembled the 1939–1952 tax.

The outstanding trend in agricultural taxation in the twenties was the growing tendency to favor the poor (*bedniaki, malomoshchnye*) as opposed to the middle peasants (*seredniaki*) and, in particular, the kulaks.

Under the 1923 law, exemptions from taxation were granted only for reasons relating to military service. This freed no more than

500,000 households or about 2 per cent of all households subject to taxation in 1923–24.[25] In 1924–25 exemptions were extended to an additional 4 million or almost 20 per cent of all households.[26] The trend continued and by 1925–26, 6 million or 25 per cent of all households were exempt from taxation. As might have been expected, receipts from the tax on peasant households declined from 346 million rubles in 1924–25 to 250 million rubles in 1925–26, whereas their money income rose from 3.3 billion to 4.3 billion rubles.[27]

In November 1927, on the tenth anniversary of the Revolution, a manifesto to all workers, peasants, and the Red Army was published.[28] Among other things, the manifesto exempted from the agricultural tax an additional 10 per cent of peasant households. This brought total exemptions up to 35 per cent.[29] The significance placed on this event by the Soviets may be appreciated by quoting Reingold:

> For 1928–1929 the law provided for a complete exemption of 35 per cent, or 8.5 million households. Obviously we are approaching complete exemption of the lower stratum of the rural population from the agricultural tax.
>
> It is hardly possible to find in the whole history of taxation another instance of such a clear-cut application of the class principle.[30]

Although the class policy of the Soviet Union may have been vigorous in this period, it is only fair to point out that, from the point of view of the tax structure as a whole, the incidence on the poorer peasant did not decline as drastically as Reingold's statement implies. By 1928–29 the agricultural tax provided less than 10 per cent of all tax revenue. The state was relying primarily on the craft and excise taxes in this period (Table 12); both of these were paid in the last analysis by the consumer, including the poor peasant.

Not only were the poorer peasants exempted en masse from payment of the agricultural tax; taxes on the middle peasants and kulaks were increased by from 5 to 25 per cent in 1928. A special schedule of rates, much higher than those for other peasants, was applied in 1930 to the kulaks.[31] As a result of discriminatory tax treatment and of income differentials between peasant classes, the private farmer paid 10 times as much tax per household as the collective farmer, and the kulak paid 10 times as much as the private farmer (see Table 39).

TABLE 39 Agricultural Taxation, 1931

Class	Tax paid	Average per household	
Collective farmer	37 million rubles	2 rubles	94 kopeks
Private farmer	300	30	80
Kulak	69	313	64

For source, see Appendix.

In 1931, the agricultural-tax law distinguished for the first time between collective and private farmers. The kulak continued to be treated as a separate and more discriminated-against category. The collective farmer was freed from taxes on income earned on the collective farm, but continued to pay a tax on private or so-called "nonsocialized" earnings. This was simply one facet of the intensive collectivization drive begun in 1930, and was designed to encourage peasants to join the collective farms. Gross income of the collective farm was, of course, taxed (see below).

In 1933 the progressive tax on the collective farmer based on income norms was replaced by a poll tax which varied from 15 to 30 rubles per household, depending on locality.[32] This appears to have been levied by the Soviets in full knowledge of its favorable incentive effects. According to Suchkov,[33] this form of tax was designed to encourage cultivation by collective farmers of vegetables, fruit trees, and so forth on their personal plots of land, as well as to encourage the development of individual animal husbandry. Aside from incentives, however, the tax may have involved an increase in the tax rate for the average collective farmer, who in 1931, for example, paid a tax of only 2 rubles 94 kopeks.[34]

The poll tax remained in force until 1939, although the amounts of tax were increased from time to time. In 1939, it was revoked, and the method of levy which had been in use until 1932 was reintroduced. The original purpose of the poll tax had been to encourage the collective farmer to cultivate his personal plot of land; the purpose of the reversion to progressive taxation was the opposite: to divert peasant labor away from private economic activity and to encourage a larger expenditure of labor time on the collective. Soviet writers claim that the old law was appropriate while the collective farms were weak and could not adequately support their members.

Now, it is asserted, the collective farms have matured and their further development depends, to a large extent, on their ability to command the labor time of their members. Furthermore, it was stated, the interests of the members now lie with the collectives because of their superior mechanization. Therefore, the old tax, which encouraged the development of nonsocialized activities, was out of step with the new needs; as Aleksandrov puts it: "The old tax under new conditions did not assure a correct union of the personal and public interests of the collective farmers." [35]

Jasny has estimated that, in 1937, 80 per cent of the money income of the collective farmers derived from their personal plots of land and only 20 per cent from the collective farms.[36] Suchkov presents figures which show the extent of private economic activity and the immediate restrictive effect of the new agricultural tax law on private agricultural enterprise (Table 40). The data indicate that in-

TABLE 40 Distribution of Collective Farm Households by Income from Private Economic Activity, 1939, 1940

Income from personal cultivation (rubles)	Percentage of households	
	1939	1940
Under 700	21.8	29.1
700–1000	19.8	23.0
1000–2000	51.2	44.7
2000–3000	6.3	2.8
3000–4000	0.7	0.3
Over 4000	0.2	0.1

For source, see Appendix.

come earned from private economic activity declined moderately. The decline cannot be attributed entirely to the new tax law, however, since other measures were taken by the Soviets to "coax" the collective farmers into devoting more time to the collective. In 1938, a new law on the distribution of collective farm money income increased the members' share of the surplus from about 50 per cent to 80 per cent.[37] In May 1939, private plots of land were limited to from 0.25 to 1.0 hectare of land per household (depending on the region), and each member of a collective farm was required to work on the farm for a minimum of 60 to 100 days a year (depending on region and type of farm).[38] There is no way of assessing the relative importance of these measures and of the agricultural tax in limiting the private economic activity of the collective farmers.

As we have already noted, the agricultural tax of 1939 reintroduced taxation according to income norms and progressive rates. The new norms were very much larger than those which had previously been in effect, as the sample contained in Table 41 indicates. Soviet

TABLE 41 Selected Income Norms under the Agricultural Tax, 1931, 1937, 1939 (rubles) *

	RSFSR			Ukraine			Uzbek		
	1931	1937	1939	1931	1937	1939	1931	1937	1939
Grain (per hectare)	46	80	540	59	80	540		140	540
Hay (per hectare)	18	28	300	30	40	400			300
Vegetables (per hectare)	210	675	2,500	230	590	2,500	210	525	3,700
Horses (per head)	22	120	500	29	140	500	17	90	400
Cows (per head)	20	105	600	24	105	600	18	80	400

For sources, see Appendix.

* The norms for 1931 and 1937 applied to the private farmers only, since the collective farmers were subject to a poll tax. The rates for collective farmers in 1930, however, were almost identical with the above-listed rates for 1931.

The norms for 1952 differ little from those for 1939 (cf. Table 37 above).

economists claim that norms were raised to correspond more closely to the actual value of agricultural output; nowhere do they comment, however, on the extraordinary degree of the increase. The value of agricultural products was, it is true, increasing in this period. But sources of peasant money income were not keeping pace with inflation. Obligatory delivery prices rose only slightly in the thirties (Chapter 7) and prices on the collective farm markets, though they skyrocketed in 1931 and 1932, declined steadily from 1932 to 1937 (Chapter 2). The peasants probably were receiving an increasing share of their total income in the form of money in 1939 and this may be one reason for the increase in norms. The norms may also have been overvalued as a device for raising the effective rate of taxation. The ratio of taxes paid to taxable income was considerably higher for the peasants in 1939 than in 1931.

There were very few changes between 1931 and 1939 in taxation of the private farmers and kulaks. Income norms increased gradually from 1931 to 1935, remained steady from 1935 to 1938, and then increased sharply in 1939 (see Table 41). The schedule of tax rates paid by the private farmer changed in minor details only from 1930 to 1935. Before 1935, incomes over 700 rubles were taxed at a flat rate of between 30 and 35 per cent; the 1935 law superimposed upon this a schedule of progressive rates rising as high as 55 per cent on incomes above 3,000 rubles.[39] Taxation of the kulaks remained relatively unchanged from 1930 to 1936. The year 1936 was the last in which kulaks were treated as a special class; in subsequent years they were taxed on the same basis as the private farmers.

In 1932, two new taxes were levied on the agricultural population, the so-called *kul'tzhilsbor* and the *samooblozhenie* (self-taxation). The kul'tzhilsbor on the rural population was the counterpart of the tax by the same name levied on the city population for the first time in 1931; after 1933, the two laws were usually published simultaneously. Like the urban kul'tzhilsbor, the rural kul'tzhilsbor was earmarked to finance cultural and housing projects. Although legally independent, the kul'tzhilsbor was calculated as a markup on the agricultural tax, i.e., its rates were applied to the same tax base as the agricultural tax. Revenue from the rural kul'tzhilsbor was of the same order of magnitude as that from the agricultural tax.

The samooblozhenie is a local tax levied upon themselves by citizens of rural communities to meet collective needs in such things as construction and repair of schools, roads, bridges, village baths, hospitals, etc. The receipts from this tax do not enter the regular budget but are kept apart and used for purposes, designated at town meetings, over and above those financed by regular budgetary funds; the tax has not appeared in the budget since 1935. The samooblozhenie is constructed like the kul'tzhilsbor but with somewhat lower rates. According to the Soviets, the samooblozhenie is a voluntary collection. Hubbard states, however, that "in practice the sums to be subscribed are fixed by the local party committee and the kolkhozniki have no choice but to vote in favour of the resolution." [40]

In addition to these taxes, the private farmers and kulaks had to pay a special levy in 1932 entitled "one-time tax on the private farmer household." [41] For the private farmer, the tax was from 100 to 175 per cent of the agricultural tax; for the kulak, it was twice as large as the agricultural tax. The "one-time tax" was repeated in 1934,[42] but never resurrected thereafter.

In August 1938 a tax was levied on private farmers who owned horses over three years of age.[43] In 1938, roughly one out of three private rural households owned a horse.[44] Private owners of horses were able to earn large "speculative" incomes, according to Soviet economists, because, although an important source of power and transportation in rural areas, horses were extremely scarce as a result of the slaughter which accompanied collectivization in the early thirties. Apparently the Soviets felt that the agricultural tax with its income norms was appropriate for taxing ordinary income from the use of horses such as cultivating personal plots of land and carrying wares to the market but not for the "speculative" gains from renting out horses. The tax varied from 275 to 500 rubles (depending on the region) on the ownership of one horse, and from 450 to 800 rubles on every additional horse. The number of privately owned horses declined from 355,000 in 1938 to 224,000 in 1939 and to 90,000 in 1940,[45] indicating that the tax had succeeded in reducing or eliminating the profit from horse ownership. The collective farms, for the most part, fell heir to the horses given up by the private farmers; and many of the private farmers themselves joined the collectives once they had been deprived of this important source of private income. These political overtones of the horse tax were undoubtedly important reasons for imposing it.

There were no changes in the basic structure of the agricultural tax from 1939 until 1952. Both rates and income norms were increased during the war, however. Preparations for war, and the advent of war in 1941, caused prices in the collective farm markets to skyrocket. This development led to a large increase in the actual income of the peasants relative to their income as estimated by norms. In 1943, the state reacted to this by increasing the norms by 3.7 times, on the average, and by increasing the progressivity of the tax schedule.[46]

Other developments in agricultural taxation paralleled those on the urban population. The tax on bachelors and small families and the subsidies to mothers of many children apply to the agricultural, as well as to the urban, populations.[47] Similarly, the war tax was levied on the peasants at the same time as on the workers. Each peasant household had to pay from 150 to 600 rubles *per person*, the amount depending on the republic.[48] The significance of this levy can be appreciated when it is compared with the prewar (1941) average tax *per peasant household* of 141 rubles.[49]

Although direct taxes on the agricultural population increased substantially during the war, they did not and could not keep pace with the increase in peasant incomes. It was administratively impossible under wartime conditions to levy and collect a tax designed to siphon off the speculative earnings of the peasants from sales on the collective farm market.[50]

At the end of the war, the peasants held huge hoards of cash. Most of the income earned in the Soviet Union during the war eventually found its way into the collective farm markets in search of food; a substantial part of this cash probably did not return to the state but remained in peasants' hoards. The Currency Reform of 1947 was directed primarily at reducing peasants' cash holdings to a noninflationary level; cash currency was converted at a rate of ten old rubles for each new ruble (Chapter 9).

The high cash-conversion ratio is an indicator of the failure of the tax system to keep peasant money incomes in line with the supply of consumers' goods during the war.

The agricultural tax of July 1, 1953[51] completes a second cycle in the history of the tax. From 1924 to 1932 income norms were used, based on the quantity of land privately held to which progressive tax rates were applied. This system was altered in 1933 to a poll tax, the ostensible purpose of which was to encourage peasant cultivation of private plots. The second cycle begins in 1939 with the reintroduction of income norms, based this time on sown area, and progressive rates and designed to discourage cultivation of private plots. The cycle is completed in July 1953 with the introduction of a tax the purpose of which, once again, is to encourage cultivation by collective farmers of their private plots. As we have seen, the new tax is essentially a property tax; payment is based on the amount of cultivable land in use regardless of how the land is used or of the extent of livestock holdings. Rates are differentiated by republic and region for type of crop typical of the region, fertility, and so forth.

Under this form of tax the peasant has an incentive to cultivate as much of his land as he can, to cultivate the more expensive (profitable) crops, and to increase his livestock holdings. Under the previous law, these activities were discouraged by high income norms on expensive crops and on livestock, and by progressive tax rates. In addition to increasing incentives to work private plots, the new tax is designed also to reduce the tax burden on the peasants. In this respect it is one of the many measures, now well known, introduced in 1953 to ameliorate the lot of the peasant farmer. In his 1953 budget speech, Zverev predicted that, in comparison with 1952, receipts from the agricultural tax would decline by 43 per cent (i.e., by 4.137 billion rubles) in 1953 and by 250 per cent in 1954.[52] Finally, the relatively simple form of the new tax is expected to result in a substantial reduction in cost of administration. For reasons mentioned earlier, the agricultural tax is particularly difficult to assess and collect and savings in this sphere may be not inconsequential.

Fiscal Importance of Agricultural Taxation. Money taxation of the agricultural population is relatively unimportant in the state budget and in recent years probably has not accounted for more than 2 per cent of total revenue. This is the result of two factors: the dominance of commodity taxation in the Soviet budget, and the tax in kind paid by the agricultural sector.

The situation was different in the 1920's, however, as Table 42 indicates. In 1922–23, the agricultural tax was the largest single tax, constituting 12 per cent of total budget revenue and 37 per cent of tax revenue.[53] From 1923–24 to 1926–27, the agricultural tax was second only to the excise tax as a source of tax revenue, although its relative importance in the budget had declined by about one-half. It continued to decline in importance as the state placed increasing reliance on commodity taxation for its revenue;[54] during the 1930's it accounted for less than 1 per cent of total budget receipts. Total direct taxation of the peasants continued at a somewhat higher level, however, owing to the introduction of the kul'tzhilsbor, samooblozhenie, and "one-time" tax. In 1939 and 1940, agricultural taxation increased sharply owing to the substitution of a progressive tax on the collective farmers for the poll tax. For the decade 1941–1951, separate figures for direct taxation of the agricultural population were not available. From Zverev's 1953 budget speech it can be estimated that the agricultural tax amounted to about 2 per cent of budget receipts in 1952 and is expected to decline to about 1 per cent in 1953 and to substantially less than this in 1954.[55]

TABLE 42 Direct Money Taxation of the Agricultural Population (billions of rubles)

	1922–23	1923–24	1924–25	1925–26	1926–27	1927–28	1928–29	1929–30
Total budget receipts	1.460	2.318	3.002	4.006	5.234	6.545	8.830	13.879
Total tax receipts	0.475	0.785	1.328	1.791	2.483	2.957		
Agricultural tax	0.177	0.231	0.326	0.252	0.358	0.354	0.449	0.406

	1931	1932	1933	1934	1935	1936	1937	1938	1939	1940
Total budget receipts	25.2	38.0	46.3	58.4	75.0	94.4	109.3	127.5	156.0	180.2
Agricultural tax	0.381	0.337	0.548	0.564	0.737	0.628	0.509	0.665	1.515	2.095
Kul'tzhilsbor	0.245	0.470	0.685	0.703	0.614	0.608	0.413	0.750	0.950	1.150
One-time tax on private peasant	0.166	0.170	0.331							
Tax on horses owned by private peasant								0.110	0.088	0.054
Samooblozhenie		—	0.504	0.448	—	—	—	—	—	—

For sources, see Appendix.
Dashes indicate that figures are not available.

Budget figures from 1922–23 to 1927–28 are incomparable with the later figures in two respects: (1) they do not include local budget receipts; (2) they include the gross receipts of state enterprises, especially transportation and communication. It should also be noted that the agricultural tax includes receipts from the collective farms up to 1927–28 — but these are negligible.

SALES OF GOVERNMENT BONDS

Economic Characteristics of Soviet Bonds. It is ordinarily possible to draw a sharp distinction between taxation of the population and the sale of government bonds to the public. The important differences are as follows:

(i) Taxes are compulsory upon all citizens with incomes falling within prescribed limits; purchase of bonds is voluntary.

(ii) Taxes immediately and permanently reduce the net worth of the taxpayer and increase the net worth of the government. When bonds are purchased the net worth of neither the bondholder nor the government changes. Furthermore, bonds can usually be cashed in with little or no loss to the bondholder.

(iii) Sale of bonds does not have a permanent place along with taxes in the budgetary receipts of most nations. Bonds are sold only when it is considered undesirable for one reason or another to finance additional expenditures from taxation; when receipts exceed expenditures, as is often the case, the amount of government debt outstanding is actually reduced.

Exceptions could be adduced; for example, the social pressure brought to bear upon United States citizens to buy bonds during World War II perhaps took these bonds out of the category of purely voluntary purchases. In normal times, however, the distinctions noted have generally been valid. The first two imply the superiority of taxation over bonds as an instrument of anti-inflationary policy: (*a*) taxes can be depended upon to secure the funds required and (*b*) taxes once and for all reduce consumer disposable income.

Bonds sold by the Soviet government have characteristics which make them more akin to taxes than to the bonds sold by most Western nations. Very strong social pressures are brought to bear on the population to purchase bonds. Apparently everyone is expected to allocate from two to four weeks' salary per year for this purpose.[56] The bonds are usually paid for by deductions from wages, as is the case with the income tax; such a payment procedure makes it much simpler to exert compulsion upon recalcitrant workers. It is difficult to believe that a people with as low a standard of living as the Soviet population would *voluntarily* spend so large a percentage of its disposable income on government bonds, especially since constantly rising prices (up to 1948) have made Soviet bonds such an obviously bad investment.

Another fact which makes one doubt the "voluntary" character of Soviet loans is that receipts from the loans, like receipts from direct taxation, are a fairly constant percentage of total budget receipts each year. This is because the Soviets issue the appropriate amount of bonds each year, and the population always subscribes, or oversubscribes, the issue. This is in contrast to bond sales in other countries, which fluctuate sharply as a percentage of total receipts. The Soviets look upon bond sales as a regular source of revenue, on a par in this respect with taxes.

It is significant that most of the bonds held by the population cannot be cashed before maturity. It is also significant that the maturity dates of bonds have been extended and the nominal interest rates lowered without the consent of the bondholders; these so-called conversions occurred in 1930, 1936, 1938, and 1947. Furthermore, the 1947 conversion, which was part of the general currency reform, also reduced the value of each person's bond holdings by two-thirds. To date, then, the Soviet citizen has had little reason to prefer being a bondholder over being a taxpayer.

The bulk of the Soviet debt outstanding is held by the population; the remainder (less than 25 per cent) is bought from the excess reserves of savings banks, state insurance organizations, trade unions, and coöperatives. The savings banks are the largest of the institutional investors, and their funds, of course, belong to the population. Therefore when the Soviets sell bonds, almost the entire amount of the sale has an anti-inflationary effect since it deprives the population of disposable income. In this sense, it again resembles a tax. Government borrowing in the United States (and other Western nations) is more often than not from banks and government agencies rather than from the population. In the United States, for example, only about 25 per cent of the federal debt is held by the population as individuals. When the government sells bonds to the banks, the results are usually inflationary rather than deflationary.

In summary, the sale of Soviet government bonds is more appropriately classified as a tax than as a noncompulsory bond sale, though it actually falls somewhere between the two classifications. Individuals are compelled to buy bonds under conditions (rising prices, high relative marginal utility of goods) which would make such a purchase, if voluntary, an irrational economic act. To the extent that the bondholder ends up with a lower net worth after his bond has been redeemed than he would have had if he had been free to dispose of his income as he pleased, he has been, in effect, taxed.[57] The tax element is increased by the conversions mentioned above, and by the fact that the bonds, with minor exceptions, are relatively inconvertible assets. For these same reasons, bond sales by the Soviets have an anti-inflationary effect very much like taxes. Finally, the Soviets treat receipts from bond sales as a stable and regular source of budgetary income — much as they treat taxes.

Description of Soviet Loans. Two types of bonds are sold to the population. The most important of these are the so-called "mass-subscription" loans. These are purchased on an installment basis, the payments taking the form of automatic deductions from the worker's wages at his place of work. With certain exceptions, these bonds cannot be cashed until maturity. For a brief period (1937–1941) it was possible without special permission to use them as security for short-term loans amounting to 30 per cent of their face value; before March 1937, special permission was required. An interest charge of 0.5 per cent a month was levied for the first 6 months, and 1 per cent a month thereafter if the loan was not repaid. The provision was revoked during the war and never reinstituted.

Much less important are the bonds purchased for cash. These are made available at savings banks and can be bought by the population at any time. They do not have to be held to maturity like the mass-subscription loans, but can be cashed.

All bonds pay interest; the present rates are 4 per cent on mass-subscription loans and 3 per cent on cash-purchase loans. Interest payments are made either by the traditional method of annual payments to each bondholder equal to the stated per cent of the value of the bond, or by payments in the form of lottery prizes. The latter method is more common. Lottery winners have their bonds redeemed at the same time they receive their prizes.

The mass-loan lotteries have been of two kinds: lotteries in which everyone wins a prize sometime during the life of the bond, and lotteries in which only a part of the bondholders win prizes.

The first type was used extensively during the thirties. The procedure was to take the total interest due on a bond issue each year and divide it up into prizes of various amounts, the winners to be determined by lot. The amount of the prizes each year was equal to one-tenth (on a 10-year bond) or one-twentieth (on a 20-year bond) of the total number of bondholders. After winning a prize, the bondholder was no longer eligible for the lottery, and his bond was redeemed. Over the 10- or 20-year period, every bondholder won one prize, which may have been smaller or larger than the nominal interest on his bond, and also received back the bond's nominal value.

The second type of lottery was used during the war and has been used exclusively in the postwar period. Instead of everyone's winning a prize sometime during the life of the bond, only one-quarter or one-third of the bondholders win prizes; the rest get back only the nominal value of their bond at maturity. Since the total amount of interest payments is distributed among fewer prize winners, the individual winnings are much larger. The change to this type of lottery was probably based on the theory that bondholders preferred a smaller chance of winning a larger prize.

Institutional bondholders purchase only the traditional interest-bearing loans and do not participate in the lotteries.

Interest income from the bonds is exempt from income taxation.[58]

Brief History of the Government Loan Program. From 1922 to 1927 numerous small loans were floated. Three of the earliest were in kind;[59] after 1923, however, all loans were monetary in form. These early loans all had relatively short terms, ranging from several months to 5 years.

The present system of so-called mass loans was instituted in 1927 with the First Industrialization Loan of 200 million rubles. It became the practice thereafter to have one mass loan a year, subscribed to by the population on an installment basis; concomitantly, bonds were sold to institutional purchasers, and small issues were sold to the population on a cash basis. The first few mass loans had 10-year maturities and paid from 11 to 13 per cent interest.[60] The loans increased in size throughout the thirties, keeping step with the growth of the budget and personal money incomes (Table 43).

The first conversion was effected in 1930. The previous four mass loans, with a total value of 1,650 million rubles[61] were converted into a 10-year 10 per cent loan entitled "The Five Year Plan in Four Years." The purposes of this conversion were to simplify servicing

TABLE 43 Major Loans by the Population, 1927–1941 (millions of rubles)[a]

Loan	Date	Planned issue	Actual sales
First Industrialization Loan	1927	200	200
Strengthen the Peasant Economy	1927	150	
Second Industrialization Loan	1928	550	499
Third Industrialization Loan	1929–30	750	829
Five Year Plan in Four Years	1930	800	1,025
Five Year Plan in Four Years	1931	1,600	1,935
Five Year Plan in Four Years	1932	3,200	2,718
Second Five Year Plan	1933	3,000	3,076
Second Five Year Plan	1934	3,500	3,402
Second Five Year Plan	1935	3,500	3,965
Second Five Year Plan	1936	4,000	4,832
Strengthen Defense of USSR	1937	4,000	4,932
Internal Lottery Loan	1937	600	926
Third Five Year Plan	1938	5,000	5,928
Third Five Year Plan	1939	6,000	7,637
Third Five Year Plan	1940	8,000	9,311
Third Five Year Plan	1941	9,500	10,945

For sources, see Appendix.
[a] The pre-1927 loans are listed in note 59 to this chapter.

the loans, to make them more accessible to the public, and to lower the rate of interest.[62]

The first change in terms occurred in the 1935 loan, when the interest rate was lowered from 10 per cent to 8 per cent. In 1936 the terms were changed again, and all previous mass loans were converted to the new terms. The interest rate was reduced to 4 per cent, and all bonds, regardless of their due date, were made payable in 20 years from the date of the conversion. The principal reason for this conversion was to cheapen the cost of the loan service and to extend into the distant future the time when the bonds would be completely paid off. Another objective was to simplify loan administration. At the time of the conversion, according to Aleksandrov, 50 million persons held 850 million obligations,[63] mostly in very small denominations; the number of obligations was reduced to 230 million.[64]

In 1938 all previous loans which had been purchased for cash — this included lottery loans issued in 1929, 1930, 1932, and 1935 — were also converted.[65] The conversion loan was valued at 600 million rubles and was for 20 years at 3 per cent.

A distribution of bond holdings and of the debt service for the late thirties is presented in Table 44.

TABLE 44 Soviet Loans: Debt Outstanding and Repayments, 1938 and 1939 [a]

	January 1, 1938		January 1, 1939	
Purchases				
Population				
Workers and salaried employees	15,992		19,651	
Collective farmers	3,900		4,562	
Others	1,042	20,934	1,620	25,833
Institutions and organizations				
Savings banks	4,653		6,203	
Others	2,958	7,611	3,534	9,737
Total purchases		28,545		35,570
Repayments to Population				
Winnings and interest		3,327		—
Principal		2,086		—
Total repayments to population		5,413		—

For sources, see Appendix.

Dashes indicate that figures are not available.

[a] Total debt-service figures for 1932 to 1953, excluding the war years, are presented on p. 330. Total debt service paid to the population in the whole Soviet period ending in 1950 has been estimated as 27.5 billion rubles (see Plotnikov, *Bol'shevik*, 1950, no. 12, p. 31).

During the war, bond sales increased somewhat, but not as much proportionately as direct taxation of the population. The mass-subscription war loans were all 20-year loans paying 4 per cent interest, and were for the amounts indicated in Table 45. The Soviets also introduced lotteries which paid off partly in money and partly in luxury commodities, such as fur coats, expensive clothes, gold watches, and so forth. Winnings in these one-draw lotteries amounted to 20 per cent of the total subscription; commodity prizes in the first loan amounted to only 5 per cent of total winnings, but this share increased to about 15 per cent in the subsequent three lotteries. The lotteries were valued at 1, 1.5, 2.5, and 5 billion rubles respectively — insignificant amounts from a fiscal point of view.

TABLE 45 Soviet War Loans by the Population (millions of rubles)

Loan	Date	Planned issue (millions of rubles)	Actual purchases			Interest and lottery payments to population (millions of rubles)
			Workers	Peasants	Total	
Third Five Year Plan, fourth year	1941	9,500	8,885	2,060	10,945	890
First War Loan	1942	10,000	9,004	2,998	13,186	531
Second War Loan	1943	12,000	12,898	6,586	20,843	859
Third War Loan	1944	25,000	16,640	10,153	28,963	1,782
Fourth War Loan	1945	25,000	17,549	8,100	26,715	2,612

For sources, see Appendix.

The postwar loan program was ushered in with two 20 billion ruble 20-year loans for "Reconstruction and Development," the 1946 issue paying 4 per cent, the 1947 issue 3 per cent. Then came the Currency Reform of December 1947, with its drastic provisions relating to the outstanding government debt. All previous mass-subscription loans with the exception of the 3 per cent 1947 loan (which remained intact) were converted into a new 2 per cent loan at a ratio of three old bonds for each new bond. The 1938 cash loan was converted to a new loan on the same terms but at the ratio of five old bonds for one new bond.[66]

The conversion sharply reduced the claims of the bondholders on the state. They fared much better, however, than persons holding cash, which cash was exchanged at a ratio of 10 old rubles for each new ruble.[67] This was because the prime objective of the Currency Reform was to wipe out the inflationary potential which had been generated during the war, and in the Soviet economy cash is potentially much more inflationary than the almost inconvertible bonds.[68] Accordingly, the existing stock of cash was converted to new currency at the ratio required to eliminate repressed inflation, given the current levels of prices and output. The conversion ratio for government bonds was based on other considerations, which had less to do with inflation than with longer-run budgetary problems (as in the case of the 1936 conversion). It was politically expedient, however, for the Soviets to have a bond conversion at the same time that a much more drastic conversion of cash was taking place; in fact, it may have been necessary to convert bonds at the same time as cash to prevent the appearance of "undue" discrimination against persons holding cash.[69]

Since the Currency Reform, the Soviets have floated 20 billion ruble 20-year 4 per cent mass-subscription loans to the population in 1948, 1949, and 1950, 30 billion ruble loans with the same terms in 1951 and 1952, and a 15 billion ruble loan in 1953. These were all substantially oversubscribed. It is interesting to note that no attempt was made to maintain the 2 per cent interest rate of the 1947 conversion loan. According to the Soviets, most of the outstanding debt at the time of the Reform had been purchased during the war with depreciated currency. It was argued that since the Reform would make the ruble a full-valued currency again, the value of and interest on the outstanding debt should be reduced. The failure of the Soviets to continue the 2 per cent rate is one indication that this argument was taken seriously.

In the past the debt service has not constituted much of a burden for the budget. Although the nominal rate of interest was very high until 1936 and moderately high thereafter, the real rate of interest was undoubtedly negative, because of the rapidity with which retail prices were rising. In addition, the several loan conversions postponed the day of redemption for the majority of loans. Since the Currency Reform of 1947, however, consumers' goods prices have declined; the real value of the outstanding debt is increasing faster than its nominal value. This is not an immediate problem, but it may pose difficulties in the future if present price trends continue. The debt service, which at present amounts to little more than 1 per cent of total expenditures, is increasing at a faster rate than total government expenditures. If prices continue to decline, debt repayments may become a substantial claim on current output.

By 1967, two-thirds of both the 1947 conversion loan (estimated roughly from data presented above to have amounted to about 50–60 billion rubles) and the 1947 "Reconstruction and Development" loan will come due; the remaining one-third will have been paid off earlier to lottery winners. Redemption of these loans, and of the succession of loans which will come due in the following years, will place a serious strain on the financial apparatus. If the long-run Soviet policy is to continue reduction of consumers'-goods prices, it is not inconceivable that loans to the population will be discontinued as a fiscal instrument, in order to avoid the problems related to a rapidly growing debt. The 50 per cent decline in planned sales to the population from 1952 to 1953, the first time in the history of the Soviet mass-subscription loans that planned sales have not been equal to or greater than those of any preceding year, would seem to be a step in this direction.

INCOME TAX ON THE COLLECTIVE FARMS (KOLKHOZY)

Since 1930 the collective farm has been the dominant form of agricultural organization in the Soviet Union, accounting for the overwhelming bulk of agricultural output. Money taxes on collective farm output have never been very important, however. Because most farms' transactions are in kind, the principal tax on them has been the tax in kind described in Chapter 7; the money tax on collective farm income typically amounted in the prewar period to less than 1 per cent of budget receipts.

Although the income tax on the collective farms is not important fiscally, it is interesting because of the variety of forms in which it has been levied in its brief history. Until 1930 the basic tax liability of collective farms was calculated in the same manner as that of independent peasants. Although the intensive drive for collectivization did not begin until that date, discrimination in favor of the farms began much earlier; in 1925 collective farm tax payments were marked down by 25 per cent, and in 1926 all new collectives were granted tax exemptions for two years after their formation.

In 1930 the Soviets began an all-out effort to collectivize agriculture. The success of this effort is indicated in Table 46. At the same

TABLE 46 Extent of Collectivization of Agriculture, 1928–1932 (per cent)

	1928	1929	1930	1931	1932
Peasant households collectivized	1.7	3.9	23.6	52.7	61.5
Sown area collectivized	1.2	3.6	30.9	63.0	75.7

For source, see Appendix.

time, taxation of the collective farms changed in correspondence with the new policy. A proportional tax of 4 or 5 per cent (depending on the form of organization of the collective farm) [70] was substituted for the progressive tax to which the farms had previously been subject. The low proportional tax was specifically designed to encourage collective farm development.

Another change introduced in 1930 was the substitution of actual income (as derived from a farm's accounts) for norms of estimated income as the basis for computing the tax. The use of accounts clearly represented an advance in taxation technique, and probably provided a much more equitable distribution of the tax burden. Nevertheless, the norm method was reinstituted in 1933.[71]

Soviet writers explained reversion to the more primitive method by the necessities of the national economic plan. It was claimed that statement of the tax in terms of each specific crop presented collectives with a much simpler chart of their obligations in relation to the economic plan of the state, and enabled them to compare *in advance* the relative profitability of producing different types of agricultural output, and thus to maximize their returns.[72]

The second reason implies that the state, by differential taxation, could guide the productive resources of the farms into the desired channels. This was in fact attempted on a large scale in the early 1930's, when a complex system of exemptions and differentials was employed to encourage certain types of cultivation. For example, exemptions in full or in part were granted on income from products of animal husbandry, industrial crops such as cotton, flax, hemp, etc., and from specialized branches of agriculture such as beekeeping.

The tax on the collective farm remained relatively unchanged until 1936. In this year the Soviets returned to taxing the gross monetary income of farms, and norms were abolished. The reasons for the change in method of levy were set forth in the text of the new decree as follows:

The present system of taxing collective farms under the agricultural tax is based on rates per hectare of crop in the plan of sowing of the current year, the bulk of the tax being collected from income of grain products, with income from industrial crops and animal husbandry almost free of tax. This system, which is pointed against the grain economy, has become unjust, and must be changed in recognition of the growth of income from industrial crops and animal husbandry. The growth of income of collective farms from industrial crops, animal husbandry, vegetables, and crafts makes it possible at this time to lower taxation of income from grains, and the strengthening of collective farms into large agricultural enterprises makes it possible to substitute for the outmoded agricultural tax on the collective farm a more just system of taxation — the income tax.[73]

The data indicate that tax discrimination against grain-producing collectives was indeed severe. In 1935, for example, grain-producing collectives paid 64 per cent of the tax on collective farms, though they accounted for only 40 per cent of total taxable income; at the other extreme, farms producing industrial crops paid only 4 per cent of the total tax, and accounted for 20 per cent of the taxable income.[74]

The 1936 edict defined taxable income to include all money income of the collective farm, plus income in kind valued at obligatory-delivery prices. The rate of tax was 3 per cent for *arteli* and communes and 4 per cent for the TOZ (defined in note 70) and was to be based on the previous year's gross income. The amount of tax collected from the farms increased sharply in 1936 and 1937, probably because there were, for the first time since the tax on collectives had been instituted in 1923, no exemptions on specific crops; also, perhaps because of the excellent crop in 1937.[75]

The tax remained essentially unchanged until March 1, 1941, when it was recast into its present form.[76] The relatively simple "gross-income" concept of the 1936 law was discarded for a much more complicated definition of taxable income. It included: (1) income in kind used for seed, food fund, children's nurseries, etc., valued at obligatory-delivery prices; (2) income in kind distributed to members, valued at decentralized-procurement prices; (3) money income from sales to the state by decentralized procurement and kontraktatsiia; and (4) money income from sales on the free market. The first and third categories were subject to a 4 per cent proportional tax, the second and fourth categories to an 8 per cent proportional tax. The following categories were specifically excluded from taxable income: money receipts for obligatory deliveries, payments to the MTS, output used for feeding animals and for stockpiling feed, receipts from insurance and interest on government obligations, receipts from the sale of capital assets, and money income used to finance expenditures of an industrial nature.

This is an extremely complicated tax, designed to encourage above-quota deliveries to state procurement agencies and to discourage free-market sales. Income in kind is valued at two different prices; income is taxed at two different rates; costs of production are treated in different ways, some deducted from gross income and others not. The Soviets themselves seem confused as to the precise nature of the tax. For example, Mar'iakhin looks upon the tax as a levy on the net income of the collective farms: "By this law the system of collecting a tax on the gross income of the collective farms was revoked, and a system of income tax established net of the basic productive expenditures of the collective farm."[77] On the other hand, Suchkov says that "the income tax is calculated . . . from income which in its structure more closely approaches gross income."[78] In our opinion, Mar'iakhin is closer to the truth, although it is clear from the listing above that not all legitimate costs are deducted from gross income.[79]

In the early postwar period the tax rates were revised upward as follows: the tax on categories (1) and (3) was increased from 4 per cent to 6 per cent, on category (2) from 8 to 12 per cent, and on category (4) from 8 to 13 per cent.[80] More recently the tax on category (3) was increased to 9 per cent and on category (4) to 15 per cent.[81] Otherwise the tax has remained unchanged since March 1941.

No data on the receipts from this tax have been available for the past 10 years, but the presumption is that it remains unimportant in the total fiscal picture.

INCOME TAX ON COÖPERATIVE ORGANIZATIONS

The income tax on coöperative organizations has never been an important source of revenue; in the prewar period it usually amounted to about 1 per cent of total budget receipts. The insignificance of the tax is explained by the special position of the so-called coöperative movement (i.e., consumer and industrial coöperatives) in the Soviet economy. Consumer coöperatives are the principal distributors of consumers' goods. As distributive organizations, however, their investment requirements are not very large; therefore, the state allows them only very narrow profit margins which leave little income to be recaptured through the income tax. The industrial coöperatives produce various handicraft products and simpler types of consumers' goods, such as furniture, pottery, and shoes. Their profits, like those of the consumer coöperatives, are limited because of their very moderate investments; in addition, they operate on a relatively small scale, and account for only a very small share of the total Soviet industrial output.

Although the coöperatives are largely guided by the state in their production and investment policies, they are nevertheless legally independent organizations with the right to distribute part of their profits among their members. State enterprises, on the other hand, have no legal independence of action with respect to profits. This difference in legal status explains why the levy on the net profits of state enterprises is called a *deduction* from profits. The income tax on the coöperatives is set up formally like any other tax; payment depends entirely on the profits (or rate of profits) of the coöperative and on the tax schedule, with nothing left to the discretion of the state. As we have seen, the deduction from profits of state enterprises is legally defined only within very broad limits; the state deducts into the budget all profits (with the exception of a small deduction into the Director's Fund) not needed to finance planned investment requirements.

At the time of the Tax Reform of 1930, the tax on all coöperatives was set at 20 per cent of profits. In 1933 the tax on consumer coöperatives was raised to 31 per cent of profits, and industrial coöperatives were subjected to an unusual type of progressive tax in which the rate of tax depended solely on the rate of profits, and not at all on the absolute amount of profits.[82] Furthermore, the rate of profits was defined as the ratio of profits to commercial cost of production. This is in contrast to the usual Western practice of relating profits to investment. The effect of this definition of the rate of profits was to discriminate against a coöperative producing a low-cost commodity, regardless of the amount of value-added in the production process.[83] The rates ranged gradually from 23.5 per cent on profits of less than 8 per cent to 55 per cent on profit rates between 28 and 32 per cent, and then rose abruptly to 90 per cent on profits which exceed 32 per cent of costs. According to Suchkov, the progressive rates were designed to discourage illegal price increases by making such activity less profitable.[84]

There is no information on how well the tax succeeded in preventing illegal pricing. It would seem reasonable that, as time passed and state economic controls were improved and expanded, control over coöperative pricing became less and less of a problem for the tax authorities.

From the Soviet point of view, the tax on the industrial coöperatives turned out to be deficient in one respect: it allowed coöperatives which had low rates of profit but large absolute profits to accumulate large sums. It was claimed that this permitted some enterprises to accumulate more funds than were needed — funds which were squandered uneconomically — whereas other coöperatives were paying so much into the budget that their development was impeded.[85] In April 1941, the law was changed to rectify this situation. The rate of tax was made to depend on the absolute amount of profits as well as on the rate of profits. This was accomplished by the use of separate tax schedules for coöperatives with profits of less than 100,000 rubles, 100,000 to 300,000, and above 300,000. Each schedule was a progressive function of the rate of profits, as in the previous law.

At the same time the proportional rate on consumer coöperatives was revoked in favor of a progressive scale of rates based on absolute profits and varying from 30 to 45 per cent.[86] This was revoked, however, in November 1946, and a proportional tax of 25 per cent on the absolute amount of profits was reëstablished for consumer coöperatives. This is the situation at present.

The government has been encouraging coöperatives in the postwar period, and receipts from the income tax on coöperatives may now be somewhat higher than in the prewar period. Should such encouragement continue, it would not be unreasonable to expect the Soviets to revoke the progressive tax on industrial coöperatives, in this way bringing the state's financial and economic policies into harmony.

OTHER SOURCES OF BUDGET INCOME

There are many sources of budget income besides taxes. The more important are noted briefly below.[87]

Customs receipts are perhaps the largest of the nontax sources of budget income. In normal times customs receipts have provided close to 2 per cent of budget income. During the war, receipts from tariffs on regular imports were strongly supplemented by the local currency resulting from sales of lend lease commodities; in the postwar period, regular receipts have been supplemented by reparations.

Soviet tariffs no longer serve any of the economic functions usually associated with tariffs, although in the early 1920's both revenue and protection were considerations.[88] At present it is probably most useful to think of the tariff on nonconsumers' goods as a device for equalizing the cost of imports with the cost of similar domestically produced commodities, and the tariff on consumers' goods as a form of turnover tax which serves to equalize the price of imports with the price of domestically produced commodities.[89]

The state also receives income from its forests, subsoil (e.g., peat), fisheries, and other properties. The most important of these incomes are the stumpage fees received from forests; such income was moderately important in the 1920's, but is insignificant at present.

The gross receipts (mostly in kind) of the MTS are included in the receipts side of the budget. But, as we indicated in the previous chapter, these receipts are valued at the low obligatory-delivery prices, and are not sufficient to enable these organizations to meet their own expenditures. On paper, then, the MTS have a net money loss; it is therefore misleading to show their receipts as a source of budget income.

At present, the Soviets do not have a tax on inheritance, although beneficiaries do have to pay a substantial fee in connection with the legal documents and procedures relating to the inheritance. A progressive inheritance tax was in force until 1942; although it cut deeply into the larger inheritances, it had no fiscal significance whatsoever.[90]

In addition to the above, other minor sources of budget revenue include fees for various state services, fines, and a large number of so-called local taxes and collections.

PART III: STATISTICAL ANALYSIS

Chapter 9

TRENDS IN SOVIET TAXATION

The more important trends in Soviet taxes for the period since 1928–29 will be traced in this chapter. The principal topics of discussion will be the changing relation between the different sources of budget revenue, the role of the budget surplus in the over-all financial plan after 1940, and the Currency Reform of December 14, 1947; the period from 1928–29 to 1940 was discussed in Chapter 2.

DESCRIPTION OF THE DATA

Since the Soviet period began there have been several important changes in the composition of the state budget. This raises the problem of comparability over time of the budgetary data. Fortunately, Soviet economists have frequently revised budget estimates of previous periods for purposes of comparison (although it is not always clear how the revisions are arrived at); for this reason, when discrepancies between earlier and later sources of data are observed, it is usually better practice to use the later figure. Some of the major changes which have been made in the five-year plan period are as follows:

(i) Before 1939 the budget was usually presented in the form of a "unified" (*edinyi*) budget. This aggregate included the union or federal budget and the budgets of the allied and autonomous republics. It did not include the county, city, and village budgets. In the larger statistical collections, however, a "summary" (*svodnyi*) budget was often presented, and this included all budgets: union, republican, and local. Since 1939 this has been the usual form of presentation; it is now called the "state" (*gosudarstvennyi*) budget.[1]

(ii) Prior to 1939, social-insurance receipts and expenditures (called the social-insurance budget) were not included in either the unified or the summary budgets. Since 1939 it has been the practice to include the social-insurance budget in the state budget.[2]

(iii) Receipts and expenditures of transportation and communications enterprises were included in the budget on a gross basis until 1931 and 1932, respectively. This resulted in a substantial inflation of budgetary receipts and expenditures, since operating receipts and expenditures of the two industries were very large.[3] In 1932, these operating expenditures and receipts were excluded from the budget, leaving receipts consisting of net income from operating the railroads, amortization, profit from loading and unloading operations, and deductions from profits of the economic associations (*ob" edinenii*) of the railroad ministry (the NKPS). Finally, in 1934 the budget received 50 per cent of the sum of the net income of the railroad ministry (total income minus operating expenditures) and receipts from the levy on loading and unloading operations.[4]

These are the major changes; many minor changes have occurred as well, but they are too numerous to be dealt with here.

Since the prewar period, only one Soviet book has been available in this country which includes fairly complete series of budget data; [5] this is Plotnikov's book, which has the additional merit of adjusting the data for comparability as far back as 1928–29. From the point of view of this chapter, Plotnikov's data have three shortcomings: (1) the series do not go back to the preplan period (before 1928–29); (2) the tax categories are for the most part very broad, and no attempt is made to present series for individual taxes (e.g., taxes on the population include at least six subcategories, but figures for the subcategories are available for scattered years only); (3) for many years, the "other receipts" category is very large, and it has not been possible to reconcile Plotnikov's estimates, particularly for the first plan period, with earlier data.[6]

In spite of these shortcomings, Plotnikov's book will serve as the main source of data for the prewar plan period. No attempt will be made to discuss trends in the preplan period.

TAX TRENDS: 1928–29 TO 1940 [7]

Size of the Budget. Budgetary receipts by main categories for the first three Five Year Plans are presented in Table 47. The outstanding trend over these years is the twentyfold increase in total receipts. Declining rates of growth mark three distinct periods in the trend: the first Five Year Plan, when the rate was more than 50 per cent annually;[8] 1933 to 1936, when the rate was about 25 per cent annually; and 1937 to 1940, when the rate was about 18 per cent

TABLE 47 Budgetary Receipts and Retained Profits of State Enterprises, 1928–29 to 1940 (billions of rubles)

Receipts	1928–29	1929–30	1931	1932	1933	1934	1935	1936	1937	1938	1939	1940
Turnover tax	3.1[a]	5.4[a]	11.7	19.6	27.0	37.6	52.2	65.8	75.9	80.4	96.9	105.9
Per cent of total	(35.2)	(38.8)	(46.4)	(51.6)	(58.2)	(64.4)	(69.6)	(69.7)	(69.6)	(63.1)	(62.1)	(58.8)
Profits tax	0.6	1.6	2.2	2.0	3.4	3.1	3.3	5.3	9.4	10.5	15.8	21.7
Per cent of total	(6.8)	(11.5)	(8.7)	(5.3)	(7.3)	(5.3)	(4.4)	(5.6)	(8.5)	(8.2)	(10.1)	(12.0)
Direct taxes on population	1.1	1.1	1.6	2.4	3.5	3.8	3.2	3.8	4.0	5.1	7.0	9.4
Per cent of total	(12.5)	(7.9)	(6.3)	(5.3)	(7.5)	(6.5)	(4.3)	(4.0)	(3.7)	(4.0)	(4.5)	(5.2)
Sale of government bonds	0.7	1.3	3.3	3.9	4.4	4.3	4.9	4.9	5.9	7.6	8.4	11.5
Per cent of total	(8.0)	(9.4)	(13.1)	(10.3)	(9.5)	(7.4)	(6.5)	(5.2)	(5.4)	(6.0)	(5.4)	(6.4)
Social insurance	1.2	1.4	2.2	3.6	4.3	5.7	7.0	8.9	6.6	7.2	7.6	8.5
Per cent of total	(13.6)	(10.1)	(8.7)	(9.5)	(9.3)	(9.8)	(9.3)	(9.4)	(6.0)	(5.6)	(4.9)	(4.7)
Other	2.1	3.1	4.2	6.5	3.8	3.9	4.4	5.7	7.6	16.7	20.3	23.2
Per cent of total	(23.8)	(22.3)	(16.7)	(17.1)	(8.2)	(6.7)	(6.0)	(6.0)	(7.0)	(13.1)	(13.0)	(13.0)
Total budget receipts	8.8	13.9	25.2	38.0	46.4	58.4	75.0	94.4	109.3	127.5	156.0	180.2
Per cent of increase		(58)	(81)	(51)	(22)	(26)	(28)	(26)	(16)	(17)	(22)	(16)
Retained profits	2.7	3.8	3.8	4.5	4.6	3.3	4.5	8.9	7.6	5.2	10.5	10.3
Per cent of budget receipts	(30.7)	(27.3)	(15.1)	(12.1)	(9.9)	(5.7)	(6.0)	(9.4)	(7.0)	(4.1)	(6.7)	(5.7)

For sources, see Appendix; discrepancies in totals are due to rounding.

[a] Summation of taxes later unified into turnover tax (see Appendix).

annually. It is difficult to determine just how much of the increment is due to growth of the "real" operations of the state apparatus and how much is attributable to price inflation, since satisfactory cost and price indexes for separating out the inflationary component of the increase are lacking. A few observations may be made, however.

The increase in budget receipts during the First Five Year Plan period is much too large to be explained solely by inflation. Excluding the period of hyperinflation in the early 1920's, Soviet costs and prices have never risen as rapidly as budget receipts did from 1928–29 to 1932. Two factors operated in this period to increase the real scope of government activity. As was indicated in Chapter 5, the private sector of the economy, which had been responsible for a substantial part of the nation's economic activity in the mid-twenties, was being rapidly supplanted in the late twenties and early thirties by state and coöperative organizations. Second, from 1928–29 to 1934 the state was deducting into the budget an increasing share of the profits of state enterprises, thereby centralizing the financing of investment and channeling the bulk of the net funds of the state sector through the budget. This is indicated by the last line of Table 47. Both of these events served to increase budgetary receipts and the role of the budget in the economy.

The importance of the state in the economy probably increased somewhat during the Second and Third Five Year Plan periods as well as the first. Statements to this effect by Soviet economists are substantiated by comparison of the rate of increase in budget receipts (Table 47) with the rate of increase in the average wage rate (Table 3). Increases in the average wage rate, deflated by increases in productivity, are probably the best single measure of the real cost of budget operations; the comparison shows that the increase in budget receipts outstrips the increase in wages, even without adjustment for changes in productivity.

Increase in Importance of Commodity Taxation. There were big changes in the structure of budgetary receipts from 1928–29 to 1940. The outstanding development in the first half of the period was the doubling in importance of the turnover tax, from 35 per cent of budget receipts in 1928–29 to almost 70 per cent in 1935. Concomitantly, the importance of all other sources of revenue declined, with the exception of receipts from government bonds; these rose from 1928–29 until 1932, and then also declined. The increasing reliance on commodity taxation can be understood in terms of the analysis in Chapter 3.

Throughout the Five Year Plan period the average rate of taxation was very high, and in the first few years the rate of taxation increased rapidly (see Table 53). The Soviets must have been seriously concerned with the social and economic effects of such a high and *rapidly increasing* rate of taxation; the changing tax structure suggests that tax policy was designed to mitigate undesirable effects. In order to minimize the negative impact on incentives of its huge tax program, the state ceased to depend on direct taxation for meeting its increasing financial requirements; the importance of direct taxes in budgetary receipts declined by almost two-thirds from 1928–29 to 1935. The average rate of direct taxation (direct taxes divided by consumer income) declined steadily in this period (see Tables 51 and 52).

The increasing importance of commodity taxation and, to 1932, of government bonds, is a counterpart of the decline in direct taxation. Although purchase of bonds is now essentially a form of taxation (for reasons advanced in Chapter 8), this was probably not the case twenty years ago. While the government strongly encouraged the population to buy bonds, purchases were still largely voluntary and there was probably little expectation at the time that the government debt would not be fully redeemed. The possibilities of further increasing receipts from this source were, however, strictly limited. To the extent that purchases were voluntary, it was not possible to induce the population to buy more bonds at a time when the standard of living was very low; to the extent that purchases could be made compulsory and increased indefinitely, their use would have involved the disincentive effects of direct taxation which the Soviets were so anxious to avoid.

The least painful way of whittling down the consumers' share in the national output is, as we have seen, to raise prices by levying higher and higher commodity taxes; the method is particularly successful when money incomes are increasing simultaneously but at a slower rate. This was the policy pursued by the Soviets, as the figures in Table 47 show. The relative administrative simplicity of commodity taxation must also be mentioned as a factor which strongly influenced the Soviets in their choice between taxes at this time.

Changes in the Structure of Commodity Taxation. There were structural changes within the commodity-tax framework. In 1928–29 the turnover tax (i.e., the taxes which were later unified into the turnover tax) and total profits (the profits tax plus retained profits) were about equal in size. As the financial requirements of the state increased, more and more of the markup over cost was siphoned immediately into the budget by the turnover tax, rather than through profits. By 1935 budgetary receipts from the turnover tax were about seven times total profits.

A similar development was occurring within the profits category itself. The profits tax was absorbing an increasing proportion of the total profits of state industry (its share increased from less than 20 per cent in 1928–29 to more than 40 per cent in 1935), while retained profits shrank correspondingly.

The factors which explain these developments were discussed in Chapter 4; they are (1) the greater effectiveness of the turnover tax as in instrument for collecting the bulk of the state revenue, and (2) the adverse effect on managerial incentives of too great an accumulation of profits — an increasingly important consideration as the markup over cost increased.

The shift away from retained profits was a natural concomitant of the state policy of financing the bulk of its investment by a tax on consumers' goods while attempting to keep the prices of producers' goods stable. In the preplan period producers'-goods industries financed investment to a considerable extent from retained profits. When their investment requirements increased sharply in the early thirties, they received large subsidies to keep prices stable; such subsidies were required primarily, of course, to offset rising wage costs (see Chapter 11). In 1936, policy reverted temporarily to the preplan period pattern: a decision was made to reduce subsidies to industry to make the cost-price system more meaningful; at the same time, investment out of retained profits was increased, presumably in order to improve managerial incentives. This was reflected in the large increase in total profits in 1936. Thereafter the Soviets apparently reversed for the second time their policy with respect to investment out of retained profits, because the percentage of profits drawn into the budget by the profits tax increased more rapidly than retained profits.

No important changes in direct taxes or sales of government bonds occurred over this period. In absolute terms, direct taxes remained quite steady from 1933 to 1937; the direct-tax laws changed very little in this period. The increases in 1939 and 1940 are attributed primarily to the change in the agricultural-tax law in 1939.

The "Other Receipts" Category. The most difficult trend to understand is that exhibited by "other receipts." One of the more annoying features of Soviet budgetary statistics is the use of a large residual category without information regarding its content. The problems in this respect are multiplied in using sources (such as Plotnikov) which attempt comparability over time, because the number of items included in the residual is usually increased.

Investigation has failed to reveal either the content of the very large "other" category in the years of the First Five Year Plan or the reasons for its abrupt decline in importance between 1932 and 1933 and its subsequent sharp rise from 1937 to 1938. The percentage decline from 1928–29 to 1932 probably occurred because the rest of the budget was increasing much more rapidly than the items in the "other" category; the *absolute* magnitude of "other receipts" increased moderately over these years.

Part of the rise from 1937 to 1938 was due to an increase in receipts from customs, and to the inclusion of gross receipts of the MTS in the budget for the first time; this, however, explains only about one-half of the increase.

No explanation is offered for the decline from 1932 to 1933. In fact, it has not been possible to reconcile Plotnikov or any other recent estimates for 1932 with earlier estimates.[9] After allowing for all known changes, the later estimates of total budget receipts are much larger than the earlier ones; this is reflected almost entirely in a larger "other receipts" category.

TAX TRENDS AFTER 1941

Figures for the major budgetary-receipts categories from 1941 through 1954 are presented in Table 48.

Size of the Budget. Some of the trends of the prewar period were reversed during the war. Total receipts, which were to have risen from 180 billion rubles in 1940 to 216.8 billion rubles[10] in 1941, reached only 191.4 billion rubles in 1941 and fell to 165 billion rubles in 1942. This was due to the territorial loss resulting from the Ger-

TABLE 48 Budgetary Receipts and Retained Profits of State Enterprises, 1941–1954 (billions of rubles)

Receipts	1941	1942	1943	1944	1945	1946	1947	1948	1949	1950	1951	1952	1953	1954 (plan)
Turnover tax	93.2	66.4	71.2	94.9	123.1	190.9	239.7	247.3	245.5	236.1	247.8	246.9	243.6	234.3
Per cent of total	(52.6)	(40.2)	(35.1)	(35.3)	(40.8)	(58.7)	(62.1)	(60.2)	(56.2)	(55.8)	(52.7)	(49.7)	(45.1)	(41.0)
Profits tax	31.3	15.3	19.9	21.4	16.9	16.6	22.6	27.2	42.2	40.4	48.0	58.5	70.3	92.8
Per cent of total	(17.9)	(9.3)	(9.8)	(8.0)	(5.6)	(5.1)	(5.9)	(6.6)	(9.7)	(9.6)	(10.2)	(11.7)	(13.0)	(16.2)
Direct taxes on population	10.3	32.5	28.6	37.0	39.8	22.7	28.0	33.2	33.7	35.8	42.9	47.4	46.1	45.7
Per cent of total	(5.8)	(19.7)	(14.1)	(13.8)	(13.2)	(7.0)	(7.3)	(8.1)	(7.7)	(8.5)	(9.1)	(9.5)	(8.5)	(8.0)
Sales of bonds	8.3	12.2	29.0	32.6	29.0	24.7	25.7	23.9	27.6	31.0	36.8	42.6	[28.0]	[28.0]
Per cent of total	(4.7)	(7.4)	(14.3)	(12.1)	(9.6)	(7.6)	(6.6)	(5.8)	(6.3)	(7.3)	(7.9)	(8.5)	(5.2)	(4.9)
Social insurance	10.0	—	—	9.0	10.4	11.7	14.9	16.2	17.5	19.6	21.4	21.9	23.2	24.7
Per cent of total	(5.7)	—	—	(3.3)	(3.4)	(3.6)	(3.9)	(3.9)	(4.0)	(4.6)	(4.5)	(4.4)	(4.3)	(4.3)
Other receipts	—	—	—	73.8	82.8	58.8	55.3	62.7	70.5	59.9	73.4	80.4	128.5[a]	147.0[a]
Per cent of total	—	—	—	(27.5)	(27.4)	(18.1)	(14.3)	(15.3)	(16.1)	(14.2)	(15.6)	(16.2)	(23.8)	(25.6)
Total budget receipts	177.0	165.0	202.7	268.7	302.0	325.4	386.2	410.5	437.0	422.8	470.3	497.7	539.7[a]	572.5[a]
Per cent of increase		(−7)	(23)	(32)	(12)	(8)	(19)	(6)	(6)	(−3)	(11)	(6)	(8)	(6)
Retained profits	13.5	—	1.8	3.0	2.0	5.5	1.5	12.1	27.4	25.1	26.9	25.0	19.0	30.6
Per cent of budget receipts	(7.6)	—	(0.9)	(1.1)	(0.7)	(1.7)	(0.4)	(2.9)	(6.3)	(5.9)	(5.7)	(5.0)	(3.5)	(5.3)

For sources, methods, and discussion of discrepancies in data, see Appendix.

Dashes indicate that figures are not available.

[a] The increase in these categories in 1953 and 1954 relative to previous years is partly spurious and due to a change in Soviet budgetary accounting methodology. See discussion below.

man invasion.[11] At its peak, the invasion encompassed an area which before the war accounted for "45 per cent of the population, 33 per cent of the gross output of industry, 47 per cent of sown area."[12] The large increases in 1943 and 1944 are to be explained, in part, by the recovery of formerly occupied territory.

Postwar percentage changes in total budget receipts have been smaller (after 1947) than was the case in the prewar period; in 1950 total receipts actually declined. This development appears to be the result of two factors. First, in the postwar period the Soviets seem to have been more successful in holding down wage inflation, hence cost inflation, so that the same volume of government activity from year to year has not required as large an increase in taxes as was required in the prewar period. Second, the rate of nonconsumption expenditures declined from 1948 to 1953 (see next chapter). Thus, the major task of the budget — the absorption of excess money income from the household — was reduced in scope. The moderate increases in receipts in 1953 and 1954 (planned) may be largely or entirely spurious, the result of a change in methods of budgetary accounting for "other receipts" (see below).

Wartime Structure of Taxation. The outstanding change in the pattern of receipts during the war was the sharp decline in the importance of the turnover and profits taxes, and an increase in direct taxation and sales of bonds to the population. After Soviet entry into the war, an extremely large share of the national output was directed into nonconsumption uses; this caused the production and sale of consumers' goods to shrink drastically. Since turnover-tax receipts are a function of the volume of consumers' goods sold as well as of tax rates, receipts were bound to fall in the absence of a large rise in prices. Reasons why prices were not increased much during the war are suggested below. Furthermore, the Soviets apparently decided that under wartime conditions, with patriotism at a peak, it was feasible to pay less attention to the "money illusion," and to offset part of the increasing inflationary pressures by higher direct taxes and more bond sales. Retained profits dropped to almost nothing during this period; financing of wartime investment was apparently completely centralized.[13]

Finally, it should be noted that substantial contributions toward financing the war effort were made through voluntary contributions by the population of both goods and money to the "Defense Fund" and "Red Army Fund." According to Voznesensky,[14] these contributions totaled 94.5 billion rubles over four war years, of which 16 billion rubles were in monetary form.

As we shall see below, the Soviets did not succeed in financing their entire war effort from taxes; they had budget deficits from 1941 to 1943, and printed large amounts of money throughout the war period. The failure of fiscal policy in these years was reflected in a shift in the center of gravity of cash holdings from the urban to the rural population, because of the war-induced food shortage.[15] The shortage of food, together with the highly inelastic demand of the urban population, enabled the peasants to sell their produce on the collective farm markets at prices admitted to be many times the official prices.[16] In other words, the terms of trade moved sharply in favor of the peasants. As a result, the urban population incurred a payment deficit with the peasants. As we shall see later, this had great significance for the Currency Reform of 1947.

Theoretically, the state could have offset these inflationary pressures by taxing either the peasants or the urban population more heavily. Its failure to do so is partly explained by the disorganized state of the economy during the war, particularly in the early years. Territory and population changed hands rapidly as the fortunes of war fluctuated. This caused rapid unforeseen changes in the number of taxpayers, supplies of consumers' goods, consumers' incomes, military requirements, and other variables which are crucial in financial planning. Plans must have been extremely short-run and were, no doubt, constantly revised. Under these conditions it would have been impossible to have varied taxes to keep up with changing fiscal needs. On the other hand, it required no long-run planning to extend bank credits and print money when new needs suddenly arose. And this the Soviets did on a scale which was for them unprecedented.

Even if careful financial planning had been possible during the war, the enormity of the fiscal task might still have made it infeasible for the authorities to prevent repressed inflation. The difficulties in taxing the peasants were twofold: first, the commodity tax is relatively ineffective in this sector because the peasants do not buy sufficiently large quantities of commodities, especially food products, from the state; second, it may have been beyond the administrative capacity of the Soviets to levy an effective direct tax on the peasants during the war.

Two difficulties also had to be faced in taxing the urban population. An indirect tax of the appropriate magnitude would undoubtedly have priced lower-income families out of the market for necessities. Furthermore, a *sufficiently* large direct tax might have played havoc with incentives even during the war. An income tax adequate to prevent the development of repressed inflation would most certainly have had an average rate of more than 50 per cent and marginal rates considerably higher.

If the state had been able to levy high enough taxes on the urban population for fiscal stability, the effective demand of the workers for commodities sold on the collective farm markets would have been severely limited. This would have had the effect of increasing the consumption in kind of the peasants, thereby reducing the amount of food offered for sale on the free markets. Since the urban population was on starvation rations during the war, any policy which increased the marketable food surplus was desirable. This is perhaps a principal benefit which resulted from the state's failure to absorb excess purchasing power generated by war expenditures.

The same result could undoubtedly have been achieved, however, with a much smaller rise in collective farm market prices. For this reason, the state's failure to maintain fiscal stability cannot be rationalized entirely as an incentive device to persuade peasants to sell their produce. In fact, it is even possible that the very large flow of cash to the rural areas satiated all too quickly the peasant demand for liquidity, and may, on balance, have reduced the amount of food the peasant was willing to part with for money, particularly in the latter stages of the war. This argument is the more cogent because the peasant could buy very little with his hoarded cash. In other words, in weighing the favorable effect of high prices on the peasant's incentive to sell food against the disincentive effects of large accumulated cash balances, it is possible that the Soviets struck the balance too high; lower prices might have reduced incentives less than smaller cash balances would have increased them.

Postwar Structure of Taxation. After the war ended, the distribution of budget income returned to the pattern which prevailed in the mid-thirties. Since 1947 there has been a shift within the commodity-tax structure away from the turnover tax and in favor of profits. Receipts from the turnover tax planned for 1954 were below those for 1947, in sharp contrast with the rapid secular increase during the thirties; the share of the turnover tax in total budget receipts has declined from 62 per cent in 1947 to 41 per cent of planned receipts for 1954.[17] On the other hand, profits of state enterprises (retained profits plus the profits tax), which constituted 6 per cent of total receipts in 1947, increased to 16.5 per cent in 1953 and 21.5 per cent planned for 1954.

These trends are the result of several recent developments. Perhaps the most important is the shift in the distribution of the national output away from nonconsumption uses and in favor of commodities sold to the consumer. This shift is suggested statistically for the years 1948 to 1953 in the next chapter. Financially it took the form of a series of price reductions on consumers' goods, beginning in December 1947 in connection with the Currency Reform; successive reductions occurred on March 1 of the years 1949, 1950, and 1951, and on April 1 of 1952 and 1953.[18] According to Soviet sources, the decline in prices saved consumers, in their purchases on *all* markets, the following amounts: 1948, 86 billion rubles; 1949, 71 billion rubles; 1950, 110 billion rubles; 1951, 35 billion rubles; 1952, 28 billion rubles (plan); and 1953, 43 billion rubles (plan).[19] A rough indication of the significance of these amounts can be obtained by comparing them with actual value of sales to consumers as estimated in the following chapter.[20] The 1950 price reduction is reported to have averaged 21 per cent for all mass-consumption commodities;[21] examination of individual price changes indicates that the price reduction, no matter how the Soviet figure was derived, was substantial.

Most of the price reductions were apparently absorbed by reductions in turnover-tax rates, hence in the budgetary receipts from this tax per unit of output sold to the consumer.[22] A small part of the price reduction may also have been absorbed by increases in productivity (reflected in lower costs). The fact that receipts from the turnover tax did not decline in this period by the amount of the "savings" to the consumer mentioned directly above is indicative of a large increase in the volume of consumers' goods offered for sale. The Soviets in fact claim that the quantity of consumers' goods supplied by the state increased, for example, by 20 per cent in 1949 and 30 per cent in 1950.[23] In summary, it appears that since 1948 there has been a substantial increase in the amount of consumers' goods offered for sale to Soviet citizens at reduced prices; financially this has been reflected in a decline in the average implied rate of turnover tax.[24]

The decline in consumers'-goods prices might have been partly absorbed by profits as well as by the turnover tax; this would not be reflected in the profits figures, however, because of a decision in 1948 to eliminate subsidies to, and increase profits of, state industrial enterprises and the transport system. This was done with the dual purpose of making the price system more meaningful for planning and of improving incentives of managers to earn profits.[25] The plan was to eliminate about 80 per cent of subsidies in 1949 and the remainder in 1950. To this end, transport rates and the wholesale prices of many industrial commodities were doubled or trebled on January 1, 1949. Although it is not known whether subsidies were in fact reduced by the intended amount in 1949,[26] total profits appear to have almost doubled, while *retained* profits more than doubled. In 1950, total profits declined slightly; in 1951, 1952, and 1953, fairly sharp increases were again registered. However, these increases were not in retained but in deducted profits; they may have served the first objective of the price increases — to limit subsidies — but it is hard to see how they could have improved managerial incentives. As of 1953, investment in the national economy apparently remained as centralized as it was before 1949. It is worth noting, however, that a 50 per cent increase in retained profits is scheduled for 1954.

The temporary decline in profits in 1950 was no doubt a result of the reductions of wholesale prices of industrial commodities which occurred in January and July 1950. The scale of these reductions and their cause are not clearly known; however, it may be doubted that they were as drastic as Jasny, for example, has affirmed. In Jasny's view, the price increases of 1949 were a "blunder" — i.e., much too large — and the 1950 price reductions had the simple purpose of rectifying the mistake.[27] *Ceteris paribus*, the reduction in prices should have reduced profits and increased the need for subsidies. If the price reductions were as substantial as Jasny claims, it is difficult to understand how subsidies could have declined *at all* in 1950 (our estimate is that the actual decline amounted to 24 billion rubles)[28] and profits by *only* about 4 billion rubles.

Before closing this section, it should be noted that a substantial part of the "other receipts" category during the war and postwar periods has consisted of customs receipts, including lend-lease aid. In the postwar period receipts from reparations and restitution have amounted, in some years, to as much as 3 per cent of total revenue. It should also be noted that an unprecedented increase in this category appears to have occurred in 1953. Although lack of information makes it impossible to deduce the precise magnitude of "other receipts," reasonable projections of other missing items indicate that it amounted to roughly 130 billion rubles, or more than 50 per cent above the amount recorded for 1952. The only plausible explanation is that the increase is the result of a change in Soviet budgetary accounting procedures in connection with the annual consumers'-goods price cuts. It is quite clear from the 1953 budget speeches that the Soviets have for the first time included in "other expenditures" the full amount of the cost to the budget of these price cuts; that is to say, the state is presumed to have subsidized the consumer through the budget by lowering prices of consumers' goods. The price cuts were expected to save consumers some 43 billion rubles; "other expenditures" are expected to increase by a like amount (from roughly 29 billion in 1952 to 74 billion in 1953). This increase in "other expenditures," it should be noted, is as unprecedented as the increase which we are attempting to explain in "other receipts." Although the Soviets make no statements connecting the category "other receipts" with the consumers'-goods price cuts, losses to the budget from these cuts can be included as an item of budget expenditure only if the same amount is first included in the budget as receipts. This must be the case, even though these receipts are never explicitly realized. Apparently the practice was continued in 1954, for "other receipts" are planned to increase still further. No explanation of this bizarre procedure is offered.

THE BUDGETARY IMBALANCE

The interrelation of banking and fiscal policy was discussed in detail in Chapter 2. An analysis of Soviet financial policy in the prewar period was also presented in that chapter; hence our attention in this section will be concentrated on the war and postwar periods. Unfortunately, scarcity of data for these years seriously limits the discussion which follows.

The net budgetary position of the years since 1928–29 is presented in Table 49. These data have been adjusted by Soviet economists so that they represent comparable coverage for each year of the period in question. To the non-Soviet economist, accustomed to deficit financing by the past twenty-five years of depression and war, the most striking feature of this table is that the budget either was in balance or showed a surplus for all years except 1941, 1942, and 1943. If the Western convention of excluding receipts from sale of govern-

TABLE 49 Net Budget Position, 1928–29 to 1954 (billions of rubles) [a]

Year	Receipts (1)	Expenditures (2)	Surplus or deficit (−) (3)	3 ÷ 1 (per cent) (4)
1928–29	8.8	8.8	0	0
1929–30	13.9	13.3	0.6	4.3
1931	25.2	25.1	0.1	0.4
1932	38.0	38.0	0	0
1933	46.4	42.1	4.3	9.3
1934	58.4	55.4	3.0	5.1
1935	75.0	73.6	1.4	1.9
1936	94.4	92.5	1.9	2.0
1937	109.3	106.2	3.1	2.8
1938	127.5	124.0	3.5	2.7
1939	156.0	153.3	2.7	1.7
1940	180.2	174.4	5.8	3.2
1941	177.0	191.4	−14.4	−8.1
1942	165.0	182.8	−17.8	−10.8
1943	202.7	210.0	−7.3	−3.6
1944	268.7	264.0	4.7	1.7
1945	302.0	298.6	3.4	1.1
1946	325.4	307.5	17.9	5.5
1947	386.2	361.5	24.7	6.4
1948	410.5	370.9	39.6	9.6
1949	437.0	412.3	24.7	5.7
1950	422.1	412.7	9.4	2.2
1951	470.3	443.0	27.3	5.8
1952	497.7	460.2	37.5	7.5
1953	539.7	514.8	24.9	4.6
1954 (Plan)	572.5	562.8	9.7	1.7

For sources, see Appendix.

[a] The figures presented here for the period 1928–1938 differ from those in Chapter 2 (Table 9, p. 57). The data presented here have been adjusted (by Soviet writers) for comparability with the period since 1938. The data presented in Chapter 2 are unadjusted.

ment bonds from current budgetary receipts were adopted, a deficit would have been returned every year except 1948. As we have demonstrated, it is more meaningful, because of the compulsory nature of Soviet bond sales, to include loan funds with current budget receipts.

The prewar budgetary surpluses were deposited to the budget's account in the State Bank, where they can be conceived of as serving to offset the Bank's short-term loans to enterprises. When the Germans invaded the Soviet Union in June 1941, the budget's account with the Bank probably totaled 25 to 30 billion rubles;[29] short-term loans outstanding on January 1, 1941 amounted to 55 billion rubles. As we indicated in Chapter 2, the budget surpluses were insufficient to achieve continuous financial stability in the prewar period.

The few scattered figures on war finance which have been published enable us to form some conclusions about policy in these years. For purposes of analysis the war and early postwar periods will be subdivided into two phases.

1941 to 1943. In the first phase, which extends from June 1941 to the end of 1943, the budget was the source of the wave of wartime inflation. There were deficits of 14, 18, and 7 billion rubles respectively in 1941, 1942, and 1943. According to Voznesensky, these deficits were financed not only by currency issue but also by drawing down commodity stockpiles: "In 1942 there was an excess of current expenditures over current receipts . . . which was covered by currency issue and the mobilization through the banking system of the commodity reserves and stocks accumulated within the economy of the USSR before the war . . . In 1943 . . . the excess of current expenditures over current receipts . . . was covered by currency issue and commodity reserves." [30]

Net credit outstanding increased little, if at all, in this period. Voznesensky states that there was a small decline in credit (of unspecified amount) in 1941–42, and an increase of 6 billion rubles in 1943.[31] This does not mean that the credit apparatus was not doing its share in the mobilization for war. The relatively small net change in loans outstanding simply reflects the fact that loans for peacetime purposes were being withdrawn (or not renewed) as fast as new loans for war activity were extended.[32] Two other writers, Gusakov and Dymshits, state that activities of the Bank *as well as* those of the budget called for new currency issue in this same period.[33]

In spite of the huge increase in monetary circulation and the precipitous decline in supplies of goods available for sale to the population, it was state policy to keep prices of rationed consumers' goods steady at the prewar level.[34] Consequently, a huge repressed inflation developed which was responsible for driving collective farm prices to about 13 times their 1940 level.[35] It is reported that by 1944 wages for all industry were 42 per cent above the 1940 level.[36] Wage increases were used to ease the transfer of workers to new jobs and to new locations, as well as to encourage harder work and longer hours. Thus the average wage in the Volga, Ural, and Western Siberian regions rose by 79, 65, and 79 per cent respectively, much more than the 42 per cent for industry as a whole.[37] The share of bonuses in total earnings doubled in many industries from 1940 to 1944.[38]

1944 to 1947. The second phase of war financial policy extends from 1944 until the Currency Reform in December 1947. In this period budget surpluses were realized again after three years of continuous deficit. The surpluses were very modest in 1944 and 1945, when merely balanced budgets had been planned; much larger surpluses were achieved in 1946 and 1947. There is no statistical information, to my knowledge, regarding operations of the State Bank in this period; it is quite conceivable, however, that loans were large and were responsible for a considerable increase in currency in circulation. There is no doubt that the legal scope of the Bank's activities was significantly extended. In 1943 the Bank was authorized to make loans to finance reconstruction in liberated areas. The legislation, as described by Atlas and Bregel',[39] appears to have provided for extraordinarily liberal use of the Bank's credit facilities to aid enterprises which had suffered under Nazi occupation. Since enormous destruction occurred, there is reason to believe that large loans were granted.

It is difficult to conjecture the net result of budgetary surpluses and Bank loans in this period. The surpluses were so small in 1944 and 1945 — a period when reconstruction loans must have been very large — that a large increase in currency circulation may reasonably be assumed. The budget surpluses were sufficiently large in 1946 and 1947 to put the net result in reasonable doubt; my guess, however, is that the currency supply was still being augmented.

Repressed inflation was reduced or released after 1943. Prices in the collective farm markets declined in 1944 and 1945, and by the latter year had fallen to a level about 43 per cent (1/2.3) below the level of 1943.[40] Three factors appear to be responsible. First, the supply of goods made available to consumers by the state increased fairly steadily after 1942.[41] Second, state "commercial trade" was reintroduced in 1944;[42] some consumers' goods sold by the state were diverted from the ration stores into special stores where they were sold freely to all buyers at much higher than ration prices. According to Voznesensky, it was this which caused the reduction in collective farm market prices.[43] Receipts from commercial trade amounted to 15.7 billion rubles in 1944 and 1945.[44] Finally, on September 16, 1946 prices of rationed consumers' goods were very substantially raised for the first time since the outbreak of hostilities.[45] The size of the increases lead us to infer that this was a serious attempt to bring household incomes and consumers' goods into better alignment. A contributing factor in the decision to raise ration prices was, no doubt, the very bad harvest in 1946.

The Currency Reform of December 1947.[46] In spite of the measures taken during and just after the war to release repressed inflation, the Soviets found it necessary to repudiate their currency before ending rationing and reëstablishing single prices for consumers' goods sold by the state (i.e., before abolishing commercial stores). The Reform decree was announced on December 14, 1947, and went into effect on December 16. The provisions which are of interest to us are summarized here; the complete text can be found in the sources cited.

The decree established differential rates of exchange for converting old to new currency. Cash currency was treated least favorably; holders received one new ruble for ten old rubles. The household is, of course, the principal holder of cash. Savings bank deposits were exchanged ruble for ruble on deposits up to 3,000 rubles, two for three rubles on the next 7,000 rubles, and one for two rubles on deposits exceeding 10,000 rubles. The provisions for exchanging government bonds were discussed in Chapter 8; in general, the face value of bond holdings of the population was reduced by two-thirds. Deposits of collective farms and other coöperatives were revalued at a rate of four new rubles for five old ones. Only deposits of state enterprises and organizations were not affected by the Reform; this made it financially possible to pay the wages and salaries of workers and employees for the first half of December in *new* money at the old rate.

The terms of the exchange are fairly drastic, and may be taken as a measure of the state's aversion to rationing and multiple-price markets, the concomitants of repressed inflation. As was indicated in Chapter 1, repressed inflation has an adverse effect upon labor incentives, and the use of rationing to distribute consumers' goods is both expensive and inefficient.

Granted that repressed inflation had to be eliminated, the question remains: why was the instrument of currency reform chosen? Why were consumers'-goods prices not raised by the necessary amounts, the technique applied successfully in the thirties? If surplus stocks of money had been evenly distributed throughout the population, this technique would probably have been used again. But as we indicated earlier in this chapter, the urban population had incurred a payments deficit with the rural population. Although most of the currency freshly printed during the war served originally to pay the wages of workers, salaried employees, and members of the armed forces, it eventually found its way into collective farm markets and thence into the mattresses of the peasants. Therefore the problem confronting the state was not simply how to reduce total currency in circulation but, more specifically, how to reduce the peasants' hoards. Obviously, this could not be accomplished by raising the general price level[47] of state-sold consumers' goods without inflicting undue hardship on the city population. City dwellers depended primarily upon current income for subsistence, and probably accumulated large quantities of cash or savings only in the first few years of the war, when supplies of consumers' goods were so catastrophically reduced. The large fall in collective farm market prices in 1944 and 1945 mentioned earlier (a decline which continued in 1946 and 1947)[48] is evidence that the excess cash held by the urban population in the early years of the war had been substantially reduced by the time of the Reform. (It is to be noted that repressed inflation in the peasant sector is not reflected directly in the collective farm market prices because the peasants are primarily sellers, not buyers, in these markets. It is reflected indirectly, however, to the extent that peasants withhold supplies from the market. There is no good indicator of how much cash the peasants may be hoarding except the detailed accounts of the currency issue department of the State Bank, which are, of course, not published.)

However, some repressed inflation continued to be generated in the urban sector until the general price rise of September 1946, owing to lack of alignment between ration prices and wages. As we have noted, wages rose steadily during the war, while ration prices were maintained at the prewar level. The price increases effected in September 1946 and again at the time of the Reform no doubt helped to remedy this.[49] Presumably these price changes established a sort of balance between the current income of workers and consumers'-goods prices.

Repressed inflation in the peasant sector could not be released in this way,[50] and this was the major reason for the Reform and for the 10-to-1 conversion ratio for cash. The Reform was put into effect at the end of a pay period for workers in state industry; presumably transaction balances from current income in the hands of the population were negligible; and *only* hoarded cash was substantially affected.[51]

At the time of the Currency Reform, the opinion was widely expressed in the West that the Reform unjustifiably discriminated against the peasants. This opinion was based on the more favorable treatment accorded savings bank deposits, held primarily by the city population, compared with cash hoards, held primarily by the peasants. Although no one would claim that the Soviets were devoid of political motivation in devising the Reform, the provisions seem to have been dictated primarily by nonpolitical considerations. First, as the Soviets have claimed, the Reform was directed not at the peasants (who are not mentioned in the decree), but at all speculators who accumulated large amounts of cash during the war. The decree states: "It is . . . intolerable that the speculative elements who enriched themselves during the war, and accumulated considerable sums of money, should have an opportunity to buy up goods after the abolition of the rationing system." It is true, of course, that the peasants were the main speculators (defined as individuals selling commodities at higher than ration prices). Second, it should be pointed out that savings deposits amounted only to about 13 billion rubles at the time of the Reform.[52] This is, of course, small in comparison with the amount of cash which must have been held by the peasants (below). Third, not all of the savings deposits were held by the urban population; some fraction, perhaps one-third, was held by rural depositors. Finally, it is pertinent to note that savings deposits were probably a much less volatile form of money-holding than cash hoarded by the peasants. Cash in the pockets of the peasants was a form of forced savings induced during the war by commodity scarcity, and held in readiness to be spent as soon as goods once more were available. This is probably much less true of savings deposits; therefore it was much less important to depreciate the value of savings deposits (and government bonds) than to reduce the amount of cash in circulation.

Currency in Circulation: December 14, 1947. An attempt will be made to estimate *very roughly* the amount of currency in circulation before the Reform. We are not interested in precise figures but only in the limits within which the correct figure probably falls. There are two reasons for attempting such an estimate: (1) to give the reader a more concrete idea of the purpose of the Reform and of the factors with which the Soviet monetary authorities had to deal, and (2) to indicate that the amount of currency in circulation before the Reform could not have been as great as most writers have estimated. The Bank for International Settlement, for example, has estimated that currency in circulation before the Reform totaled 420 billion rubles; this estimate has been accepted by Professor Condoide.[53] The estimate of the Federal Reserve Bank of New York is "over 400 billion rubles." Professor Baran more conservatively estimates circulation at 200 billion rubles, with a 25 billion leeway in either direction.[54]

For a first approximation it is assumed that the Soviets based their plans on the assumption that the income velocity of circulation of currency in the post-Reform period would remain at the level which prevailed in 1940. In other words, it is assumed that the quantity of cash required to support a given level of consumer money income was the same in 1948 as it was in 1940, and that the Soviets planned the Reform with this in mind. Letting M_{40} and M_{48} represent currency in circulation on January 1, 1940 and 1948 respectively, Y_{40} and Y_{48} the total consumer money income for the years 1940 and 1948, and k the ratio of the income velocity of circulation in 1948 to that in 1940, we can write:

$$(1) \qquad \frac{M_{40}}{Y_{40}} = k\frac{M_{48}}{Y_{48}}.$$

If k is assumed to be unity, then[55]

$$M_{48} = \frac{M_{40} Y_{48}}{k Y_{40}} = \frac{16 \times 460}{1 \times 236} = 31.2 \text{ million rubles.}$$

The assumption of unchanged income velocity of circulation is a risky one, not because the amount of money required to support a given level of income is likely to have changed significantly over this period, but because small shifts in velocity can cause fairly large changes in our results. For this reason we make alternative assumptions below. There are two reasons for thinking that velocity in the post-Reform period must have been equal to or greater than velocity in the prewar period. First, the trend in income velocity in the prewar period appears to have been fairly consistently upward. Using the currency figures of Table 8, and the consumer income figures of Table 51, the following income velocity of circulation figures are derived: 1931, 6.8; 1937, 13.9; 1940, 14.8. This trend is not likely to have been reversed, since the factors which were responsible for it have not ceased to operate. Most important of these is the fact that industrialization and urbanization have been constantly increasing; incomes earned in industry and in the cities are paid at more frequent intervals than incomes earned in agriculture. Second, the long wartime experience of "too much money chasing too few goods" is likely to have reduced, rather than increased, the desire of the population to keep part of their wealth in the form of cash.

We therefore assume that the velocity of circulation is greater in 1948 than it was in 1940. An increase of 20 per cent is considered a reasonable upper limit (k is 1.20). In accordance with this assumption, M_{48} becomes 26 billion rubles.

Although it seems unreasonable to expect a decline in the income velocity of circulation, we should at least explore the possible effect of such an occurrence for our estimates. We assume, therefore, as a lower limit, that the velocity of circulation was expected to decline by 20 per cent in 1948 relative to 1940. In this case, $k = 0.833$, and M_{48} is 37.4 billion rubles.

The second step is to relate M_{48} to the pre-Reform quantity of cash in circulation, M_{47}.[56] This can be done as follows:

(2) $$M_{48} = r M_{47},$$

where r represents the effect of the Reform. Now the quantity of currency in circulation can be subdivided into amounts hoarded out of past incomes by the peasants (H_p) and by the workers (H_w) and the money used to pay the current incomes of each group (I_p, I_w). Thus:

$$(3) \qquad M = H_p + H_w + I_p + I_w.$$

Since the Reform went into effect at the end of a pay period, it will be assumed that only the hoards were affected by the 10-to-1 conversion ratio, i.e., that incomes had already been spent. Then

$$(4) \qquad M_{48} = \left[\frac{H_p + H_w}{10} + I_p + I_w\right]_{\text{December 14, 1947}}.$$

This equation states that the quantity of money in circulation after the Reform is equal to the amount needed to pay incomes at the time of the Reform plus one-tenth of the cash balances on hand on December 14, 1947.

Values for the variables on the right-hand side of Eq. (4) must now be derived. The wage bill in 1947 was 280 billion rubles (plan).[57] Since wages are paid twice a month, this figure is divided by 24. This yields a rough estimate for I_w of 12 billion rubles (280/-24). Other currently earned money income is estimated to have been in 1947, as it was just before the war, about one-half of the wage bill,[58] or roughly 140 billion rubles. The amount of cash required to finance these income payments is not reduced by the same proportion as wages, because the income velocity of these payments is much less than that of wages (which was 24). The income velocity is estimated to have been about 10 in 1940;[59] if the same velocity is accepted for 1948, the appropriate amount of currency is 14 billion rubles (140/10).[60]

Applying the values derived above to Eq. (4), we can now solve it for hoards held by the peasants (H_p), assuming different values of k and M_{48}; then using Eq. (3), we may derive alternative estimates of M_{47} (Table 50).

The range between the estimates in Table 50 is very wide, but even the maximum figure of 136 billion rubles, which is based on an unrealistically low velocity assumption, falls far short of estimates made by Western economists. The error of these economists probably stems from a failure to recognize that only cash hoards were reduced at a 10-to-1 ratio. That is to say, they assume $M_{48} = M_{47}/10$, instead of the value given by Eq. (4). Thus, if it is as-

TABLE 50 Estimates of Currency in Circulation on December 14, 1947 (billions of rubles)

	1948	December 14, 1947			
k	M	H_p	I_p	I_w	M
1.25	26.0	0	14	12	26
1.00	31.2	52	14	12	78
(0.833)	(37.4)	(110)	(14)	(12)	(136)

Symbols: M, currency in circulation; H_p, hoards held by the peasants; I_p and I_w, the amounts of currency required to pay the current incomes of peasants and workers respectively; $k = (M_{40} / Y_{40}) / (M_{48} / Y_{48})$, where Y represents consumers' money incomes; I_w is less than I_p though Y_w is greater than Y_p because workers are paid more often than peasants. The formulas for deriving the above figures are given in the text.

sumed that 31.2 billion rubles (M_{48}) was a reasonable target for the Reform, M_{47} is estimated at 312 billion rubles instead of 78 billion rubles as we have estimated.

This fallacy can be looked at from another point of view. If 78 billion rubles was the pre-Reform currency in circulation, and 52 billion rubles was the amount hoarded by the peasants, then the 10-to-1 conversion reduced currency in circulation to 31.2 billion rubles and peasant hoards to 5.2 billion rubles (52/10). These are the results from Table 50. If the conversion ratio had been 20 to 1, the results would have been little different. Hoards would have been reduced to 2.6 billion rubles (52/20), and total cash in circulation to 28.6 billion rubles, only 2.6 billion rubles less than after a 10-to-1 conversion.

The little *direct* evidence which is available indicates that our lowest figure (26 billion rubles) is unrealistic. We have estimated currency in circulation on January 1, 1941 at 16 billion rubles (Table 8). To this can be added more than 20 billion rubles of currency issued to cover the budget deficits of 1941–1943, which totaled 39.5 billion rubles. Part of these deficits, it will be recalled, were financed not by printing currency, but by "mobilizing commodity reserves." [61] Voznesensky supplies us with our one remaining piece of information: "During three years of the Patriotic War currency circulation in the USSR increased 2.4 times." [62] Unfortunately he does not tell us to which three years of the war he is referring. If he means 1941–1943, then the currency in circulation at the end of 1943 must have been almost 40 billion rubles (16 × 2.4). If he refers to 1942–1944, currency in circulation at the end of 1944 must have been about 60 billion rubles ([16 + 8] × 2.4).[63] To these amounts can be added some currency issue as a result of State Bank operations in 1945, and perhaps also in 1946 and 1947 in spite of moderately large budget surpluses in these two years. To sum up: the direct evidence, though ambiguous, indicates that cash in circulation at the end of 1944 amounted to some 50 to 70 billion rubles; that since the *rate* of issue of new currency is not likely to have increased in the subsequent three years (1945–1947), and may have been much smaller, the amount in circulation at the time of the Reform is indicated as falling between 60 and 130 billion rubles. These can be considered fairly extreme limits; the first is a minimum figure based on the assumptions that currency in circulation at the end of 1944 was 50 billion rubles, and that in 1945, 1946, and 1947 small amounts, totaling 10 billion rubles for the whole period, were added to circulation each year; the second is a maximum figure based on the assumptions that currency in circulation at the end of 1944 was 70 billion rubles, and that 20 billion rubles a year were added to circulation in 1945, 1946, and 1947 in spite of large budget surpluses. This estimate, like the previous one, gives a range which is considerably lower than those of other Western economists.

An increase in currency in circulation from 1941 to 1947 of less than 100 billion rubles (our estimate) has at least two important implications. First, the Soviet diversion of resources to defense (and reconstruction) needs was substantially less than the amount implied by other estimates, e.g., the B.I.S. increase of more than 300 billion rubles (from 1941 to 1947, the Soviets spent, through the budget, about 700 billion rubles on defense and 500 billion on the national economy). Second, though the Soviet fiscal apparatus clearly failed to operate successfully in terms of holding inflation in check, it certainly did not disintegrate as completely as the B.I.S. and other estimates would seem to indicate.

Post-Reform Period. The Reform presumably wiped out a large part of the repressed inflation which had been generated during the war; the situation from 1948 on appears to have been quite stable. Since the Reform, the price cuts in government stores have been followed by reductions in collective farm market prices which indicate that no new repressed inflation has been allowed to develop in the market for consumers' goods. According to M. M. Lifits, prices on the collective farm markets fell by more than 75 per cent in 1947–48, by an additional 29 per cent in 1949, and still further in 1950, following reductions in state prices.[64]

The budget's role in 1948 and 1949, with surpluses of 39.6 and 24.7 billion rubles respectively, was strongly deflationary. To a considerable extent these surpluses served to offset the very large program of short-term lending undertaken by the State Bank at this time.[65] The 1948 surplus, expressed as a percentage of total receipts, was the largest in Soviet history. This leads us to believe that the Reform may not have been successful in eliminating *all* repressed inflation, and that this surplus served not only to offset newly created short-term credit, but also to "mop up" vestiges of war-generated inflation.

Both planned and realized surpluses were relatively small in 1950: 5.3 [66] and 9.5 billion rubles respectively. The planned surplus in 1951 was also small: 6.5 billion rubles.[67] A significant policy change must have occurred during 1951: the preliminary totals for that year show expenditures underfulfilled by 10 billion rubles, receipts overfulfilled by 10 billion rubles, and the surplus therefore overfulfilled by about 15 billion rubles. The surplus continued large in 1952; receipts exceeded expenditures by 37.5 billion rubles, the second largest recorded surplus. The sharp decline which was planned for 1953 (13.7 billion rubles) did not materialize; expenditures were underfulfilled by a considerably greater amount than taxes leaving a surplus of 24.9 billion rubles.[68] A sharp decline again is in prospect for 1954 with a surplus of only 9.1 million rubles planned;[69] previous experience, however, suggests viewing this Soviet plan with considerable caution.

There is too little information available on Soviet finance to make more than rough guesses regarding these trends. The very large budget surpluses of 1951, 1952, and 1953 would seem to indicate a continuation of the large short-term credit programs of 1948 and 1949 mentioned above, to which the surpluses served as fiscal counterbalances. The temporary cessation of such surpluses in 1950 may reflect the very substantial shift in the distribution of the national output toward the consumer which occurred in that year. No explanation is offered for the substantial overfulfillment of surpluses in 1951 and 1953 nor for the small surplus planned for 1954.

Chapter 10

THE "BURDEN" OF MONEY TAXATION

We saw in Chapters 1 and 2 that the principal fiscal problem in the Soviet Union is absorption of the excess purchasing power which tends to accumulate in the consumer sector for two reasons: because the rate of nonconsumption expenditures normally undertaken by the state is very high, and because the household and the state are the only significant economic sectors. In the present chapter we shall examine the consequences of this situation from another point of view. Our intent is to estimate the impact on the consumer of the state's efforts to close the inflationary gap; that is, we shall try to measure the burden of taxation which the household has had to bear in the absence of any private industry to share the cost of the state's activities.

Two time series will be presented: (1) consumer money income, and (2) money taxation of the consumer; the ratio of (2) to (1) is the average rate of taxation.

The average rate of taxation is the measure of the tax burden accepted by Shirras and Rostas in their study of British taxation.[1] It is the simplest quantitative formulation of the burden and is clearly deficient in several respects. First of all, the extent of the burden depends in part on the nature of the public expenditures the taxes are designed to finance. Taxs to finance programs of social security, education, and garbage collection may constitute less of a burden than those used to finance defense, foreign aid, or long-term investment programs, since the benefits received from the former may be more immediately perceived by the taxpayer and may to a greater extent substitute for his own expenditure. Secondly, as we pointed out in Chapter 3, the psychological impact of a tax depends to a large extent on the form in which the tax is levied: a commodity tax is probably less burdensome than an income tax; and a loan, even though it may never be repaid, is probably less burdensome than either commodity or income taxes because of the hope that it *will* be repaid. Finally, the psychological impact of the burden of taxation depends not only on the average rate of money taxation, but also on the marginal rates, and on the absolute levels of income and taxation in *real* terms. That is to say, a nation with a high per capita real income would probably find it less burdensome to pay 20 per cent of its income in the form of taxes than a nation with a low per capita real income. These are but a few of the many factors, economic and institutional, which would cause a divergence between the psychological burden of taxation and the monetary burden which we shall attempt to estimate.[2]

GENERAL METHODOLOGICAL APPROACH

Measurement of Consumer Income. Two independent methods of determining the money income of Soviet consumers are available to the research worker. The first and most direct approach is to add up all sources of income paid out to households over the course of a year: wages and salaries of workers; income earned by peasants working on the collective farms; income of the farm population from sales of agricultural products to the state and to other households; value of sales by artisans of their handicraft; pensions and other transfer payments; and other items. The second approach is to total household expenditures, i.e., to sum up the total disposition of consumer income on the purchase of consumers' goods and services, payment of taxes, purchases of bonds, changes in deposits held by savings banks, and changes in cash holdings.

Theoretically the two methods should give identical results, and the choice made between them should be on grounds of statistical convenience. American economists who have worked on Soviet national income estimates have used both approaches.[3] In a book entitled *Problems of the Balance of Receipts and Expenditures of the Population*[4] N. Margolin, a Soviet economist, has discussed the methodological problems at length, and constructed hypothetical estimates of both income and expenditure.[5]

We shall estimate consumer money income from household expenditures. In general, this approach is preferable to the income approach for an extended series of estimates, although the latter may be used advantageously for specific years. The principal stumbling block to the income approach is the ambiguity of Soviet data on the total payroll or wages bill of workers and salaried employees.[6] Since the payroll is the largest single receipts item, constituting about two-thirds of consumer money income, serious doubts would immediately be cast on any income time series based on payroll statistics which did not first explain the observed ambiguities in the magnitude of this component. On the other hand, retail trade turnover, the largest single expenditure item, is available for every prewar year and is quite unambiguous except for 1931. With regard to other receipts and expenditure categories, the difficulties seem to be about equally distributed; the advantage therefore remains with the expenditure approach.

Consumer expenditure categories are examined in greater detail below. The general problems in measuring taxation of the consumer will now be considered.

Measurement of Consumer Taxation. The approach used in constructing our principal series of money taxes on the consumer is unorthodox in terms of conventional notions of taxation, but in consonance with the ideas presented in the preceding chapters. Supplementary series based on more conventional definitions are presented later. To summarize briefly: it will be assumed that the incidence of all indirect taxes on commodities purchased by consumers (i.e., turnover and profits taxes) is on the consumer. Furthermore, since most industry is owned by the state, retained profits are also assumed to be a tax on the consumer. Social insurance (the payroll tax) is actually a transfer category; nevertheless, since it adds to the price of commodities purchased by the household, it is considered a tax for our purposes. Purchase of bonds by the population is regarded as a form of taxation for the several reasons mentioned in Chapter 8. Money taxation of coöperatives, including collective farms, constitutes a markup on price and is reflected in retail trade turnover exactly like the profits tax on state enterprises; hence the incidence of these taxes is assumed to be on the consumer (with certain exceptions noted below which apply to all indirect taxes).

At first glance it would appear quite simple to construct a time series of taxes on the consumer, since Soviet budgetary data have been relatively accessible. Actually, the available data are quite imperfect for our purposes.

The first problem arises because the cost of the consumer bill of goods is distorted by subsidies which cover losses not only in the production of consumers' goods but also in production of the producers' goods and raw materials which are subsequently used to produce consumers' goods. The major case in point is the machine tractor station complex which was discussed in Chapter 7. MTS receipts valued at the low obligatory-delivery prices have typically amounted to less than 25 per cent of their expenditures; therefore their operation nominally involves a monetary subsidy from the state. This is due in part to the fact that the receipts in kind of the MTS are valued, for budgetary accounting purposes, at the low obligatory-delivery prices. If these receipts in kind were valued at cost of production, or at retail price, the MTS might turn out to be going concerns. Furthermore, it should be noted that a part of the expenditures on MTS account are investment, rather than operating subsidies (see Chapter 7). The reader persuaded by this argument that the subsidy is illusory may discount the adjustments made below.

Industrial enterprises have also received regular operating subsidies which serve to lower the cost of consumers' goods either directly or indirectly. Should such subsidies be regarded as part of the tax burden? It might be argued that subsidized consumers' goods take on some of the character of government services, and to this extent become part of the nonconsumption expenditures of the state as we have defined them. From this point of view, the subsidies would constitute a legitimate part of the tax burden.

There seem to be two significant differences, however, between services typically underwritten by the state and the subsidies under discussion. First, the consumers'-goods products which benefit from subsidies are rarely offered to the population free of charge, whereas it is not uncommon for social services to be distributed without charge. Second, the subsidies on consumers' commodities are not the result of Soviet social policy but are rather a by-product either of the peculiar accounting relation between the state and some of its economic organizations (as in the case of the MTS) or of an economic policy designed to achieve cost-price stability.

For these reasons subsidies on consumers' goods will not be considered part of the tax burden. Instead, we shall regard them as a part of the true cost of the commodity. For example, suppose that a loaf of bread, originally sold by the state for 2 rubles, received a 1-ruble subsidy which was paid for by the consumer in the form of a turnover tax. The consumer would still be paying 2 rubles for the bread but 1 ruble would be in the form of a tax and 1 ruble would be the subsidized cost. In this interpretation, taxes which finance subsidies in consumers' goods may not properly be designated as a levy on the consumer, but should rather be subtracted from taxes collected from the consumer.

In the statistical study presented below, the desirable adjustment for subsidies to consumers'-goods industries could not in fact be made in the principal series (I and II) because of lack of data. However, an attempt is made to show for a limited number of years the effect on the tax burden of such an adjustment (series III).

Taxes which serve to finance subsidies to producers'-goods industries may properly be regarded as a levy on the consumer, since nonconsumption expenditures should include the true cost of these goods. Accordingly, no adjustment is required for subsidies in this sphere.

Our data are also imperfect because a small percentage of the major indirect taxes which appear in the Soviet budget (for example, the profits and turnover taxes on commodities purchased by the Ministry of Armed Forces) do not fall on the consumer; they are levied on producers' and consumers' goods which are not purchased by the population. This share of the indirect tax collections can in no sense be considered a burden on the consumer, but constitutes simply a bookkeeping transaction within the state sector. It is impossible to separate out precisely these two categories of indirect taxes. Nevertheless, there is enough information to make some reasonable estimates after 1931, and this is done.

A minor distortion is created by the Soviet practice of collecting the turnover tax largely at the wholesale level, i.e., before the commodities are bought by the household. As long as inventories on which the turnover tax is paid remain constant, the rate of tax on the household is not distorted; when inventories increase or decrease, however, the rate of tax is overstated or understated. No attempt is made here to correct for the lag between receipt of tax by the budget and payment by the population.

SOME SPECIFIC PROBLEMS AND ASSUMPTIONS IN MEASURING INCOME AND TAXATION

In addition to the general methodological problems discussed above, many specific problems arose in constructing our estimates, owing both to lack of data and to imperfect data. These difficulties will be considered below. Details of computations and sources are presented in the notes to Table 51.

Consumer Outlay Categories. (*a*) *Retail trade turnover.* Retail trade turnover is the largest category of consumer outlay. It includes the market value of all commodities sold in state and coöperative retail stores and on the collective farm market. Data are available for the whole prewar period under consideration (1925–26 to 1940). Few data are available, however, for the postwar period: the Soviets have published only the plan for 1947 and the plan for the last nine months of 1953. By carefully combining these figures with various scattered pieces of information which have appeared in the Soviet press, Western scholars have made estimates for the postwar years. The most recent, those of Peter Wiles (designated "*A*" estimates), have been accepted in part for our present purposes and are discussed in detail in the notes to Table 51. Reservations are expressed, however, concerning his 1950–1952 figures, and alternative estimates ("*B*" estimates) are presented for these years.

The data must be adjusted for the fact that not all retail sales are to consumers. Bergson (quoting Margolin) points out that in 1937 11.5 per cent of state and coöperative store turnover and 10 per cent of collective farm market turnover constituted sales to institutions rather than to the household.[7] This assumption seems to be in accord with independent data published for the period 1925–1930. The official figures for retail trade turnover are therefore reduced by 11 per cent for all prewar years under consideration. The percentage of institutional trade in retail trade turnover appears to have increased slightly in the postwar period and the adjustment is raised, therefore, to 12 per cent for the years 1947–1953.

(*b*) *Consumer services.* Consumers make substantial outlays for services such as rent, utilities, passenger transportation, amusements, and so forth. Bergson (again quoting Margolin) indicates that in 1934 and 1938 consumer outlays for services amounted to slightly more than 12 per cent of their outlays for goods.[8] Independent data for the period 1925–1930 suggest the same percentage; it is assumed valid for the postwar period also, although there is no evidence either to support or refute the assumption.

(*c*) *Purchases of government bonds.* For most years it was possible to obtain directly the figures for sales of bonds to the public. For some years, however, only the total increase in the national debt was available. This increase includes purchases of bonds from the free reserves of savings banks, from surplus funds of the state insurance organization (*Gosstrakh*), and by other minor investors. Since the percentage shares of these different investors in new issues has been fairly constant over time, the purchases by the population can be estimated without large error for those years in which only the total loan figures are available.

(*d*) *Trade union and other dues.* Bergson [9] estimates that expenditures by the population on dues in 1935 were 1 per cent of the total wage bill. Since wage-bill data are available for the prewar period, the 1 per cent relation is used to estimate a figure for dues for each year from 1925 to 1940. Wage-bill figures are not available for the postwar period. However, social-insurance collections, which are a function of the wage bill, are available for all years, and are used to estimate trade union and other dues for 1947–1953. In 1940, trade union and other dues were 18.8 per cent of the social-insurance collection; this ratio is applied to the years 1947–1953. The correctness of the estimate depends on two assumptions: that the ratio of trade union and other dues continued to be 1 per cent of the wage bill in the postwar period, and that social-insurance receipts were a constant percentage of the wage bill from 1940 to 1953. Both of these assumptions appear to be reasonable; in any case the item is so small that even a large error would have virtually no effect on our results.

(*e*) *Purchase of shares in coöperatives.* Data for this item are not available after 1930. Since it is small, extrapolation was not attempted, and figures are omitted after 1930.

(*f*) *Taxes.* Direct taxes on the population are a form of consumer outlay and must be included in our total consumer expenditure figure. Indirect taxes paid by the population are included implicitly as part of the value of retail trade turnover.

(*g*) *Deposits in savings banks.* A small part of consumer net income is deposited each year in savings banks. The increase in bank deposits over the year represents another form of income disposal by the household. Data on savings deposits are available for the entire period under consideration.

(*h*) *Cash holdings.* If consumer outlay is not equal to consumer income, the difference is reflected in a change in the amount of cash held by the household. That is to say, if the household receives more income than it spends, it is left holding larger cash balances; on the other hand, if it overspends its income, cash balances decline. In order to estimate consumer income from the outlay side, it is therefore necessary to add to consumer outlay the change in cash balances held by the population. This is equivalent to looking upon the change in cash balances as another way of disposing of income.

Consumer money income is assumed to have been increased or decreased each year by the increment or decrement to currency in circulation; in other words, it is assumed that the entire increment to currency in circulation is held by the population, rather than by institutions or economic enterprises. This is a reasonable assumption. Enterprises and organizations hold virtually no cash in their tills except on paydays when the local branch of the State Bank supplies enough cash to meet payroll requirements. Cash received by enterprises from sales to the population is deposited with little delay. Almost all interenterprise transactions are financed by bank account transfers rather than in cash. The amount of currency in circulation is available for the years through 1937; estimates for 1940 and 1941 were made in Chapter 2. The figures for 1938 and 1939 were then interpolated. No data are available for the postwar period. However, large budget surpluses, annual retail price cuts, and modest increases in the value of retail trade turnover in the postwar period all lead us to believe that increases in currency in circulation could not have been large. Very arbitrarily, an annual increase of 2 billion rubles is assumed for the years 1948–1953. A higher figure, 5 billion rubles, is assumed for 1947, the year preceding the Currency Reform.

Taxation of the Consumer. Estimates of consumer taxation are fairly straightforward with the exception of the two adjustments mentioned above, namely, (*A*) to allow for indirect taxes which do not fall on the consumer, and (*B*) to deduct subsidies on consumers' goods from total taxes on the consumer. The general methods used will be described briefly below. Details are contained in the notes to Table 52.

(*a*) *Turnover tax and profits*. For the period 1935–1941, Soviet sources provide a distribution of turnover-tax receipts and profits by branch of industry and by commissariat. These data are used to make rough estimates of the amounts of tax originating in consumers' and producers' goods in these years. Other Soviet sources suggest a smaller incidence on the consumer in the postwar period, due in the case of the turnover tax, for example, to the greater importance of the army in food purchases and, in the case of profits, to the reduction or elimination of subsidies and the establishment of profits in many producers'-goods industries.

(*b*) *Social insurance and other indirect taxes.* The distribution of the social-insurance markup between consumers'- and producers'-goods industries is based on Bergson's estimates for 1937.[10] The same relation is used for indirect taxes. This is an extremely crude expedient, but no better method could be found.

The category "other indirect taxes" includes such items as customs receipts, the tax on services, the tax on coöperatives, local taxes on industry, and state income from timberlands. Detailed figures for each item are not available for all years; however, since the share of "other indirect taxes" in budget income remained fairly constant (3 per cent) in the years for which complete data are available, this ratio was used to fill in the gaps.

(*c*) *Subsidy adjustments.* Subsidies are subdivided into MTS subsidies and subsidies granted directly to enterprises operating at a loss.

The MTS subsidy for 1938–1940 can be estimated directly from official data; estimates for 1937 and 1948–1950 were based on 1938–1940 relations and other scattered information (see notes to Table 52; estimates for other years were not attempted). Since most MTS activity is devoted to the production of food and industrial crops eventually purchased by the household, it is assumed, in making the deduction from taxes, that two-thirds of the MTS subsidy applies to commodities purchased by the consumer.

Direct subsidies to industry are derived as a residual figure. From Soviet sources it is known that the budget expenditure category "financing the national economy" includes the following expenditures: investment in fixed capital, investment in working capital, gross expenditures on the MTS, "operating" expenditures,[11] and subsidies. Estimates for the first three of these categories and for the total (financing the national economy) are available for the nonwar years since 1937. A residual comprising subsidies and operating expenditures can therefore be estimated. As operating expenditures are generally considered to be small, it is assumed that the entire residual is subsidies.

Soviet literature clearly indicates that the bulk of the general operating subsidies apply to nonconsumers'-goods products. However, since subsidies to the coal industry and other raw material and producers'-goods industries indirectly reduce the cost of consumers' goods, their effect should be taken into account. Accordingly, it is assumed that 20 per cent of general subsidies affect consumers'-goods costs, and should be deducted from taxes. Not too much faith is placed in these adjustments, and they are not included in our main series; crude as they are, however, the results achieved are not without interest.

Further Considerations. Soviet budget data are first published in plan form for the current year; in the subsequent year preliminary estimates of the actual results are given; another year later the final results are given. The same procedure is followed in presenting data for most other financial magnitudes. As far as possible, final or preliminary estimates were used; in many cases, however, planned figures had to be used, since they were the only ones available. No distinction is drawn between the preliminary and final estimates, which rarely differ by more than a fraction of 1 per cent; planned figures are designated as such (in the notes to the tables), and must be accepted with reservations.

STATISTICAL RESULTS: "BURDEN" OF TAXATION

Estimates of consumer money income (by outlay) for the periods from 1925–26 to 1940 and 1947–1953 are presented in Table 51. The years 1941–1946 are omitted because no usable data for our major expenditure category, retail-trade turnover, are available for this period, and because the very strong repressed inflation which pervaded the Soviet economy in these years seriously reduces the reliability of our estimates for reasons mentioned below. The estimate for 1931 probably understates consumer income by 15 to 20 per cent, because of the huge illegal trade (not reported in the retail-trade turnover figures) which occurred in this year.

Three series of estimates of consumer taxes are presented in Table 52. Series I, which covers the entire prewar period, is unadjusted for (1) indirect taxes which are not paid by the consumer and (2) subsidies on consumers' goods. Consequently this series overstates taxation of the consumer. Series II is adjusted for the taxes not paid by the consumer; the adjustment is not attempted for the period from 1925–26 to 1929–30. Series III attempts an adjustment for subsidies to consumers'-goods industries for the years 1937–1940 and

TABLE 51 Soviet Consumer Money Income (Outlay) 1925–26 to 1953 (billions of rubles)

Year		Retail sales, adjusted	Consumer services	Trade union dues	Shares in coöp-eratives	Direct taxes	Purchases of govern-ment bonds	Increment in savings	Increment in cash holdings	Total
1925–26		10.4	1.1	0.1	0	0.6	0	0.1	0.2	12.5
1926–27		12.2	1.4	0.1	0	0.9	0.1	0.1	0.3	15.1
1927–28		13.4	1.7	0.1	0.1	1.1	0.3	0.1	0.4	17.2
1928–29		15.2	1.8	0.1	0.1	1.1	0.1	0.2	0.7	19.3
1929–30		16.5	2.1	0.2	0.2	1.1	0.7	0.2	1.7	22.7
1931		24.4	3.5	0.3		1.6	1.6	0	1.3	32.7
1932		42.5	5.7	0.4		2.4	2.4	0.2	2.7	56.3
1933		54.6	7.4	0.5		3.5	3.2	0.2	−1.6	67.8
1934		67.5	9.1	0.6		3.8	3.4	0.5	0.9	85.8
1935		85.6	11.3	0.7		3.2	3.8	0.8	2.0	107.4
1936		108.8	13.9	0.9		3.8	3.5	1.1	1.6	133.6
1937		127.8	15.9	1.1		4.0	4.3	1.0	1.5	155.6
1938		146.3	17.7	1.2		5.1	6.1	2.0	1.6	180.6
1939		172.1	20.7	1.4		7.0	6.7	0.6	1.6	210.1
1940		192.5	23.1	1.6		9.4	9.2	0.2	0	236.0
1947		311.7	37.4	2.8		28.0	21.8	0.8	5.0	407.5
1948		330.2	39.6	3.0		33.2	20.3	1.5	2.0	429.8
1949		343.0	41.2	3.3		33.7	23.5	2.6	2.0	449.3
1950	*A*	350.9	42.1	3.6		35.8	26.4	1.5	2.0	462.3
	B	364.7	43.8	3.6		35.8	26.4	1.5	2.0	477.8
1951	*A*	382.9	45.9	4.0		42.9	32.6	4.0	2.0	514.3
	B	396.8	47.6	4.0		42.9	32.6	4.0	2.0	529.9
1952	*A*	393.6	47.2	4.1		47.4	36.3	4.5	2.0	535.1
	B	407.7	48.9	4.1		47.4	36.3	4.5	2.0	550.9
1953		448.0	53.8	4.4		46.1	17.3	10.0	2.0	581.6

For sources and methods, see Appendix. The reader is cautioned that some of the figures are planned rather than final magnitudes, and others are estimated very indirectly.

1948–1950. These latter two series give a much closer approximation to the actual average rate of money taxation of the consumer than does Series I; on the other hand, Series I enables us to observe the dynamics of tax policy in the NEP and First Five Year Plan periods.

Dividing each of the three taxation series by consumer income gives estimates of the average rate of money taxation; these are presented in Table 53.

In the discussion of these ratios which follows, the reader should keep the following reservations in mind:

TABLE 52 **Money Taxation of Soviet Consumer, 1925–26 to 1953 (billions of rubles)**

Year	Turnover tax	Craft and excise taxes	Profits	Other indirect taxes	Direct taxes	Purchases of government bonds	Social insurance	Total, Series I	Adjustment for taxes not paid by consumers	Total, Series II	Adjustment for subsidies	Total, Series III
1925–26	—	1.3	1.2	0.6	0.6	0	0.8	4.5	—	—	—	—
1926–27	—	1.9	1.8	0.6	0.9	0.1	0.9	6.2	—	—	—	—
1927–28	—	2.2	2.4	0.6	1.1	0.3	1.0	7.6	—	—	—	—
1928–29	—	2.9	3.3	0.8	1.1	0.1	1.2	9.4	—	—	—	—
1929–30	—	4.6	5.4	1.3	1.1	0.7	1.4	14.5	—	—	—	—
1931	11.7	—	6.0	1.1	1.6	1.6	2.2	24.2	4.9	19.3	—	—
1932	19.6	—	6.6	1.1	2.4	2.4	3.6	35.7	7.0	28.7	—	—
1933	27.0	—	7.3	1.3	3.5	3.2	4.3	46.6	8.7	37.9	—	—
1934	37.6	—	6.4	1.5	3.8	3.4	5.7	58.4	10.5	47.9	—	—
1935	52.2	—	7.8	2.1	3.2	3.8	7.0	76.1	11.6	64.5	—	—
1936	65.8	—	14.2	2.7	3.8	3.5	8.9	98.9	18.6	80.3	—	—
1937	75.9	—	16.9	3.3	4.0	4.3	6.6	111.0	22.0	89.0	6.4	82.6
1938	80.4	—	15.7	3.8	5.1	6.1	7.2	118.3	20.4	97.9	6.8	91.1
1939	96.9	—	26.3	4.6	7.0	6.7	7.6	149.1	24.9	124.2	8.9	115.3
1940	105.9	—	32.0	5.4	9.4	9.2	8.5	170.4	28.9	141.5	8.0	133.5
1947	239.7	—	24.1	11.6	28.0	21.8	14.9	340.1	64.6	275.5	—	—
1948	247.3	—	39.3	12.3	33.2	20.3	16.2	368.6	71.9	296.7	19.7	277.0
1949	245.5	—	69.6	12.9	33.7	23.5	17.5	402.7	93.9	308.8	19.0	289.8
1950	236.1	—	65.5	13.1	35.8	26.4	19.6	396.5	90.8	305.7	15.6	290.1
1951	247.8	—	74.9	14.1	42.9	32.6	21.4	433.7	98.8	334.9	—	—
1952	246.9	—	83.5	15.0	47.4	36.3	21.9	451.0	103.4	347.6	—	—
1953	243.6	—	89.3	16.2	46.1	17.3	23.2	435.7	106.4	329.3	—	—

For sources and methods, see Appendix. The reader is cautioned that some of the figures are planned rather than final magnitudes, and others are estimated very indirectly.

TABLE 53 Average Rate of Money Taxation, 1925–26 to 1953 (per cent)

Year	Series I	Series II A	Series II B	Series III
1925–26	36.0			
1926–27	41.1			
1927–28	44.2			
1928–29	48.7			
1929–30	63.9			
1931	74.0[a]	59.0[a]		
1932	63.4	51.0		
1933	68.7	55.9		
1934	68.1	55.8		
1935	70.9	60.1		
1936	74.0	60.1		
1937	71.3	57.2		53.1
1938	65.7	53.4		49.6
1939	71.0	57.2		53.0
1940	72.2	56.8		53.4
1947		67.6		
1948		69.0		64.4
1949		68.7		64.5
1950		66.1	64.0	62.8
1951		65.1	63.2	
1952		65.0	63.1	
1953		56.6		

For sources, see Appendix.
[a] These figures are untrustworthy. See p. 258.

(i) Series I is not an actual rate of taxation but rather an index of the movement in the rate of taxation over time. Series II and III are better approximations of the actual rates of money taxation.

(ii) These series include neither income in kind nor taxation in kind, both of which are much more important in the USSR than in most Western nations. Bergson estimates consumption of farm income in kind to have amounted to 30 billion rubles in 1937. My estimate for the tax in kind on grains in 1937 is 15 per cent; if this figure is assumed to be representative of all agricultural commodities in 1937, income in kind before tax is estimated to have been about 35.0 billion rubles. To this must be added 2.5 billion rubles in army subsistence. Accordingly total household income is 37.5 billion rubles greater than our estimate in Table 51, or 193 billion rubles; total taxes would be increased by 5 billion rubles, or 94 billion rubles (Series II). The rate of tax, including both income and taxation in kind, would be about 49 per cent in comparison with the money tax of 57 per cent. The money rate of tax is, of course, overstated because the turnover tax includes already the monetary equivalent of part of the tax in kind, while the household money-income series do not include any part of the income in kind. It should also be noted that the tax in kind is relatively low in 1937 because of the excellent crop in that year.

(iii) Many of the estimates upon which these series are based are crude.

BURDEN OF TAXATION: THE UNITED STATES AND SOVIET UNION COMPARED

The most striking result of the calculations summarized in Table 53 is the sheer size of the Soviet tax burden. That more than half, at times two-thirds, of personal income should return to the state in the form of taxes is indeed revealing with regard to the importance of state activities in the Soviet economy. A perspective on the significance of the Soviet rate of taxation can be gained by comparing it with the rate of taxation in a Western nation, and this will be attempted below.

Institutional peculiarities have led us to include in the category of taxes in the Soviet Union many consumer outlays which would not be so classified in other countries. For this reason the estimates of the average rate of taxation of the consumer computed in this chapter cannot be meaningfully compared with similar computations for other countries. In order to facilitate comparison, an attempt will be made to bridge the institutional gap, although the significance of such a comparison is admittedly very limited.

Our procedure will be to estimate the total of taxes (federal, state, and local) on the consumer in the United States, defining tax on the consumer in the same way as we have defined it for the Soviet Union. Thus, included in our total of taxes on the consumer will be the following unusual aggregates: purchases of government bonds by the public; the annual contribution to social insurance which is assumed to be passed on entirely to the household; the corporate profits tax, undistributed corporate profits (because retained profits of Soviet industry were considered a tax), and sale of corporate securities to the population for the purpose of financing new investment. Retained profits of unincorporated enterprises were not included because data were not available. The incidence of indirect taxes on and profits of business enterprises is assumed to be entirely on the consumer. The estimates for the United States are presented in Table 54.

TABLE 54 Average Rate of Taxation in the United States, 1940 and 1949 (billions of dollars)

	1940		1949	
	Soviet framework	Western framework	Soviet framework	Western framework
Personal income	78.3	78.3	206.1	206.1
Taxation of household				
Direct taxes	2.6	2.6	18.7	18.7
Indirect taxes	10.0	10.0	21.3	21.3
Purchases of government bonds	0.5		4.3	
Social insurance	2.3		5.7	
Corporate profits tax	2.9		11.0	
Undistributed corporate profits	2.4		9.8	
Sales of new corporate securities[a]	0.6		4.6	
Total taxes	21.3	12.6	75.4	40.0
Average rate of taxation[b]	27.2	16.1	36.6	19.4

For sources, see Appendix.

[a] Sale of new corporate securities does not include securities which were issued for the purpose of refunding previously issued securities.

[b] The gap between United States net private investment and investment financed by corporations from undistributed profits and sales of new securities suggests that the retained profits of unincorporated enterprises (not included above because figures are unavailable) may be substantial. Inclusion of this item as a tax on the household could conceivably raise the average rate of taxation, Soviet framework, to roughly 30 per cent in 1940 and 40 per cent in 1949.

We see that the rate of taxation in the United States is much lower than in the Soviet Union, even when the data are structured in accordance with Soviet institutional conditions. Under a capitalist institutional framework, the United States rates of taxation are of course lower still: 16 per cent instead of 27 per cent for 1940, and 19.5 per cent instead of 36.5 per cent for 1949. Soviet rates for these years (Table 53, Series II) were 56.8 and 68.7 per cent, respectively. The difference between the Soviet and United States rates reflects primarily the much higher rate of nonconsumption expenditures in the USSR. The real burden of Soviet taxes is undoubtedly even greater, compared to the United States, than the figures would indicate, because of the much lower level of real national income in the USSR. However, awareness of the burden is probably obscured to some extent because most Soviet taxpayers have never experienced higher standards of living, and because so large a part of their income is taken away in the form of higher prices rather than as direct levies upon income. In addition, the Soviet ratio of marginal to average tax rates appears to be unusually low, a condition which tends to minimize the impact of such taxes.

TRENDS IN THE BURDEN OF TAXATION

In this section we shall examine changes in the average rate of taxation as an indicator not only of the psychological burden of taxation, but also of changes in the rate of nonconsumption expenditures. In connection with these purposes it is important to note that the average rate of taxation is affected by changes in the degree of repressed inflation in the state sector of the economy. An increase in repressed inflation is reflected in higher prices in the collective farm markets, hence in larger household income from sales in these markets. At the same time, an increase in repressed inflation is indicative of too low a rate of taxation to support the rate of nonconsumption expenditures presumed by the state investment plan. Therefore, when repressed inflation is on the rise, taxes tend to be understated and household income overstated; the burden (taxes/income) is less than that which would obtain if taxes were large enough for fiscal stability. Conversely, when repressed inflation is being reduced, the burden of taxes tends to be overstated.

If the effects of repressed inflation could be removed from the ratio of taxes to income, the resulting series would obviously be a better index of changes in the rate of nonconsumption expenditures (though not, perhaps, of the psychological burden of taxation). If the *volume* of trade on the collective farm markets had remained relatively constant, it might indeed have been possible to remove a large part of the effect of changes in repressed inflation by deducting from the household-income series income from sales on the collective farm markets. Unfortunately, the volume of trade on these markets did not remain constant: between 1927 and 1931 sales fell gradually to zero as the state attempted to liquidate what was then called private trade; the markets were reconstituted in 1932 and the volume of trade rose steadily thereafter to 1939, and perhaps to 1940. Because the volume of collective farm market trade fluctuated, no attempt will be made to quantify the impact of repressed inflation on the average rate of taxation; its distorting effect will be taken into consideration, however, in the discussion which follows.

Other modifications in our series would be in order if we were primarily concerned with determining the Soviet rate of nonconsumption expenditures. For example, a closer approximation to the actual rate of nonconsumption expenditures could be obtained by removing transfer payments from both the income and tax series. This would have the effect of reducing the ratio of taxes to income, but would leave the trend from year to year relatively unchanged.

It would also be appropriate, in attempting to determine the actual rate of investment, to add to the total of taxes the increments or decrements to currency in circulation. To the extent that taxes, profits of nationalized industry, and receipts of the state from other sources are insufficient to cover Soviet nonconsumption expenditures (including those financed by short-term bank loans of the Gosbank), the government introduces new currency into circulation. Including changes in currency in circulation with taxes has the effect, in most years, of increasing the ratio of taxes to income, but with the exception of the years 1932 to 1934 it does not affect the trend.

Since we are primarily concerned with the rate of taxation of the population, neither of the above adjustments is made, nor are certain other minor sources of financing investment taken into consideration.[12]

The First Five Year Plan Period. Series I shows a continuous and fairly constant increase in the rate of taxation from 1925–26 until 1929–30, when the trend turns abruptly upward. The period includes the end of the NEP and the first two years of the First Five Year Plan; we may infer from the steady increase during the NEP that the state was by no means marking time while the blueprints for a planned economy were being drawn up.

It is interesting that the full impact of the industrialization drive was not felt by the population until the second year of the plan period. This seems to be in accord with other available information. It was originally planned that the net rate of investment would increase from 18.9 per cent in 1927–28 to 22.6 per cent in 1928–29 and 25.1 per cent (minimal variant) or 28.2 per cent (optimal variant) in 1929–30.[13] Apparently progress in 1928–29 was sufficiently satisfactory to warrant raising the target for investment in 1929–30 by about one-third over the original plan.[14] Our figures suggest, if anything, an even more abrupt shift to nonconsumption output in 1929–30 than was contemplated in the revised plan.

The large increase in the rate of taxation in 1931 may be largely spurious. It is reported that in the interim between the abolition of private trade and the reopening of collective farm markets in 1932 a large amount of illegal private trade was conducted, the value of which was not included in the official figures.[15] Furthermore, to the extent that trading operations were discouraged, consumption in kind by the peasants probably increased. Both of these factors would cause our rate of taxation to be spuriously high in 1931, the first by reducing computed consumer money income, and the second by causing a real shift from consumption of marketed commodities to consumption in kind.

Some illegal trade may also have been conducted in 1929–30 and our tax rate for that year may be slightly high. However, it is probable that even if illegal trade could have been taken into account, an extraordinary increase in the rate of taxation would still have occurred in this year.

As was noted in Chapter 2, repressed inflation increased steadily from 1928 to 1932, when collective farm market prices are reported to have reached a peak. Prices of some goods were 15 times the ration prices of comparable goods sold in coöperative stores. The growth of repressed inflation in this period implies that the share of the government sector in the national output was growing even more rapidly than the average-rate-of-taxation series indicate.

Second and Third Plan Periods. From 1932 to 1936 the average rate of taxation increased slowly. As an indicator of the rate of nonconsumption, this increase has an upward bias, due to the fact that from 1933 to 1937 repressed inflation was gradually being worked off[16] (Chapter 2, pp. 55 ff). It is not possible to say with certainty whether the absolute level of consumption from marketed output rose, remained the same, or declined from 1932 to 1936. The standard of living could have risen if the national output — the per capita productivity — was increasing at a faster pace than the rate of taxation; it would have fallen if national output and productivity had remained the same or declined. Soviet indexes of output and productivity for industry both show unusually rapid increases beginning in 1933;[17] the output of the major crops also increased from 1933 to 1935, with a sharp decline, however, in 1936.[18] All in all, the indications are that some increase in living standards probably did occur from 1932 to 1936.

The situation from 1936 to 1938 is unambiguous: the share of consumer income absorbed by taxes declined by 7 percentage points — fairly conclusive evidence of a rise in the consumers' share in the national output. These figures are in accord with the fact that the 1937 harvest was exceptionally good and undoubtedly affected the level of consumption in both 1937 and 1938.

In 1939 the rate of taxation rose as rapidly as it had declined in the preceding year. The increase reflects both the harvests in these years and preparation for war which apparently began in earnest in 1939; the proportion of budgeted defense expenditures to total budgetary expenditures was 18.7 per cent in 1938, 25.6 per cent in 1939, and 32.5 per cent in 1940. Failure of the burden to increase in 1940 may seem curious in view of the threatening international outlook; two developments explain this low figure, however. First, a substantial part of increased defense needs were met by a cutback in expenditures on the national economy, particularly industry. (From 1939 to 1940, absolute expenditures on the national economy as a whole and on industry alone fell from 60.4 to 58.3 billion rubles, and from 31.1 to 28.6 billion rubles, respectively. Since total budgetary expenditures were increasing, the percentage decline in these items was much greater: from 39.4 to 33.4 per cent, and from 20.3 to 16.4 per cent, respectively.) Second, repressed inflation appears to have been rising again in 1940, so that the change in the average rate of taxation probably understates the real increase in the rate of nonconsumption expenditures. Finally — a purely technical factor — our upward adjustment in 1940 of 4 percentage points for the incidence of the turnover tax on goods purchased by the military establishment (see notes to Table 52) may have been too abrupt.

Postwar Period. Soviet sources indicate that there has been little or no repressed inflation since the Currency Reform of December 1947; accordingly, we may assume that, with the exception of 1947, the postwar trend in the rate of taxation reflects the trend in nonconsumption expenditures fairly accurately. The existence of repressed inflation in 1947 explains, of course, the spurious decline in the average rate of taxation indicated from 1947 to 1948. In 1948 the burden stands higher than in any prewar year: 69 per cent of household money income was handed over to the government in the form of taxes. From 1948 to 1953, however, the burden declines every year, reaching, in 1953, 56.6 per cent, the level of the late thirties. This trend reflects the much publicized consumers'-goods price cuts of the postwar period (mentioned in Chapter 9). The decline in the burden, it should be noted, was not steady but occurred almost entirely in two years; in 1950 the burden fell by 2.6–4.7 per cent and in 1953 by 6.5–8.4 per cent. This is easily explained: the 1950 retail price cut was probably the largest of the postwar period; and it was in 1953 that the new Malenkov regime attempted to make peace with the people by reducing sharply not only prices but direct taxes and sales of government bonds as well.

The principal implication of this decline in the rate of taxation is that by 1953 the consumer was getting a considerably larger share of the national output than in 1948; since national output undoubtedly increased substantially over this period, the absolute increase in consumer income must have been very large.

This development may not support the popular conception of a Russia arming to the teeth, but it is not unreasonable. The rate of taxation in 1953 is not low even by Soviet standards; it still exceeds the rate which prevailed in many years of the prewar period. Since in 1948 the rate of taxation was 12 per cent higher than the prewar peak, the reasonable interpretation is to regard the 1948 rate of taxation as unusually high, reflecting a structure of production not yet returned to normal after the war. The decline in taxation from 1948 to 1950 may represent, then, nothing more than a return to normalcy. There are good reasons for expecting an increase in consumers'-goods output in this period. During the war years consumers' stocks and reserves must have declined to an exceptionally low level, and provision had to be made for restocking. Furthermore, the morale of the population may have been at a low ebb after a difficult war involving years of privation; the reduction in rate of taxation may have been required for reasons of internal political stability. The sharp reduction in 1953 also reflects, no doubt, considerations of political stability, those related to the shift in the reins of government. This has been discussed in detail elsewhere and nothing need be added here.[19] In conclusion, it should be noted that the shift in the distribution of national output toward the consumer does not necessarily mean that the absolute amount of investment, defense expenditures, and so forth declined commensurately, because the increases in consumption probably were met primarily by increased productivity.

ALTERNATIVE MEASUREMENTS OF THE BURDEN

The burden of Soviet taxation as presented in Table 53 is based on a rather sweeping definition of what constitutes a tax on the Soviet population; the rates are accordingly on the high side. For reasons discussed in detail in Chapter 4, certain elements of the Soviet cost-price structure have been regarded as taxes, although they contain elements of factor cost. For example, profits have been considered a tax, rather than a return to capital or a reward for exceptional entrepreneurial ability. The social-insurance markup has also been considered a tax, although a case could be made for treating it as an addition to wages. We have treated sales of government bonds to the population purely as a tax, although in Chapter 7 it was demonstrated that such sales should be classified somewhere in between taxes and truly voluntary sales of government bonds. Because some of these interpretations might be considered arbitrary, we present in Table 55 some alternative estimates of the burden of Soviet taxation, leaving the reader to his own preference.

In the first alternative estimate, both bond purchases and the social-insurance markup are subtracted from the total of taxes (Series II) as computed in Table 52. The resulting figures, divided by total income, are designated Series IV in Table 55. If the reader desires to add the subsidy adjustment of Series III, this can be approximated roughly by deducting from Series IV the difference between Series II and III (in Table 53).

In the second alternative estimate, retained profits (See Tables 47 and 48) as well as bond purchases and the social-insurance markup

TABLE 55 Average Rate of Money Taxation Recomputed, 1932–1953 (per cent)

Year	Average rates of taxation								Ratio of health, education, and transfer payments to total taxes (Total II, Table 52) VII
	Basic rate of tax (from Table 53) II		Adjusted for social insurance and sales of government bonds IV		Adjusted for social insurance, sales of government bonds, and retained profits V		Adjusted for expenditures on health, education, and transfer payments VI		
	A	*B*	*A*	*B*	*A*	*B*	*A*	*B*	
1932	51.0		42.2		36.9		38.8		30.3
1933	55.9		46.9		42.3		43.8		28.0
1934	55.8		47.4		44.9		43.3		28.4
1935	60.1		52.1		49.3		45.9		28.7
1936	60.1		53.1		48.6		43.7		32.4
1937	57.2		51.6		48.4		38.3		38.7
1938	53.4		47.3		45.4		35.4		38.7
1939	57.2		51.5		48.2		40.7		33.9
1940	56.8		50.5		47.5		40.1		34.4
1947	67.6		59.8		59.6		45.0		40.8
1948	69.0		61.8		59.9		47.8		36.8
1949	68.7		60.9		57.8		46.8		38.4
1950	66.1	64.0	57.6	55.7	54.9	53.1	44.5	42.9	39.4
1951	65.1	63.9	56.0	54.3	53.4	51.8	45.2	43.7	37.1
1952	65.0	63.1	55.4	53.8	53.1	51.6	45.1	43.6	37.3
1953	56.6		51.0		49.3		36.3		42.1

For sources, see Appendix.

are subtracted from the total of taxes (Series II), and the result is divided by total income to yield the ratio designated Series V.

The third modified series (VI) is conceived in terms of a very crude benefit theory of taxation. Budget expenditures on education and health services are deducted from the total of taxes on the ground that the household benefits directly from these expenditures, in contrast to other budget expenditures (investment in the national economy, defense, administration, etc.) which benefit the household only indirectly if at all. In addition, transfer payments—e.g., social security (pensions and other assistance, upkeep of invalid homes, rehabilitation of injured workers, etc.), social insurance (insurance for sickness and old age), subsidies to mothers, and the debt service—are removed from *both* the income and the tax series. Although taxation to finance transfer payments is not without its psychological burden, its impact is certainly offset in part by the distribution of payments. The justification for this approach is that the Soviet government does finance a relatively large program of educational and medical services and transfer payments. It might perhaps be objected that part of these expenditures serve the ends of welfare very obscurely; the education expenditures, for instance, finance a large volume of Party propaganda in various media and also scientific research which may be directed to the development of hydrogen bombs. The objection is proper; however, it is not operationally feasible to draw a distinction between budget expenditures for education and for propaganda in either the USSR or most other countries. As for scientific research, expenditures on this item have been reported independently (under the heading "Social and cultural expenditures") at least since 1949; they have amounted to about 10 per cent of the outlays on education. This provides a clue to the importance of expenditures on research when they were lumped with education. It is of course entirely possible that large outlays for nuclear research are still included under education; so far as I know, there is no reliable information on this matter. Since 1949, expenditures on the press, theaters, and so forth, have been included in the budget under education only to the extent that enterprises are not self-financing.[20] Before 1949, gross expenditures on these categories were financed by the budget. I am not sure whether or not budget expenditures on education are net of receipts from tuition fees; if not, there is an overstatement of expenditures on education from this source.

In Series VI, and in Series IV and V, a rough adjustment for subsidies to consumers'-goods industries can be made by the reader in the manner described earlier.

It can be seen from Table 55 that even after adjustments have been made the average rate of taxation is still very high. Deducting the social-insurance markup and bond purchases from total taxes (Series IV) reduces the burden by only 7 to 8 percentage points. Deducting, in addition, the retained profits of state enterprises (Series V) reduces the burden by at most another 3 points. With all these deductions, the average rate of taxation exceeds 45 per cent for all years after 1934, and is between 53 and 60 per cent in the postwar period with the exception of 1953.

The burden is reduced by as much as one-third to two-fifths when education and health services are deducted from taxes, and transfer payments are removed from both income and taxes. Even with this generous interpretation, the average rate of tax still ranges between 35 and 47 per cent of income.

A question of considerable interest is the extent to which increases in the rate of taxation served to finance increased social services and transfer payments to the population. Series VII in Table 55 is intended to shed light on this matter; it shows the ratio of budgeted expenditures for these purposes to total taxes (Series II). The ratio climbed 10 percentage points between 1933 and 1937, indicating that an increasing share of taxes on the consumer returned fairly directly to the population in this period, while less was devoted to other nonconsumption items (defense, investment, administration). In 1939, as the Soviets prepared for war, the trend was sharply reversed. In 1947 the ratio is spuriously high owing to the existence of repressed inflation. After 1948 the relative importance of expenditures on social services rises; by 1950 it exceeds the 1937 level. The ratio declines in 1951 and 1952 but increases again in 1953 by 5 percentage points to reach a new peak.[21]

FACTOR COST OF GOODS AND SERVICES SOLD TO CONSUMERS

Some interesting subseries can be derived from the figures presented above by deducting from total consumer income the increments to savings and cash balances, and all taxes. The derived series can be viewed as either receipts or expenditures. Viewed as expenditures, the series represents the cost of production of goods and services sold to the consumer. The logic behind this conception is that consumer expenditures can be divided into three broad categories: payments for cost of production, taxes, and increments to savings. If we deduct the latter two, only production costs remain.

Conversely, the costs of production of consumers' goods and services may be divided into payments to workers in the form of wages and salaries, depreciation, and payments to the agricultural sector for deliveries of produce to the state. Viewed as receipts, then, the series represents incomes earned in the production of consumers' goods, plus depreciation.

In addition, there is included on both the receipts and expenditures sides an identical entry for sales or purchases on the collective farm market.

These relations can best be visualized by examining a balance of income and expenditures:

Balance of Income and Expenditures

Incomes earned (plus transfers) =

1. Wages earned
   a. Producing consumers' goods and services
   b. Producing nonconsumption goods (investment, defense, education)
2. Sales of agricultural products
   a. To state and coöperative organizations (primarily obligatory deliveries)
      (i) For producing goods sold to consumer
      (ii) For producing goods not sold to consumer
   b. On collective farm market[22]
3. Transfer income

Incomes disposed

4. Consumer retail-trade turnover:
   a. State and coöperative stores
      (i) Cost of goods, excluding depreciation
      (ii) Markup over cost (taxes + social insurance)
      (iii) Depreciation
   b. Collective farm market.[22]
5. Purchase of services
   a. Cost excluding depreciation
   b. Markup over cost
   c. Depreciation
6. Direct taxes, purchases of government bonds, increment in savings deposits, increment in currency circulation.

These accounts can be used to represent three sets of currency-commodity flows: the labor cost of consumption goods to the state, the labor cost of nonconsumption goods, and the value of goods transferred in collective farm markets. These flows are represented by the following identities:

	Incomes earned		*Incomes disposed*
(1)	$1a + 2a(\text{i})$	$=$	$4a(\text{i}) + 5a,$
(2)	$2b$	$=$	$4b,$
(3)	$1a + 2a(\text{i}) + 2b$	$=$	$4a(\text{i}) + 5a + 4b,$
(4)	$1b + 2a(\text{ii}) + 3$	$=$	$4a(\text{ii}) + 4a(\text{iii}) + 5b + 5c + 6.$

These four equations represent, respectively, the following categories:

(1) Consumption goods (excluding collective farm market transactions)
(2) Collective farm market transactions
(3) Total of (1) and (2)
(4) Nonconsumption goods including transfer payments [23]

The first equation states that the income earned from producing consumers' goods is identically equal to the labor cost of production (or procurement) of consumers' goods to the state. The second states the equivalence of the value of goods sold and purchased on collective farm markets. The third, which is the sum of the first two, includes all income from economic activity by the household. The fourth states that the income of the state (from taxes, bond sales, use of consumer savings, printing of money [24]) is identically equal to the cost to the state of its nonconsumption expenditures excluding depreciation in consumers'-goods industries.

Next we are interested in deriving series which represent the factor cost of goods sold to the consumer. The reader is reminded that agricultural output is valued not at cost of production (which is unknown) but at procurement price. The series presented therefore understate the factor cost of goods sold to the consumer. The amount of understatement is equal to the tax on the agricultural producers, expressed in value terms. For the purpose of deriving the series, it is necessary to add the cost of depreciation in the production of consumers' goods to the first and third identities. The revised equations follow:

(1′)	$1a + 2a(\text{i}) + d$	$=$	$4a(\text{i}) + 5a + d,$
(3′)	$1a + 2a(\text{i}) + 2b + d$	$=$	$4a(\text{i}) + 5a + 4b + d,$
(4′)	$1b + 2a(\text{ii}) + 3 - d$	$=$	$4a(\text{ii}) + 5b + 6,$

where $d = 4a(\text{iii}) + 5c$ (depreciation in consumers'-goods industries).

The series which will be derived by the method mentioned at the beginning of this section will implicitly include *d*, because *d* is not explicitly deducted from the value of goods sold to the consumer. Actually, *d* is very small, and will not be considered in the discussion which follows. The reader should keep in mind, however, that both (1′) and (3′) do include depreciation cost in addition to labor cost, and therefore represent a closer approximation to the factor cost of production of consumers' goods than equations (1) and (3).[25]

Limitations of the Analysis. Let us consider (3′). The series derived from it is an aggregative value index of either side of that identity. For our purposes, it is more useful to consider the series first from an income-earned point of view (the left-hand side of the equation), since this provides us with a functional distribution of its main components. These are: wages and salaries receipts of the peasant sector from procurements by state and coöperative organizations, and sales on the collective farm markets. The enumeration suggests the limitations on the usefulness of such an index for analytical purposes; it represents the aggregation of three separate price-quantity series which have tended to vary with respect to each other in an irregular manner.

The first component, the average annual wage, has increased at a fairly steady but rapid rate — about elevenfold between 1926–27 and 1948.[26] State procurement prices have risen much more slowly, and at very irregular intervals.[27] Prices on the collective farm markets have displayed a rapid secular trend upward, but have in the short-run fluctuated inversely with the success of the state in meeting the effective demands of the household for food and other consumers' goods. The lower limit to prices on the collective farm markets has generally been the price at which similar commodities are selling in the government stores; the increase in prices in government stores was, according to Western estimates, from twenty- to thirty fold between 1926–27 and 1948.

Although it is impossible to eliminate from our series derived from (3′) the effects of unlike prices (thereby obtaining an index of the *quantity* of consumers' goods available), the series is nevertheless of interest. Since it represents the sum total of incomes earned by the population in the production or sale of consumers' goods and services (plus depreciation), it may be viewed as an index of the factor cost of consumption goods.

It is possible to isolate state and coöperative trade, since figures or estimates for private and collective farm market trade are available for all years covered except 1931. This second series, which is derived from (1′), has the advantage of fewer variables to be explained. What is more important, it represents the cost of resources devoted by the socialized sector of the economy to the output of consumers' goods; this is of interest because it is a first step toward ascertaining the amount of real resources the state is willing to use to fill the inflationary gap. Inclusion in our first series — derived from (3′) — of sales on the collective farm market obscures the answer to this question, because shortfalls of state and coöperative supplies tend to be offset in the aggregate retail sales figure by the higher prices the peasants are able to obtain for their products on the open market.

Unfortunately, it is not possible to reduce our value figures for the cost of state and coöperative retail trade to an index of physical volume, because there is no adequate deflator series to eliminate the effect of rising wage rates and procurement prices.[28] As a value index the series is likely to be misleading, not only because of the inflation of factor costs which has occurred, but also because agricultural commodities have been undervalued throughout most of the period under discussion, and the extent of undervaluation has been increasing constantly. This means that a change in the quantity of consumers' goods produced by state or coöperative enterprises has a much greater effect on the total factor cost of goods sold in state and coöperative stores than an equivalent change in the quantity of consumers' goods procured by the state from the agricultural sector of the economy and resold to the population.

Although our two sets of series (Tables 56 and 57) cannot be deflated, they are still revealing when examined in conjunction with the average rates of taxation computed earlier, and with average wage-rate and productivity data. The steady increases (except for 1929–30) shown in Table 57 for the first five years reflect the liquidation of private trade and the substitution for it of state and coöperative trade. For this reason Table 57 is not revealing with respect to the level of consumption of the population.

It will be recalled that the average rate of taxation (Series I) increased from 36 per cent to 64 per cent in this period, with half of

TABLE 56 Factor Cost of Sales of Consumers' Goods and Services Including Collective Farm Market Sales, 1925–26 to 1953 (billions of rubles)

	Series				Change [a] (per cent)	
	I	II		III		
Year		*A*	*B*		*A*	*B*
1925–26	7.6	—		—	—	
1926–27	8.4	—		—	10.5	
1927–28	8.9	—		—	6.0	
1928–29	8.8	—		—	−1.1	
1929–30	5.9	—		—	−33.0	
1931	(7.5)	(12.4)		—	—	
1932	17.3	24.3		—	—	
1933	22.1	30.8		—	26.7	
1934	25.4	35.9		—	16.6	
1935	—	39.4		—	9.7	
1936	—	49.7		—	26.1	
1937	—	63.0		69.4	26.8	
1938	—	79.1		85.9	25.6	
1939	—	86.3		95.2	9.1	
1940	—	100.2		108.2	16.1	
1947	—	123.4		—	—	
1948	—	126.6		146.3	2.6	
1949	—	132.6		151.6	4.5	
1950	—	149.5	165.0	165.1 [b]	12.7	24.4
1951	—	169.4	185.0	—	13.4	12.1
1952	—	176.9	192.7	—	4.4	4.1
1953	—	235.9	—	—	33.4	22.4

For source, see Appendix.

[a] These columns give the percentage change from year to year. The percentages are based on Series I until 1929–30, and on Series II for 1933 to 1953.

[b] This is the *A* estimate. The *B* estimate for this year is 180.0.

the increase occurring in the last year. This development is clearly reflected in the very small increase in the cost value of goods sold in 1927–28, and in actual declines in 1928–29 and 1929–30. Since costs (wage rates) were undoubtedly rising, it seems quite probable that real consumption from marketed commodities was declining even before 1929–30.[29]

In the four years from 1927–28 to 1932, the cost value of goods sold by state and coöperative stores (Table 57) roughly doubled. In the same period the average wage earned in socialized industry also doubled.[30] The effect of wage inflation on cost was probably *not* miti-

TABLE 57 Factor Cost of Consumers' Goods and Services Excluding Collective Farm Sales, 1925–26 to 1953 (billions of rubles)

Year	Series I	Series II A	Series II B	Series III	Change[a] (per cent) A	Change[a] (per cent) B
1925–26	3.2	—		—	—	
1926–27	3.9	—		—	21.9	
1927–28	5.7	—		—	46.2	
1928–29	6.4	—		—	12.3	
1929–30	4.9	—		—	−23.4	
1931	7.5	12.4		—	53.1	
1932	10.6	17.6		—	41.9	
1933	11.9	20.6		—	17.0	
1934	12.9	23.4		—	13.5	
1935	—	26.5		—	13.2	
1936	—	35.8		—	35.1	
1937	—	47.2		53.6	31.8	
1938	—	57.4		64.2	21.6	
1939	—	59.6		68.5	3.8	
1940	—	63.5		71.5	6.5	
1947	—	82.7		—	30.3	
1948	—	88.6		108.3	7.1	
1949	—	95.8		114.8	8.1	
1950	—	111.9	127.4	127.5[b]	16.8	33.0
1951	—	125.3	140.9	—	12.0	10.6
1952	—	127.4	143.2	—	1.7	1.6
1953	—	179.5	—	—	40.9	25.3

For source, see Appendix.

[a] These columns give the percentage change from year to year. The percentages are based on Series I until 1929–30, and on Series II from 1933 to 1953.

[b] This is the *A* estimate. The *B* estimate for this year is 142.4.

gated by increases in productivity: the official Soviet index of industrial productivity, which is generally believed to contain a substantial upward bias in these years, shows only a 36 per cent increase.[31] It is doubtful that much increase in the output of industrial consumers' goods occurred over these years.

The case of agricultural commodities is less clear. Although output of major crops declined from 1928 to 1932,[32] government procurements of some crops, including the most important one, wheat, appear to have increased.[33] Thus it is possible that the volume of agricultural commodities sold by state and coöperative stores to the public increased—although if it did, it was undoubtedly at the expense of peasant income in kind.

From 1932 to 1935, the cost value of consumers' goods sold by the state increased by 13 to 17 per cent a year. There are reasons for believing that although this increase was due in part to rising prices, it must have reflected quantity increases as well. It should be kept in mind that any increase in the volume of retail-trade turnover due either to the shift from consumption in kind to consumption of marketed goods (a concomitant of rapid urbanization) or to population increases does not reflect an increase in the standard of living. Wage rates were indeed rising rapidly in this period, from an average 1,427 rubles per year in 1932 to 2,269 rubles in 1935. But the effect of this inflation of the wage rate on the cost of industrial consumers' goods was offset by two factors, First, there was a relatively rapid increase in industrial productivity in these years,[34] as the Soviets gradually succeeded in mastering the new machines and techniques that had been introduced during the First Five Year Plan. Second, the policy of maintaining stable industrial prices led to distribution of subsidies on an ever-increasing scale in the early thirties to offset rising costs. Finally, it should be noted that there was a moderate increase in government procurements of grain in this period.[35]

The cost value of total retail trade (Table 56) increased still more rapidly. Collective farm market sales, which were legalized again in 1932, roughly doubled in value from 1932 to 1935; since collective farm market prices were more than halved over the same period, the increase in volume of sales on these markets is clearly understated by the value figures.

The 35 per cent increase in the value of goods sold by the state in 1936 over 1935 must be interpreted with considerable reserve. Although some increase in quantity may have occurred, the wholesale elimination of subsidies to many sectors of the national economy abruptly and substantially increased the cost prices of most raw materials and equipment, thereby raising the costs of production of consumers' goods.[36]

From 1936 to 1938 the cost value of consumers' goods supplied by state and coöperative stores increased by more than 50 per cent; there is little doubt that much of the increase was due to an increase in supply. The 1937 crop was outstanding, and the years 1937 and 1938 are usually considered the peak years of the thirties for the production of industrial consumers' goods. The rise in the retail price level in state and coöperative stores was, for the Soviet Union, very moderate; between January 1936 and July 1939 a selected group of food items increased in price by only 15.8 per cent, and clothing prices rose only 26.3 per cent.[37] Factor costs did rise moderately in this period; wages continued their upward course, and some increase in the cost of procurement of industrial crops occurred as a result of the use of premiums to encourage cultivation.

The increase in cost value of commodities sold by state and coöperative stores was only 3.8 per cent in 1939 and 6.5 per cent in 1940 (and the latter figure is spuriously high for reasons mentioned above — see p. 259). This reflects the shift from consumption to defense.[38] However, the cost value of consumers' goods including those sold on the collective farm market (Table 56) continued to increase substantially until 1940. We may infer from this that consumers were trying to buy in the collective farm markets the commodities which could no longer be obtained in state and coöperative stores.

Postwar Period. It is generally believed that the level of consumers'-goods output in 1947 was still below 1940. For this reason, and because the average rate of taxation in 1947 was still substantially above the prewar level, we may interpret the 30 per cent increase in the cost value of state and coöperative sales between 1940 and 1947 as a measure of the lower limit to the unit cost increase over this period; the actual cost increase was undoubtedly much greater.[39]

On the other hand, the increases which occurred from 1948 to 1953 may be attributed primarily to increases in the quantity of goods supplied. There was little if any rise in unit costs in this period. The average annual wage rose from an estimated 7100 rubles in 1947 to, according to reports, a little more than 8100 rubles in 1953,[40] an average annual increase of roughly 2 per cent. It seems highly probable that industrial productivity kept pace with wages over this period. Agricultural procurement prices also remained unchanged from 1948 to 1953 with the exception of the year 1953 when they were raised as part of the program to improve agricultural incentives. The increase in procurement prices may explain in part the exceptional increase in our index of retail trade at factor cost which occurred in 1953. The big years for the consumers were, according to our estimates, 1950 and 1953; without doubt there was a very large increase, in both years, in the volume of goods made available to the population by state and coöperative stores. If the "*A*" estimates, based on Dr. Wiles' calculations are accepted, the increase in the cost value of retail trade in 1953 exceeded that in 1950 by almost 250 per cent; on the basis of the "*B*" estimates, one might conclude that the increase in 1950 was greater.

It is interesting to compare our estimates of changes in the cost value of Soviet retail trade with their own volume index expressed in terms of so-called "comparable" prices (see Table 58). Correlation

TABLE 58 Increase in State and Coöperative Retail Trade, 1948–1953 (per cent)

Year	Official Soviet estimate in "comparable" prices	Writer's estimate at factor cost *A*	Writer's estimate at factor cost *B*
1948	—	7.1	—
1949	20.0	8.1	—
1950	30.0	16.8	33.0
1951	15.0	12.0	10.6
1952	10.0	1.7	1.6
1953	21.0	40.9	25.3

For sources, see Appendix.

between the two series is clearly very rough; although the direction of change from year to year is similar, the amount of change and the absolute magnitudes indicated diverge sharply for most years. With the exception of 1953 and 1950 ("*A*"), the Soviet figures indicate a more rapid rate of growth than do our own of the volume of retail trade turnover. Only a few tentative and partial explanations for the observed differences can be offered here. First, since labor productivity was probably increasing more rapidly than wages over the period in question, our measure of the cost value of retail trade turnover of industrial consumers' goods would tend to understate the increase in comparison with a measure in "comparable" prices. Second, the extraordinarily large increase in our measure for 1953 may be attributed in part to the increase in agricultural procurement prices which occurred in that year. Third, the extent to which our measure is below the Soviet measure in 1952 may be explained in part by the reduction in wholesale prices in 1952.

On the other hand, the sharp rise in wholesale prices with the elimination of subsidies in 1949 would make it more difficult to explain the relatively small increase in our measure of cost value in 1949. Another puzzle appears in considering the difference in weighting systems between the two sets of estimates. Our estimates for industrial consumers' goods are based on costs of production, primarily wages, and for agricultural commodities, on procurement prices. This procedure tends to weight industrial consumers' goods heavily since procurement prices of agricultural commodities are very low. Although we do not know how the Soviets arrive at their estimates, they may use either retail prices or 1926–27 prices (until 1950), both of which weight agricultural commodities more reasonably. Since sales of industrial consumers' goods have increased more rapidly than sales of agricultural products in the postwar period,[41] our index should tend, for this reason, to show a greater increase than the Soviet index.

Further explanation of discrepancies between the series appears to be impossible at present because of lack of information. The discrepancies should not be allowed, however, to obscure the basic trend indicated by both series: the very rapid increase in the volume of goods made available to the Soviet household in the postwar period.

PART IV: EVALUATION

Chapter 11

A CRITIQUE OF SOVIET TAXATION

Critical comments on Soviet taxes have appeared throughout the preceding pages, and particularly in Chapter 3, where the principal reasons for the Soviet choice of taxes were examined. Nowhere thus far, however, have explicit criteria of equitable and efficient tax policy been systematically applied to the Soviet tax system as a whole; this is the objective of the present chapter.

We shall ignore many of the traditional criteria which have come down to us from Adam Smith and his neoclassical successors in favor of standards which are more relevant to taxation in quasi-mobilized inflationary economies. These are: control of inflation, maintenance of economic incentives, equitable distribution of the burden of taxation, and economic allocation of resources. Furthermore, our application of these standards (which are relevant to many economies today) will be modified by considerations peculiar to the Soviet Union. Taxes are not final ends in themselves, but rather one means of implementing economic and social policy; it follows that in evaluating the Soviet tax system we can reach meaningful conclusions only if we accept some policy objectives (however perverse they may seem) as given. The most important politico-economic reality which is taken as given in this chapter is the very high level of government expenditures and the high rate of taxation this requires. In appraising the confiscatory taxes levied on kulaks in the thirties — to take an extreme example — we can hardly avoid basing our evaluation on the Soviet political objective of liquidating the kulaks as a class. There would not be much sense in substituting some other objective — encouragement of the kulak, say — and then evaluating the tax on the basis of its equitable treatment of kulaks and maintenance of kulak incentives.

Before proceeding further we must recognize that the nature of the criteria chosen precludes the possibility of arriving at precise, quantifiable results. Moreover, the criteria are sometimes inconsistent, perhaps even contradictory; they do not constitute, collectively, a touchstone by which we may determine whether the tax system as a whole is unequivocally good or bad. Each tax has both merits and demerits from the point of view of its equity and efficiency; these attributes are neither comparable nor a fortiori additive.

CRITERIA FOR TAXATION

Our criteria of good tax policy are too well known to require more than the briefest summary here.

1. *Containment of Inflation.* Few will deny that it is sound tax policy, over periods of *prolonged* mobilization or quasi mobilization, to "pay as you go," allowing neither open nor repressed inflation. Taxation short of this goal leads eventually to violations of the equity, incentive, and allocation criteria, as will be demonstrated below in the discussion of these criteria. A pay-as-you-go policy has the additional virtue of avoiding postmobilization financial difficulties of the sort which plagued most nations after World War II. Some small rise in prices or addition to liquid assets may under certain circumstances be a desirable substitute for additional taxes; the expedient cannot be employed on any larger scale, however, without experiencing the disadvantages of repressed or open inflation. The merits and demerits of the so-called disequilibrium system of repressed inflation in comparison with a pay-as-you-go policy have been discussed elsewhere at length and need not be elaborated here.[1]

2. *Incentives to Work.* A critical problem which usually must be faced at high levels of taxation is balancing the disincentive effects of additions to the liquid assets of individuals against the disincentive effects of still higher taxes. There are three reasons for preferring higher taxes over the long run. First, taxes do not have a cumulative effect, whereas increments to liquid assets are additive from year to year. Second, the speed of adjustment to higher taxes is quite rapid; in the past, increases in taxes which caused great alarm when proposed have not had most of the undesirable effects predicted for them.[2] On the other hand, nations do not adjust quickly and easily to repressed inflation, which continues to interfere with the efficient functioning of an economy until it has either been "worked off" gradu-

ally or eliminated drastically by currency repudiation and reform. Third, as was pointed out in Chapter 3, high taxes may have a positive incentive effect on many persons; the effect of repressed inflation on work incentives is always adverse. Aside from this problem, we will generally be concerned, in connection with incentives, with the degree of progression (regression) of the Soviet tax system.

3. *Equity.* The burden of mobilization should be distributed equitably among all population groups: rich and poor, urban citizen and peasant. The criterion must be applied not only to the tax burden per se, but also to the real consumption of different segments of the population, and to the distribution of forced savings. For example, the equity criterion would not be fulfilled by the use of highly progressive taxation of current income during mobilization if the wealthier persons in the community could, by spending accumulated wealth, buy a disproportionate share of the reduced consumers'-goods output. It is also important to tax during mobilization to prevent the distribution of wealth in the postmobilization period from becoming excessively skewed in favor of particular groups.

The equity objective conflicts with the incentive objective in several ways. For example, some inflation might be preferable to higher taxes because it typically induces rentiers, housewives, and others not contributing directly to the mobilization effort to join the employed labor force. Yet inflation is one of the most inequitable ways of distributing the burden of mobilization.[3] Another example: high tax rates on industry in capitalist countries, particularly high marginal rates, are probably justifiable on equity grounds during mobilization or war. Yet such rates may lead both to less efficient production and to low resistance on the part of employers to wage increases; this is because when marginal tax rates are very high and prices are controlled, the incidence of rising costs is on taxes paid to the government rather than on retained profits.

In several ways the equity objective stands in direct contradiction to Soviet political objectives.

4. *Allocation of Resources.* Our fourth criterion for a tax system is that it should not conflict with proper allocation of the components of production at the least administrative cost. Ideally such an allocation is secured by the maintenance of an economic cost-price system and the widest possible use of the market mechanism for con-

ducting transactions. As was indicated in Chapter 1, however, the state cannot depend on the market for its share of the nation's output in times of great stress and rapid change; direct allocation of critical materials, although costly to administer, is mandatory. Furthermore, prices, and especially the prices of household necessities, cannot usually be left uncontrolled. By the most primitive conception of equity those basic necessities which are in short supply during mobilization must be kept within the reach of the poorest persons' pocketbooks. It is usually necessary to freeze wages as well; failure to do so under mobilization conditions would almost certainly result in wage-price spiral inflation. The role of taxes in the mobilization period is to reinforce direct controls wherever these replace the automatic market mechanism. This criterion will be discussed later in greater detail.

5. *Political Objectives.* Like some other nations, the Soviet Union levies taxes to implement political objectives. It has discriminated against petty entrepreneurs and private farmers and in favor of the workers and collective farmers, against the commune and TOZ and in favor of the artel form of collective farm organization, and so forth. Objectives of this sort will be taken as given, and will be discussed only insofar as they conflict with other criteria which are not automatically excluded by the political objective. In other words, we shall judge "political" taxes by their success in achieving their stated purpose with the least derangement to the economic mechanism.

These are the five criteria by which we shall evaluate Soviet tax policy. No tax system could satisfy all criteria simultaneously; of necessity Soviet tax policy, like that of other nations, reflects a compromise between conflicting objectives. The nature of the compromise will, of course, differ from nation to nation.

CONTAINMENT OF INFLATION

The rapid increase in wage rates relative to productivity was probably the most important single cause of Soviet inflation in the prewar period. The average annual wage increased by more than 400 per cent from the beginning of the First Five Year Plan in 1928–29 until 1940; no one, even in the Soviet literature, has claimed a comparable increase in productivity. Since the Currency Reform of 1947, however, wage rates have risen much more slowly — probably by only a few per cent a year. By various indirect methods, Schwartz estimates a 4 per cent increase in the average wage rate from 1947 to 1948, and Barker estimates 3 per cent increases in 1949 and 1950.[4] A very recent report suggests that the average wage increase from 1947 to 1953 was no more than 2 per cent annually (see note 40, p. 366).

The relatively moderate increase in budgetary expenditures over the past five years is additional evidence that wages are no longer increasing rapidly. Until 1937, budget expenditures at least doubled every fourth year; the increase from 1937 to 1940 was somewhat less, 64 per cent. In comparison, the increases over the four-year periods ending in 1950, 1951, 1952, and 1953, though displaying considerable variability, averaged only 17 per cent. It is improbable that budget expenditures, which contain a substantial wage component, could have remained so stable (4 per cent average annual increase) if wages have been rising rapidly.

One other development damped the increase in budgetary expenditures in this period. There was a shift in the distribution of national output after 1948 from goods and services purchased by the state to those purchased by the household (see pp. 260–261). Although this shift was quite substantial in 1950 and 1953, it was probably not very significant in the other years. Primary responsibility for budgetary stability in this period must be assigned to stability of wage rates.

As long as there are no changes in tax laws, direct tax collections from the population are also closely correlated with consumer income and with the average wage rate; this provides us with another means of checking wage stability since 1947. Until 1952, the annual increases in direct taxes collected from the population have been 10 per cent or less (the decline in 1953 is attributable to a change in the tax law), which, if one considers that the labor force is continually growing and productivity increasing, implies a less than 10 per cent increase in the average annual money wage rate and an even smaller increase in unit labor costs.[5] This deduction supports the estimates of Schwartz and Barker mentioned above.

It seems fairly clear from these pieces of evidence that there has been little inflation in the labor market. It does not follow that inflationary pressures have been absent, or that tax policy has been responsible for containing whatever inflationary pressures existed.

We have seen that in the prewar period fiscal policy alone was unable to offset the inflationary effect of short-term credit policy; the ineffectiveness of the profits tax as a means of controlling enterprise expenditures on wages was demonstrated in Chapter 2. Since there is nothing in the Soviet literature to indicate that the present administration of the profits tax differs from the prewar procedure, we may assume that it is still relatively impotent in this respect. On the other hand, short-term credit policy is now even *more* inflationary than it used to be. Enterprises are financing a larger portion of their working capital needs from Bank loans than ever before; this is ostensibly to permit better administrative control by the State Bank.[6] As long as this short-term lending policy continues, inflationary pressures in the factor markets cannot be avoided. It was conjectured in Chapter 2 (p. 47 ff.) that a little inflation may even serve a useful purpose, given the Soviet disposition to plan for overfull employment of the factors of production. Planning errors may be corrected more readily when enterprises have some financial slack.

Intensification of direct controls in the postwar period confirms the hypothesis that containment of inflationary pressures in the labor market was not accomplished by fiscal policy. If the latter were adequate to contain wage inflation, there would be no need to strengthen the former. Either State Bank control over wage-fund expenditures or direct controls over labor mobility could, *if effective,* prevent the competitive bidding up of wages made possible by inflationary credit policy. Precedence cannot be assigned to one or the other on a priori grounds; it is likely that the two types of controls reinforce each other. This seems the more plausible because past evidence indicates that neither system of controls alone has been completely effective.

The situation with regard to enterprise expenditures on raw materials and equipment is similar to that of the labor market. No open inflation is possible here, since prices have always been strictly administered. Nevertheless, repressed inflation must have been widespread in the thirties; if enterprises could get excess cash to spend on wages, noncash funds for other purposes must have been even more readily available, because these funds were less closely controlled. The same is probably true today. Since open wage inflation has disappeared, we cannot be sure that repressed inflation exists in the raw-materials and equipment markets. We do know, however, that in the past few years the number of funded commodities (those which are directly allocated) has been very much expanded (p. 15). This casts suspicion on the efficacy of monetary and fiscal controls in preventing repressed inflation in these markets.

What about inflation in the consumers'-goods markets? There has been no open price inflation in state and coöperative stores; instead, as we noted in Chapter 9, prices have been reduced on six separate occasions since the 1947 Reform. Even with these lower prices, disposable income has apparently not been in excess of the supply of consumers' goods. Repressed inflation in the Soviet Union usually overflows into the collective farm markets and can be detected by the resulting differential between these market prices and state retail prices. The evidence indicates that from 1948 through 1950 collective farm market prices were very little, if at all, above state prices. In 1948, according to V. Moskvin, "Prices on the collective farm markets in most cities approached the level of unified state retail prices and in some cities the market prices of some products — meat, potatoes — were lower than state retail prices." [7] In 1949, according to M. M. Lifits, prices fell by 29 per cent in comparison with 1948 (this is certainly larger than the decline in state prices) and in 1950, collective farm prices fell *significantly* when state prices were lowered.[8]

Although there is no doubt that the Soviets have successfully contained household inflationary pressures in the postwar period, it cannot be inferred that the Soviets have once and for all found the answer to this problem. Of course, stability of the wage level vastly simplifies the problem of keeping an equilibrium between demand and supply in the consumers'-goods markets, and a continuance of such stability may well mean the end of serious repressed inflation problems in the Soviet Union. However, the period since 1948 has been atypical in that the share of the national output destined for the consumers'-goods markets has been increasing. The Soviets have undergone a period of what might be called planned deflation, in which the volume of consumers' goods has rapidly increased and the rate of taxation decreased. Fiscal planning under these circumstances is certainly simplified. There was relative price stability and little repressed inflation in 1937 and 1938, a period similar to the present in that the supply of consumers' goods was increasing. In

1939 and 1940, as defense mobilization got under way, supplies available for the population declined again. Fiscal controls did not keep pace with altered market conditions, and even though prices and direct taxes were increased, repressed inflation developed. The same may happen in the future if the Soviets again step up their rate of mobilization.

INCENTIVES

The system of monetary rewards in Soviet industry is very strongly oriented toward creating and maintaining work incentives. Differential wages are used to attract workers to jobs in which their productivity is high. About 75 per cent of all Soviet industrial workers are employed on a piece-rate basis,[9] and a large percentage of these are paid at progressively higher rates if they exceed established standards. In many factories workers also receive, as part of the regular wage system, premiums for reducing waste, economizing on raw materials or fuel, and improving the quality of the product. It is much publicized that the best workers, the so-called stakhanovites, often earn several times as much as the average worker. In addition to incentive payments paid from the regular wage fund, there are bonuses paid to workers and managers from the Director's Fund, Stalin prizes for outstanding accomplishments in all fields, and a host of nonmonetary rewards.[10]

This system of rewards does not remain undisturbed by taxes. However, it is disturbed less than one would expect in a system in which more than half of personal income is drained off into the budget. The neutrality of Soviet taxation, as we pointed out in detail in Chapter 3, is due primarily to exploitation of the money illusion — i.e., to the use of commodity taxes rather than direct taxes as the main source of budget revenue. The average and marginal rates of commodity taxation are quite difficult to perceive.

If maintenance of work incentives were the *only* concern of the Soviet tax authorities, a rational tax policy would probably dictate the use of proportional or regressive direct taxation to meet all of the budget's financial requirements. Proportional and regressive taxes do not reduce the effect of existing wage differentials. Furthermore, a regressive tax structure might increase the incentive to work; the lower-income groups would have to work harder to achieve a subsistence standard of living, and leisure would become progressively more expensive to the higher-income groups. Direct taxes would be preferred to commodity taxes because taxpayers would be fully conscious of the above effects and would be influenced by them in making economic decisions.

In actual practice this policy is politically infeasible. As we have already indicated, it is very doubtful if any nation could levy an income tax which took on the average more than half of each household's income. If such a tax were levied, it would have to be progressive or proportional; a regressive income tax would seem to be beyond the power, and certainly the discretion, of even the Soviet authorities.

Because the Soviets rely primarily on commodity taxation, the importance, from an incentive point of view, of the degree of progression-regression in the tax structure is reduced. As it happens, the tax structure appears to be, on the whole, roughly proportional and therefore incentive-neutral on this count also. The turnover tax is either proportional or mildly regressive. The low income tax is, for most social and economic groups, only mildly progressive, and should not affect incentives significantly. Government bonds appear to be sold, typically, on a proportional-to-income basis.

Incentives are a function not only of money income and the impact of taxation on income, but also of the option to spend income freely. If there is repressed inflation and the ratio of current money income to total liquid assets falls below the level dictated by the liquidity preferences of the population, the incentive to work declines. The introduction of rationing under these conditions further weakens the incentive to earn money income. As we have seen, there has been little or no repressed inflation in the consumers' goods market and no rationing since the Currency Reform of 1947, and therefore no impairment of workers' incentives from this source. In fact, the Currency Reform was followed almost immediately by a large influx of workers into the industrial labor market (p. 18).

The incentive effect of the present tax in kind on collective farms would be very powerful if the prescribed method of computing it were strictly observed in practice. Since 1940 delivery quotas have, in theory, been determined by the amount of land in the possession of collective farms. The effect of such a tax on incentives can be likened to that of a poll tax: the marginal rate of tax on effort is zero. This means that the relative prices of work and leisure are unaffected; no encouragement to leisure is granted via the substitution effect. The income effect, however, encourages work.

The average rate of the tax in kind appears to be high, so that many collective farms are left with only a small surplus to distribute to members. The rates have been so high, in fact, that some farms have been unable to meet their quotas; local authorities responded from 1947 to 1952 by levying higher taxes on the more efficient farms in order to meet local procurement goals. This practice of course vitiated the incentive effect of the tax in kind, since it resulted in high marginal rates of tax, i.e., it penalized the efficient producers. Incentives were restored, presumably in 1953 when local authorities were enjoined from further manipulation of legal delivery quotas.

The effect of taxes on managerial incentives is the most difficult aspect of the incentive problem to evaluate. In Chapter 4 it was shown that turnover taxes play some role in encouraging efficient operation by keeping profits down to a reasonable level in the consumers'-goods industries, where prices typically exceed costs by very large amounts. In addition, the profits tax in all industries is intended to prevent repressed inflation in the industrial sector by deducting into the budget excess funds which accumulate to the accounts of enterprises. The evidence indicates, however, that the profits tax has not in fact been able to perform this function (see Chapter 2).

On the whole, the significance of taxes for managerial incentives is probably small. It is in this area, in particular, that nonmonetary motivations are likely to be dominant.[11]

EQUITY

The equity of the Soviet tax system is difficult to evaluate for both methodological and statistical reasons. In applying a standard of equity to taxes, important implicit assumptions are usually made. First, it is assumed that the primary distribution of income — that is to say, distribution before taxes — is determined by economic forces, and conforms to the relative productivity of individuals except insofar as immobility, monopoly, and other deviations from perfect competition may affect the distribution. Second, it is assumed that other government policies neither reinforce nor offset the effect of the tax on the distribution of income — that the tax, per se, is an indicator of the government's social policy. If, then, the distribution of income before taxes is not in accord with the ideal of a "just remuneration" held by the community in its capacity as voters rather than as economic men, the tax system may be judged as equitable or inequitable by the degree to which the primary distribution of income is modified by taxes to conform with the community ideal of equity.

In the case of some nations, especially the USSR, the second assumption is partially invalidated by the redistributional effects of budgetary expenditures for such purposes as free medical services and education. The Soviet case also strains the first assumption, because the state is the final arbiter of all prices: it determines not only tax rates, but also the procurement prices of agricultural commodities, all wholesale and retail prices with the exception of collective farm market prices, and relative wages and salaries. Under these conditions, can taxes be considered a valid measure of state social policy?

The following hypothetical example will illustrate the problem. The state may levy very high turnover taxes on automobiles and television sets, thereby giving the impression of a severe social policy toward the few wealthy individuals who can afford these commodities. This impression would be misleading, however, if production of automobiles and television sets were heavily subsidized, if the salaries of these well-to-do persons were set at a higher level than the value of their services warranted, if the direct tax on high incomes were relatively small, or if the volume of goods and services distributed free of charge to the rich were larger than to the poor. This example indicates that when the state is free to manipulate prices, wages, and taxes, then none of these taken alone is a valid basis for judging state social policy; only the final distribution of real income is significant.

In practice, though prices are centrally administered, the authorities are not free to set all prices *as they please*. The Soviets rely on economic motivations, and this limits somewhat their area of discretion. For example, one of the most important economic constraints is that wages must be "incentive wages" if the labor market is to discharge its functions properly. As early as 1921 a member of the Central Council of Trade Unions said: "Wage scale policy . . . for the present moment, and apparently for a very long time to come must be a system of maneuvering, and not some sort of system of 'justice.'"[12]

It is interesting that the notion just expressed did not find immediate acceptance. Throughout the twenties there was a strong movement for "equalitarianism" in wages, and some sort of equality of remuneration was considered by many to be the ideal of just distribution. The great need for skilled labor in the early years of industrialization, together with an extraordinarily rapid turnover of labor in industry, led to sharp attacks on equalitarianism, although there is no clear indication that a lack of wage differentiation was at the root of the problem.[13] Stalin fired the first gun in this campaign in a speech in 1931:

> In a number of our factories wage scales are drawn up in such a way as to practically wipe out the difference between skilled labor and unskilled labor, between heavy work and light work. The consequence of wage equalization is that the unskilled worker lacks the incentive to become a skilled worker and is thus deprived of the prospect of advancement; . . . in order to get skilled workers we must give the unskilled worker a stimulus and prospect of advancement, of rising to a higher position.[14]

The wage controversy was finally resolved in the 1936 Constitution: Article 14 guarantees "to each according to his labor."

If relative wages were determined *entirely* by incentive considerations, it would be possible to take the progression or regression of the tax system as a measure of state social policy (abstracting from budget expenditures and the other factors mentioned above). It is just possible, however, that the existing wage differentials, though very large, still embody some equity considerations; if this is the case, differentials might be even larger if determined uniquely by considerations of economic efficiency. Again we see that conclusions about state social policy based only on the tax system must be drawn very circumspectly.

It is particularly important in the Soviet case to consider budgetary welfare expenditures in evaluating social policy; these are unquestionably more significant than the social considerations which may affect wage scales. Relative to the low standard of living in the Soviet Union, the level of social services is high; Bergson has estimated that education and health services, most of which are financed through the budget, amounted to about one-sixth of household consumption in 1937.[15] The budget also includes transfer payments on account of social security (disability pensions, rehabilitation of injured, maintenance of rest homes), social insurance (for sickness and old age), and financial aid to mothers of three or more children. The amount of these transfers has been rising in recent years as a percentage of budget expenditures; in 1950 they amounted to about 8 per cent of household money income. To the extent that the state implements its social policy by the so-called social and cultural expenditures mentioned above, the meaning which can be attached to its tax schedules is significantly reduced.

A major obstacle to estimating the equity of the commodity-tax system is created by the state in the exercise of its power to manipulate quite freely nonwage prices. The most important example of this difficulty is afforded by the Soviet policy of paying below-cost prices to agricultural producers for the bulk of the agricultural products delivered to the state. This means that part of the turnover tax on agricultural products is the monetary equivalent of the direct tax in kind on the agricultural producers; the remainder is, of course, a tax on the consumer. For this reason the turnover-tax rates on agricultural products are not comparable with those on industrial consumers' goods, where the tax is a markup over accounting costs of production. The problem is further complicated by the fact that many industrial consumers' goods may be produced from subsidized industrial raw materials and equipment.

There does not seem to be any acceptable way of separating the tax on the producer from the tax on the consumer of agricultural goods (with the exception of bread), nor of eliminating the effects of subsidies on the price of industrial goods. Furthermore, since Soviet procurement-price policy may not be the same for all products (i.e., procurement price may represent a different fraction of cost of production for different commodities), the turnover-tax rates on different agricultural commodities may not be comparable. Likewise the effect of subsidies on the cost of different industrial commodities may not be uniform. Since the turnover tax is the major Soviet tax, the severe limitations which these factors place on analysis are obvious.

Additional difficulties exist because the turnover tax does not constitute the total tax element in the price of consumers' goods; there are also the retained profits of state enterprises, the profits tax, and the payroll tax. Information on the incidence of these taxes by commodity is almost completely lacking. Other impediments to a study of the equity of the turnover-tax system, mentioned in Chapter 6, are lack of data on consumption patterns by income group and the multiplicity of turnover-tax rates.

Finally, in order to pass judgment on the equity of Soviet taxes it is desirable to have in mind the standard of income distribution which the Soviet people themselves consider equitable. There is virtually no information on how the average citizen thinks on this question, and the official position of the government is ambiguous. The ultimate Soviet standard of distribution — distribution under Communism — is "to each according to his needs." To this ideal, and it is unquestionably a social rather than an economic ideal, lip service is still paid. In fact, discussions have been held in the post-war period on how and when the eventual shift from socialism to communism will take place; distribution of free goods is among the topics reportedly discussed. As the following quotation from Stalin indicates, however, it is clearly recognized that the ideal cannot be put into practice:

> The principal of Socialism is that in a Socialist society each works according to his ability and receives articles of consumption, not according to his needs, but according to the work he performs for society. This means that the cultural and technical level of the working class is yet not a high one, that the distinction between mental and manual labor still exists, that the productivity of labor is still not high enough to ensure an abundance of articles of consumption, and, as a result, society is *obliged* [italics supplied] to distribute article of consumption not in accordance with the needs of its members, but in accordance with the work they perform for society.[16]

The use of "obliged" in the above context implies that distribution according to need is foregone with regrets and that distribution according to work is an economic but not an ethical ideal. If this interpretation is correct, it is safe to predict that there will be a schism between the economic and ethical ideals for many generations, for the objective conditions under which a society can permit each person to take what he needs are not likely to be fulfilled in the forseeable future, if ever.[17]

Although the economic ideal is not likely to change in the forseeable future, the ethical ideal may change; in the view of many, it has already changed. Nations usually try to justify their actions on moral grounds, and the Soviets are no exception to this rule; there are growing indications in contemporary Soviet life of the acceptance of less equalitarian standards of social justice.[18] At present, however, there is not enough information to enable us to evaluate the Soviet tax system from the Soviets' own point of view.

Despite these methodological and statistical limitations to evaluating the equity of Soviet taxes, certain aspects of the tax system will be considered from the point of view of the following two standards:

(1) Households in the same economic position (as measured, for example, by income and number of dependents) should be treated in the same way for purposes of taxation, except insofar as discriminatory treatment serves a political objective of the state.

(2) The tax system should not be regressive.

The first standard is a very simple and generally acceptable concept of equity. It is independent of the effects of income distribution from budget expenditures discussed earlier in this section, and should therefore not be objectionable on this ground.

The second criterion is based on the following two assumptions: (1) relative wages are dictated essentially by incentive considerations and satisfactorily perform their function of allocating labor; (2) the Soviet ideal of an equitable distribution of income is more equalitarian than the distribution of income dictated by incentive considerations. We are also assuming that it has been possible for us to measure the progressivity of Soviet taxes. It should be recalled that our measurement of the turnover tax was, at best, "impressionistic."

The limitations of these assumptions have been discussed and should be kept in mind. Nevertheless, if we do not pretend to a perfectly scientific standpoint, the assumptions are sufficiently valid to justify the use of the second criterion in evaluating the Soviet tax system. The results must of course be considered very tentative.

Let us first examine the progressivity of the tax system. As was tentatively decided in Chapter 6, the turnover tax is either proportional or mildly regressive; in the prewar period, because of the very high tax on bread, the tax was quite definitely regressive. The tax in kind would be roughly proportional to income if the delivery norms were accurately differentiated and strictly observed. Because differentiation of norms is not sufficiently discriminating, the tax is probably regressive, i.e., collective farms with high costs and a low rate of income pay a much higher rate of tax than average- or low-cost farms. The income tax is mildly progressive for workers and salaried employees and more progressive for other social and economic groups. The agricultural tax (i.e., the money tax on income from the collective farmer's private plot) was moderately progressive when levied on the income presumably derived from individual crops or livestock; in its present form as a property tax on land, it is proportional. Government bonds are bought on what appears to be a proportional-to-income basis.

If the turnover tax is mildly regressive, the total of taxes on workers and salaried employees is probably proportional; if the turnover tax is proportional, the total of taxes on workers and salaried employees may be mildly progressive. Whichever the structure of the turnover tax, however, *higher income* artists, professionals, other nonworkers, and nonsalaried employee groups undoubtedly pay out a slightly larger percentage of their incomes in taxes than persons with lower incomes. For example, a doctor with fewer than three dependents and an income of 50,000 rubles pays an income tax which amounts to about 32 per cent of income. Unless persons in the higher income brackets pay 15 or 20 per cent less of their income in turnover taxes than those in low income brackets, the incidence of the combination of taxes is progressive. The picture presented is that of a tax system which has little, if any, consistent effect on the distribution of income.

A progressive element is added to the tax system if subsidies to mothers are considered, as they were in Chapter 8, as negative taxes. Subsidy payments are based on the number of children in a family and are independent of the recipients' income level. Thus, a mother with five children would receive monthly payments totaling about 700 rubles a year regardless of whether the family income was 5,000 rubles or 25,000 rubles. In the first case the stipend would amount to a negative tax of 14 per cent; in the second case, to a negative tax of less than 3 per cent.

Expenditures on health and education have a similar progressive effect. In the case of education, of course, children of higher-income families are apt to go to school longer than those from lower-income families; this would raise the absolute value of educational benefits accruing to high-income families above those accruing to low-income families. Nevertheless, as a percentage of income the value of benefits received by the low-income family would be greater.

Most transfer payments (old-age insurance, disability compensation, etc.) are not redistributional because they are based on income earned.

The preceding evidence suggests that the distribution of income after both taxes *and* budget expenditures are taken into account is somewhat more equalitarian than the primary distribution of income.

Let us now examine the tax system in terms of our first standard of equity: equal tax treatment for equally situated households. The combination of income taxes and subsidies to mothers is relatively satisfactory in terms of this criterion; commodity taxes and the tax in kind, however, tend to be very unjust.

An extremely important feature of modern tax systems is allowance for dependents. As we indicated in Chapter 8, the Soviets make a crude allowance for dependency in their income and agricultural taxes; this is refined further by the tax on bachelors and small families and the subsidies to mothers of many children.[19] The subsidies undoubtedly constitute a better form of dependency allowance than exemptions from income taxes. It is a defect of income-tax exemptions that they treat alike all persons who are exempt from tax either for too low an income or too many dependents, regardless of how low their income or how many their dependents. Thus the dependency provisions are regressive (by default of action) in the lower income brackets, and of course violate the "equal-treatment" criterion.[20] The Soviet subsidy program is a step in the direction of conforming to the "equal-treatment" criterion because it yields relatively greater benefits as the number of dependents rises and as income falls. These subsidies are clearly not sufficient, however, to place a family with ten children on the same level of economic well-being as a family with two children. The significance of the income tax and mother subsidy dependency provisions is reduced still further by the fact that the commodity tax, which takes about one-third of the average family's income, makes no allowance for dependents. A family with ten children must pay the same turnover tax on bread as a family with the same income but with only two children.

Aside from dependency provisions and questions of progression, the commodity taxes are an unjust form of tax for still another reason. Consumption patterns within income groups are not uniform; therefore, unless every commodity bears the same rate of tax, persons in the same income group will find themselves paying different rates of tax. Furthermore, commodity taxes do not fall on savings, and this favors the thrifty and wealthy. Until the Currency Reform of 1947, the inequity involved was insubstantial, not only because voluntary savings in the USSR are relatively small, but because money savings were subject to a tax in the form of constantly and rapidly rising consumers'-goods prices. Since 1948, prices have been declining, placing savers in a favorable situation.

The tax in kind levied on the collective farms violates our "equal-treatment" standard of equity in two respects. The most general objection is that it places the burden of fluctuations in agricultural output on the rural population: the tax is based not on actual ouput but on the number of hectares of land held by the collective farms. Therefore in lean crop years the rate of tax is high and the agricultural population receives very little return for its effort. Bumper crops, of course, have the opposite effect. For example, in 1937, a good crop year, the tax in kind on grain was estimated to have been 15 per cent of the total crop. In 1938, when yield was lower, the rate of taxation rose to 23 per cent; in 1939 it was about 30 per cent.[21] Such a tax is very arbitrary in its effect on the relative incomes of the urban and rural populations.

Within the agricultural sector, the impact of the tax is also arbitrary. The tax in kind is a levy on gross rather than net output. If our first criterion of equity is interpreted to imply taxation based on ability to pay, then the tax in kind violates this criterion because it discriminates against high-cost farms. The tax is differentiated geographically for variations in fertility, mechanization, etc., but no amount of differentiation can eliminate the inequities which result from a tax on gross output or income. These inequities are exaggerated by large annual variability in yields. Since the tax takes on the average a large share of the net crop, the collective farms and farmers cultivating poor soil retain little for themselves except in the very best crop years. The Soviet literature indicates wide differences in earnings between collective farms, hence between collective farmers.

The tax in kind which is levied on the household plots of individual collective farmers and on private farmers also violates the "equal-treatment" criterion, since it makes no allowance either for differential costs or for dependency.

It is well known that inequities in the distribution of money income after taxes are apt to be exaggerated by inflation. In postwar years whatever degree of equity is embodied in the Soviet wage-price-tax framework has been preserved intact by Soviet success in preventing inflation. When inflationary pressures have escaped control, as, for example, in the early thirties and during the war, rationing has been used to insure that the distribution of necessary consumers' goods shall not be grossly unfair. It is significant that rationing has been differentiated according to the type of work performed, in order to preserve some of the incentive effects sought by differential wages. The use of differential rationing is concrete evidence that *both* a standard of equity and a need for incentive payments are considered by Soviet planners.

ALLOCATION OF RESOURCES

Almost all economic activity in the Soviet Union is planned, but some activities are planned in less detail than others. The allocation of the more important raw materials and equipment is, in theory, accomplished with precision by direct controls; other commodities are distributed by the market.

The importance of the price mechanism for the latter form of distribution is clear. If the market is to distribute factors to conform to plan, the following conditions must hold: (1) goods and services must be priced in an economically meaningful way; (2) there must be equality of demand and supply for each and all commodities and services; (3) the economic incentives (or rules of behavior) which insure that the planned distribution of funds leads to the planned allocation of goods and services must be maintained. The incentives referred to are familiar ones: the consumer incentive to maximize satisfaction from expenditure of money income, the worker incentive to maximize earnings, and the managerial incentive to produce efficiently and to minimize costs.

In those sectors of the economy where resources are directly allocated, conditions (2) and (3) lose their significance. However, condition (1) remains important even in this case, if money plays any role in planning decisions as a unit of account or evaluation. The extent to which planners do take price into consideration is an empirical question on which we have no explicit information. We may conjecture that although price need not be a consideration in determining *how much* steel, oil, and coal to produce, nevertheless, the prices of those funded commodities which enter into the production cost of other commodities are probably set in accordance with a positive economic policy. (See, however, the discussion of subsidies below.) Any other procedure would seriously damage the usefulness of the cost-price system in those areas where the market is the active factor in the allocation process.

In discussing the effect of Soviet taxation on allocation of resources, then, we must consider the effect of taxes on incentives, in equating monetary demand and supply both in the aggregate and in specific markets, and on relative pricing. Incentives and inflation were dealt with earlier in this chapter. The discussion which follows will therefore be confined primarily to relative pricing. It will be assumed that the relative prices of consumers' goods should be sensitive to household demands, and that relative prices of all other finished goods and factors of production should be sensitive to the demands of the planning board.

Labor. Labor allocation depends, on the one hand, on the success of the differential wage policy as modified by taxes in those areas where the labor market is free, and on the other hand, on the success with which the Soviets directly allocate labor where there is no labor market. The only careful analysis of Soviet differential wage policy, that of Professor Bergson, states that from a study of "administrative techniques used in the Soviet Union to determine relative wages . . . it may be concluded that, at least among industrial workers employed at the same stage of production, differences in earnings in the Soviet Union approximate differences in productivity." [22]

It is doubtful if the tax system seriously interferes with the effectiveness of relative wages in distributing workers. As we have seen, the income tax is only mildly progressive for most workers. Purchases of government bonds appear to depend on relative wages and therefore have the neutrality of a proportional tax. As we have indicated several times before, although we do not know whether the commodity tax is progressive or regressive, the amount of deviation from proportionality does not appear to be very great. Moreover, the impact of the tax is attenuated by the money illusion.

Nor is it likely that the discriminatory features of the income tax affect the distribution of labor adversely. The doctors, lawyers, and artists discriminated against can be classed as noncompeting groups with respect to workers and salaried employees; they are not likely to choose a different profession because they pay a higher direct tax. The extra-high tax paid by these people represents to a large extent "rent" income from a successful book, play, or symphony, or (in the case of the doctor or lawyer) from high fees charged in private practice; taxation of "rent" income should not alter the distribution of labor by profession. The discriminatory tax on individual shopkeepers, artisans, and those engaging professionally in religious activities serves the political objective of discouraging such activities. If the tax is effective and these persons turn to the state for employment, their productivity is increased from the planners' point of view.

The agricultural tax may also serve to increase productivity by "encouraging" independent peasant farmers to join collective farms. The peasant is probably more productive *over the long run*, particularly in terms of planners' preferences, if he is transplanted to the collective farm with its mechanical advantages and its susceptibility to state control and direction than when he is working by hand on his own plot of land.

As we have indicated, there is considerable direct allocation of labor in the Soviet Union today, and even where labor is not directly allocated mobility has been reduced by the introduction of labor books. Direct allocation which takes the form of placing teenage boys in schools to learn an occupation, and then forcing them to serve an apprenticeship in a job selected by the state, is not likely to affect adversely the allocation of labor. However, the use of skilled laborers, engineers, and professionals to do unskilled work on MVD construction projects represents a gross misallocation of labor, particularly in the USSR with its serious shortage of skills of all sorts. Forced reduction of mobility due to the use of labor books, though it lessens the significance of wage differentials, does not vitiate their effect entirely, since wage differentials still encourage workers to improve their position in the plant to which they are assigned. Furthermore, there is evidence that considerable labor mobility still exists in spite of controls.

Consumers' Goods. It has been pointed out that a major function of Soviet commodity taxation is to suppress consumer sovereignty in the short run, thereby freeing planners from the necessity of making the shifts in resource allocation which would be required if planning were sensitively geared to the changing demand patterns of the population. In the long run, however, some sovereignty must be allowed the consumer, or the state may find itself producing a basket of goods which satisfies the demands of the population inefficiently. This limitation on planner sovereignty is particularly significant in the Soviet Union because of the influence of rapid urbanization on household requirements. If the state paid no attention whatsoever to the changing requirements of the population, relative prices would become increasingly distorted as a result of attempts to equate supply and demand in specific markets solely by price adjustments, keeping supplies constant. Relative prices are more indicative than relative commodity tax rates because the commodity tax may include a tax on the producer as well as on the consumer.

Since we have no information on shifts in relative demand, we cannot use the available consumers'-goods price series for a rigorous test of the hypothesis that planners do pay attention to consumer preferences. There is one segment of the price series, however, which is suggestive by itself; this is the period encompassing the price changes of December 31, 1940, December 16, 1947, and March 1, 1950.[23] The trend over this period is significant because the 1947 price structure reflects war disruption, and not unconstrained state policy. Prices increased sharply from 1940 to 1947 and declined from 1947 to 1950. The interesting fact is that by and large the commodities which showed the greatest price increases in the earlier period declined the most from 1947 to 1950; this would seem to indicate a conscious effort to restore the prewar pattern of output and prices. Since the impact of war on the means of satisfying consumers' needs is capricious, the 1950 and 1940 production and price patterns are doubtless superior to those of 1947 from the consumers' point of view. The reversion to the prewar pattern was certainly dictated in part by technological and resource imperatives. It would also seem to reflect, however, at least a minimum concern with consumers' requirements. The argument is admittedly tenuous; nevertheless, it presents one type of evidence to support our theoretical inference of the preceding paragraph.

Additional evidence that the state is concerned with changes in consumers' needs is provided by the books and articles on the subject which have been published by Soviet economists since the middle thirties.[24]

The low Soviet standard of living considerably simplifies the planners' problem in determining consumers' requirements. Necessaries constitute the bulk of consumers'-goods production. The misallocation of resources which results because the planners are slow in reacting to changes in consumers' preferences is confined, therefore, to a relatively small part of the resources destined for personal consumption. As the Soviet standard of living rises in the future the problem of determining consumers' preferences may become more difficult.

Although the consumer exercises some sovereignty over the production of consumers' goods, he has virtually no sovereignty over the total amount or the distribution of resources devoted to the nonconsumption sphere. A rough indication of the extent of deprivation of sovereignty is afforded by the 50 to 60 per cent rate of taxation on the household. This does not, of course, mean that consumers in the Soviet Union are prevented from influencing the production of nonconsumers' goods merely by taxes which reduce their ability to bid for resources. This might be true in Western nations; in the Soviet Union, decisions on these matters are made by the planners and implemented largely by physical controls, though these controls are reinforced by taxes on the population. To the degree that the level of nonconsumption expenditures is maintained by physical controls, and not by taxes, the latter cannot be said to affect the allocation of resources between consumption and nonconsumption uses.

It should be pointed out that consumer control over nonconsumption expenditures is far from absolute even in Western nations. Certainly the level of government expenditures in capitalist countries is not limited by the amount of voluntary consumer savings; this is somewhat less true of the level of private investment. There would seem to be two essential distinctions which can be drawn here between the USSR and Western nations, however. First, absence of political democracy in the Soviet Union makes possible a greater rate of nonconsumption expenditures than would be possible in countries where the people's representatives must periodically place their records before their constituents at the polls. Second, a larger proportion of Soviet expenditures on nonconsumption has been for final output which is neither destined for the consumer nor instrumental in the production of consumers' goods. Under the conditions of war or cold-war mobilization, these distinctions lose some of their sharpness, of course.

Raw Materials and Equipment. We turn now to the effect of taxes on the pricing and allocation of raw materials and equipment. In addition to the prime costs of production, price generally includes a payroll tax (social insurance), profits, and, until 1949, a small turnover tax. It is generally accepted that the Soviet cost of production understates true costs because of inadequate depreciation charges and virtual lack of explicit charge for depletion, long-term interest, and rent. In theory, price would approximate cost of production if the above-mentioned taxes compensated for the understatement of depreciation and depletion and long-term interest; if differential rent were also fully compensated for, the resulting prices would be equilibrium market prices in terms of planners' preferences. Until 1949 differential rent was, in theory, accounted for primarily by differential turnover taxes levied on producers' goods;[25] in 1949, the turnover tax was removed from all nonconsumers' goods except petroleum products, where the rent element is exceptionally large. With the elimination of the turnover tax on producers' goods, profits and the payroll tax were left as the only categories which could be used to reflect rent; and since the payroll tax is levied with a different purpose in view, differential rent must be reflected in profits, if at all.

At the time the turnover tax was removed from producers' goods, wholesale prices were raised very substantially in an attempt to eliminate subsidies and increase profits, and thereby enable enterprises to finance the bulk of their investment requirements from retained profits. If subsidies had been eliminated, and if prices had been set sufficiently high so that each enterprise could finance its own investment requirements, prices could *also* have been set to reflect accurately differential rent. This could have been accomplished by planning retained profits at the level dictated by investment requirements, and adding a further markup to reflect differential rent, this latter amount to be deducted eventually into the budget. The level of profits required to reflect differential rent is not, of course, identical with the level needed to finance an enterprise's investment requirements. It is not necessarily economic for the state to invest more heavily in industries in which demand prices exceed cost by the greatest margins (i.e., where differential rent is greatest). The decision to invest should depend on the rate of return on investment rather than the rate of return on the cost of production (profit to cost ratio); these two are not the same so long as the capital-to-output ratio varies from industry to industry. Furthermore, it is the marginal, not the average, capital-output ratio which is significant. So, for example, although the quasi rent in the oil industry may be much higher than in the coal industry, there may be no new oil reserves which can be tapped at a cost comparable with that of opening up a new coal mine.

Apparently the Soviets' new profits-subsidy policy was not implemented successfully, however. Analysis of budget expenditures suggests that large subsidies are still being granted to the national economy; and budget-financed investment is presently about three times as large as investment financed from retained profits. This is a far cry from the 1949 statement of intentions. Because no other information has since been published on the structure of profits, we cannot say to what extent Soviet profits (and prices) are set to reflect differential rent.

A word about the social-insurance markup or payroll tax. It will be recalled that this tax is levied on each enterprise as a percentage of its payroll (varying from 3.7 to 10.7 per cent); the funds so collected are used to pay sickness, old-age, and accident insurance. The addition of this tax to price would seem to be in accord with good pricing policy for two reasons. First, it may be argued that to the extent that the incidence of sickness, accidents, and unemployment falls unequally on different industries, and is not taken into account in differential wages, it is a form of social cost and should be included in price. Second, since wages are a value-added component of cost, the impact of the payroll tax on final price does not depend on the degree of integration in industry, and therefore no distortion is introduced by differential industrial integration.

We have left to the last one of the most important elements in

Soviet producers'-goods pricing, namely, subsidies. Since the beginning of the five-year plan period, subsidies have been an important item of budget expenditure. Although they are not a form of tax, their effect on price is equivalent to that of a negative tax.[26] The original rationale of the use of subsidies was sound. To facilitate planning, the Soviets wanted to keep producers'-goods and raw-material prices relatively stable over time. Realizing that the preponderance of new commodities to be introduced in the twenties and early thirties would at first be relatively high-priced, they decided to subsidize such commodities until production had reached an efficient scale and costs had leveled off. Soviet economists [27] have also claimed that it was necessary to set the price of some new products below cost in order to overcome managerial resistance to the initial use of such products.[28]

In theory, such a pricing policy can be defended as not constituting a serious deviation from the principles of rational allocation *viewed over the long run.* In practice, the subsidy program was expanded far beyond original intentions. The main difficulty was caused by a wage inflation which more than offset gains in productivity and efficiency, and led to constantly increasing average costs throughout the economy. Not only did subsidies to new industries constantly increase, rather than decrease; enterprises in established industries were also incurring losses and required subsidies for solvency. When the Soviets found that costs were rising instead of declining, as had been anticipated when the subsidy program was conceived, they perhaps should have raised prices in preference to increasing subsidy payments. Producers'-goods prices were not increased, however, until April 1936, at which time subsidies were supposedly eliminated. Continuing upward pressure of wages led to the use of subsidies again almost immediately after the 1936 price adjustment had presumably eliminated the need for them. Prices were not increased again, however, until 1939 and 1940. During the war, prices of producers' goods did not change and again subsidies mounted. Finally in 1949 raw-material and equipment prices, and also transport rates, were again increased by very large amounts and subsidies presumably largely eliminated.[29]

Thus the picture in the producers'-goods and extractive industries is one of continually rising wage costs, only three significant compensating price adjustments, and very extensive use of subsidies to cover resulting losses in the periods between adjustments. This use of subsidies, in contradistinction to the use originally intended by Soviet planners, results in a very unsatisfactory system of relative prices. The principal distortion which results is the overvaluation of labor relative to subsidized producers' goods and raw materials. This distortion in relative costs is made worse by the lack of adequate charges for depreciation, depletion, interest, and rent. Furthermore, to the extent that the percentage of wage cost to total cost differs from product to product, a further distortion is introduced. For example, the coal industry, which received the largest subsidy in 1938,[30] is the industry in which wages constitute the largest percentage of total cost.[31] Other things being equal, coal was probably undervalued relative to other raw materials and producers' goods. The inconsistencies in pricing due to subsidies are the counterpart of those which would arise if the state directly manipulated wages in order to finance its nonconsumption program instead of levying taxes (see Chapter 3).

We may infer that in the years when the three big price changes occurred relative prices were nearly proportional to costs of production, and probably roughly reflected relative scarcity in terms of planners' preferences. In all other years, and especially in those years which directly preceded price changes, relative prices must have been grossly misleading indicators of the opportunity value of different economic goods. This hypothesis is supported by the fact that the increases in price of different commodities in each of the price reforms varied greatly.[32]

Our deductions regarding the inadequacy of producers'-goods prices as measures of economic value are amply supported by the writings of Soviet economists themselves. For example, T. S. Khachaturov says: "State prices generally do not reflect degrees of shortages of this or another product . . . In the USSR prices of goods in short supply are not raised, or are raised only insignificantly." [33] Soviet writings on subsidies contain many similar observations; so does the literature on the conflict between planned output and profit where product mix is involved.

It is clear, then, that the Soviet pricing of producers' goods and raw materials has been chaotic. We infer from this misallocation of resources though the extent of misallocation and consequent losses to the economy remain entirely conjectural and in practice unmeasurable.[34] Although it is unlikely that the Soviets will ever have a marginal-cost pricing system (since its advantages are not recognized by them even in theory), some improvement in pricing may be expected in the future. There is widespread recognition among Soviet economists that prices have not adequately reflected scarcity, and that the existence of large subsidies has caused serious distortions of the costing structure. It may be argued that Soviet economists have been aware of this since the mid-thirties, yet the problem still exists. In answer it should be pointed out that the planners no longer have to contend with as rapid a wage inflation as, say, before 1948. This should reduce the subsidy problem, although to date there has been no indication that it has. Furthermore, the three wholesale-price changes which occurred in 1949 and 1950 may presage an increased desire and willingness on the part of the planners to alter prices with changes in supply-and-demand conditions. Elimination of subsidies and greater price flexibility would go a long way toward enabling the Soviets to eliminate the grossest disparities in their system of wholesale prices and factor prices. Many of the more subtle pricing and allocation problems will remain to be solved, however,

ALTERNATIVE METHODS OF TAXATION RECONSIDERED

The high rates of taxation required to finance World War II and "cold war" have confronted the United States with a serious incentive-equity conflict. The income and profits taxes are considered by many to have reached a limit beyond which incentives would be seriously affected; commodity taxation, the traditional alternative, is undesirable on equity grounds. Two new devices have been suggested as possible solutions. These are the spending tax, first suggested in this country by the United States Treasury in 1942, and expenditure rationing, for which a convincing case has recently been made by a group of Stanford economists.[35] What do these taxes have to offer to the Soviets, if anything?

The spending tax as it is usually advocated is a progressive tax on spending, i.e., the more spent, the greater the tax liability. Adjustments are made for dependency just as in the case of income taxation. Spending is defined as income minus savings, and proper estimation of spending (and therefore of tax liability) requires accurate reporting of both income and savings. The United States might well consider use of such a tax for several reasons. First, it would be more equitable, as a supplement to income taxation, than sales taxation. Second, by penalizing spending, it encourages saving. By the same token, it discourages dissaving. Third, it has an advantage over commodity taxation in that it does not encourage wage-price instability by raising prices.

Because of differences in economic and institutional conditions, the advantages of the spending tax for the United States do not necessarily constitute advantages for the Soviet Union. If the Soviets wanted to increase the progressivity (i.e., the equity) of their tax system, they might consider substituting a spending tax for part of their commodity-tax system. In other respects the spending tax presents the Soviets with no startling advantages. Although they would no doubt want to encourage saving, it is not of fundamental importance, since they are successfully eliminating inflationary pressures at the current level of saving. Furthermore, the level of liquid-asset holdings in the Soviet Union is quite low, and dissaving presents no serious problem. The spending tax would also be hard to administer in the Soviet Union because of the existence of the collective farm market. Unless a system could be devised for recording income from sales on these markets, there would be a significant loophole in the tax. A final and most important disadvantage of the tax from the Soviet viewpoint is that it is essentially a direct tax, and might have serious disincentive effects. Since the incentive consideration weighs heavily in Soviet calculations, this would probably be a sufficient reason for not adopting the tax.

Expenditure rationing is similar to the spending tax in that it is basically directed at reducing expenditures rather than disposable income. It goes a step further, however. Instead of just discouraging spending by progressive levy, it absolutely limits expenditures, though still on a progressive basis. That is to say, the expenditure ration increases with income, but at a rapidly diminishing rate. The expenditure ration is a direct control over expenditures rather than a tax, and the decision on how income in excess of the ration (plus voluntary savings) is to be treated remains to be made. The program of the Stanford economists is to mop up most of the excess purchasing power by income taxation, allowing some saving for incentive reasons, and to use selective excises to meet changes in demand or to reduce demand for luxuries and for commodities manufactured from critical materials. This choice of accompanying fiscal devices would probably not be acceptable to the Soviets for incentive reasons, as we have already pointed out. Furthermore, if it is assumed that the income tax takes up all income in excess of the ration, then purchasing-power rationing would not be needed except to block dissaving. Since dissaving is not a serious problem in the Soviet Union, expenditure rationing would hardly be necessary. Expenditure rationing supplemented by commodity taxation rather than income taxation would of course not be substantially different from the present Soviet system, and in view of the absence of large-scale liquid-asset holdings by households, the rationing aspect would be quite unnecessary. There is one further drawback: expenditure rationing, as envisaged by the Stanford economists, could not be administered properly as long as collective farm markets are allowed to exist. The Stanford system requires that each ration ticket be used for one, and only one, transaction. It is doubtful that such a restriction could be applied in the collective farm market.

Neither consumption taxation nor expenditure rationing appear to offer much to the solution of Soviet fiscal problems. This does not mean that the Soviet tax system could not be improved. In particular it is difficult to rationalize the continuation of direct taxation and of sales of government bonds, since neither substantially advances the cause of equity, while both probably affect incentives more adversely than commodity taxation. (I think this is true of bonds in spite of the favorable incentive effect which stems from Soviet use of the lottery form of payment.) Sales of government bonds in the Soviet Union have most of the disadvantages of direct taxes without their principal virtue — reduction, once and for all, of the population's claim on national output. Furthermore, under present conditions of falling consumers'-goods prices, the debt service may claim a significant portion of national output in the not too distant future. The only reasonable use of bond sales is as a flexible instrument for absorbing pools of excess purchasing power which may arise because of defective planning or unplanned developments. Certainly it is much easier to alter the amount of bonds offered for sale than to change the rates of direct taxation or to raise prices. There is no indication, however, that bonds are sold in the Soviet Union with this purpose in mind; they are "levied" once a year in very much the same way as direct taxes.

It can be argued that if purchases of bonds have less of a disincentive effect on purchasers than direct taxes, they can be used to greatest advantage if they are reserved for sale to those persons whose incentives are affected most adversely by direct taxes. For example, Professor Fellner in his proposals for financing World War II suggested that compulsory loans be used in place of taxes when marginal tax rates exceed 80 per cent.[36] But high marginal rates are not the serious problem for Soviet tax authorities that they have been for other nations; therefore there is no urgent need for compulsory loans for the purpose of placing a ceiling on marginal tax rates. In practice the Soviet loans appear to be distributed among the workers and salaried employees on a basis roughly proportional to income. Such sales do not seem to offer any advantages over other forms of taxes to compensate for the disadvantage that (presumably) they must be repaid.

Some reasons for Soviet use of direct taxes on the population were suggested in Chapter 3. These reasons (e.g., the need for a means of political discrimination and for reaching rent income from private professional practice) apply only to the discriminatory income tax schedules, and not to the basic direct taxes on workers, salaried employees, and collective farmers. It is not easy to adduce strong economic or political arguments with which to defend the basic direct taxes. Some Soviet economists have argued that it is important from the standpoint of good citizenship for all citizens to participate directly in the financing of social or state activity. The implicit assumption here is, of course, that the Soviet commodity tax is not a tax on the population, or at least that the population is not aware that a turnover tax is levied on most commodities sold to them by the state. This objection aside, the argument still seems to us too weak by itself to rationalize the use of direct taxes.

It may also be contended that direct taxes are necessary to add progressivity to the over-all tax structure, and to recognize the burden of dependents. The direct taxes are much too small and insufficiently progressive to affect the progressivity of the tax structure significantly, and, as we have shown, dependency is much more adequately provided for by the subsidy-to-mothers program.

It is of course possible that the Soviets plan to rely much more heavily on direct taxes at some time in the future, in order to increase the equitableness of their tax structure. In this case, they may wish to keep the population in the habit of paying direct taxes and the administrative machinery well oiled, so that the change-over can be effected smoothly.

We conclude that there are no strong positive reasons for continuing to levy direct taxes on the workers and collective farmers. Likewise there are no very urgent reasons for immediately eliminating these taxes, although their use does increase the costs of tax administration and somewhat complicates fiscal planning. The Soviets undoubtedly could, without serious repercussions, replace the basic direct levies on income by increases in the level of commodity taxation.

FINAL COMMENTS

The Soviet tax system has been evaluated at length in terms of four criteria or objectives of taxation.

The first of these, containment of inflation, is not an independent objective but is desirable only insofar as it facilitates the achievement of other objectives. There is no doubt that the Soviets pursue this policy, and that they have been quite successful, since the Currency Reform of 1947, in preventing the development of inflation in spite of continuing adherence to an inflationary bank credit policy. Before the Reform they were largely unsuccessful, however, and in the prewar and wartime years the economy suffered from the effects of repressed inflation. Probably success of the tax policy in the postwar period would not have been possible without successful application of related policies: use of direct controls over labor, State Bank control over payroll expenditures, and the rapid increase in output of consumers' goods.

The significance of taxes and prices for efficient allocation is reduced somewhat by the use of physical controls to move resources. Labor is the least-controlled component of production, and it is quite clear that differential wages are set with an eye to efficient allocation. Taxes, it was shown, are constructed so as to minimize disturbance to the resource-allocating function of differential wages. Other components of production are priced much more haphazardly, however. This is in part the fault of the tax system, but primarily the consequence of the program of large-scale subsidies extended to the producers'-goods and extractive industries. There seem to be no compelling reasons, particularly with wage inflation under control, why raw materials and equipment should not now be priced to reflect economic scarcity. Yet the continuance of large-scale subsidies to the national economy, even after the 1949 attempt to eliminate them once and for all, would seem to indicate that they are not so priced.

There *are* compelling reasons, however, why it would be difficult for the Soviets to have a tax system which does justice to both the incentive and the equity criteria, since these are often in conflict. The greater the tax requirements of the state, the more difficult it becomes to satisfy both standards simultaneously. The Soviet system is oriented toward incentives at the expense of equity. The preservation of incentives is probably the single most important objective of tax policy. Wages and salaries are sharply differentiated for incentive purposes. From the structure of Soviet taxation, it can be deduced that a strong effort is made to minimize the disincentive effects of taxation on the average worker and salaried employee. (It is equally clear, of course, that the disincentive effects of taxes are exploited to the full where these can be mobilized in support of political and economic objectives.) The principal Soviet tax, the turnover tax, is characterized by a roughly proportional rate structure which causes it to have little effect on incentives; its neutrality is enhanced by the effect of the "money illusion." Even the fiscally unimportant direct taxes are only mildly progressive.

A tax structure which so advantageously cushions incentives against adverse impact serves very poorly the cause of social justice. Equity is clearly not a first-order objective of Soviet tax policy; the tax system does not alter substantially the primary distribution of income. Failure of the Soviet tax system to provide exemptions from taxation for the lower income stratum implies hardship for these groups. Under the present commodity-tax system, the tax paid by the lower-income groups must be of the order of 30 to 50 per cent of income, if not higher. The impact of this tax is only partially offset by the distribution of free social services and subsidies to mothers.

No other nation has ever levied as high a rate of taxation as the Soviet Union, and it may be that the cause of equity cannot be well served when the financial requirements of the state are so enormous; taxes must reach down into the last person's pocket if the program is to be successful. If this is true, the only way to achieve equity is to reduce the fiscal requirements of the state. But this decision lies in the realm of politics rather than economics.

APPENDIX

SOURCES AND NOTES FOR TABLES

TABLE 1 a. Retained profits of the collective farms which are held for investment are deposited into a so-called indivisible fund. The estimate for 1936 is interpolated from 1935 to 1937. In 1935, according to Grinko (1936, p. 9) the money income of the collective farms in 1935 was 9 billion rubles. According to S. Nosyrev, "Ustav sel'skokhoziaistvennoi arteli i finansovoe khoziaistvo kolkhozov" [The charter of the agricultural artel' and finances of collective farms], *Sovetskie finansy*, 1947, no. 1, p. 21, 14.7 per cent of collective farm income was deposited into the indivisible fund in 1935.

b. G. F. Grinko, *Finansovaia programma Soiuza SSR na 1937 god* [Financial program of the USSR for 1937] (Moscow, 1937), p. 29.

c. Planned investment in fixed capital from S. N. Prokopovich, *Biulleten'* (Prague, Czechoslovakia), March 1936, p. 30. Planned investment in working capital from G. F. Grinko, *Financial Program of the U.S.S.R. for 1936* (Moscow, 1936), p. 15.

d. At least 2.6 billion rubles of other investment from profits can be estimated from A. Smilga, "Finansy sotsialisticheskogo gosudarstva" [Finances of the socialist state], *Problemy ekonomiki* [Problems of economics], 1937, no. 3, p. 115. In 1937, 12.4 per cent of collective farm money income was deposited in the indivisible fund (Nosyrev, in *Sovetskie finansy*, 1947, no. 1, p. 21). Nosyrev, "Ukrepliat' finansovuiu distsiplinu v kolkhozakh" [Strengthen financial discipline in the collective farms], *Sovetskie finansy*, 1945, no. 11, p. 20, gives money income of collective farms in 1937 as 14,180 million rubles.

e. K. N. Plotnikov, *Biudzhet sotsialisticheskogo gosudarstva* [Budget of the socialist state] (Moscow, 1948), p. 140.

TABLE 2 TsUNKhU, *Sotsialisticheskoe stroitel'stvo SSSR* [Socialist construction of the USSR] (Moscow, 1936), p. 531.

TABLE 3 *Planned*. 1928: Gosplan, *Piatiletnii plan narodno-khoziaistvennogo stroitel'stva SSSR* [Five Year Plan of national economic construction of the USSR] (Moscow, 1929), vol. 2, pp. 208–209. 1931, 1934, 1936: *Planovoe khoziaistvo*, 1930, no. 12, p. 369; 1934, no. 5–6, p. 199; 1936, no. 2, p. 281. 1933, 1935, 1937: Charles Bettelheim, *La Planification Sovietique* (2nd ed.; Paris, 1945), p. 306. 1932 five-year plan: *Summary of the Fulfillment of the First Five Year Plan* (New York, no date), p. 296. 1937 five-year plan: I. B. Lasker and John Swift, trans., *The Second Five Year Plan* (New York, no date), pp. 624–625. 1942 five-year plan: Gosplan, *Tretii piatiletnii plan razvitiia narodnogo khoziaistva Soiuza SSR* [Third Five Year Plan for the development of the national economy of the USSR] (Moscow, 1939), pp. 228–229.

Realized. 1928: K. N. Plotnikov, *Biudzhet sotsialisticheskogo gosudarstva*, p. 72. 1929–1935: State Planning Commission, *Socialist Construction in the U.S.S.R.* (Moscow, 1936), pp. 368–369. 1936–1940: Abram Bergson, "A Problem in Soviet Statistics," *Review of Economic Statistics*, 29:236 (November 1947).

TABLE 4 *Planned.* 1931, 1934, 1936: *Planovoe khoziaistvo*, 1930, no. 12, p. 336; 1934, no. 5–6, p. 199; 1936, no. 1, p. 281. 1932: *Biulleten' finansovogo i khoziaistvennogo zakonodatel'stva* [Bulletin of financial and economic law], 1932, no. 1, p. 7. 1937–38: S. Krivetskii, "O fondakh zarabotnoi platy i ischislenii ikh" [On wage funds and their calculation], *Den'gi i kredit*, 1940, no. 2–3, p. 44. 1940: N. Sokolov, "Kontrol' gosbanka nad fondami zarabotnoi platy" [Control by the State Bank over wages funds], *Den'gi i kredit*, 1940, no. 1, p. 8. This source states that an 11 per cent increase in the wages fund was planned for 1940. 1932 five-year plan: *Summary of the Fulfillment of the First Five Year Plan*, p. 296. 1937 five-year plan: Lasker and Swift, *The Second Five Year Plan*, pp. 624–625. 1942 five-year plan: Gosplan, *Tretii piatiletnii plan*, pp. 228–229.

Realized. 1928: Plotnikov, *Biudzhet sotsialisticheskogo gosudarstva*, p. 72. 1929–1935: State Planning Commission, *Socialist Construction in the U.S.S.R.*, pp. 366–367. 1936: A. Grichmanov, "Gosudarstvennyi bank — moshchnoe orudie sotsializma" [The State Bank is a powerful instrument of socialism], *Kredit i khozraschet*, 1938, no. 3, p. 16.

TABLE 5 E. L. Granovskii and B. L. Markus, *Ekonomika sotsialisticheskoi promyshlennosti* [Economics of socialist industry] (Moscow, 1940), p. 517.

TABLE 6 N. Jasny, *The Soviet Economy During the Plan Era* (Stanford, 1951), p. 20.

TABLE 7 *Turnover tax, planned figures.* 1931: *Sobranie zakonov i rasporiazhenii pravitel'stva SSSR* [Collected laws and orders of the USSR] (Moscow, 1931), no. 5, article 61. 1932: *Ibid.*, 1931, no. 75, article 501. 1933: *Ibid.*, 1933, no. 6, article 39. 1934: *Ibid.*, 1934, no. 2, article 14. 1935: *Ibid.*, 1935, no. 8, article 71. 1936: Grinko, *Financial Program for 1936*, p. 64. 1937: Smilga, "Finansy sotsialisticheskogo gosudarstva," p. 110. 1938: A. G. Zverev, *Gosudarstvennye biudzhety Soiuza SSR 1938–1945 gg.* [State budgets of the USSR 1938–1945] (Moscow, 1946), p. 11. 1939: *Ibid.*, p. 41. 1940: *Ibid.*, p. 68. 1941: *Ibid.*, p. 95.

Turnover tax, realized figures. 1931: TsUNKhU, *Sotsialisticheskoe stroitel'stvo SSSR* [Socialist construction of the USSR] (Moscow, 1934), p. 440. 1932: *Sobranie zakonov*, 1933, no. 6, article 40; also *Pravda*, January 29, 1933. 1933: *Pravda*, January 3, 1934. 1934: *Pravda*, February 9, 1935. 1935: Grinko, *Financial Program for 1936*, p. 21. 1936: Grinko, *Finansovaia programma Soiuza SSR na 1937 god* [Financial program of the USSR for 1937] (Moscow, 1937), p. 16. States that the plan for 1937 is 16.5 per cent larger than the realized figure for 1936. 1937: Zverev, *Gosudarstvennye biudzhety*, p. 11 (preliminary). 1938–1940: Plotnikov, *Biudzhet sotsialisticheskogo gosudarstva*, p. 181. 1941:

A. Baykov and G. R. Barker, "Financial Developments in the U.S.S.R.," *Bulletins on Soviet Economic Development*, no. 3, August 1950, p. 11.

Special markups, planned. 1932: *Sobranie zakonov*, 1931, no. 75, article 501 (item entitled "commodity fund"). 1933: *Ibid.*, 1933, no. 6, article 39. 1934: *Ibid.*, 1934, no. 2, article 14.

Special markups, realized. 1932: *Ibid.*, 1934, no. 2, article 15. 1933: *Ibid.*, 1935, no. 8, article 70. 1934: *Pravda*, February 9, 1935.

The figures used in this table are not always the same as those used in later tables. The intent of this section is to compare planned and realized figures; therefore, the data were picked for comparability between these two categories, and all other considerations (e.g., comparable coverage over time) were disregarded.

TABLE 8 Currency in circulation (1929–1937) and government securities: League of Nations, *Money and Banking* (Geneva, 1938), vol. 2, p. 183.

Short-term loans: 1929–1932: A. Z. Arnold, *Banks, Credit, and Money in Soviet Russia* (New York, 1937), p. 372. 1933–1941: Gregory Grossman, "The Union of Soviet Socialist Republics," in B. H. Beckhart, ed., *Comparative Banking Systems* (to be published by the Columbia University Press).

Currency in circulation for 1940 and 1941: Estimate for 1940 derived as follows: Currency in circulation has been fairly closely related to changes in wage rates, the wage bill, and retail-trade turnover. Using these relations and projecting to 1940 gives values which vary from 15 to 17 billion rubles. The assumption that currency increased from 1937 to 1940 at the same rate as from 1934 to 1937, the last years in which we have Soviet data, gives a figure of roughly 16 billion rubles. On the basis of the correspondence between these various estimates, we assume currency in circulation on January 1, 1940 at 16 billion rubles. According to N. Voznesensky, *The Economy of the USSR During World War II* (Washington, 1948), (p. 81), currency in circulation declined slightly in 1940. We assume no change.

Income-velocity figures are calculated roughly by dividing household-income figures (Table 51) by currency in circulation.

Note on government securities: In 1931 and 1932, state enterprises which were unable to repay up to 6 billion rubles in short-term loans were relieved of these debts. In their place, government securities were substituted. This operation technically reduced the amount of short-term credit outstanding by calling part of the amount outstanding by another name. For this reason, we are interested in the total of short-term loans and government securities. It is my recollection that these securities were retired by the budget some time in the late 1930's. This operation was a bookkeeping transaction and had no impact on the economy. Therefore the retirement of the securities is not considered to have reduced the total of short-term credit at the time.

TABLE 9 The budget figures before 1938 are not consistent with those presented in Chapter 9. The figures presented in Chapter 9 have been adjusted to achieve comparable series over time. Here we are interested only in comparability between planned and realized figures for the same year; hence we use the original budget series for each year. The differences between the earlier and later estimates for the years before 1938 are described in Chapter 9.

1928–29: Planned: *Sobranie zakonov*, 1928, no. 69, article 638; realized: *Ibid.*, 1931, no. 5, article 62. 1929–30: Planned: *Sobranie zakonov*, 1929, no. 75, art. 720; realized: *Ibid.*, 1931, no. 75, art. 502. 1931: Planned: *Ibid.*, 1931, no. 5, art. 61; realized: *Ibid.*, 1933, no. 6, art. 40. 1932: Planned: *Ibid.*, 1931, no. 75, art. 501; realized: *Ibid.*, 1934, no. 2, art. 15. 1933: Planned: *Ibid.*, 1933, no. 6, art. 39; realized: *Ibid.*, 1935, no. 8, arts. 70, 72. 1934: Planned: *Ibid.*, 1934, no. 2, art. 14; realized: *Pravda*, Feb. 9, 1935. 1935: Planned and realized: Grinko, *Finansovaia programma*, p. 59. 1936: Planned: Grinko, *Financial Program*, pp. 66–68; realized: Zverev, *Gosudarstvennye biudzhety*, p. 7 (Zverev states that planned revenues were exceeded by 6.4 per cent and expenditures by 4 per cent). 1937: Planned: Grinko, *Finansovaia programma*, pp. 55–56; realized: Zverev, p. 64 (revenue fell short of plan by 1.8 per cent, expenditures by 3.3 per cent. 1938: Planned: Zverev, p. 31; realized: Plotnikov, *Biudzhet sotsialisticheskogo gosudarstva*, pp. 181, 207. 1939: Planned: Zverev, p. 62; realized: Plotnikov, pp. 181, 207. 1940: Planned: Zverev, p. 89; realized: Plotnikov, pp. 181, 207. 1941: Planned: Zverev, p. 123; Realized: revenues, A. Aleksandrov, *Finansy i kredit SSSR* [Finances and credit of the USSR] (Moscow, 1948), p. 227; expenditures, Zverev, p. 144.

TABLE 10 *Planned.* 1932: L. Gatovskii and others, "Voprosy razvertyvaniia sovetskoi torgovli" [Questions in the development of Soviet trade], *Problemy ekonomiki* [Problems of economics], 1932, no. 1, p. 27. 1934: *Planovoe khoziaistvo*, 1934, no. 5–6, p. 199. 1935: *Narodno-khoziaistvennyi plan na 1935 god* [The national-economic plan for 1935] (2nd ed.; Moscow, 1935), p. 12. 1936: Grinko, *Financial Program for 1936*, p. 20. 1937: Grinko, *Finansovaia programma*, p. 12. 1938: "Samyi moshchnyi v mire gosudarstvennyi bank" [The most powerful state bank in the world], *Den'gi i kredit*, 1938, no. 7–8, p. 55. 1940: Zverev, *Gosudarstvennye biudzhety*, p. 69, states that retail trade in 1940 was to increase by 15.7 per cent over 1939, implying a planned total of 189 billion. 1941: *Ibid.*, p. 96.

Realized. 1928–1930: State Planning Commission, *Socialist Construction in the U.S.S.R.*, pp. 407–9. 1931–1935: State and coöperative trade and public catering, *ibid.* Collective farm market, 1931 and 1935, Schwartz, p. 381; 1932 and 1933, *Bol'shaia Sovetskaia entsiklopediia* (special SSSR edition, Moscow, 1947), p. 1022. 1936–1939: Alexander Baykov, *Development of the Soviet Economic System* (New York, 1947), p. 254. 1940: Harry Schwartz, *Russia's Soviet Economy* (New York, 1950), p. 381.

TABLE 11 K. Ianbukhtin, *Nalogi v usloviiakh kapitalizma i v Sovetskom khoziaistve* [Taxes under capitalism and in the Soviet economy] (Moscow, 1934), pp. 23–24.

TABLE 12 TsUNKhU, *Sotsialisticheskoe stroitel'stvo SSSR* (Moscow, 1935), pp. 644–645.

This table does not include local taxation. In addition to these receipts, there were important sources of nontax revenue: gross receipts of the transport system and means of communication, income from state properties (especially forests), and state loans (a large proportion of which were subscribed to by state enterprises).

TABLE 13 Gordin, "O stavkakh naloga s oborota" [Turnover tax rates], *Planovoe khoziaistvo*, 1938, no. 3, p. 87.

TABLE 14 Gordin, p. 95.

TABLE 15 Retail trade turnover: see sources to Table 51; turnover taxes from Tables 47 and 48, Chapter 9.

TABLE 16 James Coogan, *Sales Taxes in the Soviet Union* (unpublished dissertation, Harvard University, 1951), pp. 161, 163, 204. The estimates for bread were computed by Coogan and include budget markups (p. 204).

TABLE 17 A. K. Suchkov, *Dokhody gosudarstvennogo biudzheta SSSR* (Moscow, 1945), p. 16.

TABLE 18 Grinko, *Financial Program for 1936*, p. 64.

TABLE 19 *Alfavitnyi perechen' promtovarov po stavkam naloga s oborota i biudzhetnykh natsenok* [Alphabetical list of turnover tax rates and budget markups on industrial commodities] (Moscow: Commissariat of Finance, 1938).

TABLE 20 *Alfavitnyi perechen'.*

TABLE 21 V. Petrov and V. Fisherov, *Nalog s oborota* [The turnover tax] (Moscow, 1936).

TABLE 22 *Cost-Price Relations for Rye Bread, 1940 (kopeks per quintal)*

	Price structure	Total tax	Substitute cost of production for procurement price	
Procurement price	766			
Value of grain in flour	807		1,500	3,000
Milling costs, including profits	250			
Turnover tax	8,850	5,900	5,433	4,433
Cost of flour at mill	9,907			
Value of flour in bread	6,679			
Cost of fabrication	202			
Cost of distribution	202			
Budget markup (16.6 per cent)	1,417	1,400 (rounded)	1,400	1,400
Retail sale value of quintal of bread	8,500			
Total tax		7,300	6,833	5,833
Rate of tax (tax divided by retail sale value)		85.9	80.4	68.6

Figures in the first column are from James Coogan, *Sales Taxes in the Soviet*

Union (unpub'd dissertation, Harvard University, 1951), p. 203. A few notes may be given in explanation of these figures. The state pays 766 kopeks for a quintal of grain. Since some grain is lost in the process of converting grain to flour, the grain required to make a quintal of flour is valued at 807 kopeks. Addition of milling costs of 250 kopeks and turnover tax on the flour of 8,850 kopeks gives the cost of flour at the mill (9,907 kopeks). When the flour is made into bread, water is added so that 1 quintal of flour makes about 1½ quintals of bread. Therefore the value of flour in a quintal of bread is only two-thirds of the cost of a quintal of flour. Similarly, only two-thirds of the turnover tax on a quintal of flour applies to a quintal of bread. Adding to the value of the flour costs of fabrication and distribution, and a budget markup, gives the retail value of bread.

Cost-Price Relations for Rye Bread, 1949 (kopeks per quintal)

	Price structure	Total tax	Substitute cost of production for procurement price	
Value of grain in flour	800		2,500	5,000
Milling costs	3,060			
Turnover tax (derived)	32,300	20,190	19,125	17,562
Cost of flour at mill	36,160			
Value of flour in bread (62.5 per cent)	22,590			
Cost of fabrication	1,500			
Cost of distribution (derived)	1,560			
Trade markdown (4.5 per cent)	1,350	1,350	1,350	1,350
Retail sale value of bread	27,000			
Total tax		21,540	20,475	18,912
Rate of tax		79.8	75.8	70.0

These figures are from A. K. Suchkov, *Gosudarstvennye dokhody SSSR* (Moscow, 1949), p. 77. We know the figures apply to 1949 because the retail price listed by Suchkov is the same retail price given by other sources for rye bread in 1949. The turnover tax and cost of distribution, although not supplied, can both be derived since they are the residual items in summations for which all the other figures have been supplied. We assumed that the cost of producing grain had almost doubled since 1940. This is in rough accord with the increase in wage rates since 1940.

Cost-Price Relations for Rye Bread, 1953 (kopeks per quintal)

	Assumption A				Assumption B			
	Price structure	Total tax	Substitute cost of production for procurement price		Price structure	Total tax	Substitute cost of production for procurement price	
Value of grain in flour	800		2,500	5,000	800		2,500	5,000

Rye Bread, 1953 (continued)

	Assumption A				Assumption B			
	Price structure	Total tax	Substitute cost of production for procurement price		Price structure	Total tax	Substitute cost of production for procurement price	
Milling and other costs	3,060				2,000			
Turnover tax (derived)	10,684	6,678	5,615	4,053	13,440	8,400	7,338	5,775
Cost of flour at mill (derived)	16,944				16,240			
Value of flour in bread (62.5 per cent) (derived)	10,590				10,150			
Cost of fabrication	1,500				1,000			
Cost of distribution (derived)	1,560				1,000			
Trade markdown	1,350	1,350	1,350	1,350	1,350	1,350	1,350	1,350
Retail sale value of bread	13,500				13,500			
Total tax		8,028	6,965	5,403		9,750	8,668	7,125
Rate of tax		59.5	51.6	40.0		72.2	64.4	52.8

In this table the basic adjustment is for the reduction in the price of rye bread since 1949 from 27,000 kopeks a quintal (2.7 rubles a kilogram) to 13,500. Both of these prices were cited in the Soviet press on the day of the price reductions of the respective years. In the first set of columns (Assumption A) it is assumed that the costs of processing and distributing grain, flour, and bread are left unchanged from 1949 in spite of the wholesale price cuts of 1950 and 1952. In the second set of columns, a one-third reduction in these costs is assumed.

TABLE 23 *Sobranie zakonov*, 1933, no. 13, art. 74.

TABLE 24 First five columns: Leonard Hubbard, *Economics of Soviet Agriculture* (London, 1939), p. 186. Last column: Naum Jasny, *The Socialized Agriculture of the U.S.S.R.* (Stanford, 1949), p. 372; these are official figures adjusted to a barn yield basis.

TABLE 25 First four columns: *Sobranie zakonov*, 1933, no. 13, art. 73; 1934, no. 10, art. 62; 1935, no. 12, art. 91; 1936, no. 13, art. 108. Last column: Jasny, p. 375.

TABLE 26 Jasny, pp. 378–389.

TABLE 27 Derived from Lazar Volin, "The Kolkhoz (Collective Farm) in the Soviet Union," *Foreign Agriculture* 11:150 (November–December 1947).

See also A. Baykov, *The Development of the Soviet Economic System* (New York, 1947).

TABLE 28 The coöperative form of the net collective farm crop (Table 27, row 3) includes obligatory deliveries, decentralized procurement, sales on collective farm markets, and payments to collective farmers. We wish to determine the element of tax comprised in the first two of these, and to express this tax as a percentage of the net crop.

Volin's ("The Kolkhoz") data (upon which Table 27 was based) do not isolate the share of decentralized procurement in gross output; we may, however, compute the share of decentralized procurement *plus* free market sales by deducting rows 4 and 6 from row 3. The results are as follows (per cent of gross crop): 1937, 4.8; 1938, 5.1; 1939, 4.0.

Free market sales must then be excluded from these figures to determine the share of decentralized procurement alone. The relative importance of free market sales and decentralized procurement in the joint total was estimated from the 1934 figures presented by Baykov (*Development of the Soviet Economic System*, p. 243); it is assumed that the former accounted for one-third and the latter for two-thirds of the total. Accordingly, the share of decentralized procurement alone in the gross crop is estimated as follows (per cent of gross crop): 1937, 3.2; 1938, 3.4; 1939, 2.7.

We may now proceed to compute the element of tax (conceived as the difference between cost of production and procurement prices) in obligatory deliveries and decentralized procurement.

It is assumed, as in Chapter 6, that the cost of production per quintal of grain in 1941 was 15 to 30 rubles. This figure must be deflated to get the cost range in the years 1937–1939. It is assumed that the rise in costs from 1937 to 1941 (Plan) is proportional to the rise in the average annual wage, which was (see Table 3): 1937, 3038; 1938, 3467; 1939, 3867; 1940, 4069; 1941 (plan), 4333. See Gosplan, *Gosudarstvennyi plan razvitiia narodnogo khoziaistva na 1941 god* [State plan for development of national economy in 1941] (published originally in the USSR in 1941 as a supplement to the 1941 State Plan; reprinted, Washington, D. C., 1941), p. 513.

The adjusted cost of production figures (rubles per quintal) are as follows: 1937, 10.5–21; 1938, 12–24; 1939, 13.4–26.8.

The obligatory delivery price remained unchanged from 1937 to 1939. It is assumed to have been 8.5 rubles, or halfway between the procurement prices for wheat and rye. See James Coogan, *Sales Taxes in the Soviet Union* (unpublished dissertation, Harvard University, 1951), p. 203.

The decentralized procurement price is assumed to have been 25 per cent higher than the obligatory delivery price, or 10.5 rubles. See Leonard Hubbard, *Economics of Soviet Agriculture* (London, 1939), p. 215. The obligatory delivery price remained stable over the years 1937–1939; the decentralized procurement price is likewise assumed to have remained unchanged.

The adjustments are made very simply. The ratio of procurement price to cost of production represents the nontax element in obligatory deliveries and decentralized procurement; this must be deducted to isolate the tax element.

In addition, the tax element contained in decentralized procurement is reduced by one-half in accordance with our assumption (presented in the text) that one-half of these sales can be regarded as voluntary, hence free of any element of tax. The calculations for 1937 are as follows. From Table 27, the obligatory deliveries were 12.2 per cent of gross crop. If the adjusted cost of production is 10.5 rubles, then

$$\text{Tax element in obligatory deliveries} = 12.2 - 12.2\frac{8.5}{10.5} = 2.3;$$

$$\text{Tax element in decentralized procurement} = \frac{1}{2}\left(3.2 - 3.2\frac{10.5}{10.5}\right) = 0.$$

If the adjusted cost of production had been taken to be 21 rubles, these figures would be 7.3 and 0.8 respectively.

The same procedure is followed for 1938 and 1939.

An Alternative Estimate of the Tax in Kind

In my dissertation, I computed a tax in kind based *not* on the differential between procurement price and cost of production, but on the differential between procurement price and an "average realized retail price" of agricultural products. In other words, it was assumed that if the collective farm had not had to sell its output at procurement prices, it could have sold it at current retail prices (for bread) or on the collective farm markets. The methodological objections to this procedure were explored at length. The principal objection is, of course, that a tax computed in this manner includes in the tax in kind on the producer the turnover tax on the consumer of bread products. The results, for those who are interested, were as follows (per cent of net crop):

	1937	1938	1939
Obligatory deliveries	18.4	24.4	25.1
Decentralized procurement	2.4	2.7	3.0
Payments to the MTS	14.7	18.1	22.8
Total Tax in Kind	35.5	45.2	50.9

Source: Holzman, *Taxation in the Soviet Union*, chap. 7.

TABLE 29 G. L. Mar'iakhin, *Nalogi i sbory s naseleniia i kolkhozov* (Moscow, 1946), pp. 61–68.

TABLE 30 Mar'iakhin, *Nalogi i sbory*, pp. 78–79.

TABLE 31 Estimated from Tables 29 and 30.

TABLE 32 I. Reingold, "The New Economic Policy, 1921–1928," in *Soviet Policy in Public Finance*, trans. E. Varneck, ed. Lincoln Hutchinson and Carl C. Plehn (Stanford, 1931), p. 174.

TABLE 33 G. L. Mar'iakhin, "Nalogovaia sistema sovetskogo gosudarstva" contained in *Finansy SSSR za XXX let* (Moscow, 1947), p. 271.

TABLE 34 Plotnikov, *Biudzhet sotsialisticheskogo gosudarstva*, pp. 17, 112, 196.

TABLE 35 Wage figures based on Harry Schwartz, *Russia's Soviet Economy* (New York, 1950), p. 460. Tax schedules from *Sobranie zakonov* 1930, no. 46 art. 482; 1932, no. 27 art. 211 b; Mar'iakhin, *Nalogi i sbory*, p. 61. Estimates are for a person with no exemptions.

TABLE 36 Same as for Table 35.

TABLE 37 *The current digest of the Soviet press*, October 6, 1951, p. 6.

TABLE 38 *The current digest of the Soviet press*, October 6, 1951, p. 6.

TABLE 39 Derived from Mar'iakhin, "Nalogovaia sistema . . . ," p. 276.

TABLE 40 Suchkov, *Dokhody*, p. 142.

TABLE 41 *Sobranie zakonov*, 1931, no. 19, art. 171; *Sobranie zakonov* 1937, no. 51, art. 216; *Finansovaia i khoziaistvennyi biulleten'* (Financial and Economic Bulletin), no. 25–26, Moscow, September 20, 1939, p. 7.

TABLE 42 1922–23 to 1925–26: V. P. D'iachenko, *Sovetskie finansy v pervoi faze razvitiia sotsialisticheskogo gosudarstva* [Soviet finance in the first phase of the development of the socialist state] (Moscow, 1947), p. 452. 1926–27 to 1927–28: V. P. D'iachenko, *Finansy i kredit SSSR* (Moscow and Leningrad, 1940), p. 202. 1928–29 to 1932: Total receipts and agricultural tax: Plotnikov, p. 17; 1931 kul'tzhilsbor: Mar'iakhin, "Nalogovaia sistema . . . ," p. 279; 1932 kul'tzhilsbor: State Planning Commission, *Socialist Construction in the U.S.S.R.*, p. 482 (take one-half of the total tax on both city and rural populations); 1932 "one-time tax": TsUNKhU, *Sotsialisticheskoe stroitel'stvo SSSR* (Moscow, 1934), p. 441, n. 2. 1933–1937: Plotnikov, p. 112 (note that 1933 kul'tzhilsbor is one-half of the total for the whole population). 1938–1940: *Ibid.*, pp. 181, 196, 190. Note that kul'tzhilsbor is estimated here as one-third of the total for the whole population — the ratio which obtained in 1936–37. Also note that Mar'iakhin, "Nalogovaia sistema," p. 285, gives the tax on horses as follows: 1938, 165 million rubles; 1939, 99 million rubles. Finally it should be noted that local taxes and collections on the popuation to a large extent fall on the rural population. However, since the tax is small and since we do not know what proportion is paid by the peasant, these figures were omitted.

TABLE 43 *Plan.* Plotnikov, pp. 47, 48, 199; D'iachenko, *Finansy i kredit*, pp. 201, 235.

Actual. A. Gordin, "Zaimy v sotsialisticheskom gosudarstve" [Loans in a socialist state], *Planovoe khoziaistvo*, 1940, no. 7, p. 18; Plotnikov, p. 199; D'iachenko, p. 235. For 1941, A. Zverev, "Uspekhi novogo zaima i zadachi finorganov i sberkass" [Progress of the new loans and tasks of the financial organs and savings banks], *Sovetskie finansy*, 1943, no. 5, p. 2.

TABLE 44 Purchases from D'iachenko, *Finansy i kredit*, p. 341. Repayments from F. Koshelev, "Gosudarstvennue zaimy SSSR" [State loans of the USSR], *Den'gi i kredit*, 1938, no. 3, p. 7.

TABLE 45 Aleksandrov, *Finansy i kredit SSSR*, p. 177, for planned figures, 1942 to 1945; Plan for 1941 from Table 43. Remaining figures from M. Naidis and A. Sakharov, "Gosudarstvennye zaimy v gody velikoi otechestvennoi voiny" [State loans during the years of the Great Patriotic War], *Sovetskie finansy*, 1945, no. 11, p. 9.

TABLE 46 TsUNKhU, *Sotsialisticheskoe stroitel'stvo SSSR* (Moscow, 1934), p. 159.

TABLE 47 *First Plan period.* The turnover tax for 1928–29 and 1929–30 is a combination of taxes which were unified into the turnover tax in the Tax Reform of 1930. The derivation is from TsUNKhU, *Sotsialisticheskoe stroitel'stvo SSSR* (1934), p. 493. The derivation follows (figures being millions of rubles).

	1928–29	1929–30
I. Payments into state budget	3,034	4,392
Taxes	2,787	4,554
Excise	1,789	2,629
Craft	886	1,797
Other	112	
Nontax income	247	377
Stumpage fees	180	290
Fee to use subsoil	66	83
Other	1	4
II. Payments into local budgets	96	126
Loading fee	71	91
Other	25	35
III. Nonbudget payments	16	297
Markup on procurement prices of agricultural products		152
Compulsory property insurance		99
Other		46
Total	3,146	5,354

It should be noted that Plotnikov (p. 21) gives different figures for the excise and craft taxes:

	1928–29	1929–30
Excise	1,798	2,634
Craft	1,056	1,989

No attempt was made to reconcile the two estimates. It seems likely that Plotnikov, in his estimates, combined with the craft tax some of the smaller taxes mentioned in the TsUNKhU figures.

The turnover taxes for 1931 and 1932 were from Plotnikov, p. 17. From this same source were obtained figures for the following categories from 1928–29 to 1932: deductions from profits, state loans, state social-insurance receipts, total budget receipts.

Direct taxes were based on the percentage figures given in Plotnikov, p. 44. The total figure was obtained by adding the agricultural tax on the population, the income tax from the population, local taxes and collections, and other taxes and collections. It is likely that both local taxes and other taxes contain items which are not paid directly by the population. The totals obtained, however, check quite well with estimates from earlier sources, and in fact may be on the low side. See, for example, TsUNKhU, *Sotsialisticheskoe stroitel'stvo SSSR* (1934), p. 468.

Retained profits were obtained by the formula: Total profits = retained profits + deductions from profits. Total profits for 1928–29 and 1929–30 were obtained from K. Shmelev, "K edinomu finplanu na 1930/31 g." [Toward a unified financial plan for 1930–31], *Finansovye problemy planovogo khoziaistva*, 1930, no. 6, p. 19. The figure for 1932 is from Suchkov, *Gosudarstvennye*, p. 131; that for 1931 was interpolated from the 1929–30 and 1932 figures.

As mentioned in the text, there is a substantial discrepancy between Plotnikov's estimates of total budget receipts for the first plan period and those of earlier writers and statistical collections. The comparison was made between the present *gosudarstvennyi* or state budget, which is the total of state, republican, and local budgets, and the old *svodnyi* or combined budget, which is equally inclusive. To the old estimates must be added the social-insurance budget, which has been regularly included in the state budget since 1938; one must also deduct from the svodnyi budget the receipts from transportation and communication, and then restore 50 per cent of net operating profits (see beginning of this chapter for references). There is not much discrepancy between most of the other receipts categories. Yet the reconciliation fails and there is a large residual between the items listed by Plotnikov and his total. Since there is no way of finding out how he made his estimates, the discrepancy remains until additional information is published. As his figures are generally accepted in other recent Soviet publications, they are also used here.

Second Plan Period. All figures for budgetary receipts are from Plotnikov, p. 102. Total profits: 1933: I. Konovalov, "Finansovyi plan na 1934 g." [Financial plan of 1934], *Planovoe khoziaistvo*, 1934, no. 5–6, pp. 177–181. It should be noted that a figure of 7.3 billion rubles, in comparison with the figure of 8 billion rubles used, is cited by S. N. Prokopovich, ed., *Biulleten'*, March 1936, p. 28. 1934: S. N. Prokopovich, ed., *Biulleten'*, March 1936, p. 28. 1935: Grinko, *Financial Program for 1936*, p. 15. 1936: D'iachenko, *Finansy i kredit*, p. 272. 1937: Suchkov, *Gosudarstvennye*, p. 131. Zverev in his budget speech for 1938 (*Gosudarstvennye biudzhety Soiuza SSR 1938–1945 gg.*, p. 11) gives the figure of 14.5 billion rubles, which is smaller than Suchkov's figure of 16.9 billion rubles. However, the Zverev figure is preliminary; therefore we accept the later estimate of Suchkov. *1938–1940*: All budgetary receipts figures from Plotnikov, p. 181. Total profits: 1938: Zverev, *Gosudarstvennye biudzhety Soiuza SSR 1938–1945 gg.*, p. 42. 1939: *Ibid.* This is the planned figure; no actual figure is available. 1940: Suchkov, *Gosudarstvennye*, p. 131.

TABLE 48 All budgeted figures for 1941–1945 are from Plotnikov, p. 259.

Turnover tax: 1941: Baykov and Barker, "Financial Developments in the U.S.S.R.," p. 11. 1942: M. Condoide, *The Soviet Financial System* (Columbus,

Ohio, 1951), p. 85. 1943: Zverev, *Gosudarstvennye biudzhety Soiuza SSR 1938–1945 gg.*, p. 129.

Profits tax: 1941 (plan): Zverev, p. 95. 1942: Plotnikov, p. 263. 1943: Zverev, p. 136.

Direct taxes and sale of government bonds: 1941: Baykov and Barker, p. 11. 1942: Loans from Baykov and Barker, p. 11. Total of loans and direct taxes from N. Voznesensky, *The Economy of the USSR During World War II*, p. 79. Subtracting loans from loans plus taxes gives taxes. 1943: Taxes from Plotnikov, p. 253; loans from *Bol'shaia sovetskaia entsiklopediia SSSR* [Great Soviet encyclopedia USSR] (Moscow, 1947), p. 1070. It should be noted that Baykov and Barker, p. 11, list this figure as 17.6 billion rubles. A different figure for loans for 1941–1945 may be obtained from K. Plotnikov, "Gosudarstvennyi biudzhet sovetskogo soiuza" [State Budget of the Soviet Union], *Finansy SSSR za XXX let* [Finances of the USSR over 30 years] (Moscow, 1947), pp. 186–187. The data are as follows (billions of rubles): sales of bonds: 1942, 13.2; 1943, 20.8; 1944, 29.0; 1945, 26.7; money-commodity lottery: 1941, 0.5; 1942, 2.9; 1943, 3.5; 1944, over 5. The reason for the discrepancies between these figures and the figures cited in the text is not known. The latter, however, are accepted because they were presented formally as complete budgetary items, whereas the former were not. The 1943 figures listed above cast doubt upon Baykov's figure of 17.6 billion rubles, and led us to choose instead the Encyclopedia's figure of 29 billion rubles.

Social insurance: 1941 (planned figure): Zverev, p. 95. The actual figure was slightly smaller (Baykov and Barker, pp. 11–12). 1942–43: No figures available.

Total receipts: 1941–1945: Aleksandrov, p. 227.

Total profits: 1941 (planned): Zverev, p. 97. 1942: Not available. 1943: Zverev, p. 137. 1944: Zverev, p. 150. 1945: A. G. Zverev, *O gosudarstvennom biudzhete SSSR na 1946 god* (Moscow, 1946), p. 11.

Turnover tax, profits tax, direct taxes, loans, and total receipts for 1946–1949 are from K. N. Plotnikov, "Biudzhet sotsialisticheskogo gosudarstva" [Budget of the socialist state], *Bol'shevik*, June 1950, p. 29. Preliminary figures for 1950 are from *Pravda*, March 8, 1951; those for 1951–1953, and 1954 (plan) are from K. N. Plotnikov, "Sovetskii biudzhet v gody piatoi piatiletki" (The Soviet Budget over the Fifth Five Year Plan), *Voprosy ekonomiki*, 1954, no. 6, pp. 4–6. For 1953 and 1954 only sales of bonds to the population were given (17.3 and 15.9 billion rubles). Since most of the bonds sold to institutions are sold to savings banks, the total bond sale planned was estimated roughly from the expected increase in savings deposits.

Social insurance: 1947: *Zasedaniia verkhovnogo soveta SSSR (tret'ia sessiia): stenograficheskii otchet*, 1947, p. 298. 1948 (preliminary) and 1949 (plan): A. Zverev, "Gosudarstvennyi biudzhet chetvertogo goda poslevoennoi stalinskoi piatiletki" [State budget in the fourth year of the postwar Stalin Five Year Plan], *Planovoe khoziaistvo*, 1949, no. 2, p. 393. 1950: *Pravda*, March 8, 1951. 1951–1954: K. N. Plotnikov, in *Voprosy ekonomiki*, 1954, no. 6, p. 5.

Profits: 1946, 1947 (plan): A. G. Zverev, *O gosudarstvennom biudzhete SSSR na 1947 god* (Moscow, 1947), p. 11. 1948, 1949 (plan): Zverev, "Gosudarstvennyi biudzhet chetvertogo," p. 395. 1950: *Pravda,* March 8, 1951. 1951–1954 (plan): K. N. Plotnikov in *Voprosy Ekonomiki,* 1954, no. 6, p. 6.

TABLE 49 For receipts: same as Tables 47 and 48.

For expenditures: 1928–29 to 1932: Plotnikov, p. 52. 1933–1937: *Ibid.,* p. 138. 1938–1940: *Ibid.,* p. 207. 1942, 1943: Voznesensky, p. 79. A. D. Gusakov and I. A. Dymshits, *Denezhnoe obrashchenie i kredit SSSR* [Monetary circulation and credit in the USSR] (Moscow, 1951), p. 159, give the deficit for 1942 as 18.9 billion rubles. 1941: Zverev, *Gosudarstvennye biudzhety,* p. 144. 1944: Zverev, *O gosudarstvennom biudzhete,* 1946, p. 6. 1945: Zverev, *O gosudarstvennom biudzhete,* 1947, p. 6. 1946–1949: K. Plotnikov, "Biudzhet sotsialisticheskogo gosudarstva," *Bol'shevik,* June 1950, p. 32. 1950: *Pravda,* March 8, 1951.

TABLE 50 Sources and methods are described in the text on pp. 278–282 and in Chapter 9, notes 55–61.

1951–1954: K. N. Plotnikov in *Voprosy ekonomiki,* 1954, no. 6, p. 4.

TABLE 51 1. *Retail Trade Turnover.* 1925–26 to 1929–30: All figures except those for public catering are from *TsUNKhU, Sotsialisticheskoe stroitel'stvo* (1934), p. 362. Public catering figures were obtained for the calendar years 1928–1930 from *Socialist Construction* (1936); these figures were interpolated to a fiscal year basis.

1931–1935: State and coöperative trade and public catering from *Socialist Construction* (1936), pp. 407–409. Collective farm market: 1931, 1935, Harry Schwartz, *Russia's Soviet Economy* (New York, 1950), p. 381; 1932, 1933, *Bol'shaia sovetskaia entsiklopediia* (special SSSR ed., Moscow, 1947), p. 1022.

1936–1939: Alexander Baykov, *Development of the Soviet Economic System,* p. 254.

1940: Schwartz, p. 381.

1947–1953, state and coöperative trade: estimates for this period are based primarily on the planned figure for 1947 of 324.6 billion rubles, from Gosplan, *O gosudarstvennom plane vosstanovleniia i razvitiia narodnogo khoziaistva SSSR na 1947 god* [State plan for reconstruction and development of the national economy of the USSR for 1947] (Moscow, 1947), p. 25, and the Gosplan results for 1953 which indicate that state and coöperative trade were expected to total 312 billion rubles (*Planovoe khoziaistvo,* 1954, no. 1, p. 15). Planned figures can be adjusted to an actual basis by assuming that the proportion of planned to actual retail-trade turnover is equal to the proportion of planned to actual turnover-tax receipts (the latter figures being available) and by making allowances for "economies" introduced in midyear (see directly below). This procedure is valid because the turnover tax constitutes a very large percentage of the value of retail trade turnover. I have accepted as my "*A*" estimates the calculations of Peter Wiles ("Retail Trade, Retail Prices and Real Wages in the U.S.S.R.," to be published in the *Bulletin of the Oxford Institute of Statistics* in November/December 1954) computed as indicated above. I have also accepted his interpolations for the years 1948–1952. According to Wiles, "The figures for 1948 to 1952 are . . . interpolated by means of the turnover tax, as follows: we have to move from a tax/trade ratio of 78.6% (1947) to one of 60.1% (1953). Large changes in the ratio are set against large 'economies,' and allowance is also made for the number of months (seasonally weighted) over which the price cut ran in the calendar year. The [retail trade] turnover value is then deduced from the interpolated tax/trade ratio." The "economies" mentioned by Wiles are the estimated savings to consumers from the annual retail price cuts which take effect every March 1 (until 1952) and April 1 (thereafter). The reduction in the tax/trade ratio is clearly closely related to the size of the "economy," since the price cuts are effected primarily by reductions in turnover tax rates.

Working independently, Naum Jasny in a recent article arrived at similar results ("Der sowjetische Staatshaushalt," *Finanzarchiv*, vol. 15, no. 1, p. 143). The two sets of figures (billions of rubles) are:

	1947	1948	1949	1950	1951	1952	1953
Wiles	308	332	348	356	385	391	445
Jasny	302	327	342	355	382	400	442 (plan)

In an article completed before Malenkov released his figure for planned turnover for the last three quarters of 1953, the present writer published estimates of retail trade turnover for 1948, 1949, and 1950 which were much higher than those of Wiles and Jasny (see my "Burden of Soviet Taxation," unpublished appendix, available upon request, pp. 1–8). Although the absolute magnitudes were clearly incorrect, reasons which I believe are still valid were presented for assuming a rather large increase in the value of retail trade turnover from 1949 to 1950. Both Wiles and Jasny, it should be noted, assume very small increases over this period. My reasons, to restate them briefly, were as follows. First, there is some basis for believing that total consumer money income increased fairly substantially in 1950. Soviet data indicate that the nonagricultural labor force increased more rapidly in that year than in any other year of the postwar period. Whether this increase represented a transfer from the agricultural labor force or a net increment to the working population, the result would still be to increase consumer money income. Second, direct taxes paid by the population and the social-insurance markup on wages (see Table 48) both increased in 1950 by a greater percentage than in 1949. Since both are closely correlated with the total wage bill, and since there were no known changes in the tax or insurance laws in 1949 and 1950, it can be inferred that total consumer income increased in 1950 by more than it did in 1949. If it is granted that consumer incomes did increase substantially in 1950, then it follows logically that consumer outlays, including savings and increments to cash balances, must also have increased substantially. The components of consumer outlay, with the exception of cash balances and retail trade turnover, are given to us directly by the Soviets. These show very little increase relative to 1949 (see Table 51). Since prices declined sharply in 1950 and no repressed inflation is reported, it can be inferred that there was little, if any, increase in cash balances. By this logic we may infer that the increase in consumer outlays must have been reflected primarily in the value of retail trade turnover, the residual item in our calculation, which, incidentally, constitutes on the average more than 75 per cent of total consumer outlays.

One additional piece of evidence: the Soviets have claimed for 1950 (*Pravda*, January 26, 1951) an increase in the volume of retail trade turnover of 30 per cent. This is higher than the increase claimed for any other postwar year. Since the 1950 retail price reduction can by no method of calculation be estimated to have exceeded 21 per cent, a larger increase in the value of retail trade turnover would seem to be warranted for 1950 than either Wiles or Jasny estimated.

For the above reasons, supplementary estimates, to be called "*B*" estimates, will be presented for the value of retail trade turnover and for all the series in which this item is incorporated, for the years 1950–1952. In other words, while I accept Wiles's estimates for 1947 and 1953, I have doubts regarding the validity of his allocation of the increase over the years 1950–1952. It seems preferable, therefore, to present the reader with an alternative set of estimates and leave him to make his own choice. The adjustment which follows is based on the Soviet claim mentioned above of a 30 per cent increase in the volume of state and coöperative retail trade turnover for the year 1950:

	1950	1951	1952
"*A*" (Wiles)	356	385	391
"*B*"	370	399	405

1947–1953, collective farm market trade: Wiles (see footnotes to his Table 11) cites Soviet sources from which it can be deduced that collective farm market trade was 12 per cent of total trade in 1949 and 1950 and 14.4 per cent in 1952. Roughly interpolating, we assume 13 per cent for 1951 and 14.4 per cent for 1953. In order to allow for repressed inflation in 1947 and 1948, 15 per cent was assumed for the former, and 13 per cent for the latter year.

The retail-trade turnover figures which have been discussed above include not only sales to consumers but also sales to enterprises and organizations. In computing consumer income from the outlay side, it is necessary to eliminate sales to nonhousehold units from the total of retail-trade turnover. Bergson, "Soviet National Income and Product in 1937," Appendix (available upon request), p. 9, states that "Sales to institutions are estimated to have amounted to 11.5 per cent of the total turnover of government and coöperative shops and to 10 per cent of the turnover in the collective farm market (based on data in N. S. Margolin, *Voprosy balansa denezhnykh dokhodov i raskhody naseleniia* (Moscow, 1940), pp. 63, 101)." We have reduced our total figure for retail-trade turnover by 11 per cent for every prewar year as a rough adjustment for the effect of nonhousehold purchases. Considerable faith can be placed in the use of the 11 per cent deduction for the earlier years. "Control figures" were published by Gosplan, *Kontrol'nye tsifry narodnogo khoziaistva SSSR na 1929–30 gg.* [Control figures of the national economy of the USSR for 1929–30] (Moscow, 1929), pp. 476–478; they include tables on the balance of income and expenditures of both city and rural populations; these figures provide us with estimates of consumer purchases in the retail markets unalloyed by institutional purchases. Unfortunately, these figures do include some transactions in kind; they are about 10 per cent larger than our retail-trade turnover figures adjusted downward for purchases by nonhousehold units. Although there is no information as to the relative amounts of transactions in kind and in money in the control figures, footnotes to the tables give the impression that the transactions in kind (which were included) are quite small. Thus the two sets of estimates appear to be fairly compatible. The adjustment was raised to 12 per cent for 1947–1953 on the basis of scattered evidence indicating that the coöperatives are now purchasing much more heavily than before in the collective farm markets.

Before concluding the discussion of the retail-trade turnover figures, it is necessary to caution the reader with respect to the validity of Soviet estimates of these magnitudes. The Soviet literature on retail trade indicates that their computations of the value of retail trade are made not directly, but by use of sampling techniques. In the late thirties the sample was fairly large and the results may have been fairly reliable. In the earlier years the samples were small and the results were probably less reliable. Since these are the only sources of such figures, however, they must be used; there does not appear to be any simple method of determining what bias, if any, the figures contain.

2. *Consumer Services.* Bergson, "Soviet National Income and Product in 1937," Appendix (available upon request), p. 9, estimates that consumer outlays for services were 13.6 per cent of adjusted consumers' outlays for goods in 1934 and 12.1 per cent in 1938. Estimates of consumer services are directly available for the period from 1925–26 to 1929–30 (Bergson, "Soviet National Income and Product in 1937," pp. 476–478). The figures for 1931–1933 and 1935–1937 are interpolated. As a rough expedient, 12 per cent is used for all years after 1938 (1938 being 12.1 per cent).

3. *Trade Union Dues.* These are discussed in the text.

4. *Shares in Coöperatives.* Figures from 1925–26 to 1929–30 are from *Kontrol'nye tsifry . . . 1929/30,* p. 476. No data were available for later years; since the item is small, no attempt was made to extrapolate it.

5. *Direct Taxes.* Sources are cited in the notes to Tables 47 and 48 except that figures for 1926–27 to 1929–30 are from Plotnikov, *Biudzhet sotsialisticheskogo gosudarstva,* p. 21, and those for 1925–26 are from *Bol'shaia entsiklopediia,* p. 1022.

6. *Loans* (purchases of bonds by population). 1925–26 to 1932: *Socialist Construction* (1936), p. 514. 1933–1937: *Gosudarstvennyi biudzhet SSSR za vtoruiu piatiletku (1933–37)* (Leningrad, 1939), pp. 8, 10. 1938–1940: It was assumed that 80 per cent of total bonds sold were purchased directly by the population. For source of total bonds sold by the government, see the notes to Table 47. 1947–1950: Total sales of government bonds from notes to Table 48. It was assumed that 85 per cent of these were sold to the population directly; this was the 1947 planned ratio of bond receipts from all sources (both figures from Zverev's budget speeches). 1951–1953: Plotnikov, *Voprosy ekonomiki,* 1954, No. 6, p. 5.

7. *Increment in Savings Deposits.* 1925–26 to 1932: *Sotsialisticheskoe stroitel'stvo* (1934), p. 502. 1933–1949: Baykov and Barker, p. 18 (1948 is based on plan). 1950: Difference between Baykov and Barker's figure for deposits on January 1, 1950 (17.0 billion rubles) and figures in *Pravda*, March 8, 1951 for January 1, 1951 (18.5 billion). 1951–1952 (plan): *Pravda*, March 7, 1952, 1953 (plan): *Pravda*, August 6, 1953.

8. *Increment in Cash Holdings.* 1925–26 to 1929–30: Arnold, *Banks, Credit, and Money in Soviet Russia*, pp. 257, 412. 1931–1936, 1940, 1941: See Table 8. 1937, 1938, 1939: Interpolated. 1947–1953: See text.

Soviet estimates of consumers' money income for 1935 and 1937 are given as 102 and 150 billion rubles, respectively (N. Sokolov, "Gosbank v bor'be za ekonomiiu v narodnom khoziaistve" [The state bank in the struggle for economy in the national economy] *Planovoe khoziaistvo*, 1940, no. 3, p. 34). This checks fairly well with our estimates of 107.4 and 155.6 billion rubles.

TABLE 52 For the period after 1928–29, most of the sources are the same as for Tables 48 and 49. This applies to the turnover tax, profits, direct taxes, and social insurance. Sources of remaining data were as follows:

1. *Direct Taxes and Sales of Bonds to Population.* Same as Table 51.

2. *Excise and Crafts.* 1926–27 to 1929–30: Plotnikov, *Biudzhet sotsialisticheskogo gosudarstva*, p. 21. 1925–26: *Sotsialisticheskoe stroitel'stvo* (1934), p. 440.

3. *Social Insurance.* 1925–26: D'iachenko, *Sovetskie finansy*, p. 290. 1926–27 to 1927–28: These two years were interpolated from the figure above for 1925–26 and the figure for 1928–29 from Plotnikov, p. 17.

4. *Profits.* 1925–26 to 1927–28. Deductions from profits in 1928–29 were 0.6 billion rubles when total profits were 3.3 billion (Table 48). Deductions from profits in 1925–26, 1926–27, and 1927–28 were respectively 0.2 billion, 0.3 billion, and 0.4 billion rubles; See *Sotsialisticheskoe stroitel'stvo* (1934), p. 441. We assume that the 1928–29 ratio of deductions from profits to total profits applied also to the earlier years, and accordingly multiply each figure for deductions from profits by 5.5 ($3.3 \div 0.6$).

5. *Other Direct Taxes on the Consumer.* No attempt will be made to detail the estimates of this category. *Socialist Construction* was used for the estimates prior to 1932. Taxes included were customs, revenue from state property, income tax on socialized enterprises, and miscellaneous fines and collections. From 1933 to 1937, *Gosudarstvennyi biudzhet Soiuza SSR za vtoruiu piatiletku* was used. Categories included were customs, income from forests, and income taxes and other (minor) taxes on enterprises and organizations. Complete statistics are not available for other years; the figures which are available indicate that the constituent figures did not change their percentage relation to total budget receipts. For these reasons, it was assumed that other indirect taxes were 3 per cent of total budget receipts for each year after 1937.

6. *Adjustment for Taxes on Nonconsumption.* It is pointed out in the text that the indirect tax figures presented in the budget include taxes paid within the nonhousehold sector by one organization or enterprise to another; the incidence of these is never on the consumer. An example of a transaction in-

volving such a tax payment would be the purchase by the Ministry of Armed Forces of food and clothing on which there is a turnover tax, or of rifles, the final price of which included profits to the producer and a social-insurance markup. The adjustment required is to some extent analogous to the adjustment of retail-trade turnover made for sales to nonhousehold units. The adjustment is different, however, for two reasons: the ratio of tax to total value on goods sold to the individual consumer undoubtedly differs from the ratio on goods sold to institutions and enterprises; and part of these taxes were levied on commodities not included in retail-trade turnover.

It is impossible to make the adjustment very precisely, since the distribution of indirect taxes between the household and nonhousehold sectors is not published. However, the distribution of turnover-tax receipts and profits by commissariat, which is available for some years, enables us to make a rough guess at the shares of the tax paid by consumers and by nonconsumers. It can be assumed, for example, that all profits and turnover tax originating in the commissariat of heavy industry were paid by nonhousehold units; on the other hand, almost all of the taxes and profits originating in the commissariats of food and procurement were assumed to have been paid by households, although some allowance was made, for example, for purchases of food by the Commissariat of Armed Forces; see Naum Jasny, "The Soviet Price System," *American Economic Review*, 40:860 (December 1950). It was estimated that about 75 per cent of turnover tax originating in light industries was paid by the household, and so forth.

Turnover-tax data are available by ministry for 1934–1937 and 1939–1941, and by commodity for 1936. The sources are: 1934, 1935 (plan): S. N. Prokopovich, *Biulleten'*, March 1935, p. 25. 1936: A. Smilga, "Finansy sotsialisticheskogo gosudarstva," p. 114. 1936 (by commodity, plan): Grinko, *Financial Program*, p. 64. 1937 (plan): Same as 1936. 1939 (plan): *Tretia sessiia verkhovnogo soveta SSSR: stenograficheskii otchet*, May 1939, pp. 328–329. 1940 (plan): *Shestaia sessiia verkhovnogo soveta SSSR: stenograficheskii otchet*, April 1940, p. 232. 1941 (plan): *Vos'maia sessiia verkhovnogo soveta SSSR*, February 1941, pp. 498–499.

The share of the turnover tax not paid by the household was estimated, from the above data, to have been about one-sixth from 1934 to 1939; this fraction was applied also to 1931–1933. For the years 1940 and 1947–1953 the fraction was raised to one fifth to allow for increased procurement by the Soviet military establishment. An increase in military procurement is indicated by N. Voznesensky, *The Economy of the USSR During World War II* (translation; Washington, 1948), p. 75; unfortunately the figures he presents are not susceptible to quantification. Bergson and Heymann's estimates for 1940 and 1948 are 20 and 23 per cent respectively; see Abram Bergson and Hans Heymann, Jr., *Soviet National Income and Product, 1940–1948* (New York, 1954), pp. 218–219. The reader should be cautioned that although the adjustment under discussion is fairly important for determining the level and burden of taxation, it is submitted with very little confidence. The available evidence is simply too scanty to permit precision estimates.

The adjustment for profits, though much less important for our results, was even more tenuous than that for the turnover tax. A distribution of total profits by ministry is available in the prewar period only for the years 1935 (Grinko, *Financial Program for 1936*, p. 16) and 1936 (Smilga, "Finansy sotsialisticheskogo gosudarstva," p. 112). The distribution of deductions from profits was available for many other years, and these aided in making judgments (especially those from the *Stenographic Reports* for April 1940 and February 1941). It was finally decided to deduct from taxes on the consumer about one-third of profits for all years until 1948; this percentage seemed appropriate for the years about which information is available. It should be remembered that many taxes levied originally on producers' goods are eventually included in the cost of consumers' goods. The adjustment was raised to one-half for the years 1949 to 1953 for the following reasons. First, the Soviets made their well-known attempt in 1949 to eliminate subsidies to industry, particularly heavy industry, and transport and to put most enterprises on a pay-as-you-go basis. The result of such a reform would be, of course, an increase in the percentage of total profits not paid by the household. Second, Finance Minister Zverev in his recent budget speeches has presented breakdowns of profits by ministry; these data support our inference that the percentage of profits not paid by the household has risen (though they by no means enable us to make precise estimates).

A ratio of one-third was used for social-insurance and other indirect taxes. The social-insurance estimate is based on data presented by Bergson ("Soviet National Income and Product in 1937," Appendix, p. 19) and is admittedly very rough; the same ratio was used for other indirect taxes for lack of a better expedient. These items are not large and, unless the one-third estimate is very far off, the final results are not likely to be significantly affected.

7. *Adjustment for Subsidies on Consumers' Goods.* (*a*) *MTS subsidy.* The MTS subsidies (billions of rubles) were derived as follows:

	1937	1938	1939	1940	1948	1949	1950
MTS expenditures	7.0	7.5	7.9	7.8	10.0	14.0	16.0
MTS receipts	1.5	1.4	1.8	2.0	2.0	3.0	3.0
Subsidy	5.5	6.1	6.1	5.8	8.0	11.0	13.0

The figures for 1938–1940 are official and are taken from Suchkov, *Dokhody*, p. 113. The figures for 1937 are estimated on the assumption that the MTS had roughly the same receipts-expenditure relation as a khozraschet organization in 1937 that it had in 1938 when it was included in the budget on a gross basis. Receipts were assumed to have been slightly higher than trend because of the excellent crop in 1937.

The estimates for 1948–1950 are extremely crude. Planned receipts for 1948 and 1949 are given as 1.9 billion rubles and 3.3 billion rubles respectively in the Stenographic Reports for those years. Because the other data are so rough, these figures were rounded. For 1950 the same receipts figure was used; the magnitude of the jump from 1948 to 1949 suggests a change in legislation (in norms of payment in kind), and this is not likely to have occurred in two successive years.

The expenditure estimates were based on three different clues, which yielded somewhat different results. The first was the receipts-to-expenditure ratio in the prewar period; this tended to give a low figure for expenditures. The second was the ratio of expenditures on MTS to total expenditures on agriculture in the prewar period. This gave a much higher figure for expenditures than the estimates we elected to use. Finally, a minimum figure for planned expenditures on the MTS in 1951 is suggested by the statement of one Soviet economist that if the cost of tractor work per hectare were reduced by 8.2 per cent, the state would save over 1 billion rubles (see I. Benediktov, "MTS v bor'be za novyi pod'em sel'skogo khoziaistva" [The MTS in the struggle for a new prosperity in agriculture], *Bol'shevik*, 1951, no. 5, p. 15). This implies that expenditures are planned at more than 12.2 billion rubles. The expenditure figures finally used are the result of juggling together information from these three sources. As was pointed out in the text, we have assumed that two-thirds of this subsidy benefited consumers' goods. (Since these estimates were made, it was stated by Zverev, in his 1952 budget speech, that expenditures on the MTS in 1952 were planned at 17 billion rubles. This supports the foregoing estimates.)

(*b*) *Subsidies to the national economy* (other than to MTS). Subsidies (billions of rubles) were estimated as follows:

	1937	1938	1939	1940	1948	1949	1950
Total budget expenditure for financing the national economy	43.4	51.7	60.4	58.3	149.6	161.9	157.3
Deduct expenditures for:							
Fixed investment	18.0	24.0	24.0	24.4	57.2	79.8	99.8
Working capital	5.5	5.4	5.6	5.5	10.7	10.1	6.7
MTS	7.0	7.5	7.9	7.8	10.0	14.0	16.0
Subsidies (+ operating expenditures)	12.9	14.0	22.9	20.6	71.7	58.0	34.8

Financing the national economy: 1937: Plotnikov, *Biudzhet*, p. 126; 1938–1940: *Ibid.*, p. 207; 1948–1949: Plotnikov (*Bol'shevik*), p. 32; 1950: *Pravda*, March 8, 1951.

Fixed investment: 1937: On the basis of the ratios which obtained in 1936 and 1938, it is assumed that budgeted fixed investment is two-thirds of total investment. Total investment in fixed capital is 27.8 billion rubles: Plotnikov, p. 129. 1938: Zverev, *Gosudarstvennye biudzhet SSSR, 1938–1945*, p. 17 (plan). 1939: Interpolated. 1940: D'iachenko, *Finansy i kredit*, p. 395 (planned figure). 1948: Zverev, *O gosudarstvennom biudzhete SSSR na 1949 god.*, p. 10. 1949: *Ibid.*, p. 16 (plan). 1950: *Pravda*, June 14, 1950 (plan).

Working capital: 1937: Smilga, p. 119. 1938: Zverev, *Gosudarstvennye biudzhet*, p. 19 (plan). 1939: D'iachenko, *Finansy i kredit*, p. 405. 1940: Interpolated. 1948: Zverev, *O gosudarstvennom biudzhete SSSR na 1948 god*, p. 23

(plan). 1949: Zverev, *O gosudarstvennom biudzhete SSSR na 1949 god*, p. 18 (plan). 1950: *Pravda*, June 14, 1950 (plan).

The major limitation on the validity of the foregoing figures is that they contain operating expenditures as well as subsidies. However, it is believed that the share of operating expenditures is very small. It must also be emphasized that the recent figures, in particular, are planned rather than actual, that some data had to be interpolated, and that the estimates of MTS expenditures are crude. In the text it was explained that one-fifth of our derived subsidy figure is assumed to affect consumers' goods.

TABLE 53 Derived from Tables 51 and 52.

TABLE 54 *Treasury Bulletin*, published monthly by the United States Treasury Department; *Survey of Current Business*, published monthly by the United States Department of Commerce.

TABLE 55 The following budget expenditure figures were used in preparing Table 55:

Year	Education	Health	Social Insurance	Social Security	Subsidies to Mothers	Debt Service	Student Stipends
1932	3.8	0.8	2.9	0.2		1.0	0.6
1933	4.9	1.0	3.2	0.2		1.3	0.8
1934	6.3	1.8	3.4	0.2		1.9	1.2
1935	8.8	4.0	3.7	0.2		1.8	1.4
1936	13.9	5.6	5.0	0.2	0.1	2.2	1.8
1937	16.5	6.9	5.2	1.3	1.0	3.5	2.2
1938	18.7	7.6	6.0	2.0	0.9	2.0	2.3
1939	20.3	8.2	7.2	2.3	1.1	2.0	2.4
1940	22.5	9.0	7.8	3.1	1.2	2.5	2.4
1947	51.5	18.1	9.9	22.0	4.5	6.5	2.5
1948	55.0	19.6	9.8	18.4	2.5	3.5	3.0
1949	57.7	21.0	11.8	21.5	3.2	2.5	3.5
1950	56.9	21.1	12.7	21.5	3.7	3.7	4.0
1951	57.3	21.7		39.0		4.9	4.5
1952	58.5	22.3		39.5		6.8	5.0
1953	61.1	24.2		40.1		9.8	5.8

1932–1937: All figures except debt service from N. Rovinskii, "Sovetskie finansy i kul'turnaia revoliutsiia" [Soviet finances and the cultural revolution]. *Finansy SSSR za XXX let* [Thirty years of Soviet finances] (Moscow, 1947), pp. 209 (for 1932) and 218.

Debt service: The figure for 1932 is from Plotnikov, *Biudzhet*, p. 52; the figures for 1933–1937 are from *Gosudarstvennyi biudzhet SSSR za vtoruiu piatiletkiu.*

1938–1940: Education: Plotnikov, *Biudzhet*, p. 220. Health: *Ibid.*, p. 223. Subsidies to mothers: *Ibid.*, p. 225. Social Insurance: 1938: *Ibid.*, p. 219; 1939, 1940 (plan): Zverev, *Gosudarstvennyi biudzhet SSSR, 1938–1945*, p. 83. Social security: 1938, 1939 (plan): *Ibid.*, p. 56; 1940: Plotnikov, p. 329. Debt service: D'iachenko, *Finansy i kredit*, p. 280. (1940 is a planned figure.)

1947–1950: Education, health, subsidies to mothers, and social insurance from: K. Plotnikov, "Raskhody gosudarstvennogo biudzheta SSSR v poslevoennyi period" [State budget expenditures in the postwar period], *Finansy i kredit SSSR*, 1953, no. 10, p. 21.

Social security: 1948: A. Zverev, "Gosudarstvennyi biudzhet chetvertogo goda poslevoennoi stalinskoi piatiletki," p. 48; 1947, 1949, 1950: Plotnikov (directly above) presents total social and cultural expenditures and all its component figures with the exception of social insurance which can then be derived by subtraction.

Debt service: 1947, 1948 (plan): *Izvestiia*, February 6, 1948; 1949: Plotnikov, *Bol'shevik*, 1950, no. 12, p. 31; 1950: K. Plotnikov, "Sovetskii biudzhet v gody piatoi piatiletki" [The Soviet budget in the years of the Five Year Plan], *Voprosy ekonomiki*, 1954, no. 6, p. 8.

1951–1953: Education, health, and total social and cultural expenditures from Plotnikov, *Voprosy ekonomiki*, pp. 9, 15. Social insurance, social security, and subsidies to mothers: the total of these three items is available from Plotnikov, p. 15, for the year 1953; 1951–1952: since these three items constitute almost the entire residual of the category, social and cultural expenditures, after education and health expenditures have been subtracted, it was possible to deduce their total by assuming they amounted to the same percentage of the residual in 1951 and 1952 as they did in 1953. Debt service: 1951: Plotnikov, p. 8; 1952, 1953 (plan): lead editorial, *Finansy i kredit SSSR*, 1953, no. 8, p. 6.

Student stipends, 1932–1953: 1934: Francis Seton, "The Social Accounts of the Soviet Union in 1934," *Review of Economics and Statistics*, vol. 36 (August 1954), p. 1 of unpublished appendix; 1937, 1940, 1948: Abram Bergson and Hans Heymann, Jr., *Soviet National Income and Product, 1940–1948* (New York, 1954), p. 20; 1953 (plan): *Pravda*, August 8, 1953; remaining years filled in by interpolation. It should be noted that for the years 1949–1952 the interpolation corresponds very closely to the change in student enrollment.

TABLE 56 Derived from data in Tables 51 and 52 and notes to these tables by methods described on pp. 264–267.

TABLE 57 Same as Table 56.

TABLE 58 Factor cost of retail trade: from Table 57.

Official Soviet data: 1947: *Izvestiia*, January 18, 1948; 1948: no data; 1949: *Izvestiia*, January 18, 1950; 1950: *Pravda*, January 26, 1951; 1951: *Izvestiia*, January 29, 1952; 1952: *Vestnik statistiki*, 1953, no. 1, p. 14; 1953: *Planovoe khoziaistvo*, 1954, no. 1, p. 15.

NOTES

INTRODUCTION

1. A. Z. Arnold, *Banks, Credit, and Money in Soviet Russia* (New York, 1937); L. E. Hubbard, *Soviet Money and Finance* (London, 1936); W. B. Reddaway, *The Russian Financial System* (London, 1935).

2. For examples of this, see Naum Jasny, "Soviet Statistics," *Review of Economics and Statistics*, 32:92–99 (February 1950).

3. Abram Bergson, *Soviet National Income and Product in 1937* (New York 1953), pp. 6 ff., esp. note 10. The other side of the issue is championed by Jasny, ref. 2.

CHAPTER 1. TAXATION AND DIRECT ECONOMIC CONTROLS

1. Some physical controls are very old, of course — drafting of soldiers and appropriation of property through eminent domain, for example.

2. During the period of War Communism (1918–1921) an attempt was actually made to do away with the market mechanism. See Chapter 5.

3. G. Bienstock, S. Schwartz, and A. Yugow, *Management in Russian Industry and Agriculture* (New York, 1944), p. 58.

4. E. Lokshin, "Voprosy planirovaniia material'no-tekhnicheskogo snabzheniia narodnogo khoziaistva SSSR" [Problems of planning material-technical supplies of the Soviet national economy], *Planovoe khoziaistvo* [Planned economy], 1950, no. 2, p. 46.

5. Bienstock, Schwartz, and Yugow, ref. 3, pp. 58–59.

6. An exception to the general freedom of the labor market in this period is provided by the agreements between collective farms and industrial enterprises, designed to shift surplus labor from the former to the latter.

7. For fuller discussion of these measures, see Alexander Baykov, *The Development of the Soviet Economic System* (New York, 1947), chap. 18; Harry Schwartz, *Russia's Soviet Economy* (New York, 1950), chap. 13.

8. See Harry Schwartz, "Soviet Labor Policy, 1945–1949," *The Annals of the American Academy of Political and Social Science*, May 1949, pp. 81 82.

9. Ia. A. Kronrod, *Ukreplenie denezhnogo obrashcheniia v SSSR, infliatsiia v stranakh kapitalizma* [Strengthening monetary circulation in the USSR, inflation in capitalist countries] (Moscow, 1950), p. 60.

10. Apparently these controls are effective. I have seen only one reference to transactions being conducted at higher than planned price. See V. P. D'iachenko, ed., *Finansy i kredit SSSR* [Finance and credit in the USSR] (Moscow and Leningrad, 1940), p. 309.

11. V. Batyrev, "Voprosy planirovaniia privlechennykh resursov gosudarstvennogo banka" [Problems of planning the attracted resources of the state bank], *Den'gi i kredit* [Money and credit], 1941 no. 1–2, p. 37.

12. The incentive role of profits is discussed in Chapter 4.

CHAPTER 2. TAXATION, INFLATION, AND THE FINANCIAL PLAN

1. A. Baykov, *The Development of the Soviet Economic System* (New York, 1947), p. 404.

2. *Ibid.*, p. 405.

3. Z. V. Atlas and E. V. A. Bregel', *Denezhnoe obrashchenie i kredit v SSSR* [Money circulation and credit in the USSR] (Moscow, 1947), pp. 241, 322, 328.

4. In 1940 about 10 per cent of cash circulation was between enterprises. See Iu. Shenger, "O metodologii planirovaniia denezhnogo obrashcheniia i nekotorykh zadachakh finansovoi sistemy" [On the methodology of planning monetary circulation and some tasks of the financial system], *Sovetskie finansy,* 1940, no. 3, pp. 13–15.

5. *Ibid.*, p. 15.

6. The funds from an extension of short-term credit to one enterprise rapidly become operating receipts of other enterprises as the funds are spent. Probably the bulk of the overexpenditures on wages which are made possible by Soviet short-term lending policy are not made in the initial expenditure of borrowed funds.

7. Shenger says (ref. 4, p. 16): "Presence in economic organizations of surplus funds in the clearing (*raschetnyi*) account (with the State bank) can lead — and, as experience shows, generally does lead — to unplanned expenditures, in particular to overexpenditures of wage funds, distribution of illegal premiums, etc."

8. The importance of financial stability in the factor markets as well as in the market for final output has only recently received the attention it deserves. Several writers have pointed out that aggregate stability requires not only equilibrium in the market for consumers' goods, but also in the market for factors of production. See, for example, Ralph Turvey and Hans Brems, "The Factor and Goods Markets," *Economica*, February 1951, pp. 57–68.

9. An increase in wage rates does not automatically increase output price, but may result in lower profits or losses. The lower profits (and profits taxes) reduce the capacity of the government to purchase the same quantity of goods and services. Losses, when they occur, are covered by subsidies which are financed through the budget, thereby increasing budget expenditures by the amount of the wage increase the subsidy is designed to finance.

10. D. H. Robertson, "Theories of Banking Policy," *Essays in Monetary Theory* (London, 1946); *Banking Policy and the Price Level* (London, 1926); *Money* (London, 1948), chap. V. Some of the more important variables mentioned by Robertson are the proportion of real income the community desires to hold in the form of money, the length of the period of production, and the percentage of circulating capital to total real income. Unfortunately, Robert-

son's model is too simple to be applied unqualifiedly to the Soviet economy, perhaps even to capitalist economies. Though he can show the relation between taxes and short-term credit which is consistent with financial stability in his simple model, this relation may not be consistent with other important aspects of an economy. The *imperfectness* of Soviet planning in a setting of high-speed industrialization, partial utilization of the price mechanism, and dependence on manager and worker incentives is, in our opinion, a case in point. This is discussed below.

11. Such an analysis would be redundant in any case, since an excellent study already exists; see Raymond P. Powell, *Soviet Monetary Policy* (unpublished doctoral dissertation, University of California, 1952).

12. Robertson, "Theories of Banking Policy," pp. 52 ff; Powell, chap. 5.

13. Powell, ref. 11, pp. 242 ff. This hypothesis is reëxamined below (Chapter 2, pp. 38–39).

14. This was true for five or six years for which data are available. See Powell, ref. 11, p. 237.

15. Alfred G. Hart, *Financing Defense* (New York, 1951).

16. Turvey and Brems, ref. 8; Bent Hansen, *A Study in the Theory of Inflation* (London, 1951).

17. Abram Bergson, "Soviet National Income and Product in 1937," *Quarterly Journal of Economics*, 64: 208–241, 408–444 (May and August 1950), pp. 236–237.

18. See Bergson, ref. 17, p. 435; Naum Jasny, "Intricacies of National Income Indexes," *Journal of Political Economy*, August, 1947, p. 300.

19. The rationale of this policy is well known. The Soviets have attempted to maintain as stable a cost structure as possible. If prices of producers' goods reflected the profits necessary for further investment in producers'-goods industries, the higher prices would be reflected in all further production in which this equipment was used. By raising the prices of consumers' goods and redistributing the profits, this cumulative effect is avoided. Furthermore, over the past 25 years of rapid industrial development the Soviets have introduced many new types of machinery and equipment. In the early stages of production, before economies of scale are achieved, costs are frequently abnormally high. In the interests of maintaining a stable cost structure and encouraging the use of new producers' goods, the Soviet policy has been to maintain the prices of such items below short-run cost by granting subsidies over the period in which short-run cost is above estimated long-run cost. It should be noted that in 1936, and again in 1949, attempts were made to reduce subsidies. The Soviets claimed that subsidies would be eliminated by the end of 1950.

20. According to Bergson (ref. 17, p. 435), defense was 7.6 per cent of net national product in 1937.

21. Voluntary savings by the population take the form of deposits in savings banks and increases in cash holdings. In 1937, these amounted to less than 2 per cent of the disposable money income of the population (see Bergson, ref. 17, p. 214). The population is subject to almost as much compulsion in the purchase of government bonds as it is in the payment of taxes. For this and other reasons to be mentioned below (see Chapter 8) purchases of bonds will

be considered a form of taxation and not a form of voluntary saving.

22. See Chapter 10.

23. See Chapter 3.

24. The implicit assumption is that Soviet planners draw up consistent plans.

25. It should be noted that this need not involve a high rate of nonconsumption expenditures, the factor responsible for anticipated inflationary pressure, though the two are not unrelated. The significance of overfull employment planning for Soviet inflation is discussed at length in a paper entitled "Financing Soviet Economic Development" given by the author at the Conference on Capital Formation and Economic Growth sponsored by the National Bureau of Economic Research in the fall of 1953. The proceedings of the Conference are to be published.

26. Naum Jasny, *The Soviet Price System* (Stanford, 1951), chap. 2; *Soviet Prices of Producers' Goods* (Stanford, 1952), *passim.*

27. See Chapter 11.

28. L. Pogrebnoi, "Stakhanovskoe dvizhenie i perestroika zarabotnoi platy" [The stakhanovite movement and the reconstruction of wages], *Problemy ekonomiki* [Economic problems], 1938, no. 5, p. 42.

29. A. Grigor'ev, "Uporiadochit' zarplatu, ukrepit' tekhnicheskoe normirovanie" [Regulate wages, strengthen technical norms], *Planovoe khoziaistvo* [Planned economy], 1938, no. 10, p. 73.

30. E.g., M. Gutman-Petrov, "Bor'ba s izlishestvami v raskhodovanii fondov zarabotnoi platy" [Struggle with excess wage payments], *Den'gi i kredit* [Money and credit], 1951, no. 2, p. 11.

31. E.g., M. Krol, "Bankovskii kontrol' za raskhodovaniem fondov zarabotnoi platy" [Bank control over wage expeditures], *Den'gi i kredit,* 1940, no. 12, p. 64; N. Sokolov, "Gosbank v bor'be za ekonomiiu v narodnom khoziaistve" [The State bank in the struggle for economies in the national economy], *Planovoe khoziaistvo,* 1940, no. 3, p. 40.

32. V. Fedulov, "Sebestoimost' i khozraschet v mashinostroenii" [Money cost and economic accounting in machine building], *Planovoe khoziaistvo,* 1941, no. 5, p. 21.

33. L. E. Gurin, *Analiz i kontrol' raskhodovaniia fondov zarabotnoi platy na mashinostroitel'nom predpriiatii* [Analysis and control of wage fund expenditures in machine-building enterprises] (Moscow 1949), p. 40.

34. N. Zabozlaev, "Fondy zarplaty—pod blitel'nyi bankovskii kontrol'" [Put wage fund under careful bank control], *Den'gi i kredit,* 1938, no. 5, pp. 33–34.

35. Gurin, ref. 33, pp. 42–44.

36. Ia. Kats, "O metodakh kontrolia za raskhodovaniem fondov zarabotnoi platy" [Methods of controlling overexpenditures for wages], *Sovetskie finansy,* 1945, no. 12, p. 18.

37. Kats, ref. 36, p. 17; also "Za bolee deistvennyi kontrol' nad raskhodovaniem fondov zarabotnoi platy" [For more control over wage fund expenditures], *Den'gi i kredit,* 1941, no. 3, p. 40 (correspondence with editor).

38. V. M. Batyrev, ed., *Kreditnoe i kassovoe planirovanie* [Credit and cash planning] (Moscow, 1947), pp. 61 ff.

39. *Ibid.*

40. *Ibid.*

41. N. Sokolov, "Kontrol' gosbanka nad fondami zarabotnoi platy" [Control of the State bank over the wage fund], *Den'gi i kredit*, 1940, no. 1, pp. 6–7.

42. L. Likhtenshtein, "Kontrol' za raskhodovaniem fondov zarplaty v stroitel'stve" [Control over wage expenditures in construction], *Sovetskie finansy*, 1940, no. 5–6, p. 53.

43. Batyrev, ref. 38, pp. 259 ff. The text of this decree and related decrees are contained in I. L. Kukulevich and M. A. Rubin, *Planirovanie i analiz trudovykh pokazatelei* [Planning and analysis of labor indicators] (Moscow, 1948), pp. 235–249.

44. The first subdivision under the ministry (formerly commissariat) is the chief administration (*glavk*). The chief administration is perhaps best defined as a subministry which controls enterprises in particular areas or producing similar products. Where the chief administrations are very large, they are subdivided into administrative units known as trusts or combines. For further details, see Schwartz, *Russia's Soviet Economy*, pp. 175–176.

45. Kukulevich and Rubin, ref. 43, p. 243 bottom.

46. Sokolov, ref. 31, p. 36.

47. Zabozlaev says that most of the overexpenditures are not primary but are made on the basis of permission from the central administration or ministry. See N. Zabozlaev, "Kontrol' gosbanka nad raskhodovaniem fondov zarabotnoi platy" [Control of the State bank over wage fund expenditures], *Den'gi i kredit*, 1946, no. 6–7, p. 8.

48. *Ibid.* See also M. Gutman and V. Turkovskii, "Posleduiushchie proverki raskhodovaniia fondov zarabotnoi platy" [Continuing check-up on expenditures from the wage fund], *Den'gi i kredit*, 1948, no. 9, p. 22.

49. See E. Granovskii and G. Nevol'skii, "Organizatsiia truda i ispol'zovanie rezervov v tiazheloi promyshlennosti" [Organization of labor and use of reserves in heavy industry], *Planovoe khoziaistvo*, 1934, no. 10, p. 119: "Wage regulation must be flexible. The highest economic organs cannot take into account the manifold conditions of different places of work. Therefore it is necessary to reserve to the directors of factories, to heads of shops, the right, within limits, to regulate wages in their shops."

50. Sokolov, ref. 31, p. 35.

51. Zabozlaev, ref. 47.

52. Gosplan, *The Second Five Year Plan*, trans. by I. B. Lasker and John Swift (New York, no date), pp. 624–625.

53. The extent of the uncontrolled inflation is, in my opinion, understated by these comparisons. After the first few years of wage inflation the Soviets probably took this factor into consideration in their plans, i.e., they assumed that wage rates would increase more than plan. With the exception of 1930–31 and 1933–34, the increases in planned figure for one year relative to the actual figure for the preceding year appear larger than one would expect the Soviets to grant if they had complete control over the situation.

54. Derived from Table 3.

55. An algebraic statement of the factors involved in the generation of

repressed inflation due to deviations from plan is contained in F. D. Holzman, "Taxation in the Soviet Union" (unpublished dissertation, Harvard University, 1952), Appendix to chap. 2.

56. See the works by D. H. Robertson cited in reference 10.

57. For discussion of the precision of Soviet planning, see Naum Jasny, "A Closeup of the Soviet Fourth Five Year Plan," *Quarterly Journal of Economics*, 66:139–171 (May 1952).

58. There are incentives designed to encourage fulfillment of the profits plans. Thus, a manager who bids up wages and reduces his profits also reduces bonuses to himself and his men from the Director's Fund. But there are compensating advantages from making unauthorized expenditures, and this explains why such practices occur. The manager may be successful in hoarding scarce materials which will boost his production at a future date, or he may be able to hire skilled workers needed by the plant. Output goals may loom more important and be in conflict with profits goals, in which case profits would suffer (see Chapter 4).

59. For a good description of illegal practices, see Joseph Berliner, "Informal Organization of the Soviet Firm," *Quarterly Journal of Economics*, 66:342–365 (August 1952).

60. *Ibid.*

61. N. Voznesensky, chairman of the State Planning Commission, reports that prices in the collective farm markets in 1943 were about 13 times what they had been in 1940. Since collective farm prices were above state prices in 1940, and since state prices had not risen since 1941, collective farm market prices must have been well over 10 times as high as state prices. See N. A. Voznesensky, *The Economy of the USSR During World War II* (Washington, 1948), p. 76.

62. A conceivable advantage of permitting some repressed inflation is that this would insure a clearing of the consumers'-goods market, albeit with some injustices in distribution. If aggregate demand and supply were exactly equal, gluts might appear in some areas due to local market maladjustments.

63. These series were collected jointly by Prof. Raymond Powell and myself. The major share of the data were collected by him, however.

64. Jasny, ref. 26, p. 31.

65. M. M. Lifits, ed., *Ekonomika sovetskoi torgovli* [Economics of Soviet trade] (Moscow, 1950), p. 319.

66. Sh. Turetskii, "Puti planirovaniia tsen" [Methods of price planning], *Planovoe khoziaistvo*, 1936, no. 3, p. 130.

67. This was first called to my attention by Professor Powell.

68. Turetskii, ref. 66, p. 133.

69. Jasny, ref. 26, pp. 36 ff.

70. See Chapter 11.

71. Turetskii reports that collective farm market prices fell by 30 to 50 per cent in 1933, prices of agricultural products fell by 20 per cent in 1934, and by 12 per cent in 1935, and at the end of 1935 were 37 per cent of the peak level of 1932. The price of bread products fell by 35 per cent in the first half of 1935 and by 70 per cent in the next two and one-half years.

72. League of Nations, "Commercial Banks," *Money and Banking 1935/36* (Geneva, 1936), vol. 2, p. 179.

73. That this must have been the case is indicated by the fact that receipts from the special markups increased from 3.2 billion rubles in 1933 to 8.4 billion rubles in 1934, in spite of the decline in the rate of markup. Receipts from the special markups, which were 11.5 per cent of total turnover tax and markup receipts in 1933, increased to 23 per cent of the total in 1934.

74. We use the average rate of taxation computed in Chapter 10 as our indicator of the changing rate of nonconsumption.

75. To designate a rise in the commodity tax as inflation is equivalent to saying that the choice between income and commodity taxation is a choice between no inflation and inflation. The price increase due to an indirect tax can be eliminated overnight by either a shift to direct taxation or a decline in the rate of nonconsumption. Inflation due to a wage spiral is not reversible, at least in the absence of drastic measures.

76. Lifits, ref. 65, p. 319.

77. A. Zverev, *Gosudarstvennye biudzhety Soiuza SSR, 1938–1945 gg.* [State budgets of the USSR, 1938–1945] (Moscow, 1946), pp. 40, 66–67.

78. Irving B. Kravis and J. Mintzes, "Food Prices in the Soviet Union, 1936–50," *Review of Economics and Statistics*, 32:165 (May 1950).

79. Jasny, ref. 26, p. 34.

80. *Ibid.*, p. 37.

CHAPTER 3. ALTERNATIVE METHODS OF TAXATION

1. An earlier version of this chapter was published in the *Journal of Political Economy*, 59:425–433 (October 1950) under the title "Commodity and Income Taxation in the Soviet Union."

2. Consistent costing may be defined as setting (factor) prices so that the minimum money cost of producing any given level of output is also the minimum real cost. An alternative definition is that the market for the factors of production will "just" be cleared, and that each factor will receive a price equal to its opportunity value in the market. The shape and position of the demand schedule will depend on whether managers are following a policy of producing up to a point at which price is equal or proportional (1) to marginal cost, (2) to average cost, (3) to some other point. The welfare position of the economy will, of course, depend on which production policy is followed.

3. For discussion, see James Tobin, "Money Wage Rates and Employment," in Seymour Harris, ed., *The New Economics* (New York, 1947), pp. 579–581.

4. As Professor Fellner puts it: "Yet one form of the so-called money illusion is precisely that the resistance to taxing away money income is substantially greater than the resistance to roundabout methods of burdening; and as to the incidence, an unpredictable distribution pattern is frequently preferred to a definite pattern which is felt to be disadvantageous by a number of groups. See William Fellner, *A Treatise on War Inflation* (Berkeley and Los Angeles, 1942), pp. 112–113.

5. G. F. Grinko, *Financial Program of the U.S.S.R. for 1936* (Moscow, 1936), p. 14.

6. James Duesenberry, *Income, Saving, and the Theory of Consumer Behavior* (Cambridge, 1949).

7. The writer is one of those who have argued this in the past; see Holzman, ref. 1, pp. 425–427.

8. The extensive use of advertising, in particular, casts doubts on the significance of consumer sovereignty, as Professor Sherrard has demonstrated. If some resources, he argues, are used to mold consumers' tastes, then consumer demand cannot be taken as an independent criterion by which the allocation of resources may be judged. See Alfred Sherrard, "Advertising, Product Variation, and the Limits of Economics," *Journal of Political Economy*, 59:126–142 (April 1951).

9. See Maurice Dobb, *Soviet Economic Development Since 1917* (London, 1948), pp. 18 ff.

10. Grinko, ref. 5, p. 64.

11. Discussed in Chapter 6.

12. For the most recent statement of this see Milton Friedman, "The 'Welfare' Effects of an Income Tax and an Excise Tax," *Journal of Political Economy*, 60:25–33 (February 1952).

13. Abba P. Lerner, *Economics of Control* (New York, 1946) chap. 9. See reference 16, however.

14. As will be pointed out in Chapter 11, the main effect of subsidies to industry is to distort the relative prices of labor and nonlabor components of production. In this section we are concerned only with the latter. If we were concerned also with labor, it would be necessary to note that a truly proportional commodity tax would have to be levied on leisure as well as on all other commodities purchased by the population.

15. In contrast to the state, which should set price and output at the intersection of marginal cost and *average* revenue to maximize consumer welfare, the private-enterprise monopolist is interested in maximizing profit. This is accomplished by carrying production to the point at which marginal cost and *marginal* revenue intersect. The Soviet state, as a monopolist, differs from the private monopolist in this respect. There is another and more important difference, however: the state must approach the pricing problem from a general equilibrium viewpoint, since the tax collected in each industry affects the receipts from other industries, i.e., it affects the demand for the products of other industries. The private monopolist takes his demand curve as "given."

16. It has been demonstrated that a better welfare position is achieved by equality than by proportionality of marginal cost and average revenue. See Lerner, ref. 13, pp. 100–105.

17. This would coincide roughly with the Soviet approach, which is to consider investment and other government expenditure as social cost borne mainly by "accumulation of socialist industry" — in our terminology, by markup over cost.

18. Professor Dobb (ref. 9, pp. 373–374) suggests that this approach, with qualifications, is used by the Soviets.

19. A. Gordin, "Formy i metody organizatsii sotsialisticheskikh nakoplenii," [Forms and methods of organizing socialist accumulation], *Sovetskie finansy* [Soviet finance], 1946, no. 6, pp. 7–8.
20. A. Gordin, "Ekonomicheskoe znachenie sistemy oblozheniia po oborotu" [Economic significance of the system of turnover taxes], *Sovetskie finansy* [Soviet finance], 1947, no. 8, p. 12.
21. Subsidies are discussed in some detail in Chapter 11.
22. See Chapters 5 and 6.
23. K. Ianbukhtin, *Nalogi v usloviiakh kapitalizma i v sovetskom khoziaistve* [Taxes under conditions of capitalism and in the Soviet economy] (Moscow, 1934), pp. 23–24.
24. Dobb, ref. 9, p. 284.
25. Naum Jasny, *The Socialized Agriculture of the USSR* (Stanford, 1949), p. 34.

CHAPTER 4. THE STRUCTURE OF SOVIET COMMODITY TAXATION

1. See Joseph Berliner, "The Informal Organization of the Soviet Firm," *Quarterly Journal of Economics*, 66:342–365 (August 1952), a study based on interviews with Soviet plant managers.
2. See Abram Bergson, "Soviet National Income and Product in 1937," *Quarterly Journal of Economics*, 64:415 (August 1950). It should also be noted in this connection that the Soviets do not take into account the costs of obsolescence.
3. Paul Baran, "National Income and Product of the U.S.S.R. in 1940," *Review of Economic Statistics*, 29:230 (November 1947).
4. Bergson, ref. 2, p. 434. Bergson indicates full awareness of the limitations of his procedure.
5. D. R. Hodgman, "A New Production Index for Soviet Industry," *Review of Economics and Statistics*, 32:335 (November 1950).
6. These details are contained in any Soviet book with a section on the turnover tax. See, for example, A. K. Suchkov, *Dokhody gosudarstvennogo biudzheta SSSR* [Income of the state budget of the USSR] (Moscow, 1945), chap. 2.
7. A. Gordin, "Formy i metody organizatsii sotsialisticheskikh nakoplenii" [Forms and methods of organizing socialist accumulation], *Sovetskie finansy* [Soviet finance], 1946, no. 6, pp. 7–8.
8. In explaining why the machine-construction industries received a larger percentage of profits into the Director's Fund than light industries, one writer says: "In light industry the importance of wages in total cost is relatively low (10–15 per cent), but profits are higher than, for example, in machine construction, where the importance of wages is 30–40 per cent." See E. G. Liberman, *O planirovanii pribyli v promyshlennosti* [Planning profits in industry] (Moscow, 1950), p. 60.
9. See A. K. Suchkov, *Gosudarstvennye dokhody SSSR* [Government receipts in the USSR] (Moscow, 1949), pp. 137–138. It should be noted that other incentive-type funds are formed from profits but these are relatively un-

important and will not be discussed here. Liberman (ref. 8, p. 61) says that in 1940, 21 per cent of the Fund was spent on housing construction, 20 per cent on cultural and welfare needs, and 6.5 per cent on individual premia. This is not strictly in accord with the law, nor with estimates published by P. Vladimirov, "Za rentabel'nuiu rabotu predpriiatii" [Toward profitable work of enterprises], *Voprosy ekonomiki*, 1948, no. 8, p. 30, who gives the following figures (billions of rubles): overplan housing for workers, 0.964; overplan cultural and welfare needs, 0.717; better conditions of work, 0.278; premiums to individual workers, 0.208; other, 0.433; total, 2.6.

10. Details are given in A. E. Shvedskii, *Otchisleniia ot pribylei gosudarstvennykh predpriiatii i organizatsii* [Deductions from profits of state enterprises and organizations] (Moscow, 1951).

11. See A. M. Aleksandrov, *Finansy i kredit SSSR* [Finance and credit in the USSR] (Moscow, 1948), p. 90.

12. Professor Moore says this with one minor qualification; see Barrington Moore, Jr., *Soviet Politics—The Dilemma of Power* (Cambridge, 1950), p. 311.

13. See Gordin, ref. 7, p. 6.

14. See A. Gordin, "Sotsialisticheskie nakopleniia—osnova sovetskogo biudzheta" [Socialist accumulation is the basis of the Soviet budget], *Sovetskie finansy*, 1943, no. 3, p. 13.

15. In those cases where the turnover tax is now calculated simply as the residual difference between wholesale and retail price, changes in retail prices would be absorbed primarily by the turnover tax.

16. Alexander Baykov, *The Development of the Soviet Economic System* (New York, 1947), p. 116.

17. Turetskii says: "Profitability is the most general synthetic indicator of the results of economic management." See Sh. Turetskii, "O khoziaistvennom raschete" [About economic accounting], *Planovoe khoziaistvo*, 1939, no. 1, p. 119. See also E. G. Liberman, *O planirovanii pribyli v promyshlennosti* [Planning profits in industry], (Moscow, 1950), p. 6.

18. See Gordin, ref. 7, pp. 8–10.

19. V. P. D'iachenko, *Finansy i kredit SSSR* (Moscow-Leningrad, 1940), p. 309.

20. Gordin, ref. 7, p. 6.

21. Liberman, ref. 8, chap. 6.

22. Professor Bienstock says: "That part of profits remaining at the disposal of the manager is divided between capital fund and a special manager's fund for bonuses and improvement of workers' living conditions. Both uses increase managers' scope of action." See G. Bienstock, S. Schwartz, and A. Yugow, *Management in Russian Industry and Agriculture* (New York, 1944), p. 95. For discussion of managerial incentives see Chapter 8 of this book.

23. See, for example, one of the best theoretical articles on the Soviet commodity tax, Gordin, ref. 14, p. 22 ff. See also Sh. Turetskii, "Khozraschet i ekonomicheskie rychagi" [Financial cost accounting and economic levers], *Sovetskie finansy*, 1947, no. 1, p. 16; L. E. Gurin, *Analiz i kontrol' raskhodovaniia fondov zarabotnoi platy na mashinostroitel'nom predpriiatii* [Analysis

and control of expenditures of the wage fund in machine-building industries] (Moscow, 1949), p. 43.

24. When the turnover tax was first established in 1930, only 45 rates, one for each combine or ministry, were used. The *assortment* problem was so acute that in the following year the number of rates was increased to 143 and the tax was levied by commodity group rather than by ministry. Partly for this reason, but also for other reasons, the number of rates continued to increase very rapidly until 1938. For discussion, see Chapter 6. See also A. Gordin, "O stavkakh naloga s oborota" [The turnover tax rates], *Planovoe khoziaistvo*, 1938, no. 3, pp. 83–96.

25. The solution in the textile industry is discussed in Chapter 6.

CHAPTER 5. DEVELOPMENTS LEADING TO THE TAX REFORM OF 1930

1. A. Arakelian, *Industrial Management in the U.S.S.R.*, trans. E. L. Raymond (Washington, 1950), p. 70.

2. For background material on this period, the reader is referred to the works of Baykov, Dobb, and Schwartz, cited above.

3. See I. Reingold, "The New Economic Policy, 1921–1928," in *Soviet Policy in Public Finance*, trans. E. Varneck, ed. Lincoln Hutchinson and Carl C. Plehn (Stanford, 1931), p. 142.

4. *Ibid.*, p. 143.

5. Schwartz, ref. 2, pp. 397–400.

6. V. P. D'iachenko, *Sovetskie finansy v pervoi faze razvitiia sotsialisticheskogo gosudarstva* [Soviet Finance in the First Phase of the Development of the Socialist State] (Moscow, 1947), pp. 240–243.

7. During War Communism the direction of industry was almost completely concentrated in the Supreme Council of the National Economy and so-called "Central Committees" (see Arakelian, ref. 1, pp. 52–66).

8. See Reingold, ref. 3, p. 147. During War Communism, of course, total receipts were handed over to the budget.

9. For example, in the early NEP period the state could not have successfully introduced universal taxation of the net profits of income in industry, since many enterprises did not have the technique to determine their own profits. The profits taxes levied on those enterprises which did keep accounts —i.e., the tax which existed until 1926 on the profits of state enterprises, and the tax (until 1932) on the income of coöperatives, were less sophisticated than the subsequent method of taxation. See A. K. Suchkov, *Dokhody gosudarstvennogo biudzheta SSSR* [Income of the state budget of the USSR] (Moscow, 1945), p. 12.

10. These are discussed below. The sales tax, known as the craft tax, was actually a combination of a license fee and a sales tax. The license fee was, of course, the simplest levy, requiring no calculations and presenting almost no opportunity for evasion. Very small private enterprises, of which there were many during the NEP, were subject only to the license fee. With larger enter-

prises the license fee was too inequitable to be used alone, and it was supplemented by the sales tax.

11. According to Lifshits, taxation of the private sector proliferated unnecessarily owing to its use in performing tasks which should have been performed by other types of administrative apparatus. See M. Lifshits, "Kak perestroit' oblozhenie chastnogo sektora" [How to reconstruct the tax system in the private sector], *Finansovye problemy planovogo khoziaistva* [Financial problems of a planned economy], 1930, no. 6, pp. 65–78.

12. "Final prices . . . were sometimes six times higher than the original factory prices." Baykov, ref. 2, p. 55.

13. S. Kniazev, "Nalogovaia reforma" [Tax reform], *Finansovye problemy planovogo khoziaistva*, 1930, no. 9, p. 15; A. A. Sokolov, "Rekonstruksiia nalogovoi sistemy" [Reconstruction of the tax system], *Vestnik finansov* [Financial news], 1929, no. 10, p. 34.

14. For example, Sokolov, ref. 13, p. 34.

15. Lifshits (ref. 11, p. 68) says that the rapid decrease in private industry and trade was partly due to "party excesses of an administrative nature" which resulted from taking too seriously slogans about the liquidation of private capitalist elements.

16. Baykov, ref. 2, pp. 65, 235.

17. TsUNKhU, *Socialist Construction in the USSR* (in English) (Moscow, 1936), p. 4.

18. A. Gordeev. "K voprosu o ratsionalizatsii nalogovoi sistemy" [The problem of rationalizing the tax system], *Vestnik finansov*, 1929, no. 11–12, p. 58.

19. *Pravda*, December 14, 1929.

20. For a detailed description in English, see Reingold, ref. 3, *passim*; James F. Coogan, "Sales Taxes in the Soviet Union" (unpublished dissertation, Harvard University, 1951), chap. 5.

21. D'iachenko, ref. 6, p. 245.

22. *Ibid.*, p. 246.

23. Each enterprise paid its license fee at the beginning of the year. If at the end of the year the equalization tax turned out to be smaller than the license fee paid, no further payment was required; if larger, however, the difference between the two had to be paid to the state. Small enterprises paid only the license fee.

24. D'iachenko, ref. 6, p. 248.

25. *Sobranie zakonov i rasporiazhenii pravitel'stva SSSR* [Collected laws and orders of the USSR] 1928, no. 50, art. 443.

26. P. Kniazev, *Rol' nalogov v politike i ekonomike Sovetskogo Soiuza* [Role of taxes in the politics and economics of the Soviet Union] (Moscow, 1930), pp. 33–34.

27. *Sobranie zakonov*, 1929, no. 62, art. 574.

28. See G. Mar'iakhin, "Nalogovaia sistema Sovetskogo gosudarstva" [Tax system of the Soviet state], *Finansy SSSR za XXX let* [Thirty years of Soviet finance] (Moscow, 1947), p. 256.

29. D'iachenko, ref. 6, p. 243.

30. Gordeev, ref. 18, p. 58.
31. *Sobranie zakonov,* 1926, no. 44, art. 315.
32. *Sobranie zakonov,* 1928, no. 53, art. 469.
33. Kniazev, ref. 26, pp. 33–34.
34. *Ibid.*, pp. 33–35; Gordeev, ref. 18, pp. 57–60.
35. Other problems discussed in connection with these taxes were at which link of the production-trade network to tax and whether to tax the current or the previous year's production. With respect to the first problem most writers agreed that it would be better to tax production than retail sales, because if the latter were chosen, the consumer coöperatives would be the main payers of the tax; as taxpaying institutions they were relatively small, less available, and less reliable in comparison with the larger state-owned industrial aggregations. With respect to the second problem, the primary consideration was that since output was increasing steadily, more revenue would be obtained with the same rate of tax from taxing current output than from taxing the previous year's output. Cf. Sokolov, ref. 13, pp. 34–36.
36. One further distinction was the use of the craft, but not the excise, tax to discriminate again private and in favor of state and coöperative enterprises.
37. It was argued that a tax based on quantity could not easily take into account qualitative differences and for this reason tended to have a regressive effect; a single rate, applied to commodities of different quality, falls more heavily on the commodities of cheaper quality. This is a common criticism of specific taxes.
38. *Sobranie zakonov,* 1929, no. 62, art. 573.
39. *Sobranie zakonov,* 1929, no. 60, art. 554.
40. D'iachenko, ref. 6, p. 250.
41. *Sobranie zakonov,* 1926, no. 64, art. 483–4.
42. *Ibid.*, 1928, no. 1, art. 2.
43. *Ibid.*, 1927, no. 25, art. 273.
44. Reingold, ref. 3, pp. 179–80.
45. D'iachenko, ref. 6, p. 253.
46. *Sobranie zakonov,* 1929, no. 76, art. 730.
47. Reingold, ref. 3, p. 230.
48. See A. E. Shvedskii, *Otchisleniia ot pribylei gosudarstvennykh khoziaistvennykh organizatsii i predpriiatii* [Deductions from profits of state economic organizations and enterprises] (Moscow, 1948), p. 41

	Deductions from profit (per cent)		
Form of deduction	Industrial Enterprises	Trade Enterprises	
		Union	Republican
Income tax	20.0	20.0	20.0
Into budget	38.0	Varies	
For technical and professional education (vtuzy)	2.8	..	..
Into fund for improving conditions for workers	9.0	2.0	8.0

Form of deduction	Deductions from profit (per cent)		
	Industrial Enterprises	Trade Enterprises	
		Union	Republican
Into bank of long term credit	20.0	8.0	. .
Into basic fund	10.0	. .	. .
Into premium fund	0.2	0.2	0.2
For reserve capital	. .	8.0	8.0
Other deductions	. .	Special Decision	
Dividends	. .	Remainder	

49. *Sobranie zakonov*, 1930, no. 46, arts. 476–483. This decree was effective as of October 1, 1930.

50. *Ibid.*, arts. 853 and 854. (Translation taken from Baykov, ref. 2, pp. 366–367).

51. Most of these taxes were revoked for the private sector as well; the principal exception was the craft tax.

52. For example, fee for judicial recourse, deductions into the welfare fund for workers.

53. The association was the link from 1929 to 1932 between the Supreme Council for the National Economy and the trusts and enterprises. It was preceded by the syndicate and followed by the *glavk* (defined in Chapter 2).

54. Kniazev (ref. 13, pp. 16–17) points out exceptions in textiles.

55. Those joint-stock companies in which less than half of the capital was owned by the state or coöperatives were subject to the income tax on private persons.

56. The tax on private enterprises was progressive, so that those with profits of more than approximately 5,000 rubles were subject to a higher rate than socialized enterprises.

57. TsUNKhU, *Sotsialisticheskoe stroitel'stvo SSSR* [Socialist construction of the USSR] (Moscow, 1934), p. 440.

58. According to Kniazev (ref. 13, p. 18), the craft tax unified 32 previous payments of which 12 were excises.

59. It will be recalled that gradual elimination of multiple-stage taxation of the craft tax in the NEP period was only with respect to the socialized sector of the economy where unification of enterprises and regularization of trade channels had been occurring.

60. As was previously the case, very small enterprises with fewer than three employees were taxed a flat amount, which varied from 6–24 rubles for persons working for themselves to 300–700 rubles for small shopkeepers.

61. See Table 47, Chapter 9.

CHAPTER 6. DEVELOPMENTS IN THE TURNOVER AND PROFITS TAXES AFTER 1930

1. I. Chistov, "K peresmotru obshchei instruktsii po nalogu s oborota" [Reëxamining the general instructions on the turnover tax], *Sovetskie finansy*

[Soviet finance], 1943, no. 5, p. 34. For a detailed discussion in English of the turnover tax, the reader is referred to James F. Coogan, "Sales Taxes in the Soviet Union" (unpublished dissertation, Harvard University, 1951).

Other sources used in preparing this chapter were A. K. Suchkov, *Dokhody gosudarstvennogo biudzheta SSSR* [Income of the state budget of the USSR] (Moscow, 1945), chap. 2; Suchkov, *Gosudarstvennye dokhody SSSR* [Government receipts in the USSR] (Moscow, 1949), chap. 4; K. N. Kutler, *Gosudarstvennye dokhody SSSR* [Government receipts in the USSR] (Moscow, 1940), chap. 3; A. Gordin, "O stavkakh naloga s oborota" [Turnover tax rates), *Planovoe khoziaistvo*, 1938, no. 3, pp. 83–96; K. N. Plotnikov *Biudzhet sotsialisticheskogo gosudarstva*, pp. 23–26; V. P. D'iachenko, *Finansy i kredit SSSR* [Finance and Credit in the USSR] (Moscow-Leningrad, 1940), pp. 237–239.

2. Kutler, ref. 1, p. 16.

3. In 1931, 93 per cent of turnover-tax receipts came from associations of national importance (see D'iachenko, ref. 1, p. 237).

4. There is some question whether this was done on the scale envisaged by the law. For example, Gordin (ref. 1, pp. 84–85) claims that the same rate of tax was applied to galoshes and to rubber tires, and that this returned large profits to the former and losses to the latter; this does not imply very extensive rate differentiation within the rubber industry.

5. D'iachenko, ref. 1, p. 238.

6. Another side of this story is presented by Coogan, ref. 1, p. 48. He points out that it would have been difficult, in 1930, to have levied the turnover tax on commodities, rather than on value of turnover, because at that time costs and prices of individual commodities had not been sufficiently unified and standardized.

7. *Sobranie zakonov*, 1931, no. 74, art. 497.

8. Kutler, ref. 1, p .16.

9. *Sobranie zakonov*, 1932, no. 15, art. 82.

10. *Sobranie zakonov*, 1931, no. 23, art. 188. The rate was lowered to 20 per cent soon afterwards (1931, no. 54, art. 352).

11. *Sobranie zakonov*, 1931, no. 49, art. 316.

12. *Sobranie zakonov*, 1932, no. 17, art. 92.

13. Gordin (ref. 1, p. 85) says: "It is difficult to draw a precise line of demarcation between the different types of markups and differences which arose in the period 1932–1935." He also notes that the special markups were levied both as markups and as differences.

14. Unlike the profits tax, which in some respects is different from the turnover tax (see Chapter 4), markups and differences are variations of the turnover tax and are not usually distinguished from it in the budgetary receipts.

15. E.g., I. Chistov, "Poriadok uplaty naloga s oborota trebuet uproshcheniia" [Payment of the turnover tax needs simplification], *Sovetskie finansy*, 1945, no. 12, pp. 13–16; M. Azarkh, "Kak uprostit' nalog s oborota" [How to simplify the turnover tax], *Sovetskie finansy*, 1947, no. 5, pp. 16–20.

16. Gordin, ref. 1, p. 85.

17. Receipts from special markups for the years 1932–1934 are presented in Table 7.

18. E.g., in the case of bread products, vegetable oils, potatoes; see Kutler, ref. 1, pp. 133–134.

19. E.g., eggs and fruit; see Kutler, ref. 1, pp. 133–134.

20. In the case of industrial commodities, Kutler (ref. 1, p. 142) specifically states that budgetary differences were required because turnover tax rates were not adjusted at the same time that new retail prices were introduced.

21. Kutler, ref. 1, p. 142.

22. Suchkov, ref. 1, *Dokhody*, pp. 67–68.

23. Azarkh, ref. 15, pp. 16–20; Suchkov, ref. 1, *Dokhody*, pp. 68–69.

24. Azarkh, ref. 15, p. 17.

25. Suchkov. ref. 1, *Dokhody*, pp. 70–71.

26. Suchkov, ref. 1, *Gosudarstvennye*, pp. 109 ff.

27. This section draws heavily on Gordin, ref. 1, pp. 86–96.

28. Both Gordin (ref. 1, p. 88) and Kutler (ref. 1, pp. 62–63) accuse the Finance Commissariat of wrecking activities and sabotage, particularly during 1936–37.

29. See Kutler, ref. 1, pp. 61 ff.; Gordin, ref. 1, pp. 88–95.

30. See Chapter 4.

31. Kutler, ref. 1, p. 62.

32. Gordin, ref. 1, pp. 88–91.

33. *Ibid.*

34. *Sobranie zakonov*, 1938, no. 11.

35. Gordin, ref. 1, pp. 92–93.

36. Suchkov, ref. 1, *Dokhody*, pp. 48 ff.

37. *Ibid.*, p. 49.

38. Suchkov, ref. 1, *Gosudarstvennye*, p. 68.

39. V. Kovylin, "Perenesti uplatu naloga s oborota so sbytovykh organizatsii na predpriiatiia" [Transfer payment of the turnover tax from the selling organizations to enterprises], *Sovetskie finansy*, 1943, no. 6, pp. 27–28.

40. Gordin, ref. 1, pp. 91–95.

41. Azarkh, ref. 15, p. 17.

42. I. Chistov, ref. 15, pp. 13–16.

43. Kovylin, ref. 39, pp. 27–28.

44. *Ibid.*

45. E.g., A. Gordin, "Formy i metody organizatsii sotsialisticheskikh nakoplenii" [Forms and methods of organizing Socialist accumulation], *Sovetskie finansy*, 1946, no. 6, pp. 8–9.

46. See Chapter 11.

47. Cf. D'iachenko, ref. 1, p. 239; Plotnikov, ref. 1, p. 27; *Sobranie zakonov*, 1931, no. 26, art. 205, and no. 57, arts. 366 and 367.

48. This is essentially the situation as it exists today except for minor revisions in the rates.

49. *Sobranie zakonov*, 1931, no. 70, art. 471.

50. *Sobranie zakonov*, 1936, no. 20, arts. 169–170.

51. A. M. Aleksandrov, *Finansy i kredit SSSR* [Finance and credit in the USSR] (Moscow, 1948), pp. 138–139. According to Kutler (ref. 1, pp. 170 ff)

and Suchkov (ref. 1, *Dokhody*, p. 93), measures in this direction were first taken in 1935 and in 1939 respectively.

52. Aleksandrov, ref. 51, p. 135.

53. Suchkov, ref. 1, *Gosudarstvennye*, pp. 137–38.

54. R. Shneider and A. Shapiro, "Fond direktora promyshlennykh predpriiatii" [The director's fund of industrial enterprises], *Sovetskie finansy*, 1947, no. 3, p. 36.

55. Firms for which losses have been planned have to fulfill only the first three conditions.

56. This is discussed in greater detail in Chapter 4.

57. Cited by Donald R. Hodgman, "A New Production Index for Soviet Industry," *Review of Economics and Statistics*, 32:333 (November 1950).

58. E. G. Liberman, *O planirovanii pribyli v promyshlennosti* [Planning profits in industry] (Moscow, 1950), chap. 7; K. Denisov, "Izmenit' praktiku otchislenii ot pribylei promyshlennosti" [Change the method of deducting profits from industry], *Sovetskie finansy*, 1942, no. 3, pp. 11–18.

59. Liberman, ref. 58, p. 64.

60. Denisov, ref. 58, p. 12.

61. *New York Times*, August 4, 1952 (signed article by Harry Schwartz).

62. Lenin, in an article entitled "Capitalism and Taxes," said: "Workers [in the United States] pay 7 kopeks per ruble in indirect taxes whereas the capitalist pays but 1/3 kopek. The worker pays proportionally twenty times more than the capitalist. Systems of indirect taxes inevitably take this structure . . . in all capitalist countries." Quoted by K. Plotnikov, "Biudzhet strany sotsializma" [Budget of a socialist nation], *Den'gi i kredit*, 1938, no. 5, p. 7.

63. For example, in 1885 direct taxes accounted for 24.1 per cent of the total revenue from taxation, indirect taxes for 66.7 per cent, and customs for 9.2 per cent. In 1913 the corresponding figures were 12.9 per cent, 76.1 per cent, and 11.0 per cent. See M. Bogolepov, "The Financial System of Pre-war Russia," in *Soviet Policy in Public Finance*, ed. Lincoln Hutchinson and Carl C. Plehn (Stanford University, 1931), p. 21. It should be noted that a tax on beverages accounted for about 60 per cent of the indirect taxes in both years.

64. E.g., I. Reingold, "The New Economic Policy," in *Soviet Policy in Public Finance*, pp. 160, 185–86.

65. E.g., D. Kuzovkov, "Perevozhdenie kosvennykh nalogov v perekhodnyi period" [Rebirth of indirect taxes in the transition period], *Problemy ekonomiki*, 1929, no. 7–8, pp. 49–82. This argument dropped from sight after the wage principle "to each according to his labor" had been officially introduced (see Chapter 11).

66. A disjunction is made between "self-taxation" and "class taxation"; see Kuzovkov, ref. 65.

67. E.g., V. Katz, "O raspredelitel'nykh i nalogovykh otnosheniiakh v SSSR" [On distributive and tax relations in the USSR], *Problemy ekonomiki*, 1929, no. 3, pp. 25–41; also M. Sobolev, "K voprosu o prirode naloga" [On problems of the nature of taxation], *Finansovye problemy planovogo khoziaistva* [Financial problems of a planned economy], 1930, no. 9, pp. 36–44. This article contains references to many other articles on the question.

68. Sh. Turetskii, "Puti planirovaniia tsen [Methods of price planning], *Planovoe khoziaistvo*, 1936, no. 3, p. 125.

69. Naum Jasny, *The Soviet Price System* (Stanford, 1951), p. 74; A. Yugow, *Russia's Economic Front for War and Peace* (New York and London, 1942), pp. 132–133.

70. Some guidance was obtained from a German study published in 1938 and relating to the year 1936. Household-expenditure patterns for two worker families, one with an income of 2,600 rubles and four members, the other with an income of 4,500 rubles and six members, were constructed on the basis of information contained in a large number of previous studies, both Soviet and Western. See "Lohn, Preis, und Lebenshaltung in der Union der Sozialistischen Sowjetrepubliken," *Vierteljahreshefte zur Statistik des Deutschen Reichs*, vol. 47, 1938, no. 4 (Berlin, 1939).

71. Commissariat of Finance, *Alfavitnyi perechen' promtovarov po stavkam naloga s oborota i biudzhetnykh otsenok* [Alphabetical list of turnover tax rates and budget markups on industrial commodities] (Moscow, 1938).

72. V. Petrov and V. Fisherov, *Nalog s oborota* [The turnover tax] (Moscow, 1938).

73. Expenditures on bread and flour by the 2,600-ruble-income family of the German study cited above amounted to more than 25 per cent of total income; see ref. 70, p. 160.

74. Maurice Dobb, *Soviet Economic Development since 1917* (London, 1948), pp. 371–372 (footnote).

75. *Gosudarstvennyi plan razvitiia narodnogo khoziaistva SSSR na 1941 god* [State plan for the development of the national economy of the USSR in 1941] (prepared in the Soviet Union in 1941 and reprinted in 1951 in Washington, D. C.), p. 584.

76. Discussed in Chapter 7.

77. See Chapter 7.

78. Naum Jasny, *The Socialized Agriculture of the USSR* (Stanford, 1949), pp. 436 ff.

79. The average rate of turnover tax for 1940 was estimated as 60.8 per cent (Table 15). If the tax on the producer could be removed from all agricultural commodities, the average rate would be somewhat less than 60.5 per cent, and therefore less than the tax on bread.

80. Suchkov, *Dokhody*, p. 113.

81. See Zverev's 1938 and 1939 budget speeches.

CHAPTER 7. TAXATION IN KIND

1. Useful discussions of the Soviet tax in kind may be found in the following sources: Naum Jasny, *The Socialized Agriculture of the USSR* (Stanford, 1949), chap. 16; L. Hubbard, *The Economics of Soviet Agriculture* (London, 1939), chaps. 18 and 19; M. Moiseev, "Progressivnyi kharakter pogektarnogo ischisleniia obiazatel'nykh postavok sel'skokhoziaistvennykh produktov gosudarstvu" [Progressive character of per-hectare calculation of obligatory deliveries

of agricultural products to the state], *Sotsialisticheskoe sel'skoe khoziaistvo* [Socialist agriculture], 1947, no. 7, pp. 3–16.

2. See I. Reingold, "The New Economic Policy, 1921–1928," in *Soviet Policy in Public Finance*, ed. Lincoln Hutchinson and Carl C. Plehn (Stanford, 1931), pp. 138 ff; K. Schmelev, "Public Finances During the Civil War," *ibid.*, pp. 83–98.

3. Reingold, ref. 2, p. 139.

4. *Ibid.*, p. 151. Lifshits says that the costs of collection averaged 15 kopeks a pood (36.07 lb. avoirdupois), whereas receipts were generally 50 kopeks a pood, although as much as 70 kopeks was sometimes obtained (quoted by V. P. D'iachenko, *Sovetskie finansy v pervoi faze razvitiia sotsialisticheskogo gosudarstva* [Soviet finance in the first phase of the development of the socialist state] (Moscow, 1947), p. 267, footnote).

5. See Reingold, ref. 2, pp. 138 ff.

6. Roughly three-fourths of the receipts were in money (see D'iachenko, ref. 4, p. 266).

7. Alexander Baykov, *The Development of the Soviet Economic System* (New York, 1947), pp. 89 ff.

8. K. Ianbukhtin, *Nalogi v usloviakh kapitalizma i v sovetskom khoziaistve* [Taxes under conditions of capitalism and in the Soviet economy] (Moscow, 1934), pp. 39 ff.

9. Maurice Dobb, *Soviet Economic Development Since 1917* (London, 1948), p. 214.

10. *Ibid.*, pp. 214–220.

11. Jasny, ref. 1, p. 722.

12. For example, in a government regulation (*Sobranie zakonov*, 1929, no. 65, art. 610) it is stated that under *kontraktatsiia* the peasant obligates himself (1) to fulfill the state order to produce the proper quantity and quality of output, (2) to surrender these commodities at the proper time under planned conditions, (3) to execute measures which will raise productivity and secure the technical reconstruction of agriculture.

13. Jasny, ref. 1, p. 723.

14. According to the same regulation cited in note 12, the collecting organizations were obliged (1) to fulfill orders of unions of peasant households on procurement of means of production and, wherever possible, objects of consumption, (2) to organize agronomical-technical services for peasants, supply productive credit, and give organizational help.

15. See Hubbard, ref. 1, pp. 183–185; Moiseev, ref. 1, p. 6.

16. This situation is very similar to the situation in 1921, when the shift from "distributive quotas" to produce taxation took place.

17. See M. Rabinovich, "Progressivnaia rol' sistemy obiazatel'nykh postavok sel'skokhoziaistvennykh produktov v razvitii ekonomiki kolkhozov" [Progressive role of the system of obligatory deliveries of agricultural products in the development of the kolkhoz economy], *Sotsialisticheskoe sel'skoe khoziaistvo*, 1950, no. 7, pp. 18–28.

18. Moiseev (ref. 1, p. 13) says that regional differentials reflect differential rent.

19. Jasny (ref. 1, p. 363) says: "Since 1931 the claim of the state for its dues from the kolkhozy has been termed the 'first commandment.' 'Sacred obligation' is another favorite term for the deliveries by the *kolkhozy*, *kolkhozniki* and individual peasants to the state. Since a somewhat later date, the term 'second commandment' has been applied to the obligation to store seed grain."

20. Hubbard, ref. 1, p. 187.

21. Jasny, ref. 1, pp. 370–371.

22. *Ibid.*, pp. 374–375.

23. *Ibid.*

24. *Ibid.*, p. 377.

25. For the text of the regulation see *Sbornik rukovodiashchikh materialov po kolkhoznomu stroitel'stvu* [Collection of leading materials pertaining to collective farm development] (Moscow, 1948), pp. 178–183; or *Sobranie zakonov*, 1940, no. 9, art. 235. The collective farmers are taxed on the *actual* (rather than planned) number of hectares sown; the private farmers are taxed on the same basis as the collective farm for grain and rice, but at a higher rate.

26. Moiseev (ref. 1) claims that as a result of the new system deliveries increased, that the cultivated land increased by 3 million hectares in 1940 in comparison with an increase of only 1.4 million in the preceding three years, and that the number of animal farms increased by 194.5 thousand in 1939 (when the new system was introduced for meat) in comparison with 52.7 thousand in the preceding three years.

27. *Sobranie zakonov*, 1940, no. 9, art. 235.

28. *Vazhneishie resheniia partii i pravitel'stva po sel'skomu khoziaistvu, 1946–1949 gg.* [The most important decrees of the party and government on agriculture, 1946–1949] (Kirov, 1949), p. 46.

29. See "O merakh dal'neishego razvitiia sel'skogo khoziaistva SSSR" [Measures for the further development of agriculture in the USSR], *Pravda*, September 13, 1953.

30. Lazar Volin, "The Kolkhoz [Collective Farm] in the Soviet Union," *Foreign Agriculture*, 11:150 (November–December 1947).

31. The coöperative approach, as used here, should not be taken to mean that the collective farms are true coöperatives in the Western sense of the word. All that is implied is that the peasants are the residual claimants on the output of the collective farms — that the collective farms are coöperatives in form.

32. This can be demonstrated with reference to Table 27. The two rates of tax are calculated as follows:

$$\text{Rate of tax (coöperative form)} = \frac{\text{obligatory deliveries}}{\text{net crop (coöperative form)}},$$

$$\text{Rate of tax (corporate form)} = \frac{\text{obligatory deliveries}}{\text{net crop (coöperative form)} - \text{payment to collective farmer}}$$

The numerator, in both cases, is fairly insensitive to variations in crops due to climatic conditions, etc. The denominator of the first equation, however, varies directly with fluctuations in crops, so that the rate of tax declines when there is a good crop, and increases when the crop is bad. This is illustrated by the years 1937 and 1938. The 1937 crop was the best in the Soviet period, whereas 1938 was only average; hence the rate of tax for 1937 is much lower than 1938:

1937: 12.2/52.9 = 23.1 per cent,
1938: 15.0/47.0 = 31.9 per cent,
Percentage increase 1938 over 1937 = 38 per cent.

The denominator of the rate of tax (corporate form) is not sensitive to fluctuations in the crop. This is because both net crop (coöperative form) and payments to collective farmers are sensitive, and in subtracting the second from the first, the fluctuation cancels out:

1937: 12.2/(52.9–35.9) = 71.7 per cent,
1938: 15.0/(47.0–26.9) = 74.6 per cent,
Percentage increase (1938 over 1937), 4 per cent.

Thus, the large difference in crop yield between 1937 and 1938 is reflected in a much larger relative increase in the rate of tax in the coöperative form of tax than in the corporate form of tax.

33. See Chapter 6, pp. 152–153.
34. Hubbard, ref. 1, p. 209.
35. Abram Bergson, "Soviet National Income and Product in 1937," *Quarterly Journal of Economics*, 64:416 (August 1950).
36. Jasny, ref. 1, pp. 289–290.
37. Hubbard, ref. 1, pp. 150–151.
38. Sir John Maynard, *Russia in Flux* (New York, 1948), pp. 543–544.
39. Jasny, ref. 1, pp. 293–294.
40. The reader is referred to Chapter 6 for a detailed discussion of MTS finances.

CHAPTER 8. DIRECT TAXATION OF THE POPULATION AND MISCELLANEOUS SOURCES OF BUDGET INCOME

1. See W. J. Schultz and C. L. Harriss, *American Public Finance* (New York, 1949), p. 306.
2. Minor changes were made by the Ministry of Finance on March 27, 1947; see V. S. Dankov and others, *Spravochnik nalogovogo rabotnika* [Handbook of tax workers] (Moscow, 1949), p. 76.
3. Abram Bergson, *The Structure of Soviet Wages* (Cambridge, 1946), *passim*.
4. Harry Schwartz, *Russia's Soviet Economy* (New York, 1950), p. 460, estimates that the average wage in 1948 was 7400 rubles. If this figure is correct, the average wage must be about 8000 rubles at present. Since there are wide disparities in incomes earned in the USSR, it may be inferred that a large part of the distribution of incomes is above the 12,000-ruble level.

5. In the original law (1943), the nontaxable minimum was 150 rubles a month for workers and 210 rubles a month for students.

6. G. L. Mar'iakhin, *Nalogi i sbory s naseleniia i kolkhozov* [Taxes and collections from population and collective farms] (Moscow, 1946), pp. 77–80.

7. I.e., the subsidies can be looked upon as negative income tax payments.

8. By a decree of the Supreme Soviet dated November 27, 1947.

9. The total amount of subsidies paid out in different years is given in the notes to Table 55.

10. V. P. D'iachenko, *Sovetskie finansy v pervoi faze razvitiia sotsialisticheskogo gosudarstva* [Soviet finance in the first phase of development of the socialist state] (Moscow, 1947), p. 250.

11. The text of the law is not available to me. Judging from the commentaries of D'iachenko, ref. 10, p. 250, and I. Reingold, "The New Economic Policy, 1921–1928," in *Soviet Policy in Public Finance*, ed. Lincoln Hutchinson and Carl C. Plehn (Stanford, 1931), pp. 168 ff, the property tax seems to have been a levy on purchasers of property, presumably denationalized property.

12. G. Mar'iakhin, "Nalogovaia sistema sovetskogo gosudarstva" [The tax system of the Soviet State], *Finansy SSSR za XXX let* (Moscow, 1947), p. 254.

13. *Sobranie zakonov*, 1924, no. 20, art. 196.

14. Table 32 actually understates the bias of the tax in favor of the worker by excluding from the first four columns the large number of workers and workers' incomes which are below the taxable minimum.

15. *Sobranie zakonov*, 1931, no. 31, art. 238.

16. K. N. Plotnikov, *Biudzhet sotsialisticheskogo gosudarstva* [Budget of the socialist state] (Moscow, 1948), pp. 271–272. Workers earning less than 300 rubles a month were exempt, those earning from 300 to 500 rubles a month were subject to a 50 per cent markup, and those with wages of more than 600 rubles a month paid a 100 per cent markup. Persons who ordinarily should have been mobilized into the armed services, but for some reason had not been, were subject to a markup of from 100 to 200 per cent.

17. See Plotnikov, ref. 16, p. 277. The receipts for individual years were: 1942, 14.0 billion rubles; 1943, 17.1; 1944, 20.7; 1945, 20.3.

18. See Chapter 9.

19. Before 1936, a single tax, called the unified agricultural tax, was levied on the collective farms as well as the individual peasants.

20. The 1952 agricultural tax was based on an edict of the Supreme Soviet of September 1939. Changes by the Supreme Soviet were made in June 1943 and July 1948 and by the Ministry of Finance in April 1949. See V. S. Dankov and others, *Spravochnik nalogovogo rabotnika* [Handbook for tax specialists], (Moscow, 1949), p. 5.

21. *Pravda*, August 10, 1953.

22. See Edwin R. A. Seligman, *The Income Tax* (New York, 1914), pp. 10–15.

23. D'iachenko, ref. 11, pp. 267–268; *Sobranie zakonov*, 1923, no. 42, art. 451; *Sobranie zakonov*, 1924, no. 58, art. 570.

24. See especially *Sobranie zakonov*, 1926, no. 30, art. 192; *Sobranie zakonov*, 1928, no. 24, art. 212.
25. Reingold, ref. 11, p. 161.
26. *Ibid.*
27. *Ibid.*, p. 167. These figures are somewhat higher than the figures presented by other Soviet sources.
28. *Sobranie zakonov*, 1927, no. 61, art. 613.
29. *Sobranie zakonov*, 1927, no. 61, art. 617.
30. Reingold, ref. 11, p. 166.
31. *Sobranie zakonov*, 1930, no. 13, art. 144. The maximum rate on kulaks was 70 per cent on income over 6000 rubles annually.
32. *Sobranie zakonov*, 1933, no. 32, art. 188b.
33. A. K. Suchkov, *Dokhody gosudarstvennogo biudzheta SSSR* [Income of the state budget of the USSR] (Moscow, 1945), p. 138.
34. Mar'iakhin, ref. 12, p. 276.
35. A. M. Aleksandrov, *Finansy i kredit SSSR* [Finance and credit in the USSR] (Moscow, 1948), p. 165.
36. Naum Jasny, *The Socialized Agriculture of the USSR* (Stanford, 1949), p. 692.
37. *Sobranie zakonov*, 1938, no. 18, art. 116; no. 55, art. 308.
38. *Sobranie zakonov*, 1939, no. 34, art. 235.
39. *Sobranie zakonov*, 1935, no. 30, art. 232.
40. L. Hubbard, *The Economics of Soviet Agriculture* (London, 1939), p. 200.
41. *Sobranie zakonov*, 1932, no. 78, art. 476.
42. *Sobranie zakonov*, 1934, no. 49, art. 380.
43. Plotnikov, ref. 16, pp. 189–191.
44. Jasny, ref. 36, p. 788.
45. Plotnikov, ref. 16, p. 191.
46. *Ibid.*, pp. 278–279. The text of this law was not available to me.
47. See earlier in this chapter for details.
48. Plotnikov, ref. 16, p. 276.
49. *Ibid.*, p. 272.
50. See Chapter 9, pp. 224–225 for discussion.
51. See *Pravda*, August 10, 1953.
52. *Pravda*, August 6, 1953.
53. The latter percentage is more comparable to the present because, in the 1920's, the budget included the gross revenues and expenditures of many enterprises. In 1923–24, for example, gross revenues of transportation amount to about 40 per cent of total budget revenue. See D'iachenko, ref. 10, p. 452.
54. Cf. Chapter 9 for discussion of the main trends in taxation.
55. Ref. 52.
56. This is the opinion of Western economists who have written on the subject. Although it has not been possible to obtain documentation from Soviet sources, conversations with Soviet refugees tend to confirm this opinion. Most Soviet economists maintain that bond purchases by the population are

purely voluntary and an expression of the patriotism and faith in his country of the Soviet citizen.

57. Dr. Shoup constructs examples to demonstrate the amount of tax in a forced loan: "If the current rate of interest for a 10-year bond is, for instance, 2.9 per cent, there is no difference to the individual between (*a*) paying $25 in tax, and (*b*) loaning $100 to the government without interest in exchange for a negotiable certificate redeemable at par in ten years. The forced-loan certificate would have a market value of $75, which is what the individual would have left after paying $25 in tax."

"For example, a certain individual is required to purchase for $100 the noninterest-bearing 10-year bond used in the illustration above, except that it is now nonnegotiable, and will not be redeemed until the ten years are up. This individual has not accumulated savings, is spending all his current income, and has a high preference for present over future goods. Suppose that he would voluntarily purchase this kind of a bond only if it were offered to him at $30, that is, he would be willing to cut his current consumption by no more than $30 in order to obtain $100 ten years hence; and if in addition the government were collecting a tax from him of, say, $80, he would be willing to offer no more than $20 for the bond, in view of the larger total decrease in current consumption he would be enduring. Under these circumstances a forced loan of $100 is to him a tax of $80 and a voluntary loan of $20. From his point of view the forced loan of $100 leaves him just as he would be if the government taxed him $80 and simultaneously offered him, for voluntary purchase, a $100 certificate (due in 10 years) for $20. In this sense his present net worth is decreased $80 by the forced loan of $100." See Carl Shoup, "Forced Loans," in a symposium conducted by The Tax Institute entitled *Curbing Inflation Through Taxation* (New York, 1944), pp. 127 ff.

If, in the second case, the individual's preference for present goods should be independent of changes in the level of prices, i.e., independent of expectations of price increases, then it would seem that the net worth of the individual should also be deflated by the increase in the price index.

58. The material presented in this section was derived primarily from the following sources: Aleksandrov, ref. 35, chap. 11; Suchkov, ref. 33, pp. 176–183; V. P. D'iachenko, *Finansy i kredit SSSR* [Finance and credit in the USSR] (Moscow and Leningrad, 1940), chap. 11.

59. Suchkov, ref. 33, p. 177. As of October 1, 1927, the following public debt from previous years was outstanding (in millions of rubles): First State Loan of 1922, 104.3; Second State Loan of 1924, 39.1; First Peasants' Loan of 1924, 0.6 (46.8 was outstanding October 1, 1925 of which 46.2 was repaid); Second Peasants' Loan of 1925, 95.6; Internal 5 per cent Loan of 1925, repaid (10.0 outstanding on October 1, 1925); Internal 8 per cent Loan of 1925, 223.0; Internal Loan of 1926, 27.4; The commodity loans, repaid by 1924 were: First Grain Loan of 1922, 2.5; Second Grain Loan of 1923, 27.4; Sugar Loan of 1923, 0.1. See TsUNKhU, *Sotsialisticheskoe stroitel'stvo SSSR* [Socialist construction of the USSR] (Moscow, 1934), pp. 512–513.

60. Suchkov, ref. 33, p. 178.

61. Strengthen the Peasant Economy Loan (1927), 150 million rubles; First

Industrialization Loan (1927), 200 million rubles; Second Industrialization Loan (1928), 550 million rubles; Third Industrialization Loan (1929–30), 750 million rubles. The amounts listed for these loans are the planned issues, not the actual amounts sold. The Soviets have typically oversold their loans.

62. Aleksandrov, ref. 35, p. 185; Plotnikov, ref. 16, p. 47.

63. Aleksandrov, ref. 35, p. 185.

64. F. Koshelev, "Gosudarstvennye zaimy SSSR" [State loans of the USSR], *Den'gi i kredit,* 1938, no. 3, p. 7.

65. D'iachenko, ref. 58, p. 338; Aleksandrov, ref. 35, p. 185.

66. Aleksandrov, ref. 35, p. 186.

67. Persons with savings deposits fared best, receiving one new ruble for each old ruble on deposits under 3,000 rubles, 2 for 3 rubles on deposits between 3,000 and 10,000 rubles, and 1 for 2 rubles on deposits in excess of 10,000 rubles. Two possible reasons for this preference are: the Soviets may have wanted to encourage savings deposits which are the principal form of voluntary saving in the USSR; savings deposits are held primarily by the higher-income urban population — the managerial class, government officials, artists, etc. — and there is a tendency to favor this group in the population.

68. Rough estimates indicate that in the late 1930's the Soviet annual income velocity of cash was between 10 and 15. A 20-year bond issue, inconvertible until it matures (or until a lottery is won), has virtually no velocity.

69. As it happens, the discrimination against cash hurt the peasants most. The peasants accumulated most of the economy's cash during the war by selling produce on the collective farm markets at very high prices. Nevertheless, they purchased less than one-third of the war bond issues, and held an even smaller fraction of the prewar issues (see Plotnikov, ref. 16, p. 290; D'iachenko, ref. 58, p. 341).

70. "Three types of *kolkhozy* were distinguished: communes, arteli, and TOZ . . . The commune was a full realization of the communist ideas of the earliest period . . . Everything in the commune was in common, even dwelling houses and meals . . . The TOZ, an abbreviation of the Russian 'co-operative for working of the land,' was the loosest form of organization. All productive livestock and most workstock remained private property. Even the working of the soil and the machinery for this were only partly collectivized in the TOZ. The artel was intermediate between the commune and the TOZ, with field work almost entirely collectivized and productive livestock partially so." Jasny, ref. 36, pp. 299–300.

71. The norms were different from those used earlier in one respect: previously norms had been used to calculate taxable income, to which was applied a schedule of tax rates; after 1933 the norms were expressed directly in the form of so many rubles of tax per hectare of crop sown. Since the per-hectare rate does not vary with the number of hectares, the tax is proportional.

72. For discussion see Mar'iakhin, ref. 6, pp. 46–47; K. Ianbukhtin, *Nalogi v usloviakh kapitalizma i v Sovetskom khoziastve* [Taxes under capitalism and Soviet economy] (Moscow, 1934), p. 44.

73. *Sobranie zakonov,* 1936, no. 40, art. 339. It should be noted that, from

this time on, the income tax on the collective farm was a distinctly separate tax from the agricultural tax on the agricultural population.

74. Plotnikov, ref. 16, p. 116.

75. During the Second Five Year Plan, the following income-tax receipts were collected from the collective farms (in millions of rubles): 1933, 222; 1934, 247; 1935, 258; 1936, 413; 1937, 535 (Plotnikov, ref. 16, p. 118).

76. Cf. *Sbornik rukovodiashchikh materialov po kolkhoznomu stroitel'stvu* [Collection of directives concerning collective farms] (Moscow, 1948), pp. 191–195.

77. Mar'iakhin, ref. 6, p. 48.

78. Suchkov, ref. 33, p. 108.

79. E.g., fertilizer, seeds, depreciation of equipment.

80. N. N. Rovinskii, *Gosudarstvennyi biudzhet SSSR* [State budget of the USSR] (Moscow, 1950), vol. 2, pp. 120–121.

81. V. I. Gavrilov, *Raspredelenie dokhodov v kolkhozakh* [The distribution of income in collective farms] (Moscow, 1953), p. 84.

82. Suchkov, ref. 33, pp. 96–97.

83. Let us assume we have two equally equipped woodworking coöperatives making tables, and that A manufactures its tables from cheap pine costing 300 rubles per table while B uses mahogany costing 1000 rubles per table. Furthermore, both coöperatives use about the same amount of labor and equipment to produce a table, so that the amount of value added in both cases is 500 rubles; both coöperatives are allowed a 200 ruble profit. The rate of profit of A would be 200/800 or 25 per cent; that of B would be 200/1300 or about 15 per cent. Coöperative A would pay a higher tax than B because it has a higher rate of profit.

84. Suchkov, ref. 33.

85. *Ibid.*, p. 98.

86. *Ibid.*, p. 99; Aleksandrov, ref. 35, p. 140.

87. Suchkov (ref. 33, *passim*) has a fairly comprehensive discussion of most of the minor sources of budget income.

88. *Ibid.*, p. 129.

89. For discussion in English, see Schwartz, ref. 4, pp. 503–505. Schwartz's account is taken from Suchkov, ref. 33, chap. 10.

90. Plotnikov, ref. 16, pp. 281–282. In 1940, for example, receipts from the inheritance tax were only 5.6 million rubles. A summary of the inheritance tax in effect in the mid-twenties can be found in Reingold, ref. 11, pp. 182–183.

CHAPTER 9. TRENDS IN SOVIET TAXATION

1. See Alexander Baykov, *The Development of the Soviet Economic System* (New York, 1947), pp. 388–389.

2. *Ibid.*

3. For example, in 1932 these amounted to 2.9 billion rubles, compared with total budget receipts of 31 billion rubles; see TsUNKhU, *Sotsialisticheskoe stroitel'stvo SSSR* (Moscow, 1936), p. 644.

4. See K. N. Plotnikov, *Biudzhet sotsialistcheskogo gosudarstva* [Budget of the socialist state] (Moscow, 1948), p. 18; also *Gosudarstvennyi biudzhet soiuza SSR za vtoruiu piatiletku 1933–37* [State budget in the Second Five Year Plan] (Leningrad, 1939), pp. 3–4.
5. Plotnikov, ref. 4, *passim*.
6. See notes to Table 47.
7. Until 1931, the budget year was from October 1 to September 30. The transition from 1929–30 to 1931 was bridged by a special period, the fourth quarter, 1930. The results for this period are not sufficiently significant to merit inclusion, particularly since they reflect seasonal variations.
8. The 81 per cent increase of 1931 over 1929–30 is artificially high, owing to the omission of the fourth quarter of 1930.
9. E.g., TsUNKhU *Sotsialisticheskoe stroitel'stvo SSSR* [Socialist construction of the USSR] (Moscow, 1936), p. 644.
10. From Finance Minister Zverev's budget speech of 1944.
11. This explanation appears to have escaped Professor Bettelheim. See Charles Bettelheim, *L'Economie Sovietique* (Paris, 1950), p. 409.
12. N. Voznesensky, *The Economy of the USSR During World War II* (Washington, 1948), p. 94. It is surprising in the light of this information that total receipts in 1942 were not still lower.
13. This trend may indicate simply a decline in investment in those industries which normally financed investment out of retained profits.
14. Voznesensky, ref. 12, p. 82.
15. *Ibid.*, p. 81.
16. *Ibid.*, p. 76.
17. See Table 15, Chapter 6 for another measure of the decline of turnover taxation.
18. Reported in the Moscow press on those dates.
19. For 1948–1951 see A. V. Bachurin, "Povyshenie pokupatel'noi sily sovetskogo rublia i obestsenie kapitalisticheskikh valiut" [The increased purchasing power of the Soviet ruble and the depreciation of capitalist currency], in A. I. Pashkov, ed., *Voprosy sotsialisticheskoi ekonomiki* [Problems of socialist economics] (Moscow, 1951), p. 142. For 1952 see Moscow press on date of price cuts.

The 1952 savings are estimated as 23 billion for state and coöperative stores and 5 billion for collective farm market sales (Moscow press). A summary of the distribution for 1948 to 1951 is contained in United Nations, Economic Commission for Europe, Research and Planning Division, *Economic Survey of Europe in 1951* (Geneva, 1952), p. 146. The distribution follows (billions of rubles):

Year	State retail trade	Collective farm + coöperative trade	Total
1948	57	29	86
1949	48	23	71
1950	80	30	110
1951	27.5	7	34.5

20. See Table 51. The comparison follows:

Year	Total sales	"Savings"	Savings ÷ sales
1948	330	86	26.1 per cent
1949	343	71	20.7 per cent
1950	351–365	110	31.3–30.1 per cent

Unfortunately the Soviets nowhere state precisely how their figures for savings were estimated, so that the above percentages are not to be taken for more than a rough indication of the magnitude of the price cuts.

The price cuts, by individual commodities, can be found in the Moscow newspapers for the days on which the reductions went into effect.

21. N. S. Margolin, *Balans denezhnykh dokhodov i raskhodov naseleniia* [Balance of money income and expenditure of the population] (Moscow, 1951), p. 7.

22. See Tables 15 and 48.

23. See *Izvestiia*, January 18, 1950; *Pravda*, January 26, 1951. For discussion see Chapter 10, pp. 260–261, 272–274.

24. We do not have sufficient material on turnover-tax rates in the postwar period to make direct comparisons.

25. For fuller discussion of these developments see A. Zverev, "Gosudarstvennyi biudzhet chetvertogo goda poslevoennoi stalinskoi piatiletki" [The state budget in the fourth year of the postwar Stalin Five Year Plan], *Planovoe khoziaistvo*, 1949, no. 2, pp. 38–50; P. Vladimirov, "Za rentabel'nuiu rabotu predpriiatii" [For the profitable operation of enterprises], *Voprosy ekonomiki*, 1948, no. 8, pp. 28–32; M. C. Kaser, "Soviet Planning and the Price Mechanism," *Economic Journal*, 60:81–91 (March 1950).

26. Subsidy estimates for 1948 and 1950 are presented in the notes to Table 52, and the methodological difficulties of making such estimates are indicated. For what the estimates are worth, they indicate a substantial decline in subsidies in 1949 and 1950, as planned. However, recent data would seem to indicate an increase again in 1951 and 1952, almost to the 1948 level.

27. Naum Jasny, *The Soviet Price System* (Stanford, 1951), pp. 39–40. Still another wholesale price reduction occurred on January 1, 1952 (*Pravda*, March 8, 1952).

28. See Chapter 10, p. 329. The subsidy estimate must be treated with considerable reserve since it is based on planned rather than actual figures.

29. Estimated roughly as the sum of the budget surpluses in the prewar years.

30. Voznesensky, ref. 12, p. 79. It is not at all clear what sort of transaction "drawing down commodity stockpiles" is, from the point of view of budgetary accounting.

31. *Ibid.*, pp. 80–81.

32. *Ibid.*

33. A. D. Gusakov and I. A. Dymshits, *Denezhnoe obrashchenie i kredit SSSR* [Monetary circulation and credit in the USSR] (Moscow, 1951), pp. 159–160. Their remarks would seem to imply a larger currency issue to finance

short-term credit operations than is admitted by Voznesensky. However, they speak very loosely and may not be taking into account the fact, noted by Voznesensky, that short-term loans for peacetime purposes were being withdrawn rapidly.

34. Voznesensky, ref. 12, pp. 72–77.

35. *Ibid.*, p. 76. Most economists consider this a minimum estimate of the collective farm market inflation during the war.

36. *Ibid.*, p. 70.

37. *Ibid.*

38. *Ibid.*, p. 69.

39. Z. V. Atlas and E. Ia. Bregel', *Denezhnoe obrashchenie i kredit SSSR* [Monetary circulation and credit in the USSR] (Moscow, 1947), p. 241.

40. Vosnesensky, ref. 12, p. 76.

41. *Ibid.*, p. 74. Some of this increase may represent recapture of previously occupied territory.

42. This technique was used under similar circumstances in the early thirties (see pp. 53–54).

43. Voznesensky, ref. 12, p. 76.

44. Gusakov and Dymshits, ref. 33, p. 162.

45. Jasny, ref. 27, p. 34.

46. No attempt will be made to present a thoroughgoing analysis of the Reform and its effects, since this has been done by P. A. Baran, "Currency Reform in the U.S.S.R.," *Harvard Business Review*, 26:194–200 (March 1948). Professor Baran also describes the provisions of the Reform at considerable length. The text may be found in *Pravda*, December 15, 1947. A summary in English was given in *The New York Times* of the same date. A Soviet analysis of the Reform is that of G. Kosiachenko, "Sovetskaia denezhnaia reforma," [Soviet monetary reform], published originally in *Planovoe khoziaistvo*, 1949, no. 1, and reprinted in *Narodnoe khoziaistvo SSSR, II* [National economy of the USSR] (Moscow, 1948).

47. Since the peasants buy primarily industrial consumers' goods, it is the prices of industrial commodities which would have been most important in putting into effect the policy under discussion.

48. A. Baykov, "Internal Trade During the War and Its Post War Development," *Bulletins on Soviet Economic Development*, no. 4 (1950), p. 5.

49. Commercial stores were eliminated at this time. Since the new prices were below the former commercial-stores prices, the prices of goods formerly sold through these channels can be considered to have declined.

50. Baran (ref. 46, p. 199) says: "A general price increase would have affected the population very inequitably. The urban population, especially the workers whose wartime savings were very small, would be completely cut off from the market and would need large adjustments of their current incomes to make up for the rise in prices. The peasantry, on the other hand, in possession of large money hoards, would still have been able to clear from the shelves whatever goods were offered for sale."

51. Harry Schwartz, *Russia's Soviet Economy* (New York, 1950), p. 434.

52. *Ibid.*

53. Bank for International Settlements, *Eighteenth Annual Report* (Basle, Switzerland, 1948), pp. 35–36; Mikhail V. Condoide, *The Soviet Financial System* (Columbus, 1951), p. 69.

54. Baran, ref. 46, pp. 8, 197; Federal Reserve Bank of New York, *Monthly Review*, January 1948.

55. The value of M_{40} is taken from Table 8; Y_{40} and Y_{48} are from Table 51. The value $k = 1$ represents no change in income velocity of circulation.

56. Currency in circulation in M_{47} is taken to include not only currency actually in circulation at the moment of the Reform, including cash in the hands of the population, collective farms, coöperatives, state enterprises, etc., but also that part of the deposit accounts of state enterprises, collective farms, etc. which was to be paid out to workers, collective farmers, or members of coöperatives who had not received income payments since December 16, 1947. This definition is justified by the timing of the Reform to take effect when currency in circulation was temporarily reduced below normal, particularly in those cases (e.g., agriculture) where income payments are made very infrequently.

57. *Pravda*, March 1, 1947.

58. S. Krivetskii, "O fondakh zarabotnoi platy i ischislenii ikh" [The wage fund and its calculation], *Den'gi i kredit*, 1940, no. 2–3, pp. 41–44.

59. This is estimated as follows: The total wage bill in 1940 was approximately 124 billion rubles (Table 4). If this was paid twice a month or 24 times a year, the currency requirement was 5.2 billion rubles. Since total cash in circulation was 16 billion, this leaves 10.8 billion rubles to finance nonwage income plus hoards (and we assume hoards were negligible). Nonwage income is equal to total income (236 billion) minus the wage bill (124 billion), or 112 billion rubles. This implies an income velocity of about 10 (112/10.8). We are treating other income here as peasant income. Actually it is composed of: peasant income from the collective farms which is paid out only a few times a year; peasant income from sales on the collective farm markets which is received somewhat more often, but seasonally; pensions and stipends which are received monthly; earning of members of producers' coöperative associations; and others. See N. S. Margolin, *Voprosy balansa denezhnykh dokhodov i raskhodov naseleniia* [Problems of the balance of money income and expenditure of the population] (Moscow and Leningrad, 1940), p. 114.

60. Unfortunately, we do not know how much of this income had been spent, and how much was on hand on the day of the Reform. In the case of wages, it can be assumed, without much risk of error, that virtually no cash balances from current income remained by December 16, 1947. In the case of the peasants, it is conceivable that the whole 14 billion rubles had been spent. The peasants were so "liquid" before the Reform that it may be reasonable to assume they spent new income almost as fast as it was received. On the other hand, since most of their income is typically received after the fall harvest, some current balances may still have remained unspent by December 16th. Whichever is the case, the results are not altered significantly, since the balances which remained unspent would have been depreciated, along with the much larger hoards, at a 10-to-1 ratio.

61. The deficits were covered both by introducing new currency into circulation and by "mobilizing commodity reserves" (Voznesensky). The relative importance of these two methods of deficit financing is unknown but may be revealed by Atlas and Bregel' (ref. 39, p. 233), who claim that in the budget and other economic organizations drew upon their past savings (in the case of the budget, upon past surpluses), for more than 20 billion rubles. It should also be noted that to assume that the whole budget deficit resulted in new currency is inconsistent with the statement of Voznesensky quoted directly below in the text.

62. Voznesensky, ref. 12, p. 82.

63. We assume that currency in circulation in 1941 increased by a little more than half of the budget deficit of 1941 or by about 8 million rubles (cf. note 61).

64. M. M. Lifits, *Ekonomika sovetskoi torgovli* [Economics of Soviet trade], (Moscow, 1950), p. 322.

65. See the article by K. Plotnikov in *Pravda*, May 18, 1949: "In the postwar years, even more than before the war, the temporarily free funds of the budget are used to extend short-term credit to the economy. The 1949 budget provides for an excess of receipts over expenditures of 30.7 billion rubles. This not only strengthens monetary circulation, but serves as a most important source of extension of short-term credit to the economy."

66. *Pravda*, June 14, 1950.

67. *Pravda*, March 8, 1951.

68. Expenditures for 1953 were preliminarily estimated at 514.8 billion rubles and receipts at 539.7 billion rubles. (See *Pravda*, April 21, 1954.)

69. Expenditures were planned at 562.7 billion rubles, receipts at 571.8 billion rubles. (*Ibid.*)

CHAPTER 10. THE "BURDEN" OF MONEY TAXATION

1. G. F. Shirras and L. Rostas, *The Burden of British Taxation* (New York, 1943), chap. 1.

2. The reader may be interested in the quantitative relation between the burden of taxation as measured here and the so-called inflationary gap. The term inflationary gap has been used to refer to both (1) inflationary purchasing power *before* taxes, and (2) inflationary purchasing power left unabsorbed *after* taxes. The two magnitudes are related by the following identity: (1) = taxes + (2). If the tax program were completely successful in absorbing inflationary pressures, then taxes would be equal to (1), and the tax burden (i.e., total money taxation on the consumer) would be equal to the inflationary gap *before* taxes. If there is a shortfall in taxes, then the tax burden is equal to (1) minus (2). The effect of repressed inflation on the average rate of taxation is discussed below.

3. Baran built up his estimates of household income in 1940 from the income side; see Paul Baran, "National Income and Product of the USSR in 1940," *Review of Economic Statistics*, 29:226–234 (November 1947). Bergson worked basically from the outlay side in making his estimates for 1937; see

Abram Bergson, "Soviet National Income and Product in 1937," *Quarterly Journal of Economics*, 64:208–241, 408–441 (May and August, 1950).

4. N. S. Margolin, *Voprosy balansa denezhnykh dokhodov i raskhodov naseleniia* (Moscow, 1940).

5. These estimates are reprinted in Alexander Baykov, *The Development of the Soviet Economic System* (New York, 1947), pp. 476–479. Although the figures are not designated as representing any particular year, they are quite close to figures estimated for 1935.

6. For discussion of this problem see Abram Bergson, "A Problem in Soviet Statistics," *Review of Economic Statistics*, 29:234–42 (November 1947), and Maurice Dobb and Harry Schwartz, "Further Appraisals of Russian Economic Statistics," *Review of Economics and Statistics*, 30:34–41 (February 1948).

7. Bergson, ref. 3, Appendix, p. 9.

8. *Ibid.*

9. *Ibid.*, p. 10.

10. *Ibid.*, p. 11.

11. Operating expenditures (*operatsionnye raskhody*) are expenditures on training workers, scientific research, and other projects administered by enterprises but not part of the normal operating expenses of production.

12. For a more elaborate attempt to measure the Soviet rate of nonconsumption expenditures, the reader is referred to my paper "Financing Soviet Economic Development," delivered in the fall of 1953 to the Universities-National Bureau Conference on Capital Formation and Economic Growth. The proceedings of this Conference are to be published in 1955.

13. Maurice Dobb, *Soviet Economic Development Since 1917* (London, 1948).

14. *Ibid.*, pp. 242–3.

15. The official figures for retail-trade turnover were as follows:

	1929–30	1931	1932
State	4.1	6.5	14.5
Coöperative	12.4	18.2	25.8
Kolkhoz	. .	. .	7.5
Private	1.1	. .	. .

For sources, see notes to Table 51.

16. Sh. Turetskii, "Puti planirovaniia tsen" [Methods of price planning], *Planovoe khoziaistvo*, 1936, no. 3, p. 133. There was a sharp decline in the amount of currency in circulation in 1933, certainly circumstantial evidence that a deflationary policy was being pursued. The movements of other financial magnitudes indicate a similar policy. It is interesting to note that if we included the change in currency in circulation along with taxes in computing the average rate of taxation (as suggested on p. 257), the trend in the rate of taxation for the years 1932 to 1934 is altered as follows:

	1932	1933	1934
Series II, unadjusted	51.0	55.9	55.8
Series II, adjusted	55.8	53.5	56.9

The rate of tax is spuriously low (as an indicator of investment) in 1932 because of the increase in repressed inflation, and spuriously high in 1933 because repressed inflation was being reduced.

17. See Alexander Gerschenkron, "The Soviet Indices of Industrial Production," *Review of Economics and Statistics*, 29:218 (November 1947); W. Galenson, "Russian Labor Productivity Statistics," *Industrial and Labor Relations Review*, 4:500 (July 1951). The indexes computed by Professor Donald Hodgman, which are presumably free of the specific Soviet weighting bias, bear out the statement in the text; see D. R. Hodgman, "A New Production Index for Soviet Industry" (unpublished dissertation, Harvard University, 1950), pp. 185, 216. Hodgman's results are to be published shortly.

18. Naum Jasny, *The Socialized Agriculture of the USSR* (Stanford, 1949), p. 792.

19. See, for example, Lazar Volin, "The Malenkov-Krushchev New Economic Policy," *The Journal of Political Economy*, 62:187–209 (June 1954); F. D. Holzman, "Soviet Economic Growth," *World Politics*, 7:133–156 (October 1954).

20. See N. N. Rovinskii, *Gosudarstvennyi biudzhet SSSR* [State budget of the USSR] (Moscow, 1949), p. 292.

21. We have made no adjustment for the fact that a ruble used to buy a unit of equipment is probably worth a lot more than a ruble used to buy a unit of education or health. See Naum Jasny, *The Soviet Price System* (Stanford, 1951), *passim*.

22. For simplicity we assume that collective farm market transactions are entirely intrahousehold.

23. This category also includes depreciation in consumers'-goods industry and to this extent is nonhomogeneous. Adjustment for this will be made in subsequent equations.

24. Printing of money is the residual element which always insures an *ex post* balance of accounts.

25. Total depreciation for the whole national economy was 5.8 billion rubles in 1937 (Bergson, ref. 3, p. 216) and has been estimated at 9.15 billion rubles in 1940; See V. P. D'iachenko, *Finansy i kredit SSSR* [Finance and credit in the USSR] (Moscow and Leningrad, 1940), p. 399. Only a small fraction of these amounts related to consumers'-goods production; hence we feel justified in ignoring depreciation in the discussion which follows. It should be noted that Western economists are of the opinion that Soviet depreciation estimates are on the low side.

26. Jasny, ref. 18, p. 23. See also Table 3.

27. See Chapter 7.

28. The following difficulties are encountered: (1) Average annual wage rate figures for the period from 1925 26 to 1940 are available for the economy as a whole, and for specific sectors of the economy, but *not* for nonagricultural consumers' goods. (2) If such wage rates are available, they would have to be adjusted for changes in productivity; productivity series for consumers'-goods industries are not available. Furthermore, Soviet series for changes in aggregate labor productivity suffer from the same sort of bias as the production index.

(3) Procurement prices of agricultural commodities over time are available for only a few commodities and for a few years. (4) The share in total agricultural procurement of commodities subject to further processing in state factories is not available for many years.

29. The average wage (rubles) in the entire socialized economy increased as follows:

	1925–26	1926–27	1927–28	1928–29	1929–30
Average wage	571	624	703	800	936
Change (per cent)		9.1	12.7	14.5	17.0

See TsUNKhU, *Sotsialisticheskoe stroitel'stvo SSSR* (Moscow, 1934), pp. 316–317.

30. The annual wage increased from 703 rubles in 1928 to 1,427 rubles in 1932 (*Ibid.*).

31. Galenson, ref. 17, p. 500. Hodgman's figures (ref. 17) indicate an actual decline in productivity from 1928 to 1932. The productivity and wage data cited refer to all industry rather than to consumers'-goods industry; however, the trends for the latter were in the same direction, even though they differed in extent.

32. See Jasny, ref. 18, p. 792 (Table 28). For example, grain fell from 73.3 to 66.4 million tons; potatoes from 46.4 to 43.2; sugar beets from 10.1 to 6.6; sunflower seed from 2.13 to 2.27, etc.

33. *Ibid.*, p. 794. Procurements of wheat increased from 11.0 to 22.8 million tons, even though gross grain output declined.

34. Galenson, ref. 17, p. 500.

35. Jasny, ref. 18, p. 794.

36. Naum Jasny, *Soviet Prices of Producers Goods* (Stanford, 1951).

37. I. Kravis and J. Mintzes, "Food Prices in the Soviet Union, 1936–1950," *Review of Economics and Statistics*, 32:166 (May 1950).

38. The extent of the decline in real terms is underlined by the fact that an index of food prices in state stores rose by 49 per cent and an index of clothing prices by 83 per cent between July 1939 and July 1940. In addition, many commodities are reported to have been unavailable in this period (Kravis and Mintzes, ref. 37, p. 166).

39. Part of the increase is attributable to territorial expansion after 1940.

40. Wage for 1947 estimated by Harry Schwartz "Soviet Labor Policy, 1945–1949," *The Annals of the American Academy of Political and Social Science*, 263:80 (May 1949); Peter Wiles reports that the new Soviet economics textbook reports the average annual wage for 1953 to be 8163 rubles. See his "Retail Trade, Retail Prices and Real Wages in the U.S.S.R.," *Bulletin of Oxford Institute of Statistics*, to be published November/December 1954.

41. For example, in 1949 and 1950 industrial goods increased by 25 and 35 per cent, respectively, while agricultural commodities increased only 17 and 27 per cent, respectively. See *Izvestiia*, January 18, 1950 and *Pravda*, January 26, 1951.

CHAPTER 11. A CRITIQUE OF SOVIET TAXATION

1. T. Scitovsky, E. Shaw, and L. Tarshis, *Mobilizing Resources for War* (New York, 1951), pp. 106 ff., 133 ff.; A. G. Hart, *Defense Without Inflation* (New York, 1951), pp. 95 ff., 159 ff. These writers favor the pay-as-you-go system, although they admit the disequilibrium system may have some advantages. With the exception of preservation of incentives, the advantages they list are advantages for an economy operating in a capitalist institutional framework, and have little relevance for the Soviet economy.

2. Klaus E. Knorr, "Welfare-State Measures and the Free Market in International Trade," *American Economic Review (Proceedings)*, 41:434–442 (May 1951).

3. See William Fellner, *A Treatise on War Inflation* (Berkeley, 1942). Professor Fellner says: "Uncontrolled or incompletely controlled inflation is much more harmful than the usual types of regressive taxation" (p. 13), and later "Indeed it would be hard to invent a tax which would be as harmful as an inflationary gap of unmanageable size" (p. 21).

4. Harry Schwartz, "Soviet Labor Policy, 1945–1949," *Annals of the American Academy of Political and Social Science*, 263:73–84 (May 1949), p. 80; G. R. Barker, "Soviet Labour," *Bulletins on Soviet Economic Development*, 2:21 (June 1951).

5. The large increase in direct taxes collected in 1951 may have been due to an increase which occurred in the agricultural tax rates.

6. V. Batyrev, "Rol' kredita v narodnom khoziaistve SSSR" [The role of credit in the national economy of the USSR], *Bol'shevik*, 1951, no. 12, p. 58.

7. V. Moskvin, "Sovetskaia torgovlia v tret'em godu piatiletki" [Soviet trade in the third year of the Five Year Plan], *Bol'shevik*, 1948, no. 15, p. 32.

8. M. M. Lifits, ed., *Ekonomika sovetskoi torgovli* [Economics of Soviet trade] (Moscow, 1950), p. 322. Lifits also points out that collective farm market prices fell to 25 per cent of their previous level after the currency reform.

9. E. L. Manevich, *Zarabotnaia plata i ee formy v promyshlennosti SSSR* [Forms of wages in Soviet industry] (Moscow, 1951), pp. 80, 137; Barker, ref. 4, p. 18.

10. Barker, ref. 4, p. 18.

11. Joseph Berliner, "Informal Organization of the Soviet Firm," *Quarterly Journal of Economics*, 66:342–365 (August 1952).

12. Quoted by Abram Bergson, *The Structure of Soviet Wages* (Cambridge, 1944), p. 184.

13. *Ibid.*, chap. 14.

14. J. Stalin, *Problems of Leninism* (Moscow, 1940), pp. 371–373.

15. Abram Bergson, "Soviet National Income and Product in 1937," *Quarterly Journal of Economics*, 64:426 (August 1950).

16. Stalin, ref. 14, p. 518.

17. "To each according to his need" is hardly an operational goal. Except for necessities required to support life, "needs" are difficult to define; what people need seems to vary from society to society and from group to group

within a society. Needs are acquired by individuals when they hear about or experience new goods and services. If the Soviets produced only the physiological necessities, and kept all knowledge of other commodities from the population, they might soon allow people to take as much as they want of everything produced. But they produce commodities such as nylon stockings, automobiles for private use, and cameras, which can be bought by only a small percentage of the population. The distribution of these "incentive" goods makes it impossible for them to achieve distribution according to need, since it creates more needs than it satisfies. As long as new commodities are developed which cannot be produced in sufficient quantities to be distributed to everyone immediately, the Soviet goal will remain a mirage.

18. Alex Inkeles, "Social Stratification and Mobility in the Soviet Union: 1940–1950," *American Sociological Review*, 15:465–79 (August 1950); Barrington Moore, Jr., *Soviet Politics — The Dilemma of Power* (Cambridge, 1950), chap. 10.

19. See Table 31.

20. The most symmetrical system for handling dependency, as some writers have suggested, would be to pay a negative income tax, based on a continuation of the positive rate schedule below the exemption line, to households who are exempt from taxation.

21. These are the B estimates from Table 28.

22. Bergson, ref. 12, p. 209.

23. Naum Jasny, *The Soviet Price System* (Stanford, 1951), p. 169.

24. Some of these are cited by Maurice Dobb, *Soviet Economic Development Since 1917* (London, 1948), p. 376, and by E. M. Chossudowsky, "Rationing in the U.S.S.R.," *Review of Economic Studies*, 8:143–165 (June 1941).

25. A. Gordin, "Ekonomicheskoe znachenie sistemy oblozheniia po oborotu" [Economic significance of the turnover tax system], *Sovetskie finansy* [Soviet finance], 1947, no. 8, p. 12.

26. It should be noted that subsidies on producers' goods and raw materials which do not eventually lower the price of consumers' goods do not affect taxes on the consumer. Such subsidies involve simply a transfer within the state sector of the economy. For example, a subsidy to an enterprise which produces tanks constitutes an expenditure by the state which is *offset exactly* by the reduced cost to the state (on behalf of the Ministry of Armed Forces) of purchasing the tanks. On the other hand, subsidies which lower consumers'-goods prices require increased household taxation for monetary stability, all other things remaining equal.

27. See, for example, Sh. Turetskii, "O khoziaistvennom raschete" [Economic accounting], *Planovoe khoziaistvo*, 1939, no. 1, p. 118.

28. This, it should be noted, is not necessarily in contradiction with the assertion that important Soviet raw materials and equipment are directly allocated. True, funded commodities are directly allocated. But it is only after the managers of plants have included them in their plans that allocations to them are scheduled. Managers may be unwilling to alter their production functions in the first place if the price of new equipment is relatively high.

29. See Jasny, ref. 23, pp. 85 ff., and elsewhere indicated in the index.

30. Naum Jasny, *Soviet Prices of Producers' Goods* (Stanford, 1951), p. 48 (cites a Soviet source).

31. In 1934, wages were 57.3 per cent of total cost in the coal industry. This is somewhat higher than the percentage in other extractive industries, and about twice as high as in many manufacturing industries. The percentages for each industry are available in *Socialist Construction*, 1936.

32. This is indicated by indexes computed by Jasny, ref. 23, p. 168.

33. T. S. Khachaturov, *Osnovy ekonomiki zheleznodorozhnogo transporta* [Foundations of railway transport economics] (Moscow 1946), part I, p. 49.

34. I think there is merit in Peter Wiles' contention that "The loss of 'welfare' or 'efficiency' through an incorrect micro-economic allocation of resources [in the Soviet Union] is surely less than that brought about [under capitalism] by unemployment, restrictive labour practices, the refusal to share trade secrets, or the suppression of workable patents, could any of these losses ever be measured." See Peter J. D. Wiles, "Scarcity, Marxism, and Gosplan," *Oxford Economic Papers* (New Series), 5:315 (October 1953).

35. Scitovsky, Shaw, and Tarshis, ref. 1, *passim*.

36. Fellner, ref. 3, p. 97.

INDEX

RUSSIAN RESEARCH CENTER STUDIES

1. *Public Opinion in Soviet Russia: A Study in Mass Persuasion*, by Alex Inkeles
2. *Soviet Politics — The Dilemma of Power: The Role of Ideas in Social Change*, by Barrington Moore, Jr.
3. *Justice in Russia: An Interpretation of Soviet Law*, by Harold J. Berman ‡
4. *Chinese Communism and the Rise of Mao*, by Benjamin I. Schwartz
5. *Titoism and the Cominform*, by Adam B. Ulam
6. *A Documentary History of Chinese Communism*, by Conrad Brandt, Benjamin Schwartz, and John K. Fairbank
7. *The New Man in Soviet Pyschology*, by Raymond A. Bauer
8. *Soviet Opposition to Stalin: A Case Study in World War II*, by George Fischer
9. *Minerals: A Key to Soviet Power*, by Demitri B. Shimkin
10. *Soviet Law in Action: The Recollected Cases of a Soviet Lawyer*, by Harold J. Berman and Boris A. Konstantinovsky
11. *How Russia is Ruled*, by Merle Fainsod
12. *Terror and Progress USSR: Some Sources of Change and Stability in the Soviet Dictatorship*, by Barrington Moore, Jr.
13. *The Formation of the Soviet Union: Communism and Nationalism, 1917–1923*, by Richard Pipes
14. *Marxism: The Unity of Theory and Practice*, by Alfred G. Meyer
15. *Soviet Industrial Production, 1928–1951*, by Donald R. Hodgman
16. *Soviet Taxation: The Fiscal and Monetary Problems of a Planned Economy*, by Franklyn D. Holzman
17. *Soviet Military Law and Administration*, by Harold J. Berman and Miroslav Kerner
18. *Documents on Soviet Military Law and Administration*, edited and translated by Harold J. Berman and Miroslav Kerner
19. *The Russian Marxists and the Origin of Bolshevism*, by Leopold H. Haimson
20. *The Permanent Purge: Politics in Soviet Totalitarianism*, by Zbigniew K. Brzezinski
21. *Belorussia: The Making of a Nation*, by Nicholas P. Vakar
22. *A Bibliographical Guide to Belorussia*, by Nicholas P. Vakar
23. *The Balkans in Our Time*, by Robert Lee Wolff

24. *How the Soviet System Works: Cultural, Psychological, and Social Themes*, by Raymond A. Bauer, Alex Inkeles, and Clyde Kluckhohn *
25. *The Economics of Soviet Steel*, by M. Gardner Clark
26. *Leninism*, by Alfred G. Meyer
27. *Factory and Manager in the USSR*, by Joseph S. Berliner *
28. *Soviet Transportation Policy*, by Holland Hunter
29. *Doctor and Patient in Soviet Russia*, by Mark G. Field *
30. *Russian Liberalism*, by George Fischer
31. *Stalin's Failure in China, 1924–1927*, by Conrad Brandt
32. *The Communist Party of Poland*, by M. K. Dziewanowski
33. *Karamzin's Memoir on Ancient and Modern Russia, A Translation and Analysis*, by Richard Pipes
34. *A Memoir on Ancient and Modern Russia*, by N. M. Karamzin, the Russian text edited by Richard Pipes
35. *The Soviet Citizen: Daily Life in a Totalitarian Society*, by Alex Inkeles and Raymond A. Bauer *
36. *Pan-Turkism and Islam in Russia*, by Serge A. Zenkovsky
37. *The Soviet Bloc: Unity and Conflict*, by Zbigniew K. Brzezinski †
38. *National Consciousness in Eighteenth-Century Russia*, by Hans Rogger
39. *Alexander Herzen and the Birth of Russian Socialism, 1812–1855*, by Martin Malia
40. *The Conscience of the Revolution: Communist Opposition in Soviet Russia*, by Robert V. Daniels
41. *The Soviet Industrialization Debate, 1924–1928*, by Alexander Erlich
42. *The Third Section: Police and Society in Russia under Nicholas I*, by Sidney Monas
43. *Dilemmas of Progress in Tsarist Russia: Legal Marxism and Legal Populism*, by Arthur P. Mendel
44. *Political Control of Literature in the USSR, 1946–1959*, by Harold Swayze

* Publications of the Harvard Project on the Soviet Social System.

† Published jointly with the Center for International Affairs, Harvard University.

‡ Out of print.

Bei Fragen zur Produktsicherheit wenden Sie sich bitte an:
If you have any questions regarding product safety,
please contact:

Walter de Gruyter GmbH
Genthiner Straße 13
10785 Berlin
productsafety@degruyterbrill.com